Old Newfoundland:
A History to 1843

Patrick O'Flaherty

Old Newfoundland: A History to 1843

LONG BEACH PRESS

Long Beach Press,
Box 2676,
St. John's, Nfld.
Canada, A1C 6K1

Cover: Detail from Herman Moll's map, "NewFoundLand, St. Laurence Bay, The Fishing Banks, Acadia, and Part of New Scotland," c. 1732. (Marjorie Doyle collection)

Canadian Cataloguing in Publication Data

O'Flaherty, Patrick, 1939-

    Old Newfoundland: A History to 1843
    Includes bibliographical references and index

    ISBN: 0-9680998-2-3

1. Newfoundland — History — To 1763. 2. Newfoundland — History— 1763-1855. I. Title

FC2172.O45 1999   971.8'01   C99-900765-3
F1123.O45 1999

Contents

Preface

This book is a compact narrative history of Newfoundland to the 1840s. My main area of interest is the first half of the 19th century, but to place that period in context I decided it would be best to start from the beginning and move towards it. Why end where I did? Properly understood, at least as I've come to see it, the period 1833-43 illuminates not just the view to the rear but the road ahead. I wonder how much of Newfoundland's modern history can really be surprising after we explore that turbulent decade. But in a later work I hope to investigate aspects of the post-1843 era.

I hope this new survey of the colony's early and formative years will be of interest to the general reader. But I use endnotes to direct the curious to my sources and carry on limited ancillary discussion.

I've drawn on my previously published work in Newfoundland studies, together with that of recent scholars, and some not so recent, in history, geography, religious studies, archaeology, and a few other disciplines. Their publications are acknowledged in the notes and Bibliography. Of course, none of my errors is to be blamed on them. I rely more on my own research in the latter stages of the work. The chapters get longer as I move towards and into the 19th century, when the colony, with a growing population, ceases to be an extension of European commerce and comes into its own as a discrete entity, heading towards nationhood.

I owe particular favours to Priscilla Renouf, who steered me through the archaeological shoals, and Alan Macpherson, who looked over Chapter 2 and offered his usual shrewd comments. I thank them both. John Mannion, Edward-Vincent Chafe, Hans Rollmann, Robert McGhee, David Liverman, Joan Ritcey, and William Kirwin responded cordially to my inquiries. I thank them too. Irene Whitfield's expert assistance is gratefully acknowledged. Much of the work for this book was done at Memorial University's Queen Elizabeth II Library, and I am grateful for the cooperation and help I received from librarians there, especially those in the Centre for Newfoundland Studies. I was also made welcome at Memorial University's Maritime History Archive, the A.C. Hunter Library in St. John's, the Provincial Archives of Newfoundland and Labrador, and various libraries and archives in England and Scotland.

Access to Marjorie Doyle's fine Newfoundland collection has greatly facilitated my work. But her contribution went far beyond that. I thank her for her support, patience, and insight.

P. O'Flaherty
June 30, 1999

Chapter 1

Beginnings

AROUND 25,000 YEARS AGO, for reasons only dimly understood, the earth's climate cooled. One year the winter snowfall in Labrador-Ungava and the island of Newfoundland lingered in late spring on the higher ground. Years went by; the snow stayed longer, into summer. Then, fatally, it stayed until the onset of the next winter. More snow was added in succeeding winters. The accumulating snow shortly turned to ice which, as decades and centuries passed, thickened into ice caps. At a certain critical point, driven by gravity and their own mysterious inner forces, the ice caps began moving off hills and mountains, slowly and irresistibly, towards the sea. An Ice Age had begun that would last more than ten thousand years.

The icy battering rams moved at first through the river valleys, pulverizing vegetation, plowing great mounds of clay and debris in front of them, grinding and rounding off the rocks along their sides. They spread in fan shapes over the marshes and lowlands, filling in the lakes and destroying whatever life was in them. Snow kept falling, the ice caps got thicker. They overflowed the valleys and butted their way over the hills, crushing, scouring, scraping, plucking up and carrying great chunks of bedrock. On the continent, land animals could escape the approaching ice by migrating south. On the island, they were doomed. Soon, land forms disappeared altogether. The ice caps congealed into sheets, perhaps more than a kilometer thick, extending over the whole island and Labrador and far out over the continental shelf. The Labrador sheet crossed into the northern tip of Newfoundland, blocking off the sea passage between the two land masses. The whole northeastern corner of North America formed a white, frigid, lifeless wilderness.

At about 12000 B.C. the processes that caused the Ice Age were reversed or modified. The climate changed. The ice sheets over Labrador and Newfoundland couldn't go backward, but they started melting. Rivers of meltwater formed under the sheets, eroding the earth anew. The ice bridge from Labrador broke away. Hilltops and plateaus reappeared and warmed in the sun, which speeded up the melting. Vast quantities of clay, rock, and drift picked up by the ice over the centuries were deposited back on the land, to be reshaped or washed away by the glacial rivers; as much or more was dropped onto the continental shelf. By about 8000 B.C. the island of Newfoundland was glacier-free. A littered, silent and desolate landscape was left, featuring numerous narrow lakes inland carved by the ice, deep fiords and ragged shreds of islands along parts of the coast, and vast stretches of denuded outcrop. Gradually, as the climate got warmer, the vegetation of grass, flowers, low brush, spruce, and other evergreens reappeared in areas where coarse glacial drift could sustain them. Plant decomposition made the skin of soil a little richer and deeper. Insects returned. Deciduous trees grew. Songbirds and waterfowl flew in from the south. Fish that could migrate through salt water made it back to the island's rivers. Some land animals returned on spring ice. The ecology of the continental shelf, which must have been ravaged by the intrusive ice sheet,[1] was, in time, restored. Groundfish reappeared, including the voracious and abundant cod; in the water above them, herring, mackerel, and caplin swarmed in vast schools. Great whales found their way to the waters nearshore; seals and walrus to the islands and coastline.

At around 7000 B.C., perhaps as the retreating ice sheet was still visible inland, another species, Homo sapiens, made an appearance in Labrador. With him and her, our story begins.

* * *

These first inhabitants were Stone Age Indian hunter- gatherers from the southwest, migrants from the earliest Indian bands of North America. Having moved to the continent's east coast, they found their way along the south shore of the Gulf of St. Lawrence, across the mouth of the great river, and into southern Labrador. After about 1500 years, they had developed an "elaborate and distinctive complex of artifacts and ideas,"[2] i.e., a "tradition," that makes them definable to archaeology. They are said to belong to the Maritime Archaic Tradition. The people are termed Maritime Archaic Indians. As centuries passed, their descendants migrated further. By 3000 B.C., they had taken possession of the Labrador coast as far north as Ramah Bay, where they collected a pale gray translucent chert, prized for use as spear tips. By that date they had also moved into Newfoundland, and soon spread throughout the island. They disappear from the island's archaeological record about 1200 B.C., but what Tuck calls "a slender thread of evidence" points to their survival in southern Labrador. This thread of evidence suggests, but does not prove, that they are the distant ancestors of the Innu of Labrador and the Beothuck of Newfoundland.[3]

What we know of them derives solely from study of gravesites and cultural debris. In Labrador, their habitations varied from small pit structures to more elaborate rectangular longhouses, the latter perhaps being skin-covered summer dwellings used by a number of families.[4] Most house sites were on the littoral, though the Indians moved to less exposed places at the head of bays in winter, and perhaps moved with the seasons in search of food. But they were mainly a coastal people, living by exploiting sea resources, birds, fish, walrus, seals, and sometimes whales. They hunted with harpoons and lances "probably launched from large dug-out canoes."[5] They also pursued caribou; an Indian site at Nulliak Cove in northern Labrador has remains of a rock funnel to drive caribou towards waiting hunters. They buried their dead, apparently with elaborate ceremony, and believed in an afterlife. A surprisingly intact burial mound at L'Anse-Amour in Labrador, carbon-dated at c. 5500 B.C. — 3000 years before the building of the Great Pyramid of Khufu in Egypt — contained the body of a child about twelve years old, laid face down with a large stone on its back. The grave was lined with red ochre. Among items left with the body were a bone whistle, perhaps used for calling birds, a walrus tusk dagger, and the head of a toggling harpoon, part of a tool kit evidently thought to be needed in the next world.

This harpoon head pierced the animal being chased, but then twisted inside the flesh to form a crude hook or toggle. By means of a "skin line"[6] attached to the harpoon, the hooked animal could be pulled towards the thrower, or at least prevented from escaping. Once the seal or walrus was hauled within reach, the killing would be completed with lances. Even by the early date of c. 5500 B.C., the Indians appear to have been hunters of great skill and daring, since it would have taken both to retrieve a wounded seal or walrus with such a device. As time passed, their technology became more sophisticated. A Maritime Archaic cemetery at Port au Choix on Newfoundland's Northern Peninsula, dated c. 2300-1400 B.C., contained an assortment of ornaments and household implements, including "awls and bone needles with remarkably fine eyes [which] attest to the working of hides and the manufacture of tailored clothing."[7] One item found in this dig is a six-inch killer whale effigy carved from stone.[8] Its significance is unknown. Possessing it might have been thought a means of keeping the creature itself at bay. Or it might just have been sculpted for fun! It is in any case an object of great beauty, produced by a person or persons with both artistic talent and the leisure to indulge it.

The Indians lived on the coastline of Labrador and Newfoundland for thousands of years. Such impressive longevity dwarfs the subsequent 400-year European occupation (as does, to a lesser extent, the record of the ancient peoples who followed them). It implies not uneasy coexistence with a harsh environment but mastery over it. Yet the Indian population was perhaps never large, though some dwellings are thought to have occasionally housed "at least 7-15 families, thus group sizes of up to 50-100 individuals."[9] The evidence suggests a small, scattered, and somewhat nomadic people, finely adapted to the sometimes scarce, sometimes plentiful resources along the perimeter of a vast homeland. The nature of the resources was such that they kept the population low but allowed its continuance. But the survival of even durable inhabitants like these would be severely tested during a prolonged series of crises in the food supply, perhaps caused by climatic change. This might partly explain their apparent extinction on the island, or at least their complete emigration from it,[10] and their near extinction in Labrador.

A further complication in their lives was what must have been the startling (if not initially terrifying) appearance of another race in northern Labrador, close to the chert deposits on which the Indians depended for some parts of their weaponry. These so-called Palaeo-eskimos were descendants of Siberian hunters who moved across the Bering Strait into Alaska c. 2500 B.C. Over the next 500 years, pursuing, with their hunting dogs, their principal food supply, muskoxen, they traversed the high Arctic to Greenland, living on the northernmost islands and peninsulas of that bleak immensity. Around 1800 B.C. they found their way into Labrador and gradually migrated south along the coast. The Palaeo-eskimo move southward seems to correspond somewhat with the decline of the Maritime Archaic. It may not be altogether idle to conjecture a lengthy history of animosity between the two peoples, though perhaps "structured avoidance"[11] (staying out of each other's way, using different sites) is a more likely scenario. Still, the Palaeo-eskimo expansion no doubt put pressure on the Indians. A cooling climate would have favoured the new arrivals since they were an Arctic people, and hastened the latter's decline. As with the Maritime Archaic, we depend on archaeological reconstruction for insight into this people's way of life. Among their artifacts is one extraordinary item: a small ivory mask about 3500 years old, depicting a human face, perhaps that of an old woman, either in death or repose.[12] The eyes and mouth are tightly shut, the skin deeply and symetrically etched with lines. Who can tell what the object meant or was used for? Since they were racially distinct, the Palaeo-eskimos must have spoken a language the Indians couldn't understand; they also looked different, dressed differently,[13] built a different style of habitation — a skin-covered, circular home with a complex construct (including a hearth) across the diameter[14] — and used at least one weapon unfamiliar to those whose lands they invaded. This was the bow and arrow. We can imagine the feelings of the Indians when they first saw this formidable killing tool in use by interlopers in the land of their ancestors. The Indians appear to have adopted it themselves, and from them it could have spread throughout most of continental North America.[15] In turn, the Palaeo-eskimos might have adopted the toggling harpoon from the Indians.

By 800 B.C. the original Palaeo-eskimos' descendants, who are termed Groswater Palaeo-eskimos, had moved to the island of Newfoundland and spread throughout it, "excluding the Avalon Peninsula."[16] Excavations carried out at Port au Choix, a location highly valued by most of Newfoundland's early inhabitants, provide some insight into Groswater activities. They appear to have been expert seal hunters, likely employing boats and maybe even nets. They were migratory, moving to the coast when seals and fish were abundant, and inland at other times to chase caribou and smaller animals, including beaver, fox, and marten. Wolf bone has been found in one site. If they chased wolves, they were surely accomplished hunters. Their great weapon during their occupation of the island of Newfoundland was the harpoon, used to hunt the harp seal. A great number of Groswater harpoon end-blades (tips) were found at Port au Choix. Two chert end-blades in particular were "beautifully crafted [with] tiny and uniformly spaced edge serrations, and a ground facet on one face."[17] Such attention to craft in the making of a harpoon blade could signal the weapon's preeminence.

Over time, for whatever reason, the signposts of the original and Groswater Palaeo-eskimos[18] disappear from the archaeological record and are replaced by another distinct but apparently related culture. These people are called Dorset Palaeo-eskimos. They appear c. 600 B.C. in Labrador and around the beginning of the first century A.D. in Newfoundland. Exactly how they were related to earlier groups is unclear. They could be descendants, but it is possible that they represent a new migration from the north.[19] For the first time, we have some hint of what one of these shadowy early peoples called themselves or were called by a group they encountered. In Inuit oral history the Dorset were termed Tunit.[20] The Dorset occupied the entire island and may well have outnumbered other insular aboriginal peoples.[21] Around 800 A.D. they either withdrew from the island or became extinct. By c. 1400 A.D. they had also left northern Labrador. Not long afterwards, in their final retreat, the high Arctic, they vanished altogether.

The Dorset way of life seems to have centered, moreso than that of their ancestors, on the exploitation of ice-edge mammals — walrus, smaller whales, and seals of all types, but especially the harp seal.[22] Perhaps cooler climatic conditions during the period in which they flourished encouraged this kind of hunting. More sea mammals were available; one could specialize in, say, killing seals and walrus, and these would provide sustenance for much of the year, supplemented by caribou, birds, and fish as needed. Aspects of the earlier Palaeo-eskimo tradition of hunting muskoxen far from shore with dogs and bows and arrows would be discarded. Something like this happened, though over centuries. The Dorset people abandoned the bow and arrow, and there is no evidence they used dogs. Their boats and sleds were small, the latter likely hand-drawn. They used tools "efficiently and elegantly designed for their purposes":[23] lances and harpoons, thrown from standing positions on the ice, ice picks, bone creepers attached to the bottoms of boots to prevent slipping. They used seal oil lamps carved from soapstone to heat and light their houses in addition to the Palaeo-eskimo central stone hearth.[24] Food was heated in soapstone pots, gouged from well known quarry sites. Their winter houses were sturdy constructs of turf, sod, and stone, though some were skin-covered in the manner of their high Arctic predecessors.

The Dorset were prolific carvers and artists, and here again they specialized. Inuit legend depicts the Dorset as a culture of "large people possessing great physical strength who rejoiced in building with great boulders."[25] But their art and even many of their tools were carved or chipped in miniature from bone, ivory, tooth, wood, or soapstone. Carvings of seals, walrus, bears, belugas, muskoxen, and birds are normally tiny, though exquisitely crafted. The polar bear, doubtless a creature that inspired awe and terror in Dorset hunters, was a favourite model for the miniaturist. Sometimes the bear is shown simply sitting and bellowing. But the animal is also depicted as thin and extended, with rear legs stretched behind and the elongated front legs held tightly to the sides, as if the carver conceived it as diving or in flight — an early instance of abstract art. A miniature man is also shown as if in flight. Another tiny carving is of a seated man, dressed in the garb of a hunter.

The mysterious Dorset withdrawal from Newfoundland and Labrador (or extinction there) coincided with a period of global warming. This likely had a drastic effect on ice conditions along the coast, which in turn affected patterns in mammal migrations. The Dorset focus on the harp seal, which ensured the people's survival in periods of bountiful annual harvests, might have been fatal if the spring ice bearing the seals and pups stayed far offshore and inaccessible for even a single year.[26] Another factor in their decline, however, might have been the appearance of competing and possibly hostile intruders.

In Newfoundland, the intruders were Indians who crossed over from Labrador "sometime during" the first five centuries A.D., while the Dorset were still occupying the island.[27] These begin what is called the "Recent Indian" stage of Newfoundland "prehistory." One scholar has said they "were almost certainly descended from Maritime Archaic peoples," who he thinks continued to inhabit southern Labrador.[28] This second wave of prehistoric Indian migrants from Labrador to Newfoundland were possibly the ancestors of the Beothuck, the name given to the island's aboriginal Indians in the "historic" period, i.e., the period after 1497. (It was what they called themselves, though this wasn't known until the 19th century.) But archaeology has not yet established, and may not establish, a continuous line of descent between the historic Beothuck and the first Recent Indians. However, by 1000 A.D. the ancestors of the Beothuck had appeared in Newfoundland and can be identified.

As the Dorset were failing in Newfoundland, Indians were able to survive there. Why? We have to enter yet another "ill-lit lane of speculation"[29] for tentative answers. The new immigrants seem to have been more capable of adapting to changing climatic and ecological conditions. Whereas the Dorset were seal-killers of the headlands and outer islands, these perhaps made fuller use of the resources of the land as well as the sea, adopting "a somewhat more generalized strategy"[30] for survival. Their hunting and foraging practices were the ones needed in the circumstances. If the two peoples occasionally "resorted to fighting," as has been suggested,[31] it is likely the Indians would have had the upper hand. The Dorset had had a long sojourn as sole occupants of the island; the arts needed to resist attack — if attack there was — do not thrive in such a context. In Inuit legend they were pictured as a gentle, timid race. And now the Indians were evidently the ones with bows and arrows.[32]

The intruders in Labrador, whose impact on the Dorset culture was possibly just as severe, were the Thule Eskimo or, as they called themselves, the Inuit. At about 1000 A.D. these migrants from Alaska swept across the high Arctic, reaching Greenland in the 12th century, and Labrador in the 13th; during the following centuries they moved along the coast towards Hamilton Inlet, making occasional forays as far south as the Strait of Belle Isle.[33] As they moved east through the Arctic and into Labrador, they displaced the Dorset, who withdrew or were killed off, perhaps by disease, as they approached. (Though another possibility is that the Dorset had already disappeared in most parts of the Arctic before the Thule's arrival.)[34] The Inuit were aggressive and efficient whale hunters. They were capable of killing the bowhead right whale, and perhaps left Alaska to find a better supply of these large creatures, which conveniently stayed amidst the northern ice fields throughout the year. Of course, they hunted seals, walrus, and caribou as well. With their big skin-covered boats (umiaks), kayaks, dogs, dogsleds, and Mongol-style bows "powered by a thick cable of twisted sinew,"[35] they were a formidable new presence along the Labrador coast.

As we approach the historic period, then, at least three, and maybe four, aboriginal groups were present, either as permanent residents or regular visitors, in Labrador and/or Newfoundland. Inhabiting Labrador with the Inuit were the pre-contact[36] Innu (later termed Montagnais), who now mostly lived along the southern coast of the peninsula and in the interior as nomadic hunters of caribou and other game.[37] As stated earlier, they were possibly descended from the ancient Maritime Archaic. On the island of Newfoundland another Indian group, perhaps distant cousins of the Innu, ranged over most of the island in small bands, moving back and forth between the interior and the coast as seasons changed and different species of animals became available. Their total population might have been less than 1,000. It is likely that some of these pre-contact Beothucks crossed into southern Labrador to hunt, and that the prehistoric Innu sometimes hunted in Newfoundland too.[38] Similarly, the seagoing Eastern Micmacs (or Mi'kmaqs) of the Maritime Provinces may have hunted in southern Newfoundland, and possibly on other coasts, in the prehistoric period.[39]

Around 1000 A.D. one of the three last-named races, the prehistoric Innu, Micmac, or (most probably) Beothuck,[40] encountered yet another new breed of men and women at the northernmost tip of Newfoundland. There were the Norse, the first Europeans to see and occupy part of North America.

* * *

The Norse mini-empire in the North Atlantic had expanded to Iceland in the 9th century, and to Greenland by the 10th. From the *Grønlendinga Saga* (written in the late 12th century, but surviving in a late 14th-century text) we learn that in 985 or 986 A.D., Bjarni Herjolfsson, a trader, was blown off course for "many days" on a voyage from Iceland to Greenland, and eventually sighted land "not mountainous, but ... well wooded and with low hills."[41] This was probably Newfoundland. Bjarni didn't go ashore but sailed north, sighting land twice more, likely Labrador and Baffin Island, before finding his way to Greenland. In or about 1000 Leif Eiriksson, with a crew of thirty-five, retraced Bjarni's route from Greenland, naming the last country Bjarni saw Helluland, and the second Markland. Leif's and Bjarni's ships were probably not longships, which were coastal vessels, but heavier craft made for ocean voyaging; they were driven by single square sail at midship, and steered by an oar or rudder hung over the starboard side.[42] Two days after finding Markland, Leif saw land again, the first coast Bjarni had spotted. On landing on an island near the coast, Leif and his men saw dew on the grass. They got some on their hands and put it to their lips, "and to them it seemed the sweetest thing they had ever tasted."[43] They proceeded to the mainland, where Leif, having decided to overwinter, built "large houses." Leif named this new country (after his crew found grapes[44] there) Vinland, i.e., Wineland. The place in Vinland where Leif and his crew landed and built houses became known as Leifsbúðir (Leif's booths or camp). The following spring, they returned to Greenland. Over the next decade, according to the *Grønlendinga Saga*, four more voyages to Leifsbúðir were attempted. The last two were fairly elaborate efforts at settlement. In both instances some of the settlers were women.

The remains of eight unquestionably Norse buildings, three of them large halls with ample living and working space, were found at the tip of Newfoundland's Northern Peninsula in the 1960s; they were excavated, studied, and carbon-dated. Evidence points to a date c. 1000 A.D. The precise location is in a shallow bay[45] around whose edges lies an open, meadow-like peat bog, through which runs a brook. The buildings are about 100 yards from the shoreline. The woods lie well back. The terrain was possibly much the same in 1000 as it is in 1999. The spaciousness was perhaps a particular attraction to the visitors. If, on landing, they saw signs of human life along the shore and sensed danger, they had room to maneuver; they had a clear view for hundreds of yards and time to prepare for any attack from natives.

They looked around, and decided to stay.

There were men and women in the colony, if such it can be called.[46] They may have brought sheep with them (but perhaps only wool). They may have had pigs. They built sod houses over supporting frames of wood, cut from the nearby forests after they discovered it was safe to enter them. They dug a foot or two down in the marshland and found a dark brown layer of bog iron ore, which they smelted in a forge to make nails. The women cooked, spun wool, knitted, sewed, picked berries; the men hewed timber, repaired boats, fished, hunted, explored. Slaves did most of the menial labour. Somebody lost a bronze pin used to fasten a cloak, and never found it. Someone else misplaced or discarded part of a spindle. A quartzite needle hone (used to sharpen needles) was left behind, as was a small lamp made from a soapstone rock. A wooden arrowhead could have been a child's toy. The people lived off the land and sea. For how long? We don't know. But the nature of the remains suggests the Norse occupation lasted "a maximum of only a few years."[47]

This may or may not be the site of Leifsbúðir, as described in the *Saga*.[48] If the two are indeed the same, we know why the settlement failed, for the *Saga* describes in some detail the always tense, and latterly hostile, relations between the newcomers and native peoples (termed by the Norse "skraelings")[49] — hostilities caused more by the former than by the latter — and the murderous betrayals within the settler group itself. But even if the site discovered by archaeologists was not Leifsbúðir, we may perhaps deduce that, after an initial period of enthusiasm and hope, a single tiny group of settlers, feeling far from home, outnumbered by the unknown people among whom they found themselves,[50] sensing they were on the fearful edge of a vast new continent, would have found reason to withdraw.

They left, were killed by the skraelings, or just perished. Five centuries went by, during which the memory of a northerly route to Vinland faded. The native peoples of Newfoundland and Labrador had the place to themselves. It was a long interlude, but one destined not to last.

Chapter 2

European Outpost: 1497·1604

THE NEXT PART of the Newfoundland story is not without drama, for it encompassed ocean-going adventure and discovery. But the main ingredients, destined to be enduring ones in the years stretching ahead, were cod, peril, toil, and trade.

A few Bristol merchants had become interested in western exploration as early as the 1480s, and John Day, the English merchant who left the most complete account of the Cabot voyage, reported it was "certain" they had found "the Island of Brasil," a legendary place in the Atlantic. It is possible that they were sending out voyages in the early 1490s.[1] But there was no royal endorsement of such ventures until 1496. In that year, John Cabot, a Genoese-born citizen of Venice, but now master of an English ship, sailed westward from Bristol into the north Atlantic. Letters patent from Henry VII, King of England, authorized him to conquer "whatsoever such towns, castles, cities and islands" he might discover, and to give Henry one-fifth of "all the fruits, profits, emoluments, commodities, gains and revenues" he accrued.[2] Cabot turned back after becoming confused and running into bad weather. In May of the following year he struck west again; this time we know his crew numbered eighteen to twenty,[3] and there is some "very slight"[4] evidence that his ship was called the *Mathew*. On June 24, after a voyage of about thirty-five days, someone on board the ship sighted what Cabot later claimed was "the country of the Grand Khan"[5] (i.e., China, of whose longed-for wealth and spices he had read in Marco Polo). But it was North America, likely Newfoundland.[6] Disembarking with a crucifix near the point first seen, Cabot and a few men raised banners with the arms of the English king and of Pope Alexander VI. Not daring to go inland further than "the shooting distance of a cross-bow," they went back to their ship and spent a month "discovering the coast," without landing again. Then they recrossed the Atlantic in fifteen days.[7] Cabot was back in England by mid-August and was granted a pension by Henry. "Vast honour is paid to him and he goes dressed in silk, and these English run after him like mad," one observer noted.[8] News of the "new fund Yle" (to quote the Scottish poet William Dunbar),[9] spread rapidly through Europe. Cabot undertook a more elaborate western voyage in 1498, from which, it seems, he never returned. In 1501 a Portuguese crew landed in Newfoundland, or somewhere near there, and recovered from natives "a piece of broken gilt sword" and two Venetian earrings.[10] Perhaps these items had been taken from a Cabot shipwreck.

Cabot's planting of Alexander VI's banner at the landfall might have had more than just pious significance. It was that Pope who, in a papal bull in 1493, drew a line of demarcation on a north-south meridian, passing through the Atlantic 100 leagues west of the Azores. The line divided the non-Christian parts of the globe between the two great sea powers, Spain and Portugal. Spain was to get the New World, while Portugal had to be content with Africa and points east. In the Treaty of Tordesillas in 1594 the line of demarcation was moved farther west in the Atlantic, thereby giving Portugal a claim to Brazil and parts of North America. The raising of the Pope's banner in Newfoundland might have signalled English defiance of this arrogant partitioning.[11] (Then again, it might simply have marked an extension of Christendom.) In any event, Cabot's landing had little immediate effect on European imperial arrangements. Henry might think he owned New-foundland,[12] but the Portuguese seemed to regard it as part of their overseas empire, and even Spain fancied it had a claim.[13] Before long, France was to entertain the same notion.[14]

The Portuguese, however, were first off the mark to follow Cabot to New-foundland. In 1500 Gaspar Corte-Real of Terceira, an island in the Azores, headed north, found Cape Farewell in Greenland, which he mistook as Asia, and might have gone on to see parts of North America. A second expedition in 1501, on which Corte-Real's own ship, and he himself, were lost, cruised along parts of Labrador and Newfoundland, and other coasts, landing at least once.[15] A 1502 Portuguese map derived largely from this voyage seems to depict the island of Newfoundland, which is boldly called "Terra del Rey de Portugall" (land of the king of Portugal).[16] The island is shown to be covered with tall trees. Reports of the voyage stressed the "great store of wood" that had been seen, "above all of pines for making masts and yards of ships."[17] The crew of the 1501 voyage "forcibly kidnapped about fifty [native] men and women" — almost certainly Indians, perhaps Beothucks — thereby greatly pleasing King Manoel, who anticipated shortly having "plenty of men-slaves, fit for every kind of labour."[18] The method by which this large group was captured, and the conditions under which they were transported, have not been recorded. Neither has their ultimate fate, though a slave trade had already com-menced and they were likely sold.[19] Nothing was more pleasing to 16th-century Christian Europeans than the prospect of getting someone besides themselves, slaves, convicts, or aborigines, to do menial labour for nothing, or next to nothing. Corte-Real's brother Miguel sailed from Lisbon in 1502 to find his sibling; he too was lost. Another Portuguese obscurely involved in western exploration was João Fernandes, a landowner (labrador) in the Azores, who might have accompanied Cabot on his 1498 voyage and charted the coast known as Labrador, so called on maps by the 1520s.[20]

As news of Cabot's discoveries spread throughout Europe, shrewd observers took note, amidst the talk of spices, silk, and Brazil wood, of a more mundane commodity he had come upon, namely codfish. Cabot himself bragged that fish near the new isle could be caught "not merely with nets but with baskets, a stone being attached to make the basket sink in the water." Raimondo di Soncino, the

Duke of Milan's envoy in England, told his master this as if he were describing an Eldorado.[21] And there surely was reason for excitement. To a trader the humble cod had many appealing qualities. Once found, it was easy to catch and process. Its flesh wasn't bony like herring, or oily like salmon or mackerel. Since it wasn't fatty, it was easier to cure than other species and could be preserved for long periods. As for its taste, it was bland, hence acceptable to all, except perhaps to those with refined palates. Ribald jokes might be made about the cod, but it was, to quote Humphrey Gilbert, "a principall and rich and everie where vendible merchandise."[22] Yet if fortunes were to be made on it, it had to be found in great quantities.

England had traditional cod-fishing grounds off Iceland, but here was another allegedly abundant source of that valuable species.[23] Cabot's English crew said their country had "no more need of Iceland."[24] In 1502 a ship sent from Bristol brought back eighteen lasts (216 barrels) of salt cod — perhaps the first such cargo from Newfoundland and, if so, the beginning of one of the world's great fisheries.[25] Other voyages followed, but after 1505 English interest in Newfoundland enterprises appears to have slackened.[26] By then the French fishery had already begun; and the Portuguese were fishing in Newfoundland waters in 1506. The French fishing fleet, operating at first mainly from ports in Normandy and Brittany, but soon from La Rochelle and other places in the Bay of Biscay as well, grew rapidly. A report from 1517, albeit in a poem, numbers it at above 100 sail.[27] John Rut, an Englishman who led an expedition to Newfoundland, entered St. John's in early August, 1527, and found in that harbour alone "eleven saile of Normans, and one Brittaine,[28] and two Portugall Barkes, and all a fishing."[29] But the report he gave of the "mayne Land" he saw — "all wildernesse and mountaines and woods, and no naturall ground but all mosse, and no inhabitation nor no people" — would hardly have encouraged others to follow.[30] The Portuguese fleet, from ports such as Vianna and Aveiro, might well have equalled that of the French in the early decades of the century.[31] Fishermen from the Basque regions of Spain and France were active in Newfoundland waters from the 1520s. These nations, and the English as well, were already accustomed to conducting long-distance fisheries. It was a small adjustment, perhaps, to transfer effort and technology from waters off Iceland or Spitzbergen to the New World. The distance to Newfoundland was not great. Portugal's King Manoel noted that the resources found by Gaspar Corte Real were "very near to his kingdom."[32] And so the fleets sailed.

Before long cod-fishing, in elaborately equipped ships of between 30 and 100 tons, was carried out from dozens of ports along the French, Portuguese, and Basque coasts.[33] While much is known about the organization of the cod-fishing enterprise in Europe,[34] we know little about the actual fishing that went on in and around Newfoundland. Catching cod for a few months a year on the New World frontier left few marks apart from place names; and fishing was, in any event, a secretive business. It was also far down the list of occupations a man might follow, dirty, dangerous, low work, attractive mainly to the poor and illiterate — and of course to the shipowner-trader, who was normally back home with clean hands. Much depended on the "beastly trade,"[35] but few bothered to take notice of it. Amidst the numerous representatives of the common folk in Shakespeare — sailors, shepherds, pages, bawds, wenches, soldiers, constables, watchmen, jailers, grave-diggers — fishermen appear just once.[36] Yet he had smelled "not of the newest Poor-John."[37] (Poor john or poor jack being the familiar 16th-century name for "New land fish.")[38]

Until the mid 1500s, the Newfoundland fishery was evidently a shore fishery. Given the documentary void, we can speculate about how the fishery was carried out by looking backward from first-hand accounts in the next century. The men, having crossed the Atlantic, selected a harbour, landed, cut wood, built some rudimentary premises — stages (wharf-like, wooden structures, partly covered in, extending some distance into the sea on shores),[39] huts, cookhouses, flakes (platforms for drying cod) — and worked from there, fishing initially, perhaps, from the ships themselves but then using smaller keeled boats (shallops)[40] that were rowed or sailed to the nearby shoals. There the cod were caught on handlines with baited hooks. They were then brought to shore, pronged onto the stages, headed, gutted, and split (meaning the backbone was removed), and underwent one of two processes. They were either salted and immediately stowed for shipment (wet fish, also called green fish and cor[41] fish); or, after being salted for a time in stacked piles, they had the salt and brine washed off and were put out in the sun to dry, either on the flakes or directly on beaches (dry fish). As far as is known, in the early decades no nation had a monopoly on a particular coastline, though most Portuguese fishing went on around the Avalon peninsula, while the Strait of Belle Isle was chiefly occupied by Bretons.

It was soon discovered that there was no need to land in Newfoundland to fish. A great breeding ground of cod, the Grand Bank, lay southeast of the Avalon Peninsula, in area almost as large as the island and "coming within a few metres of the surface in numerous shoals."[42] By 1550 a bank fishery had emerged. Bank fishermen left continental European ports, fished far offshore, salted and stowed the fish in the ships' hold as it was caught, and sailed back home, perhaps without even touching land.[43] This was a faster way to make a voyage. If a ship left home very early in the year, it was possible to make a second voyage. Bank fishermen would go ashore, if at all, only to get firewood and water. To obtain meat, French bankers (and doubtless others as well) often went to Funk Island, thirty miles off Cape Freels, and dispatched a landing party for a supply of easily killed great auks, tricked by evolution into flightlessness. As the bank fishery expanded, a ship's master could tell without sounding that he was nearing Newfoundland "by the incredible multitude of sea foule hovering over the [Grand Bank], to pray upon the offales & garbish of fish throwen out by fishermen, and floting upon the sea."[44]

Cod and cod liver oil[45] were not the only merchantable commodities sought in Newfoundland waters. When Jacques Cartier visited the Strait of Belle Isle in 1534, one of the harbours on the Labrador side, Red Bay, was already known as

Whale Harbour.[46] Great numbers of right whales (including bowheads) and other species passed through the narrow Strait on their migrations into and out of the Gulf of St. Lawrence. From the 1530s[47] the experienced whalers from the Basque regions of Spain and France were going regularly to the Labrador side of the Strait, where they supplanted the Breton cod-fishermen. By mid-century a large whaling industry operated out of Red Bay (called Butus by the Basques), and other harbours between Cape Charles and the St. Augustin River.[48] Galleons of about 500-750 tons burden, about 20 to 30 in number, arrived each year in Labrador from ports such as San Sebastián, Orio, Guetaria, and St. Jean-de-Luz, carrying around 2,000 men. These proceeded to build or repair shore installations: cooperages to make barrels (out of staves brought from Europe), cabins (more substantial than fishermen's huts), forges, tryworks containing stone firepits, and landing stages or wharves — in effect, whaling factories. Imported Iberian red tile, the remnants of which, sprinkled on beaches and rock, ultimately gave Red Bay the name it bears, was used on roofs. Moravian missionaries were taken aback to find such "red tyles" amidst the ruins of a house on Henley Island in Chateau Bay in 1765, and correctly surmised the house had been "built by Europeans."[49] Whales were chased in rowed shallops, normally with a crew of seven.[50] They were killed with harpoons and drogues (heavy floats at the end of the harpoon line to slow the whale and tire it). The dead whales were towed to stages along shore, where the fat was cut off and minced into blubber. Copper cauldrons placed over the crude furnaces rendered the blubber into oil, which was put into barrels for shipping to Europe. Around 18-20,000 barrels of oil (each 400 pounds in weight) were exported each year[51] in the heyday of the industry, c. 1545-85. The Basques shipped oil directly from Labrador to England and France as well as to their home ports. Baleen, the bone-like flexible strainers in the mouths of right whales by which they collect food, was another valued export. Overall, Labrador whaling was a major contributor to the Basque economy. So familiar did Labrador become to the whaling crews and investors that while initially it was referred to in documents as "las partes de Tierra nueva," after 1560 it was often called "la Provincia de Terranova," as if it were part of the Basque country, which in a sense it was.[52] (In the 16th century the term Terra Nova, applied by the Basques to the Labrador side of the Strait of Belle Isle, could refer to a wide expanse of territory in the general area of Newfoundland.)[53]

A Basque graveyard with the remains of about 140 bodies has been excavated on Saddle Island in Red Bay harbour.[54] One grave contained seven skeletons lying in a row — perhaps a longboat crew had been killed in the highly dangerous activity of harpooning a whale. We might get more of the human side of the Basque story as more documents pertaining to whaling are found in Spanish archives.[55] One of the skeletons could be that of Joanes de Echaniz, who perished in Carrol's Cove, Labrador, on December 24, 1584, after dictating his will to the surgeon. Only two witnesses were on hand to see the will executed "because it was midnight and some of the sailors of the ship were working on land rendering whale to make train oil and the others were sleeping on board exhausted due to sheer work."[56] No priest was present, though priests sometimes accompanied the crews to Labrador.[57] The will is one of the earliest known pieces of writing done in the New World. The vignette it provides of men boiling blubber at midnight on Christmas Eve gives a clue about the toilsome life the whalers led. The late date of Joanes de Echaniz's will points to another feature of the whalers' experience. Unlike cod-fishermen, the whalers stayed in Labrador until the onset of winter, often mid-January.[58] So they endured colder weather on shore and stormier seas on the way home. The late departure also brought the danger of being iced in and having to overwinter. This happened to a ship and its crew in 1574.[59] Inadvertently, no doubt, the Basques may have proved that the coast of Labrador could sustain a European population year-round.

The Basques had better relations with native peoples than other Europeans.[60] This could mean they had more respect for the natives they encountered. There is, for instance, no evidence that they captured "salvages"[61] and brought them back for display in Europe, as others, including even Cartier, were prone to do. An Inuit woman and child from Labrador, seized by Frenchmen after they murdered the woman's husband, were on exhibition at Antwerp and in the Bavarian cities of Augsburg and Nuremburg in the 1560s. Handbills were printed to attract the curious.[62] By contrast, the Basques actually employed Indians (likely Innu) in their whaling work. Richard Whitbourne, writing in the early 17th century but recalling a Newfoundland career stretching back forty years, said the Indians helped the Basques "in the killing, cutting, and boyling of Whales ... without expectation of other reward, then a little bread, or some such small hire."[63] This, if described accurately, was undoubtedly exploitation, but it at least shows human interaction, and might even be a cut above trading practices of some other Europeans in North America, for example buying fox fur with "petty haberdasherie wares"[64] such as glass beads, or exchanging a tin plate for twenty buffalo skins.[65] Basque whalers probably had a greater need to make friends of the natives than fishermen. When they sailed home in winter, they left a sizeable establishment, their onshore factory, behind, together with their shallops.[66] To rebuild these every summer was impractical. By contrast, the fishermen left little in the way of huts and stages that couldn't be readily reconstructed the following year, though leaving behind boats was equally risky for them. Despite the generally harmonious relations between whalers and natives, two Basques were killed in 1574,[67] possibly by Inuit, who, over time, no doubt with good reason, seem to have become more hostile towards all European intruders.

The real threat to fishermen and whalers in the New World came less from the native peoples than from other Europeans. When war broke out — and war, as Keith Matthews noted, was "a normal condition"[68] of the day — no ship was safe from raids by enemy privateers[69] or men-of-war, especially as the fishing fleet neared home ports with full loads. Records from 1523 and 1531 show the English busily robbing French fishing ships; in the latter case a Breton boat had sought shelter from a storm at Ramsgate, only to be plundered. No fewer than twenty-five French ships with cargoes of cod were seized by the English in 1547. Bretons responded by attacking English shipping.[70] Skirmishes could also take place on or near the overseas fishing grounds. Shipowners sent vessels to Terra Nova not to catch fish but to steal it from competing enemy nations. This naturally led to bloodshed. When French Basques attacked Spanish Basques "by sea and by land" at a whaling harbour in Labrador in 1554, the fight lasted a day and night, one man was killed and several wounded.[71] The following year more deadly encounters occurred. In a "great fight" at a port "in the northern part of the New Land," Spanish Basques approached French "forts and bastions" in a surprise attack from land, killed seventy-two, wounded many more, and captured eight ships. So, at any rate, goes one report.[72] Violence continued until 1559, when the Treaty of Cateau-Cambrésis, signed by France, Spain, and England, ended decades of conflict. A period of peace followed, but war soon broke out again, with more bloody reverberations in the New World. In wartime fewer fishing ships left for Newfoundland, yet such was the lure of profit that many still chanced it. Small fishing vessels would be virtually helpless when caught by a privateer, but the large Basque galleons could offer a stiff fight. In addition to anchors, cables, tiles, and other gear for whaling, they brought to Newfoundland heavy artillery in the form of iron cannon (protruding, when in use, from ports along the deck), swivel guns (smaller pieces, set on pivots on the ship's gunwale), harquebuses (early rifles), gunpowder, crossbows, pikes, corslets (body armour), and helmets.[73] Native peoples might well have been astonished to see arriving on their shores such technologically advanced apparatus for human slaughter.

English interest in the Newfoundland fishery, intermittent since early in the century, revived in the 1570s. Anthony Parkhurst, a Bristol shipowner with first-hand knowledge of the migratory fishery, reported that only four[74] "small barkes" went to Newfoundland from England in 1572, but that the number had grown to forty by 1577. Half of these were "worthy shippes," some so big that each could bring home as much fish "as all the navy did before."[75] The number had grown to fifty the following year, when Parkhurst wrote an elaborate report on Newfoundland in which he noted that the Spanish cod-fishery, which had commenced a major expansion in the 1550s, stood at 100 sail, while the French stood at 150.[76] Add to these a Portuguese fleet numbering about fifty and Basque whaling galleons at between twenty and thirty. The fishery was crowded. Thousands of men and boys were going annually to Newfoundland, either as bank- or shore fishermen (though an English bank fishery didn't begin until much later). When Humphrey Gilbert arrived in St. John's on August 3, 1583, to take possession of the island for Elizabeth I of England, he found thirty-six Portuguese, French, Basque, and English ships there. One of his captains, Edward Hayes, said the harbour "seemed a place very populous and much frequented."[77]

Reports on the extensively documented Gilbert expedition shed light on conditions and practices in St. John's and on the fishery generally. When the first of his four ships, the *Squirrel*, arrived at the port, the English fishing captains refused her entry, suspecting, with good reason,[78] that she was a pirate or privateer. On arriving, Gilbert had to send a boat ahead to explain that he had a "Commission from her Majestie" and had arrived "for no ill intent"; he was then allowed in through the Narrows. The English masters did not assume that the arrival of an English ship was necessarily fortuitous. Instead, they took steps to protect themselves and the ships of other nations from an anticipated assault. The thirty-six vessels in port formed a community of self-interest, and appeared to coexist in Newfoundland more happily than their squabbling mother countries did back in Europe. There may have been more of this international collaboration in Newfoundland than the documents show. The fishermen may also have had some attachment to the land, or at least a reluctance to deface it. When the Hungarian poet Stephen Parmenius, who sailed in the *Swallow*, suggested that the woods be set afire in the vicinity of St. John's so that "we might have space, and entrance to take view of the Countrey,"[79] Gilbert would probably have done it but for the protests of fishermen. They claimed the turpentine "and rosen of the trees" would flow into the sea and spoil the fishery. Parmenius was a man of sensitivity who could sing of "shapely cedars" and "lofty firs" in other settings.[80] But Newfoundland was "a very wildernesse" to him. Burning the scrub and low trees along the coast in order to "have space" was a thought that occurred to many other European visitors. And sometimes more than a thought; a deed. Even Whitbourne, who complained of "good timber trees" being "spoiled or burned" by fishermen, recommended burning "unnecessary bushes" and "unserviceable woods" in order to "lessen" fogs and improve the climate and soil.[81]

Gilbert's formal act on behalf of the Queen, important as it was, in a sense merely recognized a reality, at least as far as the east coast of Newfoundland was concerned. The English were "commonly lords of the harbors where they fish," as Parkhurst saw in 1578.[82] This fact had become evident in the way the harbours were governed or regulated. In St. John's, Hayes wrote, masters of English vessels were now "alwaies ... Admirals" over the fishing fleet in the harbour.[83] This meant that the master of the first English ship to arrive in the spring became admiral, and as such was responsible for adjudicating disputes and protecting the other ships.[84] In return, he likely had the choice of the best fishing room in port. (A room is a waterfront space suitable to carry out fishing.) He could also ask for help in fishing or demand salt or a boat. By the 1570s, as Parkhurst makes clear, the role and powers of the admiral had become "an old custome of the countrey."[85] Before the English became dominant on the east coast, the first in port became admiral, no matter what his nationality was.[86] At Renews as late as 1582 a French Basque was admiral.[87] Whoever entered the harbour after him took the next best room and accepted the admiral's authority. The position of admiral was naturally much sought after;

captains held offshore by contrary winds would send longboats ahead to secure the top spot. This informal structure on a lawless frontier, an unwritten international code, possibly worked well in the early fishery. It was eventually incorporated in statutes, and endured into the 18th century.

Before Gilbert's arrival in St. John's, fishing rooms there, as in other harbours, were available to all comers on a first-come, first-served basis. There was an "absolute freedom of fishing which forbade the reservation of beach space from year to year."[88] Gilbert changed this by granting, in free-farm (i.e., perpetual possession but subject to fixed rent) "divers" rooms "both in this harbor of S. John and elsewhere" to certain "owners."[89] This appears to be the earliest European attempt to establish property rights on the island of Newfoundland. How long the grantees remained attached to particular rooms is unclear. They were obliged "yeerly to maintain possession," a hard condition to meet, and later fishermen would have resisted the intrusion on well-established liberties, and doubtless found means to circumvent it.[90] Gilbert also tried to establish a religion in Newfoundland. The "publique exercise" of religion, he directed, "should be according to the Church of England."[91] He issued a decree against treason, and declared that anyone uttering words of dishonour to Queen Elizabeth "should loose his eares, and have his ship and goods confiscate." (Those who knew of Gilbert's brutal record as a pacifier of Ireland would not have been disposed to take his threats lightly.) The attempt to impose such laws on a coastline without onshore establishments to enforce them, or even carry a memory of them from year to year, seems quixotic. His decrees were likely more honoured in the breach than in the observance. Gilbert himself perished on his way back to England a month after taking possession of Newfoundland, and his plan to construct "a colonial Utopia" somewhere in North America in which he would be "the governor and universal landlord" came to nothing.[92] The poet Parmenius left his bones in the Atlantic too.

In the 1580s and '90s the English fishery continued to expand, while the Spanish fleet declined, and with it that of Portugal, which was conquered and absorbed into Spain in 1580. When Spain closed her ports to English ships in 1585, the raider Bernard Drake rushed to Newfoundland to warn English ships not to proceed directly to Spain with their fish, an indication that a "triangular trade" (from the West Country[93] to Newfoundland, and from there directly to European ports, where cod would be exchanged for specie or wine, spices, olive oil, aniseed, almonds, raisins, etc. for the English market) was already established.[94] While in Newfoundland, Drake captured sixteen Portuguese fishing ships, a severe blow. The defeat of the Armada in 1588 dealt a similar crushing blow to the Spanish Newfoundland fleet, since the Armada was composed partly of embargoed fishing and whaling vessels. Despite disruption in trade caused by the closing of Spanish and French ports in the late 1580s, English fish would not be shut out of Europe. As the end of the century neared, the fishery had grown to perhaps 150 sail, operating mainly out of West Country ports, from which cod was supplied to the

English and Irish markets, and to the continent, either through the triangular route or re-export. European vessels awaited the English fleet to transship cod. In one fortnight in September, 1595, fifty English fishing ships from Newfoundland arrived in Plymouth, where they were met by Flemish and French ships ready to take their cargo.[95] When war with Spain ended in 1604, English merchants were ready to move briskly into that market as well. In fact, they began to do so as early as 1599.[96] And English fish was reaching Spain via France before then. War did not always obstruct the serious business of making money.

England was now a rising power in Europe and on the high seas. Rising as well were her imperial ambitions in North America. Her great rival, France, was not to be easily dislodged from Newfoundland, but in the century's closing decades the French shore fishery was likely being nudged into harbours on the south coast and north of Cape Bonavista.[97] Yet the French fleet was still numerically dominant. Meanwhile, with the decline of whaling in the Strait of Belle Isle, harbours on the island's west coast were beginning to be occupied by Basque cod-fishermen.[98] England was paramount over the east coast, between Cape Race and Cape Bonavista, a wide area to be sure, but only a fraction of the island. The English followed the "dry" method of curing fish, which meant they made greater use of onshore establishments than their rivals from other countries. With this use came closer adherence to the coastline and greater knowledge of it. Perhaps even more liking for it. As the century closed, English cartographers were depicting Newfoundland, not as an archipelago or peninsula, but as an island onto itself.[99] (Though Hayes seemed still uncertain whether it was "An Ilande or ... sundry Ilandes and broken landes.")[100] Inevitably, parts of the hinterland were becoming known as well. Parkhurst had evidently been "up in the land" (likely meaning a short distance back of the coast) "toward the South" (doubtless the coast used by the English) where, he said, the island, far from being cold "as foolish Mariners doe say," was "hotter then in England."[101] He also planted seeds of various grains and herbs to show "the fertilitie and goodnesse of the countrey." The island, he said, was "full of little small rivers all the yeere long proceeding from the mountaines," and "lakes with plentie of fish." It was "most covered with woods of firre, yet in many places indifferent good grasse."[102] He was among the first to see that there was more to Newfoundland than fish, something later commentators, including not a few historians, would at times fail to notice. Hayes found much to enjoy and praise in this new country, though he saw it only briefly. Neither of these seamen was a dreamer. Yet both recommended a new approach[103] to Newfoundland, one that would soon be widely discussed: settlement. Hayes in fact drew up an elaborate plan for colonization, one calling for the renting of shore space, fortification of harbours, construction of guesthouses, production on the island of pitch, tar, soap ash, cordage, linen, hides, and fur, and employment of convicts to row galleys and do other forms of menial labour. Newfoundland "may become the richest Corner of the World," he said.[104] Such schemes had to be put on hold as war heated up with Spain. The disastrous

Virginia experiment of 1587 also gave men reason to pause.[105] Yet before long settlement in Newfoundland would be tried — and proved.

Of course, the island and Labrador were already settled, by the aboriginal populations. By the end of the 16th century, these peoples had already been affected by contact with Europeans. They traded with the intruders, learned the use of iron from them, and likely caught their diseases. They learned more efficient ways to kill. They saw the the emblem of the Christian God erected on their land. In time, these and other influences would change their lives profoundly, often, but not always, for the worse.

No expulsion of the invaders was possible. There was no turning back; the Europeans had come, and would soon dominate. The way to survive was to adapt to their ways, to interact with them and learn from them. For the 500[106] or so Beothucks on the island, tragically, for reasons we can only guess at,[107] the kind of adaptations that were needed to ensure survival proved to be beyond their grasp.

Chapter 3

Unsettled Settlement: 1605-64

IN THE EARLY 1600s Newfoundland remained a frontier which Europeans visited and exploited, and from which, once their business was done, they quickly departed. But while dispatching fishing ships on annual voyages was understood to be a fast way to make money,[1] it was also fraught with peril. Amidst the prosperity and optimism following the peace with Spain in 1604, some Englishmen, not buccaneers like Raleigh and Grenville who had botched the Virginia settlements of the 1580s, or visionaries like Gilbert, but mostly practical men of affairs, began to think again along the lines suggested by Parkhurst and Hayes. They fancied there was a better way than the ship fishery to exploit Newfoundland. If a coastal region was granted or purchased, and men and women settled on it, their work would, it was believed, somehow create big profits for the investors back home. The settlers might find gold, silver, iron, tin, pearls; they would trade in furs, tax foreign shipping, lease property, try farming, lumbering. And go fishing too. Wealth would flow to England as it had to Spain from Mexico. Such were the mercenary motives behind the founding of the early English colonies in Newfoundland. It was also the thinking behind the Jamestown plantation of 1607 and some of the New England colonies. Nor was this the only initial similarity between American and Newfoundland settlement experience. Yet colonial development on the island would in time take a strikingly different path from that on the continent.

While profit was the main objective behind the early Newfoundland colonies, it was not the only one advanced by promoters.[2] In an age of empire building, the island was seen as "a new accesse of Dominion" that would bring "perpetuall Honour" to the King.[3] It was a "Sister land,"[4] not far off, closer to England than to any other European state. So it was natural that England should settle and own it. If England didn't, some other country would.[5] (Fears of rising Dutch power were now commonly expressed in the imperialist literature.) Once Newfoundland was taken, the next step might be to annex the adjacent portions of the North American continent; thus the island was a stepping-stone to bigger things. Settling Newfoundland would also drain off the excess population of vagrants, idle unemployed, loiterers, criminals, and "fatherlesse children," widely thought to be pestering the commonwealth.[6] (It was around this time that the Earl of Gloucester's son, Edgar, in *King Lear*, decides that the best way to escape pursuers is to disguise himself as Poor Tom, since "The country gives me proof and precedent/ Of Bedlam beggars.")[7] Again, possessing Newfoundland would strengthen the navy and enlarge trade, thereby adding to the wealth and security of the kingdom. And there was a religious argument. Newfoundland had a number of "poore mis-beleeving Inhabitants," "Infidels" living in "Barbarisme"; the way to bring them to "the knowledge of God, and the light of his truth" was by planting[8] a colony, and "by that meanes onely."[9] But it was also claimed, as one of the attractions of Newfoundland, that there were no "savage people" there; or at least none on the east and south coasts of the island, "which is the fittest place for a plantation."[10]

Some of these arguments were expressed or implied in the documents relating to the first English attempt at year-round settlement on the island.[11] This attempt was financed by the London and Bristol Company,[12] which was granted a royal charter[13] on May 2, 1610. The grantees included the essayist Francis Bacon, John Guy, a Bristol merchant who had visited Newfoundland in 1608, the London merchant John Slany, and Sir Percival Willoughby, a country squire from Nottinghamshire.[14] In their petition for a charter, the investors stressed the contribution a colony would make to the already well established Newfoundland trade, namely the ship fishery. They were making a plantation "for the good of the fishinge trade," they said. A colony would be a means of securing "the places of fishing forever ... for our nation," by keeping foreign countries from gaining possession. Colonists would also supply the visiting fishermen with "manie necessaries," assist them during sickness, and keep "their boates saufe for the right Owners &c." As for themselves, they would expand the fishery by frequenting "manie places" not used by the fishing ships owing to lack of harbours. They asked for "a small parte of the saide Countrie," but with the rights of fishing ships, both English and foreign, to be reserved. In describing their own anticipated activities in Newfoundland, they emphasized whaling, agriculture, furs, lumber, seals, and mines — all of which "might easily raise greate proffitt" — more than fishing.[15]

The company was granted the land south of the parallel passing by Cape Bonavista, and east of the meridian passing by Cape St. Mary's, together with "seas and islands" within ten leagues (roughly thirty miles) of the coast. This was much more than "a small parte" of the country. It was, if the stated boundaries were adhered to, a sizeable territory, comprising the Avalon and Bonavista peninsulas, part of the eastern interior, and the islands off the east coast and in St. Mary's and Placentia bays.[16] Yet even that area was considered too small. In addition to the specific grant, the company was given "all" the land and islands "commonly called Newfound Land" between latitudes 46°N and 52°N — in effect, the whole island.[17]

The charter stipulated conditions and conferred certain powers. The "singular liberties" enjoyed by Englishmen "and persons of what nation soever" to fish in Newfoundland were not to be disturbed but were to be continued "in as large and ample manner" as before, "anything in these presents to the contrary notwithstanding." King James was to get a fifth of all the gold and silver ore found (a standard clause in such charters). The company had power to tax British and foreign ships trading in merchandise unrelated to fishing, at rates of 5% and 10% respectively, for twenty-one years, after which the taxes would go to the King — a considerable power it appears not to have used.[18] It could "take and lead" into the plantation as many colonists as would willingly come, but all such colonists had to take the Oath of Supremacy. This oath, which declared the monarch supreme in spiritual and ecclesiastical matters as well as temporal, obviously eliminated all "suspected to affect the superstitions of the Church of Rome."[19] The colony would be Protestant. The company could make laws for the government of the colony, provided such laws were "as near as conveniently" agreeable to the laws of England, and had "full and absolute power and authority" to "correct punish pardon govern and rule" both inhabitants and those "who adventure themselves in any voyage thither." This last instruction, since as written it embraced both settlers and non-settlers, might well have been construed as applying to visiting fishermen, as John Guy later seemed to think it did.[20] But the "notwithstanding" clause quoted above placed the ship fishermen outside any laws made by the company.

Guy, an energetic, able, and literate man, was appointed governor of the colony. He "had supreme authority and was to govern without assistance," Cell writes.[21] The colonists sailed in a single ship from Bristol on July 5, 1610, but the loss of the ship's anchor, along with contrary winds, caused delays. Guy finally left the Welsh seaport of Milford Haven for Newfoundland on July 22, arriving in Conception Bay in August. The tossing of the ship on the voyage killed one of the goats on board. But the thirty-nine[22] colonists, all men, survived, even one who caught smallpox in Bristol. Only nine were to be engaged in catching and processing fish; the rest were "land men."[23] The plan was to create a varied economy, with the colony functioning, in part, as a hub in triangular trade[24] with continental Europe and the West Country. It was to be, in part, a trading and supply post.[25] Guy had already determined that either Colliers Bay, which he had visited in 1608, or Cupers Cove (later Cupids), both near the head of Conception Bay, would be the place "to beginne our plantacion."[26] The phrase is significant: he didn't intend to confine himself to one spot. He wanted to settle Renews as well — he hoped to find pearls in clams discovered near there — and perhaps other locations.[27] In the event, he chose Cupids over Colliers Bay "for the goodness of the harbour, the fruitfullnes of the soyle, the largenes of the trees, and many other reasons." This would be the "cheefest place"[28] for the colony.

The big cove in which Cupids is located, called by Guy Salmon Cove, is open to northeast winds, as are so many coves in Conception Bay; but Guy chose a location behind a natural breakwater — a rocky spit, open to the sea at one end, forming a protected harbour. A brook flowed from a large pond just in back of the site. The land he built on[29] was low-lying but not marshy, giving hopes of agriculture. The large trees he saw might have been a sign that the place was little used by migratory fishermen; but when he landed there were fishing ships in the area, their summer's work done, waiting for a fair wind home. In his letter to Willoughby in October, he reported favourably on the climate, fish, birds, "hills full of woods," herbs, scurvy-grass,[30] and berries. The men had a sawpit in place and were at work building a storehouse, dwelling house, and other structures. Guy's examination of the soil showed it was "deepe in some places without stones." He summed up: "there wanteth nothinge to make a flourishinge Country but cattle and the industry of men, without which" — he added in an apparent slip of the pen — "our Country [i.e., England] would be as bad as this." But the colony would soon be able to support itself, he said, "and cattle undertakers and tennents to take land of the Company wilbe in aboundance drawn hether."[31] It is moving to have such a testament from a settler not long off the boat, overlooking the rugged coastline of Conception Bay. Guy's optimism lasted throughout the first winter, which luckily was mild. Even so, four of the colonists perished, including the smallpox victim and one who died "of thought." By the following May chicken were hatching, grain was growing, swine prospering.[32]

One of the advantages of settling was to be certain of a good room to go fishing. That, at least, was Guy's view. If the rule was that the first arrival would get the choice of rooms, then, he said, the colonists, who were "sure to be first be first here every yeare," would take "what stage they shall have need of." In 1610 Guy calculated this assurance of "a good place" as worth more than £100 or £200 per year.[33] How this could be reconciled with the freedom of the fishery as explicitly guaranteed in the charter was, however, a problem, one that, on paper at least, was insoluble. Guy had been instructed, if, on arriving, he saw evidence that the fishermen regarded his enterprise with suspicion, to read his "patent" (i.e., charter) and commission to "Some few of the cheife of them."[34] They would then be assured that "their former right of fishing" was assured. He decided he would wait until the following year to do this. After wintering in Newfoundland and perhaps having considered the problem at length, Guy did indeed reserve a space in Cupids for one of the company's ships, but the "spaces desired" for a second ship supposed to come earlier had all been "possessed" by other boats when it arrived. It evidently had to choose an inferior room. So he risked reserving one room only, though obviously two ships needed two. Guy appears to have had doubts as well about the one room he did reserve — he may not have selected the best one available, and when the ship turned up the master in fact decided to go on to Ferryland.[35] The episode reveals Guy's unwillingness to take undue advantage of his position. As for the ship fishermen, if they resented the prior appropriation of a room by a settler this was not immediately apparent, since the earliest to come in 1611 "most willingly" supplied the few wants of Guy's men.

Yet by mid-August, 1611, before he left for a winter in England, Guy felt the need to issue a proclamation aimed directly at the visiting fishermen, not just those in Conception Bay, and not only Englishmen but "all persons of what nation soever." A "plantation and government is begun to be settled" in Newfoundland, he stated, and "among those persons that use the trade of fishing ... many disorders, abuses and bad customs" have crept in, though more from "corrupt usage" than malice. He then listed his commands and fines. No ballast was to be thrown into harbours. Fishing premises were not to be destroyed or damaged or made use of to repair other premises; timber for repair was to be taken out of the woods, not from structures already in place. Fishermen (even admirals, who must have been taken aback to find themselves dictated to) were not to take up more space in the harbours than they really needed.[36] Identifying marks left on boats were not to be cut away or defaced. Boats left behind were not to be made use of without the owners' consent. The woods were not to be set on fire. Fishermen at the end of their voyage were not to destroy their stage, cook-room, or flakes. No master of a fishing ship was to "receive into his ship or custody" any planter, without the governor's special warrant.[37] (He was already worried about deserters.) Some of these clauses would be repeated as a matter of course in later regulations for the fishery. Here they appear to come from direct observation. Newfoundland in the early 1600s was evidently often rowdy and brutal, governed, if that word can be used at all, by custom, not law. But with Guy's regulations, the frail hand of law had dared to interpose itself on an unruly coast.[38]

Guy returned from England in 1612 with additional settlers — sixteen women.[39] Soon more men arrived. The population peaked at 100 in the summer of 1612, then dropped to sixty-two the following winter.[40] This was a considerable advance over the original thirty-nine. But difficulties and disappointments had already occurred. The threat of piracy in the summer of 1612[41] led Guy to cancel his plan to settle Renews. A report done on the possibilities for agriculture was not encouraging. Efforts to grow grain were unsuccessful. Complaints came from settlers of "usage far woorse than we expected" (presumably at the hands of Guy), "labour verie much and harde," and doubts "of the goodnes of our land."[42] In November contact was made with the Beothuck in Trinity Bay — the only known friendly encounter between the Indians and Europeans — but prospects for extensive trade did not look promising.[43] Now a harsh and long winter set in. By late February, half the settlers were suffering from scurvy. Eight died. But the first child was born in the colony on March 27, 1613. Seventy goats, many pigs, and all but one of the cattle perished when fodder ran out. Guy left again for England in the spring of 1613, and likely never came back. The population was down to thirty the following winter. In 1614 Guy complained of lack of financial support for the colony. The company, he said, had not even paid his men's wages.[44]

A new governor, John Mason, was in Cupids in 1616, and over the next few years busied himself in exploring the south coast of the island. These explorations were in time incorporated in a famous map (1625), perhaps the first to show an accurate detail of the interior (a pond with an island, near the head of Trinity Bay).[45] Mason also wrote a *Briefe discourse* on the island (1620) in which he answered "maligne persons" who "bl[e]mish the good name thereof."[46] But by the 1620s the colony was in decline, Bristol merchants had split off from Londoners to form their own company, and investor interest in the Cupids venture had virtually disappeared.

By then, other settlement schemes were in progress or being planned. One, indeed, had already collapsed. That was the colony established in 1617 by the Welshman William Vaughan on land obtained from the London and Bristol Company on the southern Avalon Peninsula. His colonists were Welsh. At any rate, in 1619 they were termed "the Welch fooles" by a settler at Cupids. They settled in 1617, evidently at Aquafort.[47] In 1618 Whitbourne found they had spent the winter "most shamefully" in fishermen's huts, not having bothered to build a proper house.[48] He moved some of them to Renews, but the following year they went home. Another colony, of which few records survive, was established in 1617 or 1618 by Bristol merchants on the west side of Conception Bay. Called Bristol's Hope,[49] the colony was centered in Harbour Grace but extended north to Carbonear and some distance south. Whitbourne in 1622 said the colonists "have builded there faire houses" and "live there very pleasantly," but his account is so short and so vaguely worded as, perhaps, to be unreliable.[50] The colony was reportedly doing well in 1631.[51] In 1623 Henry Cary (Lord Falkland), the Lord Deputy of Ireland, seems to have dispatched settlers to a six-mile-wide strip of territory granted to him by Vaughan. The strip included both Fermeuse and Renews harbours, the latter especially popular with fishermen owing to the number of desirable rooms and, perhaps, the appealing flatness of surrounding land. Renews was apparently the site of Cary's settlement. Much is known of the preparations for the colony; practically nothing of the activities of the colonists.[52]

George Calvert (later Baron Baltimore), a principal secretary of state (1619-25) in the court of James I, also caught the colonizing fever. He too procured land from Vaughan, north of Falkland's allotment, and in 1621 sent a group of twelve men under a Welshman, Edward Winne, to settle Ferryland. Winne built in the big harbour to the north of Ferryland Head, a picturesque finger of land that he rightly said was "almost an island."[53] The harbour mouth was protected by islands and shoals, while in the inner harbour a curving spit of rocky beach formed an inviting sanctuary for boats and stages. In 1622 the number of settlers rose to over thirty, of whom seven were women. So impressed was Calvert by reports from the colony that in April, 1623, he obtained a royal charter expanding his holdings as far north as Petty Harbour and the head of Conception Bay. (Initially he was granted the whole island.) The charter, which gives Calvert's lot the name of Avalon, resembles that of the London and Bristol Company, but there were important differences. The freedom to fish was asserted, but with the restriction that the fishermen will cause no "Injury or notable loss or detriment" to Calvert or the inhabitants, "especially in the Woodes growing within the said Province," under penalty of incurring the King's "heavy displeasure."[54] No such clauses were in the earlier charter. No Oath of Supremacy was required,[55] possibly because the king knew of Calvert's leanings towards Roman Catholicism. The specific right of inhabitants to "have, hold, buy, and possess, ... occupy & enjoy, give, sell ... & bequeath" land was affirmed. It had only been implied in the charter of 1610.[56] Calvert was given the power to make

laws for "good and happy Government," but with the "advice, Consent & approbation" of the "freeholders of the sayd Province," a clause which had the same
general intent as instructions given to the Virginia colony and might have led to the
early establishment of democratic institutions in Newfoundland. (Virginia had a
resident governing council — which elected a president — in the early years of
settlement, and an assembly in 1619.) Again, the 1610 charter contained no such
statement. Another clause seemed to imply that Calvert could impose customs
duties on merchandise passing through ports in his colony.[57] It is not clear whether
he ever used this power.

Calvert announced his conversion to Roman Catholicism and resigned as
secretary of state in 1625. In that year he appointed a new governor in Ferryland,
Sir Arthur Aston, a Catholic, who may have brought fifteeen Catholic settlers with
him to Newfoundland, thereby making Ferryland a community of mixed faiths.[58]
When Aston was killed in France in 1627, Calvert himself went to Ferryland to
deal with unspecified difficulties in the colony. He took two Catholic priests with
him, Anthony Smith (alias for Anthony Pole) and Thomas Longville. Also in
Ferryland in 1627 was a Church of England minister, Erasmus Stourton. (Richard
James, another minister, had been there earlier.) The place was well stocked with
clergy. Calvert and Longville went back to England after the summer, but Pole
remained in Ferryland, awaiting Calvert's return. Ferryland was becoming a fairly
elaborate settlement, with a stone "mansion house" and other dwellings within a
palisade (perhaps with a drawbridge), a cobblestone street, forge, warehouse,
wharves, and cleared land under cultivation outside the fortified area — a colony
intent on farming as well as fishing, though mainly the latter. Evidently deciding
to make it his home, Calvert returned in 1628 with his wife and all but one of his
children, about forty more Roman Catholics, and another priest named Hacket. The
population was now perhaps 100. While Calvert's intention seems to have been to
"make his new province one in which Catholicism was fully represented,"[59] he
planned no assault on Protestantism. On the contrary, he was a tolerant man, even
permitting Catholic and Protestant services to take place "under one and the same
roof." News of this scandal reached Rome. Ferryland was to be a "noble experiment" in religious freedom.[60]

The experiment was not destined to succeed. The minister Stourton, dismayed
to see the Catholic mass openly celebrated, was soon back in London telling tales
about a forced Baptism and other "papist" "ceremonies."[61] The fact that Calvert
took most, if not all, of the Catholics with him when he left in 1629 could mean
that Ferryland Protestants were as shocked as Stourton with the goings-on, and as
hostile. The English "hatred and fear of Catholics"[62] reflected in the minister's
actions would be a lingering theme in much subsequent Newfoundland history. It
was perhaps the most distasteful import from 17th-century England. But other
factors contributed to Calvert's decision to go. He found himself on an undefended
coastline, and soon was forced to take action to protect the fishery. "I came to builde,

and sett, and sowe," he complained in 1628, "but I am falne to fighting with Frenchmen."[63] On one of his actions against French raiders, his men captured sixty-seven of the enemy, and he was "troubled and charged" with them for the summer. His charter authorized him to put them to death, but he declined to do this. He wrote home, explaining his "difficulties and Incumbrances," and asking for military protection.[64] By December, 1628, in the middle of an "intolerable" winter, during which half the settlers were sick at the same time and about ten died, he asked for a grant of land in Virginia. The winter didn't end until mid-May. "It is not to be expressed with my pen what wee have endured," Calvert wrote in 1629; he was "almost undone."[65] In late summer, thinking himself deceived by glowing accounts from the first settlers in Ferryland, and having lost thousands of pounds,[66] he and most of his Catholic followers fled to America, where more trouble awaited them. Ferryland was left with perhaps thirty residents.[67]

The hopes of making huge profits, quick profits, or any profits, from the English colonies in Newfoundland were, so far at least, illusory. Projectors seemed to grasp fully neither the enormous difficulties inherent in colonization nor the "large capital investments"[68] required in such ventures. Lack of capital was the likely cause of Guy's failure. *Loss* of capital, with loss of nerve, contributed to Calvert's. But capital wasn't the whole story. Extracting wealth from any North American colony or creating a comfortable and independent life there for inhabitants would take ingenuity, persistence, and ruthlessness. The difficulties faced by the early colonies in Newfoundland were experienced in other places on the Atlantic seaboard. This wasn't a continent for dreamers or the faint of heart.

Settlers in Newfoundland, as elsewhere, had to face grinding labour, hunger, disease —especially scurvy — and danger from a variety of sources. Pearls and gold were less likely to be encountered than famine and defeat. But not everyone turned tail and went home. Despite drawbacks, the underemployed tradesmen who came to Newfoundland, the farmhands, younger sons, and orphans, could have land virtually for the taking. There was little or none for them in the "low farms" and "poor pelting villages"[69] of England. It is true, they could have had better land by going on to Virginia and some other colonies in America, and in time many were to do just that.[70] Yet some stayed. By 1630, a tiny population of English-born livyers and their Newfoundland-born children clung to the shoreline of the Avalon Peninsula, at the sites formally colonized and doubtless in the coastal nooks and crannies nearby to which settlers would naturally drift in search of unclaimed land and new rooms. There was a plantation in St. John's too, barely mentioned in the early documents.[71] How the population was added to in the years immediately ahead has been studied. Handcock said it was apparently more by "temporal linkage through replacement populations" (i.e., people coming and going, with the former slightly outnumbering the latter) than by "generational succession" (people staying and having families).[72] His research showed few family links between the early colonists and late 17th-century inhabitants. But Pope has questioned this, finding "remarkable continuity" in settlers' names at Ferryland during the century.[73] Whichever view is right, one fact we do know: the population stayed small, while that of most American colonies, after slow starts, grew rapidly. Matthews notes there were 250,000 people in the mainland colonies by 1700.[74] By comparison, Newfoundland's population was puny.

Pope has warned us not to "misconstrue conditions in 17th-century Newfoundland as unique," and notes that Newfoundland's slow population growth had analogies in the colonies of Acadia and Maine.[75] New Scotland too could be pointed to as a "marginal" colony.[76] But it is perilous to compare and contrast the progress of individual colonies, since the factors influencing the development of each so widely differ. To look at the overall picture of colonial development in North America, Newfoundland undeniably stands apart; it "was different."[77] Not merely in population growth but, as we will see, in many aspects of civil society, it was slow to develop. To some extent, this can be explained by geography. The New England colonies didn't have the Labrador Current running by them, often, as Calvert found, extending winter well beyond the calendar limit and chilling spring and summer. Again, while some parts of the Atlantic seaboard had their share of bog, scrub, and rock, the soil *was* better, and there was too a fertile hinterland behind the coast, much more usable than Newfoundland's, that could absorb settlers and ameliorate life.[78] But to counter these points, we might note there were reasons, considered in the abstract, for Newfoundland to enjoy the same success as any other American colony, if not more. It was closer to England, well known to thousands of Englishmen, comparatively free of hostile aborigines, and it had a "cash crop," i.e., cod, as readily available as Virginia's tobacco. As for cold, deprivation, scurvy, and other such hazards, as Pope says "there is no reason to assume Newfoundland a significantly less healthy environment than, say, Salem, Massachusetts."[79] It seems illiberal to pin all the blame on climate and terrain, since Newfoundland later proved capable of supporting a population of over half a million and is without doubt much more than "a rather impoverished piece of the boreal forest," which is how Pastore describes it.[80] There were reasons beyond geography, reasons rooted in policy and attitude, for its comparatively slow progress.

One early and often repeated argument for settling Newfoundland was that it would be in England's interests to do so. But this was by no means universally accepted. As indicated, from the inception of the chartered colonies a guarantee was given of a fishery open to all. Here lay the germ of what would become a major problem. Within a decade, West Country merchants, the leading investors in the ship fishery, started submitting petitions alleging various abuses perpetrated against them. The leading complaint was that the planters were driving the ship fishermen "from the chiefest places of fishing,"[81] i.e., taking up the best rooms. This, simply stated, was the main thrust of 17th-century mercantile argument against the expansion, or even the existence, of Newfoundland settlement. By 1620 the Newfoundland migratory fleet had grown to about 300 ships, a huge industry, one of the major sources of employment and revenue in the West Country. What would happen if settlement grew as it did in America?[82] There, from the 1620s, Englishmen found themselves increasingly shut out of fishing. Charters granted in 1620 and 1621 covering a huge portion of the coastline gave monopolies on the fishery and trade.[83] Many feared the same would take place in Newfoundland. Settlement would constrain, and perhaps destroy, the ship fishery.

The issue quickly found its way into the House of Commons. A bill was presented in 1621 calling for freedom of the fishery in Newfoundland, New England, Virginia, "and other the sea-coasts and parts of America," with fishing rooms to go to first arrivals, and fishermen having the right to cut wood.[84] Guy, now representing Bristol in the Commons, spoke against it, arguing that there were "but three real plantations in Newfound-land" and that "there never will be above twenty, or thirty." Newfoundland had room "for 500 ships to fish," he said,[85] sensibly, for though protected harbours are few on the Avalon Peninsula those that do exist can accommodate hundreds of boats, and fishing can also be carried out from numerous exposed beaches and coves. For that matter, it would one day be done from clifftops, using trolleys and booms. The bill passed the Commons, but never found its way into law. Similar bills were presented in sessions until 1628. With the influx of population into America, and the growing importance and power of institutions there, the West Country effort to control that fishery was given up. But it persisted in Newfoundland. There a "free" fishery had to be maintained.

A hint of bias against inhabitants was soon to be found in official documents. In new regulations for the Newfoundland fishery drawn up in 1634 (the so-called Western Charter), no encouragement is given to settlers. They are, rather, pictured as troublemakers, for they have the "conceipt"[86] that for whatever "wronge or Injuries" they do, they cannot be "impeached" in England[87] — they fancy they are above the law. Thus the preamble. The charter corrected that notion by laying down eleven laws that were to "bee obeyed and put in execution." Two were aimed directly at the inhabitants. One forbad setting up taverns for selling wine, beer, "stronge waters" (spirits), and tobacco, since in them fishermen "are debauched," neglecting their work and spending "most part of their shares before they come home." This more than hints at an already robust alcohol-centered culture and trade in the fledgling settlement.[88] Another law applied to anyone "on the land there" (i.e., settler) who committed murder or stole goods to the value of forty shillings. The accused was to be arrested, brought to England, and delivered to the Earl Marshal for trial, which meant he would be tried under martial law.[89] The testimony of "two witnesses or more" would suffice to condemn him to death. This hurried justice was an answer to those who thought residence in Newfoundland removed them from the rigors of law. A subsequent paragraph empowered the mayors of Southampton and certain West Country towns to proceed against anyone who broke "these Ordinances upon the land."[90] The mayors were to receive complaints, go to trial, and punish delinquents by fine or imprisonment, or by seizing property "in the partes of Newfoundland, or in the Sea." Both the London and Bristol Company Charter and the Charter of Avalon had authorized the appointment of magistrates in Newfoundland; the latter envisaged the making of laws on the island.[91] That approach was now changed, or at least said to be changed.

Yet the laws incorporated in the 1634 charter were mostly intended to apply to both ship fishermen and settlers, so even if justice were to be administered at a distance, the latter had some protection. One of the laws might even be seen as a concession to settlers. The "auncient custom" of making the first arrival admiral of the harbour was affirmed, and as in Guy's regulations he was allowed a little extra space to go fishing beyond what he strictly needed. He was also given the option of laying claim initially to a number of rooms as long as his final choice of one of them was made within forty-eight hours. But an inhabitant was evidently not required to wait until the fishermen selected rooms before he made his own choice.[92] So under this charter, if strictly interpreted, the visiting fishermen could not always choose the best room in the harbour. The choice the admiral and aftercomers made, supposing they obeyed the law, was from *available* rooms, whether these were the best ones or not. This was either a tacit recognition of the rights of settlers or an oversight. The charter was to be publicly proclaimed in every harbour.

West Countrymen doubtless recognized the potential for encroachment on their old liberties in the loophole just described. An effort to plug it was made in 1637, in the last royal charter given to a colonizing enterprise in Newfoundland. This time the whole island was again granted, the beneficiaries being the Marquis of Hamilton, the earls of Pembroke and Holland, and Sir David Kirke.[93] Former grantees, the King (Charles I) asserted, had "deserted the Province and Plantacion," and it was of "greate consequence" to "our poore Subiectes" there that it "bee cherished and speedilie promoted." But the cherishing of the plantation seems merely notional. The first new rule in the charter was this: that neither the new grantees nor the inhabitants "nowe or at any tyme hereafter" should cut trees nor "builde any house or houses whatsoever or plant or inhabitt within six miles of the Sea shore" between Cape Race and Cape Bonavista, i.e., the area of English fishing and settlement. People could go fishing, but there was a catch: they couldn't live on the coast where the fishing took place. That was "some catch"![94] As for the freedom of the fishery, this was fully, not to say repeatedly and verbosely, restored. No inhabitant was to take up "the beste or moste convenient Beaches or places for fishing" before the arrival of the fishing ships. This could only mean that the ship fishermen were to have first pick of *all* rooms. The grantees could "make and enacte" any law whatsoever, according to their own discretion "together with the common assente and approbation of the freeholders." The freeholders were to attend from time to time when summoned. But ship fishermen were to be immune from such laws; they were answerable only to the King. Relieving these dictates somewhat was the recognition that the inhabitants "shall have like libertie of fishinge there" as other subjects. (Though how could they, if ship fishermen had the right to choose rooms before them?) While they had to build houses six miles inland, they could build premises to go fishing on the coast and they could also erect forts on the coast to protect the fishery with "convenient habitacions therein." Sufficient ambiguity existed in these clauses to permit inhabitants to live where they had always lived, which is what they did. But there is evidence that the six-mile rule drove some of them to New England.[95] For the rest, it could only have made life more uncomfortable.[96]

Another clause in the charter required settlers aged twelve and older, before leaving England or on arrival in Newfoundland, to take both the Oath of Supremacy and the Oath of Allegiance, the latter also anti-Catholic in tendency, but less so.[97] Visiting fishermen had to take neither. The oaths were so long — the Oath of Supremacy alone had 500 words — that to force many hundreds of men, annually, to take them would have caused delays and been an obstacle to business. Men would be "tied up all over the squadron signing [and] pledging."[98]

Kirke, a Dieppe-born English adventurer who had, with his brothers Lewis and Thomas, captured Quebec in 1629 and occupied it until 1632, was to be the governor, and he duly arrived in Newfoundland in 1638 to take charge. He installed himself in the "mansion house" in Ferryland, thereby, as Matthews has pointed out, promptly breaking "the terms of his own patent" by settling on the seashore.[99] The house was in the hands of the second Lord Baltimore's agent, William Hill, who had to be dispossessed. It had likely deteriorated since George Calvert's departure; the contents were little more than a table, chair, and bedstead. One old boat was later said to be all that was left of Calvert's fishing enterprise. About 100 colonists followed Kirke to Ferryland, which was now, at least according to one scholar, "the principal settlement of Newfoundland."[100]

The charter gave Kirke and his associates the right to collect a 5% tax on the fish and oil taken by foreign fishermen off Newfoundland and a slightly lower tax on fish and oil bought by foreign sack ships (trading vessels, also called sacks), giving one-tenth of the "profitt and Commodity" collected to the King. In addition, they were to have control of trade. No other Englishmen were to go to Newfoundland "for Merchandizing, buying, or Exchanging of any Merchandize or Commodityes whatsoever" (except for fishing). West Country merchants had, however, taken steps to ensure that any fish of theirs that might normally be bought by foreign sacks would instead be bought by the grantees.[101] Guy had been given a similar power to tax but evidently didn't have the will or muscle to enforce it. Kirke was of different mettle. Given rights, he acted on them. Before long he "was heavily engaged in a trade in alcohol,"[102] not just importing it but licensing and supplying taverns in various harbours. He took immediate steps to collect the authorized 5% of fish and oil, no easy matter on a coastline where no such impost had ever been taken, apart from Gilbert's "tax" on fishing ships in August, 1583, and where hundreds of foreign vessels fished annually. (Kirke's estimate was 500.) But he is said to have erected forts at key points along shore, which must have given a hint that he meant business. He was also not one to shy away from a fight, or to be driven off by bad weather. He soon had the foreigners paying up, though not without complaint at the highest level.[103] Grumbles from inhabitants and petitions from the West Country, starting in 1639, at least showed that Kirke played no favourites. He took money from one and all. He was not one to consult with freeholders or merchants before taking action. In 1640 he evidently grabbed fishing ships' rooms and let them out to "Biscayans and other aliens."[104]

One of the arguments now being advanced by those who opposed settling Newfoundland was that since adventurers "of excellent partes" like Guy and Calvert had "never thryved" there,[105] settlement was hopeless. Yet Kirke was apparently getting rich. His record seemed to show that colonies on the island could pay, after all. The alarmed West Countrymen renewed their assault on him in 1646, accusing him of various "insolencies and oppressions." Meanwhile the planters, they said, were still taking up "the principall places for fishinge" and "setting up tavernes and tiplinge houses whereby the seamen are much deboyshed."[106] This news might not have made an impression in a nation convulsed in a Civil War. Out of sight in Newfoundland, Kirke, it seems, was taking few if any steps to enforce the parts of his charter that might constrict his activities,[107] but many steps to line his pockets. The merchants ultimately brought him to heel by accusing him of robbing the portion of the tax assigned to the King, whose decapitation in 1649 did not invalidate the clauses in the charter pertaining to his share of the loot. Kirke was recalled to England in 1651, and the charges against him duly investigated. While awaiting justice, he submitted a remonstrance to the government. The real purpose of the West Countrymen in charging him with "great and heynous crimes," he said, was not so much to prosecute him as to dispute "the contynuance of the Plantation" in Newfoundland.[108] He went on to list the many attractions of the island. The document is remarkable in that it comes from someone who had lived there more or less continuously for over a decade. It derives from experience. As if to illustrate the "certainety of advantage" from investing and living in Newfoundland, he noted he had given £40,000 security to answer the charges brought against him. Kirke had many rough edges, and he taxed and charged rent to planters[109] as well as taxed foreigners. The fact that he imported wine and set up taverns does not seem to us as monstrous a crime as it did to some contemporary observers. He also was a shipowner, supplier, and fish merchant.[110] His colony "was run by a practical man to make money."[111] Not only did he make money but he wished to return there to make more. As for the charges against him, none was proven, though he was known thereafter as a "bad Governor."[112] Kirke died in England in 1654, "probably in the Clink."[113]

In 1652 four commissioners were sent to Newfoundland to probe the accusations and claims against Kirke, the principal one being from Cecil Calvert, George

Calvert's son, the second Baron Baltimore, who asserted his ownership, not just of the mansion house in Ferryland, but of the whole island.[114] Six witnesses, three men and, remarkably, three women (one of whose names was Philip, no doubt short for Philippa), were examined at Ferryland in late August.[115] Only summaries of their testimony survive, but these bring us close to the voices and attitudes of ordinary mid-17th-century settlers — not new arrivals, but seasoned veterans. All but one, a man named John Slaughter, were illiterate. (Documents from the earliest days of the Cupids and Ferryland colonies suggest a far higher degree of literacy among the first comers.) If the men were something other than fishermen, and the women other than housewives, this is not indicated. Their home communities are given as Ferryland, Renews, Fermeuse, and Caplin Bay.[116] A trace of humour and cynicism may be detected behind the formal abstracts. When asked if he preferred the second Baltimore to Kirke, John Stevens said "hee affects Sr David best, but as far as hee knowes my Lord Baltemore may be as bad." Asked how well she knew Kirke, Philip Davies said "a little too well and [she] wisheth she had not knowne him." (But Amie Taylor said "she loves Sr David Kirke best.") William Poole, asked if he had done business with Kirke or Baltimore, said no, adding "he doth not thinke that he shall gett a farthinge by either of them." None of them seemed to care which litigant prevailed over the other, though one liked Kirke because he wasn't "a Papist." They expected nothing from their would-be rulers. They expressed no grievances. They made no demands for more effective government, or for any government.[117] It is sometimes said that government is a blessing, and indeed it is, especially to those doing the governing, or hoping to do it. A commoner attitude among ordinary people is to see it as an affliction. 17th-century Newfoundland colonists, recently informed they would have to build homes amidst marshes and gullies six miles from the coastline, and soon to be told they were to vacate the island, would have had reason to regard it in just that way.

In 1653, the first year of the Protectorate, another set of regulations were devised for Newfoundland by the Council of State.[118] These mostly repeat earlier rules, but two new ones, while restricting settlers somewhat, at least acknowledged their existence. Planters were not to take up more "stage room than [they] had fishing-men in possession for the managing of it," and, moreover, were to occupy stages "together in one part of the harbour and not scattering as they now do."[119] Also, they were not to build houses, make gardens, or keep pigs or cattle "upon or near the ground where fish is saved or dried." This was a considerable improvement over the regulation driving them back in the woods. The new rules reflect an awareness of changes in Newfoundland. Planters were now employers of "fishing-men," i.e., indentured servants[120] who came to Newfoundland from England as passengers on sacks or fishing ships and normally (but not always) returned once their apprenticeships were over. The planters also were tilling the soil and keeping farm animals. In a given harbour they were spread out in the various coves along shore. A place such as Renews was more a composite of separate fishing rooms than a real community.

These regulations were to be implemented by John Treworgie, a West Countryman who was appointed commissioner for Newfoundland in 1653 and directed "to take care for the Government and well ordering of the said country."[121] He was to govern both inhabitants and fishermen — the first time such power was given to a resident authority — though his chief responsibility was to collect the taxes from foreign ships "due to the Commonwealth or Adventurers."[122] Little is known of how he governed, apart from the fact that he "took impost"[123] as Kirke had done, but he stayed in Newfoundland, apparently in charge, until the end of the decade. The 1650s were years of tumult and war for the home country, with the ship fishery severely diminished owing to embargoes, press gangs, and fears of Dutch attack. English statesmen had much to occupy them besides Newfoundland. The island, fated often to be low on the English agenda, at times dropped off it altogether. This was one of those times.

Soon after the Restoration, however, a new regulation was thought necessary. In 1661 a twelfth rule was added to the Western Charter, requiring fishing ships to bring to Newfoundland none other than their own ship's company (or that of other ships) "or such as are to plant and do intend to settle there."[124] The purpose of this was to exclude a different kind of migrant to Newfoundland, the boat owner who came each year as a passenger (or joined with others of like mind to freight a ship),[125] fished with the men he'd hired, sold the fish to sacks, left his boat or boats behind, and returned to England in the fall. These small operators in the long-distance fishery were termed by-boat keepers or by-boatmen.[126] West Country merchants viewed them as a great threat, arguing that by-boat fishery stole their best servants, drove up wages, didn't breed good seamen for the navy, and encroached on trade, which "properly belongeth" to merchants alone. They were leading Newfoundland towards the "decayed" fishery of New England.[127] Some by-boat men, and some of the servants they brought with them, stayed in Newfoundland to add to the stock of residents, which by the 1660s (not counting aboriginal peoples, but counting servants) was around 1,000.[128] Far from disdaining settlers, by-boatmen needed them to look after their boats and gear over the winter. For that matter, as the century wore on it became clear that ship fishermen too needed the inhabitants, at least a certain number of them, as caretakers, suppliers of wood, makers of oars, and boat-builders.[129]

Whatever merchants might think of by-boatmen, by the 1660s settlers and fishermen appeared at times to coexist quite happily. We can gather this from the journal of James Yonge, a youthful surgeon[130] who made his first voyage to Newfoundland in 1663.[131] That year his station was Renews, a harbour having five planters, among them a woman. As already suggested, the word "planter" now meant more than simply inhabitant; it meant an inhabitant who hired servants, one with a fishing room and boat or boats. The Renews planters had about forty servants working in the fishery. How many of these forty could be called inhabitants, and how many seasonal transients, is unclear.[132] There is no suggestion in Yonge's journal that the settlers could not occupy a room before the ships arrived. It appears that as time passed a system had evolved whereby some rooms in a harbour were informally reserved for the visiting fishermen, while others were taken by planters. There were, in any case, few planters in the harbours Yonge visited in 1663-9, with the exception of St. John's,[133] so plenty of space was available. Presumably there was a relationship between the planters and the admiral of the harbour, with the latter having authority over the former; but that relationship, as yet not closely defined, was amicable in Renews, at least according to Yonge. The master of Yonge's ship, who was vice-admiral, even hired a "sloop" from a settler to secure possible rooms in other harbours, a sign of cooperation and interdependence. (In 1664, arriving late in Bay Bulls, Yonge's ship hired a planter's stage in order to proceed quickly to fishing.)[134]

Though his main responsibility was obviously to his own ship, Yonge made an arrangement with another surgeon to serve the planters too. His remarks on medical matters are often poignant. He tells of curing "a little boy," clearly an inhabitant, who had lost the top of his nose, several fingers and toes, both heels "to the bones," and part of his penis, through frostbite. On a later voyage "Our people brought the small pocks among the inhabitants; I cured many, and bled several children and others, all which escaped."[135] His account of the laboriousness of the servants' lives is moving too. He later said "the Twelve labours of *Hercules*" could not compare with the toil he'd witnessed, "which is so great as no tongue is able to express it."[136] The scenes evoked by his journal are tranquil. He did indeed collect arguments pro and con the "boat-keepers" and later published a pamphlet giving his views. But the source of controversy wasn't the inhabitants; it was "the byboats."[137]

Yet it is clear from Yonge what class of entrant into Newfoundland was dominant. The fishing ships at Renews in the summer of 1663 used about fifty-five boats, to the inhabitants' nine. Ship fishermen outnumbered the inhabitants nine to one. By the late 1660s, perhaps thirty harbours on the English shore were settled, but most if not all were little more than fishing stations. Ferryland had become such a station. The number of inhabitants at Cupids had dwindled to a handful.[138] People clung to the foreshore. Many of their houses were perhaps not far above sodden tilts. Their small gardens intruded on flake space. To the rear stretched mile upon mile of mostly craggy woodland, acidic bog, and bald rock, terrain that would long defy occupation by Europeans and their descendants. (Which is not to say it was of no use to them.) Whereas 17th-century Maine, though initially just a place to fish, developed land-based industry and became "a society in which land assumed an increasing economic importance,"[139] Newfoundland remained, overwhelmingly, tied to the sea, a producer of fish. Even Maine between 1636 and 1652 had a form of local government, "conducted chiefly by magistrates who were also large landowners."[140] Other American plantations were further along the path to local control of their affairs. We cannot think of 17th-century Newfoundland as being on any such path.

It is when the experience of the colonial America is examined that we can see the true impact of the failure of Newfoundland's chartered colonies. In America, the charters were "the umbilical cords which attached the colonies to the mother country." They transferred considerable legal authority from Britain overseas. They conferred rights to the colonists, sometimes surpassing those of Englishmen at home. They told the colonies "what kinds of governments to set up."[141] In effect, they authorized forms of limited but democratic self-government that led, in time, to the standard apparatus of colonial administrations: governor, council, and assembly. The success of the colonies meant that the charters continued as legitimate statements of rights and privileges to which the colonists could tenaciously and legally cling. Whenever "a dispute arose between the [American] colonies and the home government, the former fell back on their charters to obstruct and resist."[142] What is more, the structures set up by charters gave many Americans, from early in their history, practice in democratic government. As we have seen, charters conferring similar privileges were granted to Newfoundland projectors. But when the colonies failed, the charters and the rights they contained died with them. (And even before they failed, the grantees made little or no effort to implement key portions.) The Newfoundland inhabitants were left with no foundation to build on, supposing they wanted to start building an authentic society.

Chapter 4

Laws, Old Saws, and Dogs of War: 1665-1713

"IF IT WERE NOT FOR WOOD, water, and fish, Newfoundland were not worth a rush": so went a West Country proverb that, at least once, found its way into high level government discussion about settlement on the island. So barren a rock! Not even worth a marsh reed! But the proverb, self-contradictory in any event — it's like saying, if it weren't for wheat and oil, Alberta wouldn't be worth a gopher — gives a false idea of the value placed by West Countrymen on Newfoundland. For they did think it worth a rush. Even those who chose not to settle there, and who spurned, or said they spurned, the ones who did, needed the beaches and coves of Newfoundland as places to carry on trade. They not only needed them; at times they demanded exclusive access to them. Some drowned in their hurry to get to them before their competitors from other ships.

As Defoe would testify, Newfoundland was in fact indispensable to the economies of West Country towns like Poole, Bridport, and Dartmouth.[1] And many from Devon and Dorset of course did settle. Some grew to like it. Rough as it was, it could bear comparison with fenny and rocky parts of the West Country itself. The peasants cutting gorse in Wessex, soon to make an appearance in literature, do not seem much better off than their fisherfolk cousins overseas. One 17th-century immigrant even fancied that Newfoundland "passeth England."[2] To look beyond the perspective of individual settlers and fishermen and towns to national and international levels, it was there clearly seen that Newfoundland had value. That is shown by the extent to which, in time, it figured in treaties and wars among nations. An area fought and haggled over by mighty combatants for so long can only be thought of, not as a rush, but as a prize. And not one of the "lesser prizes."[3]

So, at any rate, it was regarded by France. From the late 1650s, after a long period of decline, the French migratory fishery off Newfoundland expanded rapidly. Around 1658 the youthful Louis XIV granted Nicolas Gargot de la Rochette, a naval captain from La Rochelle, land on the west side of the Avalon Peninsula.[4] The grant included Placentia (termed Plaisance by the French), a fine protected harbour fronted by an immense rocky beach well suited for curing and drying fish. Behind the beach lay splendid land for settlers. In 1660 Gargot was named Compte de Plaisance and made governor of Newfoundland. Two years later "a great French ship full of men and women" (around eighty in number) put into Placentia to establish a colony. An English planter, soon forced to leave,[5] reported that the harbour had been fortified with eighteen pieces of ordnance. He saw Governor Thalour Du Perron's commission, which gave him "command of the whole country of Newfoundland." So began France's effort to settle and possess the island. Du Perron was killed by some of his own men during the first winter, but from this bloody beginning the colony crept to a population of 128 in 1670 and 2-300 in the mid-1690s.[6] Other small settlements, including one at St. Pierre, were established to the south and west. One estimate puts the French population of Newfoundland in 1687 at 1,000[7] — rivalling, but not equalling, the number on the English shore. Though referred to by one governor as "a collection of wretched shacks,"[8] the fortified and garrisoned settlement at Placentia became the center and supply base of a vigorous fishery, and functioned too as a stopping-off port for shipping between France and Quebec. Administratively it was part of New France. England might ruminate over whether or not Newfoundland should be settled and have civil government, but France's intentions were clear. Placentia was vital both for its fishery and as a North American "bastion of French power and influence."[9] Newfoundland was to be settled and eventually conquered. To the French, as English settlers would quickly discover, the island was worth fighting for. Yet before war was declared the English and French coexisted without undue friction. At Trepassey, it was reported, they "fish together without quarreling."[10]

In the event it was England's other great 17th-century imperial rival, the Dutch, who first decided to transport large-scale European warfare to Newfoundland settlements. Dutch traders were active in Newfoundland waters from early in the century; they well knew what a valuable asset England had in the fishery there. In the first Dutch War (1652-4), a sea war fought in the English Channel and North Sea, the island was left unmolested. But in the second Dutch War (1664-7), Admiral Michiel Adriaanszoon De Ruyter took a fleet of twenty ships, including twelve warships, to the West Indies, from whence, in June, 1665, he sailed to Newfoundland. On arriving, he divided his fleet and proceeded to raid Bay Bulls, Petty Harbour, and St. John's.[11] De Ruyter entered St. John's on June 16. The harbour was undefended, apart from a cable across the Narrows, which was easily cut. The ships in port were deserted, those on board having fled into the woods at the sight of the approaching men-of-war. Perhaps they had heard of the Dutch proficiency in the slave trade and feared being shipped to Surinam. The extent of the plundering is unclear. An English report states that the Dutch "took all the ships and goods, and destroyed cattle and houses,"[12] but there is contrary testimony from Dutch accounts, at least as it pertains to houses. It is said that De Ruyter was so struck by the "very poor condition" of the people in St. John's that he decided not to burn their houses. (But Petty Harbour and Bay Bulls likely suffered a more complete demolition.) Sack ships laden with victuals and salt were captured. One calculation placed the damages caused by the Dutch at £36,000.[13] Some 300 ship fishermen, taken as prisoners, were given enough provisions to get them to New England or back home. The pillaging ended on June 20.[14] Yet another Anglo-Dutch war broke out in 1672, and again Newfoundland was the object of attack. This time Ferryland was thoroughly ransacked. Four Dutch men-of-war, commanded by Captain

Nicholas Boes, arrived in early September, robbed dried fish that was stored for transport to market, burnt fishing boats, took prizes, and destroyed the inhabitants' cattle and stores.[15] Again, it appears houses were spared.[16] Nearby Caplin Bay too was raided. When Boes approached St. John's, a battery either offered, or seemed about to offer, some resistance, so the Dutchman steered clear and likely raided other settlements. The tally of his destruction is unknown, but it included "at least 150 sloops" (i.e., fishing boats) burnt or ruined, and four prize ships captured.[17] There was undoubtedly much thievery and burning of stages and flakes. Few records of these forays have been brought to light. We are left to guess their full impact on ordinary settlers, though the raids of 1665 did provoke one unheeded petition[18] and the horror and rage such assaults provoked among innocent bystanders of European warmongering can well be imagined.

The Dutch menace and the evidently permanent French presence in Newfoundland caused anxiety and argument among English merchants. By 1667 there was agitation for the appointment of a governor and construction of forts to protect the fishery — eminently sensible suggestions.[19] Immediately a counter petition was presented from the West Country opposing the notion of a governor as a "Useless and insupportable Charge,"[20] and no action was taken. More strong arguments for "the settlement of Newfoundland and the trade under Government" were offered in 1669, bringing a lengthy rejoinder from merchants. The French, they said, had fortified Placentia in order to protect themselves from the "solvages"; there was therefore no threat to England's fishery. They noted that the English in Newfoundland fished in forty-eight places spread out over 300 miles. To fortify St. John's would still leave the other sites unprotected. So there was no point in erecting a fort in that one harbour. As for settlement, "barren and rocky" Newfoundland "is productive of no commodities as other Plantations, or affords anything of food to keep to keep men alive or employment for the people." The "inhabitants' increase" caused lawbreaking and destruction of trees and stages. The merchants concluded from this that "some" of the settlers should "be brought away, and the rest transported[21] where they may not live so idle, and dishonourable to God and this nation." If settlers were allowed to continue there, the fishing trade "in a few years will be removed from this kingdom, and become as that fishery of New England, which at first was maintained from these parts, but is now managed altogether by the inhabitants, so that not one ship hath gone on that employment out of England these seven years."[22]

Here, then was a solution to the Newfoundland problem — remove the settlers. That was how to prevent the place from becoming another New England. The government accepted the proposal. Matthews claims that this was "the first time" the West Country traders had made the recommendation of expulsion — as if the late timing somehow constituted a virtue.[23] Thus a wife-beater might say, in expiation of his crime, that he hadn't decided to hit her until he'd reached the age of fifty. Pope, following Matthews, says the mid-1670s were "the one period" in the 17th century characterized by "overt official hostility" to settlement on the part of British "authorities."[24] He pleads the brief duration of the hostility. ("I only hit her for three years, M'Lud.") His point at any rate is historically unconvincing. If the six-mile rule, dating from 1637 and imposed nowhere else in North America,[25] wasn't a sign of "overt" hostility to settlement, how should it be described? Instead of being an eccentric development, the recommendation to expel settlers was more likely the culmination of an attitude long held by influential merchants and, through their lobbying, in time, by government.

In 1671 the British government,[26] acting on the advice of the Council for Foreign Plantations, as the agency responsible for shaping colonial policy was now called,[27] promulgated harsh new official rules that somewhat indirectly and clumsily implemented the clarified approach to Newfoundland. The traditional freedom of the fishery for "all the subjects of his Majesty's Kingdom of England" was lengthily asserted in rule 1; they were free to fish anywhere in Newfoundland, to "go on shore" anywhere to cure fish, and to cut wood for building stages, boats, and "other necessarys." It is apparent that this rule was intended to apply only to visiting fishermen.[28] Different laws applied to settlers. For them, the six-mile rule was again proclaimed, this time with no directly stated provisos (as had accompanied the rule in 1637) giving them liberty to fish, to build premises for fishing, or to build forts. Settlers were not to "erect or make any houses, buildings, gardens, &c." (the intent of the "&c." must have been to forbid them to build *anything*) or "fell, cut down, root up, waste, burn, or destroy any wood, or timber trees," or "inhabit or plant" —within six miles of the shore[29] between Cape Bonavista and Cape Race, or upon any island inside those limits within ten leagues from the shore. The rule was categorical.

The regulation against making "gardens" here appears for the second time in fishery regulations, on this occasion as an unqualified prohibition.[30] (It reappeared in the rules of 1676.) It is sometimes said that agriculture was never forbidden in Newfoundland. Under these rules, gardens, i.e., "enclosed [pieces] of ground devoted to the cultivation of flowers, fruit, or vegetables,"[31] certainly were banned within six miles of the shore (though raising livestock, an aspect of agriculture, could obviously be regarded as outside the interdiction). Forbidding the cutting, rooting up, or burning of trees was also, in effect, an indirect prohibition of agriculture.

Rule 4 specified that no inhabitant was to take up "any of the stages, cook-rooms, &c. beaches, or places for taking bait, or fishing, before the arrival of the fishermen out of England, and that they be all provided."[32] So, then, by implication, the settlers *were* permitted to fish, or at least not denied that right, but only after the ship fishermen had taken their pick of rooms (though it would have been virtually impossible to fish if they could cut no trees and erect no buildings within six miles of the shore). Rule 5 forbad the transportation of passengers to Newfoundland. A master or owner of fishing ships was to carry to Newfoundland only "such as are truly belonging to his or other[33] ships company, and such as are engaged in the voyage and share, or shares, or hire of the said ship." *No* "other persons." No exception was made (as in the rule of 1661) for "such as are to plant." Masters of ships were to give bond before setting out that they would carry to Newfoundland only those engaged in the voyage and, further, bring "all" of them back to England. The penalty for acting otherwise was severe: £100. Informers were to get a third of any forfeitures or penalty imposed on those who broke the new laws. Another rule specified (as if this hadn't been made plain) that no fisherman or seaman was to remain in Newfoundland once the fishing season was over. His Majesty's orders "forbidding" this were to be read by the admirals of the harbours on or about September 20 yearly.

Admirals, vice-admirals, and rear-admirals were authorized "to preserve peace and good government" among seamen and fishermen in their harbours "as well as on the shore," to execute the new orders for the fishery, to apprehend offenders (against the "rules and orders") so that "they may be punished," and to apprehend anyone committing a crime in Newfoundland "on shore, or at sea" and bring the accused to England. These regulations gave the admirals extensive defined powers over settlers, no small matter in view of the recurrent tensions and animosities on this fishing frontier.[34]

The main intent of the regulations of 1671 was clear: new settlers were to be kept out. They were not directly forbidden to go to Newfoundland, but English fishing ships were forbidden to take them there and seamen on the ships were forbidden to stay there over the winter. The effect was the same. There was no "enforced removal" of planters authorized by the 1671 regulations, as Matthews points out.[35] But if the settlers could get no servants from England to work in the fishery, and if the six-mile rule were applied, their position was untenable. Most, if not all, would have to leave. This wasn't "enforced" removal, but the effect again was the same. Verbally, settlement wasn't outlawed, but to insist on this in an effort to extenuate British policy seems pedantic.[36] After the new regulations were approved, a further paragraph was added. "Encouragement" was to be given to the inhabitants of Newfoundland, presumably by convoy commanders and admirals, "to transplant themselves" to the West Indies or other English colonies.[37]

The regulations were publicized in Newfoundland in the summer of 1671 and, as might be imagined, caused some consternation. Convoy captain Davis of H.M.S. *Success* — men-of-war were now sent out to ensure safe passage for the fishing ships — reported that the inhabitants were so "affrighted" by the "order for their removing" that he feared they would abscond to the French who "are very kind to the English who come to them."[38] He judged that the West Countrymen were at fault for the troubles in Newfoundland. The removal order might well have put a stop to inhabitants' efforts to clear new ground for farming.[39] (Such activity was in any case forbidden in the stricture against clearing woods.) But before the full effort against settlement could be tried, war broke out with the Dutch, and in London the Newfoundland problem faded from sight.

It came back into official notice in 1675, when again a governor was asked for, but the West Countrymen once more said nay. One spokesman for them, a certain Mr. Perrot, was much inclined to distrust reports of French expansion in Newfoundland. The French had settled there only for the beaver trade, he averred, repeating the claim that they had built a fort solely as protection against the Indians. Only two English ports were worth defending, and there was no point to doing it anyway since "they were sufficiently defended by ice in winter,[40] and in summer by our own strength at sea." The inhabitants were unruly, took up the best places for fishing, and debauched the seamen by selling them wine and brandy.[41] The unlikely charge of debauchery was repeated in various West Country documents. Newfoundland, once summer ended, was pictured as a cesspool of vice, laziness, and drunkenness.

Mr. Perrot's points hit home. Now in charge of colonial business was a Committee for Trade and Foreign Plantations. It rejected all talk of forts and defence: "'tis needless to have any such defence against Forreigners, the coast being defended in the Winter by the Ice, and must in Summer by the resort of your Majesties Subjects, for that place will allwayes belong to him that is superior at Sea." It took due note of the inhabitants' idleness and debauchery, the latter allegedly brought on by French brandy and Madeira wines. A sore point, however, was that these products were reportedly imported from New England, "without depending for any supply from hence" (i.e., England). The objection of the Committee to the establishment of civil government in Newfoundland was, at bottom, economic. If such a structure and official colony were created, the settlers "would rather adhere to New England, and in time tread in the same stepps, to the losse of those many advantages, which at present, by the Method things are in [i.e., the ship fishery], we yet enjoy." The Committee proposed that "all Plantation and Inhabiting" in Newfoundland "be discouraged." The commander of the 1675 convoy was to tell the planters His Majesty's pleasure, "that they come voluntarily away." If this were to be disobeyed, beginning the following year "the ancient Charter, which strictly forbidds any planters to Inhabit within six Miles of the Shore" should "strictly" be "putt in execution." Settlers found within the six miles would then be seized, brought away, or sent home "to answer their Contempts." The convoy was to assist settlers who chose to come home, while the governors of other colonies were to be told "to receive them with all favor."[42] The Committee's proposals were accepted. The order to the commander of the convoy, dated May 5, 1675, to "admonish" the settlers to leave Newfoundland, was duly delivered.[43] The governor of Barbados was told to receive and assist the transplanted islanders.

The commander obliged to deliver the news was Sir John Berry, the son of a Devonshire vicar and, possibly as a consequence, a man of some moral principle. As instructed, he made the King's wishes known to "all the Planters" between Cape

Bonavista and Cape Race. Those in St. John's, he said, promised to obey, but "the greatest part are too poor to remove unless his Majesty will send a ship for them." Wherever they come, he added, "they must be put on the Parish,"[44] for although "a labouring man" can earn £20 in summer and get his daily food free, "such a person would not get 3 [pounds] in England." We might bear this comment in mind when we read that Newfoundland had "almost nothing to offer," whereas life in "old established and comfortable villages" in England had a lot.[45] Similarly, when told that "many of the planters did not really intend to live and die on the island,"[46] we might note Berry's comment that Newfoundland settlers, having been told to leave, "implore his Majesty's favour to continue."

After diligent inquiry into charges made against settlers, Berry found "most of them false." He stood "in admiration" that "so many untruths" were told to his Majesty. It was the masters of the fishing ships, not the settlers, who took down stages and houses and sold the wood to the sack ships. The settlers did not entice seamen to stay behind, as had been suggested; instead, the masters of the ships persuaded the men to stay, to save the expense of their passage home. Far from finding that the New Englanders brought wine and liquor to Newfoundland, he learned that they purchased the wine and liquor in St. John's, to which it was conveyed on English ships. Importing alcohol to Newfoundland from the West Country had in fact become big business.[47] The settlers "are not so bad as the Merchants make them," said Berry. What was happening, in his view, was that the latter "have a mind to engross all into their own hands." Berry called the admirals and ship captains together and ordered them to pull down no stages, flakes, storehouses, or "anything else." He cautioned the government that if the inhabitants are removed from Newfoundland, "the French will soon possess it," a warning that might well have caused some tremors at a time of rising fear and loathing of French power in England. Some settlers, having been badgered to quit their homes in 1671 and 1675, and pillaged by the Dutch in other years, evidently thought French ascendancy in Newfoundland might not be such a bad idea. They told Berry that rather than leave "they design to settle amongst the French on the other side of Cape de Race." Berry provided an exact count of the overwintering settlers. There were now 1,655 men, women, and children on the English shore. The value of their fishery was two-fifths that of the West Country merchants.[48]

Berry's reports, which accused the merchants of being outright liars, led Secretary of State Sir Joseph Richardson to the conclusion, not far wide of the mark, that the merchants' design in Newfoundland "was to exclude the poor from being sharers in anything."[49] But the reports did not prevent the issuing, in 1676, of yet another charter for the Newfoundland fishery, one that combined the Western Charter of 1634, the additional clause of 1661, and the rules of 1671.[50] The result was something of a hodge-podge, but in fact the laws of 1671 were given priority over the others. In the summer of 1676, the order to expel was evidently still thought to be in force. The new commodore, a Captain Russell, declined to execute it. At this the fishing admirals, "quite naturally incensed," writes Matthews, seized the initiative and in St. John's "at least attempted" to remove the settlers.[51] It is not clear exactly what happened, though there was violence.[52] The masters of the fishing ships, Russell reported, had been made "insupportably insolent" by the renewal of the 1671 charter and "extremely oppress [the] inhabitants." There could be "cutting of throats next year between them."[53] In the fall of 1676, a St. John's planter, John Downing, went to England and the following March appeared before the Committee on Trade. He effectively rebutted the self-serving arguments and distortions of the merchants. It was the ship fishermen who pulled down stages, he said, partly to make fires "to brew drink." He stressed the usefulness of the planters to the fishermen; he himself one year had stored 600[54] hogsheads of salt for their use. As for the six-mile rule, it was "impossible" for the planters to live so far from the shore. None of their houses was farther inland than a quarter of a mile. He indicated the size of the resident population and explained their employment during winter, arguing as well that the people in Newfoundland had "settled there by virtue of former patents, whereby the soil is granted to them." In his opinion, they had the legal right to live there. (This was doubtful in view of the failure of the chartered colonies.) He stressed as well, rightly as events would show, the threat posed by the French, whose "colony" was "so near to ours." The notion that the French had built forts solely as protection from Indians he dismissed out of hand. No Indians "ever come near" the French plantations, he said.[55] In a separate petition, Downing returned to the problem of defence. The inhabitants were "left naked and defence-less to the Invasion of others especially the ffrench," he said. If a governor could be appointed, settlers would pay his salary and, once a "Competent number of guns" were supplied, would themselves erect and maintain forts.[56] Such requests for fortifications, made by both convoy captains and inhabitants, were long ignored. Made aware, at last, not just by Downing's testimony but by that of naval commodores, that it had been lied to and manipulated by spokesmen for the West Country, the government retreated, and in March, 1677, issued an order to masters of the fishing ships "not to disturb or injure his [Majesty's] Subjects the Planters inhabiting & Fishing" in Newfoundland, and suspending the six-mile rule.[57] A crisis had been averted. The following year the restriction against transporting passengers was also suspended.[58] To say that the British government had "decided ... to accept settlement"[59] is perhaps overstating the case. But at least, for now, they withdrew the order to ban it. In 1680 the Committee on Trade even agreed to send out a governor "for the security of Newfoundland," but then, perhaps thinking this altogether too radical a step, decided not to.[60] Resistance to settlement would characterize official English thinking about Newfoundland until well into the 18th century. Indeed, traces of it lingered into the 19th.

Sending out a resident governor would have meant the formal recognition of Newfoundland as a community separate from the mother country, though of course ultimately under its control. It would have led to a degree of local autonomy, with year-round civil institutions such as courts and schools and some kind of representative body — a Massachusetts in embryo. Such was not to be. Massachusetts was trouble enough. But while there would be no governor, there had already been quasi-governors. Guy, Calvert, and especially Kirke had played, or tried to play, the role of governor. More significantly, since 1675 the commander (or commodore) of the naval convoy had been giving instructions to the fishing admirals and generally acting as a governor during his stay. In 1680, in an intriguing incident outlined by Pope, the commodore Sir Robert Robinson, with two fishing admirals and another officer, held criminal court at Bay Bulls and sentenced four inhabitants to be "duck[ed] att the Maine yard Arme of the Shipp."[61] No statute or order in council pertaining to Newfoundland settlers[62] authorized him[63] to hold such a court, but he held it anyway. This is a reminder that while Newfoundland late in the 17th century lacked the normal institutions associated with colonial administration elsewhere, it was not, at least in the fishing season, entirely lacking in figures of authority. As already indicated, the admirals had been "authorized and required" to preserve "peace and good government" in their harbours, and the men-of-war were at hand, though very briefly, to show the flag and offer protection, usually when it wasn't needed. Once the fishing season ended, this apparatus of course vanished, and the settlers were on their own. But nothing stopped them from sending a principal inhabitant like Downing overseas to present argument.

With the threat of expulsion at least temporarily removed, the settlers resumed their normal routines. Their lives are all but invisible owing to the lack of a descriptive literature, though not impossible to reconstruct from late-century censuses taken by convoy commanders and other documents. By the 1680s settlers on the English shore had drifted north of Cape Bonavista at least as far as Salvage and likely beyond that. James Cook made inquiries in the next century and reported that Bonavista as well as "Keels, Salvages, Gooseberry Islands, Greenspond, [and] Cat Harbour [i.e., Lumsden] [were] settled on or before the year 1660."[64] There were settlers at Fair Islands by 1681. In the south, they had gone beyond Cape Race to Trepassey.[65] They occupied about thirty-five harbours.[66] The most populous was St. John's; Old Perlican, Carbonear, Harbour Grace, Bay de Verde, Bonavista, and Ferryland were also substantial places. In 1677 the settlement of Old Perlican was bigger than Carbonear and Harbour Grace, and about twice as big as Ferryland.[67] St. John's and its immediate environs, Conception Bay south of Carbonear, and the coast between Renews and Petty Harbour were the most developed areas. Baudoin noted in 1697 that the coast of Conception Bay, meaning from Carbonear south, was "much better established and more populated than that from Renews to St. John's."[68] The shoreline between Carbonear (including the immediately adjacent settlements of Clowns Cove, Freshwater, and Crockers Cove) and Bay de Verde was apparently not yet permanently occupied, though of course fishing would go on there in summer and it is possible that some coves might have winter houses.[69] (The distinction was drawn between winter houses, homes or tilts in wooded areas lived in during winter, and summer houses, more permanent residences near the fishing rooms.)[70] Settlement in Trinity Bay was sparse. Men outnumbered women by as much as ten to one,[71] but a high proportion of planters,[72] in certain harbours — St. John's, Carbonear, Old Perlican, for instance — were married with children.[73] Some planters were widows. The bulk of the male population consisted of unmarried male servants, hired to work for planters. The shortage of female servants, and of females generally, was overcome somewhat by an influx of Irish. In 1681 it was reported that Irish traders, themselves newcomers to Newfoundland, brought to the island, in addition to clothing, butter, and other merchandise, "many women passengers whom they sell for servants." Soon after coming, these "marr[ied] among the fishermen that live with the planters."[74] There were also many Irish men about in the 1690s. Thus was pure English blood diluted. By the late 17th century, and certainly by the early 1700s, when the Irish were moving with some rapidity into the southern Avalon, the term "English" shore had perhaps become a misnomer.

The settlers were far from idle after the ship fishermen left for England in late August. They fished into November,[75] and had much to occupy themselves in the way of productive work over the winter. The fishery itself, supposing someone focused exclusively on it, left little room for idleness. Repair of boats, gear, fish-houses, and flakes was time-consuming; it is likely as well that in certain locations, if not in most, parts of stages extending farthest into the ocean were laboriously taken down in fall in anticipation of winter storms.[76] Building boats for sale to the ship fishermen, as Pope has pointed out, was now an important part of the economy.[77] Boat-building was a complex and time-consuming process. Not the smallest part of it was searching in the woods for timber of the right sizes and shapes for knees, ribs, and stems, which might lead the boat-builder far afield. Once located, the timber had to be sawed and chopped into usable boards and planks — back-breaking work. Cutting and hauling firewood were other onerous tasks. Cattle-rearing was a major activity; scores of cattle roamed through and in back of Carbonear, Harbour Grace, St. John's, and elsewhere. Carbonear and Harbour Grace alone had 200 head.[78] Pigs, sheep, goats, and chicken were kept as well. All had to be housed, fed, and cared for. Despite prohibitions, clearing land for gardens and pasture evidently went on, doubtless mostly outside the fishing season, whenever weather permitted it. This meant digging up ubiquitous large rocks as well as cutting trees, hauling out stumps, and clearing away gorsy thickets and scrub. In some places very little land could be made arable. Even a sympathetic observer thought "It is a Colony not of husbandmen but of fishermen."[79] The future would show how right he was. Yet small-scale farming would be an important adjunct to fishing in Newfoundland until well into the 20th century. With cattle wandering around, fences or rock walls had to be erected to protect vegetables. Once carved out of the bush, gardens for turnips, carrots, cabbages, and other vegetables (not potatoes, which were introduced in the mid-18th century) were manured and made ready for planting. Tilling the land was very hard work, there being few horses in 17th century Newfoundland, though more than is generally realized.[80] To transport a horse to Newfoundland, and land it, was no easy matter.[81] Vegetables were harvested late in the fishing season or shortly after it. Berry-picking, while it went on at the same time as fishing, also extended beyond it, as did hunting for the assortment of animals needed for food. There was some furring as well, beaver, fox, and otter being available, if not plentiful. Some furriers went on long winter treks outside the English shore. Settlers became expertly knowledgeable about the resources in the woods and barrens behind their home. They wandered far from home, hunting, looking for timber, and stealing from the French. The Avalon interior has been called an "intractable wilderness"[82] as if it were darkest Africa, but paths were beaten through this wilderness, both towards the interior and along shore between settlements. Yonge walked on such a path between Fermeuse and Renews in 1663.[83] By the end of the century the settlers had broken trails between settlements throughout the English shore.[84]

Life was burdensome but, through the 1680s, evidently peaceful. With England beset with intrigues and rebellion as it moved to rid itself forever of Catholic kings, Newfoundland affairs went unnoticed. But a month after William of Orange ascended the throne in April, 1689, he declared war on France, noting in his declaration that of late "the encroachment of the French upon Our said Island [of Newfoundland], and our Subjects' Trade and Fishery have been more like the invasions of an Enemy, than of becoming Friends."[85] Ten days later, on May 18, perhaps prompted by the thought that this mention of Newfoundland might be fancied a provocation, the King in Council decided "that a Governor be forthwith sent to Newfoundland" and that he carry materials to build a fort at St. John's. Prudence dictated that the cost of the fort was not to exceed £3,000.[86] An elaborate fort could have been built from such a fund. But for some reason, once again there were second thoughts. Someone said Newfoundland wasn't worth a rush, or perhaps not worth the candle. Or that there was a poor sign of fish. Or that ice offered sufficient protection. No governor was sent. Nor was the £3,000 fort built, though in fact a number of fortifications, in varying states of readiness — mostly unready — existed in St. John's by the mid-1690s. The only effective one within the harbour was "King William's Fort," built (or begun) in 1693 by the inhabitants under plans laid out by a military engineer, Christian Lilly.[87] By the mid-1690s batteries and forts, most rudimentary, had been set up as well in some other harbours.

Reverberations from the War of the Grand Alliance, known in North America as King William's War, were soon felt in Newfoundland. French accounts, likely exaggerated, tell of an assault on Placentia by a 45-man raiding party in February, 1690, in which the governor, Antoine Parat, was tortured and the population (numbering now in the hundreds) imprisoned in the church.[88] After this, fortifications at Placentia were strengthened. Now followed a series of skirmishes. In

September, 1692, five ships under the command of Commodore Francis Williams appeared off Placentia and demanded surrender. The governor, Jacques-François de Mombeton de Brouillan, a soldier from Gascony, declined; an exchange of fire followed, whereupon Williams withdrew. Before leaving Placentia, he burned whatever buildings there were at the settlement of Point Verde, which overlooked the harbour. Having provoked the French, Williams now sailed off to England, leaving settlers on the English shore once again to be defended by the ice. (No warships were left in Newfoundland over the winter until well into the 18th century.) Phillipe Pastour de Costebelle, an officer at Placentia, distinguished himself next spring by sallying forth to Trinity Bay and returning with six prisoners. This slight was not to go unnoticed. Sir Francis Wheler, who in 1690 had commanded a ship in the disastrous battle with the French off Beachy Head on England's south coast, appeared off Placentia in August, 1693, with about twenty vessels, but had no better luck. He evidently tried to enter the harbour, but either withdrew or was repulsed.[89] As recompense he burnt the fishing station at St. Pierre. The following year, on September 10, the Norman officer Pierre de Saint-Clair, leading a squadron of three warships with a combined total of 140 guns, a Saint-Malo privateer, a fire-ship,[90] and a bomb-ketch[91] — enough firepower to take Southampton — arrived in Ferryland. Captain William Holman defended the settlement, but perhaps the day was saved when one of Saint-Clair's warships, the *Aigle*, having, it seems, unwisely entered the tricky harbour without prior knowledge of sunkers, ingloriously ran aground. At this the crew mutinied; and after cannonading for several hours, the French sailed away, taking the winged *Aigle* with them.[92]

Plans were soon afoot for a more deadly attack.[93] The contest for control of North America was now bloody and in earnest, and as part of its general stategy France decided to drive the English out of Newfoundland. Two were selected to lead the assault. Pierre Le Moyne d'Iberville et d'Ardillières, born in Montreal to a wealthy family, was young, daring, hungry for glory, and hence dangerous. By 1696 he had exhibited a soldierly ruthlessness, if not something beyond it, in the assault on Schenectady (1690) and in encounters with the English in Hudson Bay. Iberville was to recruit Indians and Quebec voyageurs, then lead them in the raid on Newfoundland. But the overall command was to be under Brouillan, governor of Placentia, in his 40s, known for his vanity and violent temper.

Iberville sailed from France to Canada in spring, 1696, did some good work of destruction at the Saint John River and vicinity, assembled his hardy band, and proceeded to Placentia. He had 124[94] men, including about fifty voyageurs and twenty-eight Indians (of whom three were Micmacs, the others Ottawas or Abenakis.)[95] To this number Brouillan was to add about 100 when their joint campaign began. This is the total which the scholar Williams thinks fits "all the evidence,"[96] but it could well have been much higher. Iberville had a Sulpician priest with him as well, Abbé Jean Baudoin, who had worked as a musketeer before taking holy orders. He was to serve as chaplain to the Canadians and keep an account of the expedition. Iberville arrived in Placentia September 12.

Brouillan, anxious for booty and reputation, had left for the English shore three days earlier with a squadron of Saint-Malo privateers, so Iberville had to await his return, which didn't happen until October 17. After rounding Cape Race, Brouillan sailed first to St. John's, hovered off that port, but did not try to enter or attempt a landing nearby. Instead, he went south to Bay Bulls, where he found fishing ships about to sail to England under the protection of the 32-gun English frigate *Saphire*, commanded by Captain Thomas Cleasby. In the ensuing encounter, Cleasby not very helpfully scuttled the *Saphire* in the harbour rather than risk capture, and beat a retreat to Ferryland. Brouillan's men stormed and burnt Bay Bulls, then went to Ferryland and burnt it too, this time including houses. Some settlers were deported; 150 were living in poverty at Barnstaple, Devon, in December, apparently not much enjoying being "surrounded by their kinfolk and friends ... at home."[97] Others were taken captive, while some were just left behind. In early November, a ship from Poole calling at Bay Bulls found 115 men, women, and children living amidst the ruins of their settlement. News of Brouillan's assault reached England in October. No retaliation or relief effort from the mother country was attempted. Commodore William Whetstone, indeed, on board H.M.S. *Dreadnought*, came within a hundred miles of Newfoundland in November, but hearing of the raids from a captured French fly-boat,[98] decided to sail home.[99] Matthews notes that British authorities had "far more pressing problems of defence in the English Channel and Ireland" to occupy them.[100]

Back in Placentia, Brouillan found Iberville itching to go into battle with his Canadians and Indians. A clash of egos between the two commanders caused delay, but at last points of honour were settled and a strategy worked out. Iberville and his men were to go overland from Placentia to Ferryland and rendezvous at Renews with Brouillan, who would take his troop there by sea. The assault northwards would then commence. Iberville left Placentia on November 1, and in nine days reached Ferryland, now without settlers. But he did find a dozen horses, which his men killed and ate. On November 12, he sent a detachment to Cape Broyle, where twelve prisoners were taken. One of these, a woman, flung herself off the *Profond* — Brouillan had arrived — and drowned, evidently choosing death over prolonged incarceration on a French warship. Brouillan's blundering had already alerted the coast north of Bay Bulls to what was afoot. After another quarrel, Iberville and the governor proceeded in tandem to Bay Bulls, where they arrived in sloops on November 23 to find settlers rebuilding their homes. The crew of a 100-ton sack ship took to the woods. Late November is winter in Newfoundland. A winter war was underway. Leaving the defence of Newfoundland to the ice was now seen for the foolish policy it was. What the inhabitants had dreaded,[101] an overland assault by the French and Indians, had come about. Iberville's voyageurs and Indians were well used to fighting in winter conditions, though they had brought no snowshoes and would have to take time later to make them. But this was a minor hitch. Newfoundland fishermen and their families were overmatched.

Opposition was nonetheless mounted. On his way to St. John's, Iberville met Petty Harbour men. Thirty-six[102] of these were killed and others captured. Petty Harbour was occupied. St. John's was now less than ten miles away. On November 28, after a day of heavy snow, Iberville moved closer to that harbour, along a track over the hills. Eighty-odd[103] men — not soldiers; there were no soldiers in Newfoundland — confronted him "in a burnt wood full of boulders." After receiving absolution, his men attacked and "killed many"; the remainder retreated to St. John's. This battle lasted half an hour.[104] The French entered St. John's, took two forts, captured sundry folk, and watched others (around 180 men, plus women and children) retreat into Fort William. About 100 residents wisely made their way to a ketch in the harbour and fled through the Narrows. Others went into the woods. Fifty-five settlers were killed on November 28; the French lost one man (though five were wounded). These are Baudoin's numbers. Next day some who had escaped into the woods were rounded up, and at night many of the fifty or so[105] houses — those nearest the fort, the best ones — were burnt. The men, women, and children in the fort were thus treated to the spectacle of their houses aflame, lighting up the night sky, with winter hard upon them. On November 30, a settler named William Drew was scalped and sent into Fort William, with a reminder that a like fate awaited those holed up inside if they didn't surrender. With this inducement to consider, the defenders handed over the fort. St. John's had fallen. Who thought up this stratagem is unknown, but the Abenaki chief Nescambiouit, a notorious scalper known to New Englanders as "a bloody devil," was in Iberville's party.[106] There is no mention of the scalping in Baudoin. He does say the "Canadians" (by which he may here mean the Indians) "frightened" the people. They had heard of "the terrible war with the Iroquois," he comments, "in which, *as in this one,*[107] it was better to be killed on the field than to be wounded or cut off from all aid." Fear of Indian atrocities may well account for much of Iberville's success in Newfoundland.

Another tiff between Brouillan and Iberville now broke out. The former wanted to dig in and hold St. John's, the latter wished to press on north. Iberville won. The remaining buildings in St. John's were burnt, apart from some to shelter the wounded. The battery in the harbour entrance was destroyed. Fishing sloops were burnt. Neighbouring settlements like Torbay and Quidi Vidi were ransacked. Williams calculates that by the end of 1696 the French had killed ninety-two and taken about 565 captives, of whom 471 were dispatched to Europe and seventy-five to Placentia.[108] One of the ships, sent to France with eighty prisoners, was wrecked. Brouillan went back to Placentia. Iberville pressed on, leaving a number of captives, including women and children, behind in St. John's with sick and wounded Frenchmen. The ultimate fate of these captives is unknown.[109]

Conception Bay now lay open to the "great offensive"[110] of the Franco-Indian raiders. They crossed to Portugal Cove and headed south on foot towards Harbour Main. One of Iberville's officers, Jacques Testard de Montigny, a veteran backwoods brawler who was to take a leading role in the weeks ahead, fell into a river en route from Portugal Cove, but lost only his musket and sword. It was he who took Harbour Main. Port de Grave, where there were seventeen houses, fell; settlers were sent to Brigus with orders to the leading men in that settlement to surrender and deliver their arms. They gave up without a whisper of protest. Iberville now took to the water. He left Harbour Main in commandeered boats, and reached Carbonear, a "well-established" settlement with the "best built" houses Baudoin had seen in Newfoundland, on January 24. Montigny had preceded him, and had gone house to house, killing and creating havoc, chasing and catching many who tried to escape into the woods. A great number of settlers from Carbonear, Harbour Grace, and other places (around 200 men, plus women and children) had taken refuge on Carbonear Island, a cliffy wedge of rock at the mouth of the harbour with just one secure landing place. They had built "barracks" on the exposed rock and fortified and provisioned it. Some cattle were taken there as well. As Iberville reconnoitered in pillaged shallops, cannon were fired at him.

This was something unexpected — resistance. He demanded the islanders' surrender. They replied "that they would fight." Iberville's progress had stalled. He did indeed busy himself during the following week looting and burning. (Harbour Grace was burnt on January 28.) But how could he take the island? "God be blessed," Baudoin prayed, "He can bring this about if it pleases Him." But it did not please Him. A landing was tried on January 31, but again the French were fired on. Another attempt on February 1 failed. "The most renowned son of New France"[111] hesitated. He decided it would be unwise to risk a frontal assault on settlers willing to do battle with him. The path to victory was to attack the defenceless. So he proceeded to take Bay de Verde, Old Perlican, Hants Harbour, Scilly Cove, New Perlican, and Heart's Content. A fortified house at Heart's Content quickly surrendered, perhaps because news of the St. John's scalping had reached them.

On returning to Carbonear, a piqued Iberville issued orders to burn Port de Grave, Brigus, and "autres habitations" — likely every house at the head of Conception Bay. He now had about 2-300 prisoners. He sent Montigny to attempt a parley with those on Carbonear Island, who had dared to take a few of his men, including three Irish deserters, captive. (Baudoin reported that the English in Newfoundland treated Irish Catholics "like slaves.") The effort failed. Montigny fancied the officers of the King of France had been mocked, so he took prisoner those sent from the island to parley, hardly an honourable proceeding. Carbonear Island held out. Iberville burnt Carbonear on February 28. He had now reduced the settled shore of Conception Bay (except for Bay de Verde) and the south coast of Trinity Bay (except for Old Perlican) to rubble. His "multitude of prisoners"[112] were to be led or ferried to Placentia, via Heart's Content and Bull Arm at the head of Trinity Bay, which lies only a few miles from Placentia Bay across the isthmus of Avalon.

At the end of March raids were carried out along the north side of Trinty Bay as as far as Trinity harbour. In mid-April Bay de Verde and Old Perlican were put to the torch. An unburned Bonavista remained; to destroy it had been one of Iberville's main objectives. Salvage, too, and other places beyond Bonavista, or between Bonavista and Trinity,[113] were intact. But time was running out on our hero. The English fishing fleet was about to arrive, likely accompanied by warships. An expected French fleet was late in coming; Iberville spent much time in Placentia twiddling his thumbs, waiting for it. Captives, including women, were escaping from Placentia, where there was no prison, and heading back overland to the English shore. Some who had eluded the French in the woods were coming back to the coast. On May 18 Baudoin noted that Iberville "was no longer going to Bonavista." The winter war was over.

It is difficult to place a value on the amount of damage done and goods looted, but everywhere fishing premises as well as houses were burnt, boats and gear destroyed, cattle, horses, and provisions eaten, salt discarded, and fish and oil robbed. About 200 settlers were killed, about 700 taken prisoner. There were few casualties among the invaders. "I have never seen a better example of God's protection," said Baudoin.

As news of this this mass mugging reached England, it was greeted by — more discussion. Late in 1696 anxious petitions reached the House of Commons from Dartmouth, Poole, and other towns. These stressed, not the bloodshed and upheaval among inhabitants, but the threat to English fishing interests.[114] There had been similar threats to the trade in Africa, which had prevented "supplying his Majesty's plantations with negroes."[115] Black slaves and Newfoundland settlers had to compete for the attention of legislators. The fishery petitions were referred to a committee of the Commons, which reported at the end of January, 1697. The committee noted the many ways in which the Newfoundland trade "is profitable to this nation." It promoted navigation, was "a nursery of seamen" for the navy, gave employment to about 140 ships in peacetime and about 5,000 men and boys, produced marketable fish and oil. The French in Newfoundland had seized "about thirty-three vessels, loaden with fish and train-oil; to the ruin of very many families." These were evidently West Country families. Steps had to be taken, using both men-of-war and land forces, to regain the places taken, otherwise "that very beneficial trade will be wholly lost to the nation." Early in February, the House was told that His Majesty would "take all imaginable care for the retrieving of so beneficial a trade." In the meantime, the Board (or Council) of Trade and Planta-tions[116] had been conducting its own inquiry, and had determined that settlers were indeed "convenient to preserve the boats, oars, stages, etc." of the fishing ships, but should be limited in number to 1,000 lest by increasing "they engross the fishery to themselves."[117] This represented some advancement in official thinking. But sober second thought intervened. The report was never presented to the King.

In due course, long after Iberville had departed, a fleet commanded by Sir John Norris was sent with a large number of troops.[118] It arrived in Newfoundland on June 7, to find "nothing but destruction." St. John's had "not a house standing but one, and but four families upon the place." French leave had been taken, and with avengeance. Apart from Bonavista and Carbonear Island, Colonel John Gibsone noted, "nothing escaped the barbarous fury" of the enemy. South of St. John's "there is not an inhabitant left" apart from two or three in Bay Bulls and two in Brigus South. Even Ferryland, "always looked upon...as the best harbour and the pleasantest place in the whole island," was deserted.[119] So, at any rate, he was told. But with the belated appearance of the military, the lives of the remaining inhabitants began returning to something close to normal. Work began on reconstructing Fort William. Farming and (once boats were built) fishing resumed. Terror subsided, though Norris's failure to engage a French squadron that appeared off St. John's in July might have left some wondering just how safe they were. (It was later alleged his men-of-war were too encumbered with prize goods to fight.)[120] After the signing of the Treaty of Ryswick with France in September, the process of rebuilding doubtless speeded up. Most deportees to England came back; the population rebounded.[121] The main body of soldiers returned to England in the fall of 1697, but a garrison was left to defend St. John's and continue work on fortification.

Matthews writes that "the ramshackle houses and stages" in Newfoundland were rebuilt quickly and "by the Autumn of 1698 one would hardly have known than an attack had ever taken place."[122] Yet Baudoin indicates that many of the houses were far from "ramshackle." And as for "one" "hardly" knowing an attack had taken place, the displaced and brutalized inhabitants who had lost all or most of their possessions, the wounded and their relatives, and the families of the slain, certainly knew an attack had taken place, and would never forget. Williams says the "folk-memory" of the winter war was "quickly eradicated" by rapid "turnover" in the population,[123] but this too is unconvincing. Prowse in 1895 said that outport people still retained "a traditionary remembrance" of 17th- and 18th-century Canadian raids.[124] Janzen claims that the destruction caused by the French "had no lasting significance."[125] As for inhabitants, he writes, "most were newcomers, too seasonal and transient to have developed any kind of loyalty to what was, after all, a very harsh environment."[126] Nothing whatever is known about the "kind of loyalty" the inhabitants had. Even if "most" were "newcomers," which in itself is speculative, that didn't mean they had no loyalty to their new setting. "An Englishman transplanted," even a newcomer, "was not the same kind of Englishman."[127] He (and she) might sink roots quickly overseas. In 1697 Arthur Holdsworth sailed the *Nicholas* from Dartmouth with 100 passengers returning to Newfoundland following the disruption of their residence by the French. To those people, New-foundland was home.[128]

It is astonishing how the consequences of this fierce raid can be so smugly understated by such gifted scholars. The fact is, we have no settlement literature to open our eyes to the effects of the winter war on individual families and harbours. It is also hard to gauge its overall impact on the small society that had taken root and was slowly growing. But clearly the stability and progress of that society had been shattered. Presumably that gives the attack some "significance." Leaving the people to be protected in wartime only by the winter ice, with the enemy 40-50 miles away, was at best an indifferent, at worst a cynical and shameful tactic. But it was in keeping with the official English policy towards Newfoundland, as stated in 1698 by William Popple, secretary to the Board of Trade: "there are no planters nor any manner of Government in that Island as there are in other Plantations."[129]

With peace restored, the migratory fishery rebounded, and the House of Commons resumed its consideration of Newfoundland. In May, 1699, "a bill for encouraging the trade to Newfoundland" was passed by both houses of Parliament and given royal assent.[130] The preamble to the act (often called King William's Act) indicated its purpose, which was to preserve and strengthen the migratory fishery. That fishery, the preamble stated, employed seamen and ships, made use of English provisions and manufactures, created work for "tradesmen and poor artificers," brought wine, oil, plate, iron, wool, "and sundry other useful commodi-ties" into England from foreign countries "to the increase of his Majesty's revenue," and encouraged trade and navigation.[131] Most clauses in the act were aimed at keeping Newfoundland a free fishery,[132] readily accessible to English ships. There was to be no encouragement to civil society or government on the island, which would, as West Country merchant petitioners had repeatedly stressed,[133] in time prove an impediment to their interests. The vulnerability of settlers to attack was now painfully evident; but there was no hint in the act that a winter war had even occurred.

The inhabitants (and "other persons," presumably by-boatmen) were, how-ever, brought into a number of clauses. Those who, since 1685, had taken up rooms which before that date had "belonged to fishing ships," had to relinquish them (clause 5). Nor were they to take up rooms that, since 1685, "did or at any time hereafter shall belong to" fishing ships, until all the ships arrived from England, Wales, and Berwick,[134] and were provided for (clause 6). But — the famous clause 7 — all persons who, since March 25, 1685, had cut out or made houses, stages, cook-rooms, train-fats, or other conveniences for fishing (or hereafter will build such) that did not "belong" to fishing ships since 1685, "shall and may peaceably and quietly enjoy the same." The concession made to inhabitants in clause 5 was that those who had possessed rooms *before* 1685 were evidently secure. (Why the year 1685 was selected as a boundary is unclear.) Clause 7 also conferred rights, although it might be thought to conflict with clause 6 in that any new land that might be cleared by an inhabitant could be claimed by a fishing ship under the "any time hereafter" phrase. Yet its intention seemed to be: if you moved outside the areas used by the fishing ships and cleared land, you could hold it for your exclusive use, without disturbance. It will be noted that clause 7 appeared to recognize the clearing of land only "for fishing." Cutting or burning trees or damaging them "for any Use or Uses whatsoever" apart from getting wood for fuel ("for the Ships and Inhabitants"), building and repairing houses, and uses connected with the fishery was specifically disallowed in clause 12, which is therefore, like the 3rd 1671 regulation, an indirect prohibition of agriculture.[135] How far these clauses went towards conferring legal ownersip of property is another question, later to be much brooded over.[136] Handcock says unequivocally that the act "made settlement legal,"[137] but it is doubtful that it did. If the act legalized settlement in clause 7, it did so by nuance or implication, not directly, and by contravening the whole tenor of the clauses generally, which was known to be decidedly "in disfavour of the Newfoundland-men [i.e., settlers]."[138] Legalizing settlement, had that been the intention, would surely have been couched in plain language. But while the act did not specifically make settlement legal, neither did it forbid it.

Another clause (14) in the act specified that it was the duty of fishing admirals to see that the "Rules and Orders" in the Act "concerning the Regulation of the Fishery" were "put into Execution" in their harbours, at sea and on shore, "in order to preserve Peace and good Government among the Seamen and Fishermen." It was later determined that the last phrase was not a general directive to admirals to keep the peace and preserve good government (as was evidently intended by the almost identical wording in the 1671 rules). The clause did not make the admirals magistrates, though they apparently fancied it gave them equivalent powers and continued to have "a stupid notion" of the act until well into the 18th century.[139] They were given the responsibility to ensure that the fishery regulations in the act were executed, and by clause 15 to settle disputes over fishing rooms. The process through which they were to make such decisions was not specified. Presumably they were to hold court in some fashion; but this was not required in the act. If someone were "aggrieved" by the admiral's "judgement or determination" on fishing rooms, he could appeal to the commander of the convoy, who was to make the final adjudication. So the naval commodore, monarch of the quarter deck, was given, by statute, an appellate role above the admirals, whose only qualification to make delicate decisions on property and interpret the sometimes cloudy language of the act was their speed in getting to a harbour. This was justice. (This is not to say that the commodores' actions in Newfoundland were always harsh or unjust; they were often the opposite.)

The commodore had already been functioning as a sort of proto-governor. Under the new laws he found his labours greatly increased, for though the act failed to indicate who should determine what land was possessed by inhabitants prior to 1685 and what after, the commander had to do it and, if necessary, on his return the following summer — for he was still only a temporarily resident proto-governor — re-do it.[140] Confusion as to who had a right to many fishing rooms persisted into the 1720s and even later.[141] The act was complex and, as hinted, in places ambiguous. To attempt to implement its clauses fully without a magistracy[142] or other permanent administration in place was problematic. Few of the admirals were capable even of keeping a journal (as they were also required to do in the act), and as for solving disputes, as one commodore said, they were "generally the greatest [ag]gressors themselves."[143] By 1701 admirals were said to be leaving "all" such work to the commodore, who to ease the burden was already sending his lieutenant to coves outside St. John's to solve disputes,[144] thereby inaugurating a "surrogate" system that remained in place until 1825. But some admirals did their duty as outlined in the act, and governors, once they were appointed, were instructed to assist them and not to interfere with their statutory functions.

The long-term effects of King William's Act have not been carefully studied. Matthews, the historian who has given it closest attention, says it was "unworkable and disregarded by every one in the fishery," yet "formed the basis of British policy towards Newfoundland throughout the eighteenth century"[145] — a somewhat contradictory judgment. How "unworkable" it was depended on the will of those who enforced it. From time to time parts of it were enforced, and then it did "work" well for those whose interests it chiefly protected. It gave the admirals authority to hold court, and they did. Admiral William Orchard and rear-admiral Elias Rendell held court in St. John's as late as 1786.[146] The act was certainly not "disregarded by every one in the fishery." Merchants, fishing admirals, and lobbyists for the migratory fishery clung to it as their bible. The extent to which it gave general satisfaction to the West Country may be inferred from the fact that no further substantial legislation pertaining directly to the fishery was enacted until 1775. King William's Act was not repealed until 1824.

The immediate effect of the 1699 legislation on the inhabitants was to put some of them out of their rooms; how many is unclear.[147] The act also had an unexpected consequence in the West Country. Matthews says it created a rush by merchants "to seize the best rooms."[148] Exactly why it led to this is not apparent, but perhaps on the surface the act seemed to provide a means for getting a more permanent hold on the rooms, or for preventing others from grabbing them. The merchant Arthur Holdsworth of Dartmouth certainly saw an opening. He brought no fewer than 236 passengers to Newfoundland in 1701 (when he was also admiral of the harbour) and placed them in fishing ships' rooms. When more ships arrived, several had to hire rooms from planters.[149] Other merchants snatched places too. They would dominate the fishery, not just through petition and influence in England, but by direct "engrossing"[150] of land in Newfoundland — though ironically this must have contributed to the increase in settlement that some of them, on paper at least, deplored. The interests of many leading West Country men had in any case expanded well beyond fishing by the late 17th century. They were diversifying, becoming importers and suppliers. Yonge had noted this happening in 1671.[151] That melancholy fixture of Newfoundland history, indebtedness to merchants, was now in place. Some "wheedle a Poor planter into debt [and] either take his fish by force from him, or break open his house (to take it), if lockt," Commodore John Graydon said in 1701.[152] A report by barrister George Larkin that same year gives a similar account of fish being "stript by night" off rocks by creditors and other images of planters entangled in debt, being left at season's end with "not one penny wages."[153] "Stripping" debtors' fish to prevent it being seized by other creditors or sold would remain a feature of life for some time.[154]

Meanwhile, and with good reason, the 3,500[155] residents lived "in daily fear of the neighbouring French."[156] Queen Anne's War (1702-13) saw them once again afflicted not just by French warships and privateers but by murderous overland raids. The first of these assaults occurred in the summer of 1702, when "40 or 50" Frenchmen came from Placentia to Scilly Cove,[157] killed "3 or 4," stole a ship with 1,000 quintals of fish on board, but "took no fish from the rocks."[158] The following year Commodore Graydon led a squadron to Newfoundland for an assault on Placentia. A council of war was held in St. Mary's Bay in August, and a decision was made to return to England. The famed Articles of War often did not seem to apply in Newfoundland waters. Engish warships regularly approached Placentia, hovered offshore, then withdrew. They were efficient enough in taking French prizes,[159] but were loath to attack Placentia itself. (Though *stages* were said to be destroyed at Trepassey, St. Mary's, Colinet, and St. Lawrence in 1702.)[160] The main port was left intact to provide a base for winter campaigns against settlements on the English shore. Some residents of Trinity, realizing England could not be counted on, retreated to an island in the harbour in the fall of 1703 and drew up elaborate plans for defence. This time, apparently, they were prepared to fight to the death.[161]

The French were bold, by sea and land. In August, 1704, privateering surgeon Jean Léger de la Grange attacked Bonavista and caused great havoc, making off with a 250-ton ship heavily laden with dried cod.[162] One of his partners in the venture was a Quebec baker. More money was to be made in pilfered *morue* than in *petites bouchées*. That same year another overland assault was planned on a scale resembling, and perhaps exceeding, Iberville's. It was under Placentia's governor, Daniel d'Auger de Subercase, a Frenchman with wide experience in Canadian frontier warfare. He was joined by Iberville's brutal officer Montigny, and by around 100[163] Canadians and Indians, including the Abenaki Nescambiouit. The total force, about 450,[164] left Placentia on January 8, 1705, crossed the peninsula slowly in bitter cold, and took Bay Bulls and Petty Harbour. They then entered St. John's, all of which, except for Fort William, they captured with apparent ease. The fort held out. The commander of the fifty-man garrison (or Newfoundland Independent Company, as it was sometimes called) was Lieutenant John Moody, who resisted all appeals and threats, and fought off assaults, for thirty-three days — a victory of sorts but, since it saved neither the town nor any other settlement, more symbolic than real. There was perhaps something incongruous, if not ludicrous, in having the fort hold out while all else was overrun, but Matthews' inference[165] that it shows the virtual impossibility of defending Newfoundland (as sundry West Country merchants had claimed) seems unwarranted. As the engineer Michael Richards later told a House of Commons committee, such forts were impractical. He "could think of no better way" to defend Newfoundland "than to repel force by force, by equalling at least, if not outnumbering, the enemy."[166] That was the real lesson of the winter wars. Others drew the same conclusion as Richards.[167]

Moody lost two men in the seige; twelve more perished of cold. His estimate of the number of raiders killed, likely highly exaggerated, was "about 200."[168] The vicious maneuvers to force surrender might be imagined. The invaders "committed many barbarities and sent many threatenings," said the historian Penhallow.[169] One inhabitant was sent to the fort carrying the body of a child whose throat had been cut.[170] All but four houses in St. John's were burnt, together with all boats and ships. Subercase gave up, retreating to Ferryland on March 5, letting the Canadians and Indians ravish the coastline in his rear. From there he sent Montigny with about seventy men (Canadians and Indians again) northwards to Holyrood, where he proceeded, with as much "dash"[171] as he had shown under Iberville, to re-enact the events of 1697 — killing, looting, burning, and taking captives in Conception Bay. In this campaign, Nescambiouit "as usual, distinguished himself."[172] Carbonear Island again provided a refuge for about 300 settlers. Other islands had by now been occupied, from fear of the French; perhaps these too were unmolested. On returning to Placentia, Montigny crossed the isthmus to Trinity Bay and forced the surrender of Bonavista. It is not clear what happened to the contingent on the island in Trinity harbour. The victors' tally for the entire expedition included the figure of 1,200[173] prisoners — an astonishing number when the total population is considered. Subercase took about 150 of the "ablest men" to Placentia and forced them to work in the French fishery. Some, "particularly the Irish," joined the French military.[174] First-hand accounts of the atrocities are scarce. Having rebuilt their stages and settlements after 1697, the residents now had to turn to it again. The very foundations of the fledgling society had been demolished once more.

There was now good reason to retaliate, and some thought was given to punishing Placentia by sea when news of this second winter war reached London. But no attack was made. More discussion ensued.[175] Instead of plundering on the south coast around Placentia, the English turned their attention to the north of Bonavista, where there were no French settlements (owing to fear of the Beothucks)[176] but only fishing ships and stages, signs of a large French migratory fishery. The assaults in 1707 on the non-settlements of Fleur de Lys, Conche, Croque, St. Julien's, and other places along the unfamiliar northern shoreline were successful. A number of French vessels were taken as prizes. (A prize officer to handle business was now stationed at St. John's.) As for St. John's, the residents formed themselves into a militia, probably reflecting, with the men of Trinity, that they had better look to themselves for protection against the enemy. A new fort was built with this militia in mind. The garrison commander who had preceded Moody, Thomas Lloyd, was back in charge and, it appeared, displaying some vigour in preparing defences against any further attack. Commodore Timothy Bridge, however, reported ominously that he had often gone into and out of a fort under Lloyd's command and had "not seen one [s]entinel upon duty."[177]

This observation was soon validated. Late in 1708 preparations for yet another foray from Placentia were underway, under the general direction of the governor, Pastour de Costebelle, a veteran raider. The expedition was to be led by Joseph de Monbeton de Brouillan, called Saint-Ovide, the nephew of the governor who accompanied Iberville. Saint-Ovide, with "about 170"[178] men, including Indians, set out overland in mid-December; a frigate bearing munitions and supplies would meet them at St. John's. All went as planned. Saint-Ovide arrived at St. John's early on January 1, 1709.[179] Proceeding in moonlight, he stormed Fort William, which appears to have been less than adequately manned with sentries, and, once the new fort surrendered, was master of the town. Having taken it, he held it (with 800 prisoners) only until March, when he destroyed the forts, burnt the houses residents could not afford to ransom, stole the cannon and munitions, sent the garrison to Quebec, and, on the 27th, departed in glory. Even though an effort to take Ferryland had been repulsed, this was the most "distinguished"[180] action in his career. A military response from the British, anticipated by the French, was not forthcoming. The new naval commodore, Joseph Taylour, turned up in mid-August to find the town, once again, in ruins.

Before he left, Taylour had Fort William rebuilt, and appointed a resident, the merchant John Collins, as governor and commander of the fort and harbour for the winter (there now being no garrison). This appears to be the first time a civilian was formally appointed to such a position, though residents had on occasion chosen their own winter governor. "Governor Collins" remained in his post until 1720. This innovation was succeeded by another. Commodore Josias Crowe in 1711 called an assembly of ships' captains and "chief inhabitants." After holding "several" such "courts" during which witnesses were examined, the commodore issued a series of sixteen "laws and orders"[181] dealing with fishing rooms, defence, taverns, and other local business, all presumably approved by the captains and inhabitants, or at least discussed by them. This practice was followed up in 1712 by Crowe's successor, Sir Nicholas Trevanion, who was even more prodigal with his laws.[182] Such proceedings indicated both the need for local regulations far beyond what was in King William's Act and the willingness of inhabitants to help draw them up. But these were isolated events. Government through formal consultation with inhabitants was a long way off.

What was in the offing was a long peace. Negotiations with France began in 1709, and climaxed in the Treaty of Utrecht in 1713. From the beginning of the talks Queen Anne insisted on "the restitution of Newfoundland," though it was she who ultimately permitted negotiator Henry St. John to concede extensive fishing rights.[183] France was indeed obliged to yield and give up its settlements on the island, including Placentia, in article 13 of the treaty. "From this time forward" Newfoundland and the islands adjacent were to "belong of right wholly to Great Britain," an assertion that would, in fifty years, be slightly modified, and in a later century changed utterly. But the French were not driven out altogether, though that might well have been appropriate in view of the barbarities they committed. While subjects of France were forbidden to "resort to" Newfoundland beyond the fishing season, or to erect any buildings there apart from "stages made of boards, and huts necessary and usual for fishing and drying of fish," they were "allowed" to catch fish and "dry them on land," on the northern and western coast between Cape Bonavista and Point Riche, and "in that part only." Seventy years later, these limits too would be altered, but the the so-called French shore (also termed Treaty shore or Petit Nord), defined at Utrecht for the first time, would provide a source of contention in Newfoundland history until 1904.

Chapter 5

Colonial Twilight: 1714-63

OR *PRE*-COLONIAL. The British Empire comprised different types of colonies, but before the 19th century Newfoundland could hardly be said to conform to any of them. To have the status of "a conventional colony"[1] meant having structures of government and society to some extent separate from those of the mother country. A colony was thought of as a community, albeit a subservient one, tied to England in various ways yet with a degree of control over its affairs. English statesmen would not grant Newfoundland this recognition. Its "colonial existence" was "denied."[2] The British were determined that the island (when it crossed their minds) would not take the path of a regular colony. It would not go the route of Nova Scotia where, to offset the Acadian influence, vigorous and expensive measures were put in place to attract English settlers and make them comfortable and secure.[3] It would not go the way of America, which by the early 18th century was seen as less a prop to Britain than a stern competitor in trade and "too much inclined to Independence."[4] Colonial news from Boston and Williamsburg and Halifax and St. John's passed through the hands of the same officials and was considered by the same ministers. In what was happening in other settlements, they could see what might happen in Newfoundland. For various reasons, though the economic ones preponderated, it was important that Newfoundland's affairs be run from London. If kept wholly under control, the island and adjacent ocean would remain a training ground for the navy and a place for British merchants to trade and migrating British fishermen to find employment, not a colony but rather "a very important branch of the British Commerce."[5] In short, a moneymaker.

It hardly needs saying that to foster a resident population formed no part of this policy. English politicians and thinkers knew that an expanding colonial population meant expanding colonial power and wealth.[6] Which also meant enlarged colonial presumption. And trouble. The larger the American population got — it famously doubled every twenty-five years — the more trouble America was. Even so, imperial policy might dictate that, as in Nova Scotia, a colonial population should be raised. Nothing remotely equivalent was tried in Newfoundland. The opposite path was followed. The number of people, which had fortunately remained low, was to be kept low, and at times a lofty pretence maintained that those who stayed might not in fact exist.

And so, until comparatively late in North American imperial history, the island lacked many of the institutions that go to form a community, notably a permanent, year-round governor[7] and, until grand juries convened in the 1750s,[8] any constitutional mechanism to give the people a say over their affairs. There would be no council and assembly until well into the 19th century. As we begin this chapter, there were still no magistrates on the island. Some of the North American colonies in the 1700s acquired not just developed structures of government but a veneer of high culture: academies, newspapers, printers, public entertainment, an intelligentsia. Newfoundland lacked these too.

Not that it was ignored. While it had no legislature, it was, as we have seen, regulated by a statute of the British parliament and on occasion discussed both there and in the highest councils of government. There was no shortage of facts and views on which to base decisions and, mostly, non-decisions. Annual reports by commodores or governors were demanded; statistics relating to trade and population were sought and analyzed; inquiries were held. If 18th-century British policy towards the island can be termed one of neglect, it was a studied neglect. It certainly wasn't indifference. It only looked like indifference. Delay, neglect, apparent lack of foresight, failure to correct certain abuses — these reflected not so much negligence or ignorance as (to use a phrase of Burke's) "design artfully conducted."[9] Design clumsily conducted might be a more precise description. There is, perhaps, a danger of crediting British colonial administrators with too much cleverness. We might recall Benjamin Franklin's conclusion, after spending time in London observing parliamentarians at work, that "they appear'd to have scarce Discretion enough to govern a Herd of Swine."[10] Yet a consistent policy towards Newfoundland had evolved by the end of the 17th century; and that policy — of trying to keep the island a sub-colonial British fishing berth, an outlying cod abattoir — remained in place for more than a hundred years. How effective it was can be debated. Matthews says the policy was "always ineffective,"[11] but this seems a rash judgment. If the overarching British project with regard to all the Empire was "to spend as little as possible on, and to make as much as possible out of, the colonies,"[12] then the Newfoundland policy didn't fail, for the migratory fishery brought great dividends to Britain until well into the century, and there were no clamours from an insurgent population to slow the flow of the loot. On balance, the policy worked.

But as the population, though stagnant in the early decades of the century, slowly grew, the island acquired some of the institutions, personnel, and objects normally thought of as marking the appearance and growth of civilized, or at least organized, community life: courts, officials, clerics, stocks, jails, a few schools and churches. There is no question that Newfoundland, as a political and social entity, developed more slowly than, say, Nova Scotia. We can concede too that factors other than a self-regarding British colonial policy slowed it down. Some of these have already been listed. Yet it did develop. History is not a race to see who gets the first post office. In a little noticed but nonetheless valued corner of the Empire, Newfoundland kept the noiseless tenor of its own slow, odd way.

* * *

After Utrecht, Placentia Bay and the south coast of the island, soon termed the "western shore," lay open for both ship fishermen and settlers. Though it was reputed to be "the best place of fishing in Newfoundland as also for furrs and masts,"[13] neither group moved quickly to exploit the new region. In 1716 it was reported that not a single Englishman had gone there. To the English, this was an uncharted and virtually unknown coast. A rough survey was conducted by the Newfoundland-born William Taverner in 1714-18, yet other difficulties remained. The movement of the French inhabitants out of Newfoundland to Île Royale (Cape Breton, ceded to France in the treaty) was slow. An effort was made to induce them to take the oath of allegiance[14] to King George and stay; some did, but most moved on in time. Those who took the oath but left anyway claimed a right to return.[15] Yet only one French family remained at Placentia in 1735.[16] Some who left the easterly French settlements moved to the western extremities of the coast and squatted illegally at Cape Ray alongside migrants from Île Royale. By 1734 the French from Île Royale who had settled at Port aux Basques were said to have "become a little Commonwealth."[17] As Janzen has shown, there was a persistent French presence at and near Cape Ray until 1744.[18] Settlers on the old English shore who contemplated moving into the vacated areas knew this meant either encountering, or in any event getting closer to, both the French and their dreaded Indian allies. Among the latter, the Micmacs were now known to come routinely to the south coast from Cape Breton to hunt. In addition, in any attack emanating from New France someone living in St. Pierre or Burin would be on the front line. The surest way to keep your scalp was to stay close to home.

Other complications were caused by an experiment in government. In 1712, as peace approached, Placentia was placed under the governor of Nova Scotia,[19] and a lieutenant-governor, Lieut.-Col. John Moody, renowned for his defence of Fort William, was appointed in 1713. Officially part of Nova Scotia, Placentia now had what the rest of Newfoundland was denied —year-round resident government, though under a soldier in command of a garrison. British authorities had decided that Placentia, not St. John's, was to be the island's "military centre,"[20] so the garrison was moved there. The French inhabitants had been given the right to sell their rooms before departing, and Moody promptly bought many of them and proceeded to get into the fishing, leasing, and tavern business. Seeing this, the surveyor Taverner bought rooms to lease in St. Pierre. The ship fishermen had grounds for protest, for a "free" fishery could hardly take place if they had to rent space. This was too Kirke-like for them to swallow. Complaints poured in. The Board of Trade was soon informing the King that soldiers should not be involved in the fishery. Moody was recalled.

But an an even more troublesome lieutenant-governor was ensconced at Placentia from 1719. He was Samuel Gledhill, a Yorkshire captain of foot whose character combined greed, vanity, obduracy, and no small measure of energy and ability. (Grant Head's view that he was "apparently mad" is not to be taken seriously.)[21] He has left a memoir[22] — among the earliest in Newfoundland's literary history. It boldly declares how rich he became, through renting fishing rooms, trading in merchandise, and shipping. It was said that only liquor imported by him could be sold in Placentia, and that he had become "the general Banker of the town."[23] As with Kirke, Gledhill's success brought him into collision with the West Country merchants, who, out of "malice" and "envy," so he claimed,[24] soon petitioned against him. The enmity of the West Countrymen has led their chief modern apologist to judge Gledhill rather harshly, saying he was "concerned almost completely with [his] own self-interest."[25] (As contrasted, perhaps, with West Country selflessness.) But Gledhill had an affection for Newfoundland. He called one of his daughters Placentia! Under his regime the harbour rebounded from its desolate situation after the French departure. Masters of ships might resent paying rent, yet they did pay it and their men bought his wine. The postwar years brought a serious downturn in the Newfoundland fishery, but Gledhill soon revived it in his area. He started shipbuilding, and even proposed opening a road linking Placentia, St. John's, and other settlements. Neither plan was encouraged in London. He suggested a hemp industry. He suggested a fortnightly post.[26] Placentia's civilian population jumped to 179 by 1731. A high proportion of these were Irish. Gledhill, who employed them,[27] insisted they take the required oath, yet the growth of a disaffected Irish population in the southern Avalon — "scum," according to one commodore[28] — was a source of anxiety to British authorities and, initially, to West Country merchants. The latter's squawking about them in petitions would soon change, however, as the Irish were seen as a pool of cheap labour for the fishery. Placentia and its immediate environs would remain largely an Irish Catholic enclave. Settlers of English descent who in time ventured to the south coast tended to pass by the Irish into the bays and islands farther west. Though some Irish were at Cape Ray before 1744,[29] and pockets of Irish established themselves elsewhere on the coast, Fortune Bay and beyond were destined to become largely a Protestant shore.

The Irish threat, or perceived threat, was but one of many largely self-created "difficulties and disorders"[30] confronting those charged with administering the island. It was now understood that King William's Act was flawed, but to recast it and bring it back to Parliament was inconvenient, so the British muddled through with it. Had there been any serious rethinking of the act's fundamental aims, it would have been amended, of course. But there was no such rethinking. Suggestions for changes that from time to time occurred to those who visited the island were ignored. The policy embedded in the act was the policy subscribed to. Rather than legislate anew or introduce wide-ranging changes in government, the British tinkered, hesitantly consenting to small bureaucratic improvements as circumstances required. Courts for trying pirates, with a local merchant as registrar, had been created in 1701; a prize officer, in place in St. John's from 1704, added customs duties to his labours in 1708.[31] These offices were filled intermittently and, it appears, ineffectively. A vice-admiralty[32] judge, James Smith, was appointed in 1708, together with a registrar and marshal, but none of the three proceeded to Newfoundland.[33] Smith finally went in 1713, but stayed very briefly.[34] On returning to England, he reported that a vice-admiralty court could accomplish little in Newfoundland since the place lacked both a permanent governor and a naval officer[35] to take bonds and clear ships inwards and outwards. (A vice-admiralty court was appointed in 1736, a naval officer in 1741.) In the absence of officials to enforce the Navigation Acts,[36] smuggling flourished, with New England and European merchants — mostly English — taking advantage of the unregulated mid-Atlantic coastline to trade in a wide variety of contraband. It was, in fact, thought that, strictly speaking, Newfoundland was not a plantation within the meaning of the Navigation Acts, and so was immune from their provisions.[37] This was one cost to the British of leaving the island in an ungoverned or half-governed condition. Another was an annual drain of seamen to New England. Despite efforts to get English vessels to bring their men back each year, many were left behind. They most often stayed to avoid the press gangs at home or because they couldn't afford the passage back,[38] whereupon large numbers were coaxed onto New England ships for transport to labour-short America. Some American traders got forty shillings for each man carried off.[39] "One cannot give it a better term than kidnapping," a commodore said in 1715.[40] The presence of New England factors[41] in St. John's facilitated this dubious trade. Many commodores tried to stop the practice, which struck at the very heart of the notion that Newfoundland was a "nursery of seamen" for the British navy. None did. It could only be stopped by year-round vigilance. American recruiters simply waited for the commodores to sail off home before going into action.

But the chief failing in the system of ruling Newfoundland was in the area of law and order. Once the fishing admirals and commodore departed, there was no official law-enforcing authority at all on the island (save at Placentia). The admirals were far from scrupulous in their dealings, indeed were widely viewed, even by the commodores, as corrupt, ignorant, and harsh. They were quite capable of expelling planters from rooms that were long inhabited, and of insolent resistance to a commodore's explicit commands.[42] Yet they were at hand. Their presence alone was a deterrent. Even when admirals and commodore were in port, no authority existed for dealing with capital crimes,[43] a category which in the eighteenth century encompassed much more than treason and murder. In King William's Act (clause 13) "robberies, murders, and felonies, and all other capital crimes" committed in Newfoundland were ordered to be tried in "any shire or county" of England by commissioners of oyer and terminer, and jail delivery.[44] That meant they had to be sent overseas with witnesses, a procedure entailing trouble and expense. Because such trials interrupted their work and cost them passage back to the island, some witnesses absconded. Outside the fishing season, the arrest and deportation of a murderer might have to be carried out by a civilian, acting on his own.[45]

The lack of an effective year-round legal system encouraged crime, bullying, and exploitation. So, at any rate, the reports by the commodores repeatedly aver, with the Irish often pointed to as malefactors. The dearth of regulation might even have drawn a certain ornery type of immigrant to the island. One commodore noted that "a place without Government" such as Newfoundland attracted a "set of people" who "can't live in Great Britain or anywhere else."[46] (Similarly the lack of priests likely drew some of the Irish to the island.)[47] But official reports tended to emphasize crises and problems rather than the normal, peaceful routines of daily life, and as such likely provide a somewhat distorted picture. Amidst the evidence pointing to the (mostly Irish) drunkards, malcontents, and criminals, it is well to bear in mind the opinion of one high official, who thought the reports were the product of malice. He found the "seafareing" people of Newfoundland to be "much the same" in their "behaviour" as those "in other seaport towns in England."[48]

In any event, in 1716 the Council (or Committee) of Trade, responding to numerous reports of vice, debauchery, etc., formally recommended that winter magistrates be appointed, the appointees having first been elected by the planters.[49] Secretary of State James Stanhope chose not to act on this sensible and uncharacteristic suggestion. Two years later, the Council thought better of it and in two separate sets of recommendations reversed the previous finding. Now noting that "it might be of ill consequence" to alter the "ancient usages" practised in Newfoundland, the Council in its first presentation thought it advisable "to use all proper methods" to get the inhabitants to move to Nova Scotia. (In the second and lengthier document, the recommendation was simply "to remove" them.) It was the "several ill practices of the inhabitants," after all, that had caused the "inconveniences" to the fishery; furthermore, the settlers persisted in trading with New England rather than with "their Mother Kingdom." A clinching point: if the "few remaining inhabitants" were removed, the French would not regard it as worth their while to attack the island.[50] In case the recommendation for removal was thought "a hardship," the Council supplied the draft of a new bill for the fishery, including several harsh measures directed at inhabitants.[51]

Once again, the British government was considering deportation. By official count, the permanent population of Newfoundland in 1717 (excluding native peoples) was still only 2,822.[52] But they were well scattered along a tortuous coast, with deep woods in back to hide and live in. It might have been a hard task to root them out. Yet if they were persuaded to move, their presence in Nova Scotia, it was thought, could counterbalance that of the intransigent Acadians. In June, 1719, the Governor of Nova Scotia, Richard Phillips, was told to "use all proper methods" to induce the inhabitants of Newfoundland to move to his province, and as well to reduce the size of the Placentia garrison. He gave orders to Gledhill (who was not only lieutenant-governor of Placentia but "Commander-in-Chief," i.e., military commander, of Newfoundland) to send all but forty soldiers back to Nova Scotia[53] and to publish proclamations to inform people "of His Majesty's desire of their removing to this country." Gledhill sent the soldiers, but refused to publish the proclamations unless he received instructions directly from the Secretary of State. No such instruction was received.[54] The revised Newfoundland bill sent to the King by the Council on Trade was not enacted. In 1721, the Council was still finding reasons for sending settlers to Nova Scotia.[55]

By the 1720s a small society was beginning to take shape in Newfoundland, the hub of which was the "metropolis"[56] of St. John's. The little town already had a number of resident merchants, whose premises were built alongside the taverns, boarding-houses, suttling-houses,[57] stages, and flakes.[58] It was the commercial sector which now took the lead in providing for the administration of justice. In November, 1723, the "Merchants, Factors, Principal Inhabitants, or Masters of Families" of St. John's, together with the Church of England minister Richard Jago, proceeded to "embody [themselves] into a Community for the mutual Preservation of His Majesty's Peace ... during the Winter."[59] The document in which they announced the formation of this "community" (a Lockeian word) began with a quotation from the philosopher John Locke's *Essay on Civil Government*, 4th ed., (1723), which affirmed: "Men being by nature all free, equal, and independent, no one can be put out of this estate, and subjected to the political power of another, without his own consent." It is intriguing that someone possessed, not just Locke, but Locke in the most recent edition. There was possibly already a book culture in the city, hidden from view owing to the lack of a body of settlement literature. (Gledhill's memoir, it might be said, is full of references to classical and English writers.) The document had fifty-one signatures, of which fourteen were marks. This suggests a fairly high degree of literacy at the merchant and planter level. While Locke's prefatory words might have been thought to carry a whiff of menace, the document made it clear that the steps to be taken as a result of the spread of crime — listed are "insolences," rapines, frequent burglaries, cattle rustling, insults to merchants, the cajoling of servants to leave their masters, and trespasses, all "daily committed" — were only to be in effect "until the arrival of a British fishing ship in this harbour." The assembly was loyal. Nonetheless, without authorization from Britain, Jago and two merchants were selected as "justices" to hold weekly courts. Fourteen such courts were held. No serious crimes were brought before them. However, a servant named Thomas Slaughter, evidently an Englishman, was convicted of insulting and striking his master, and of spitting in the face of the master's wife and calling her bitch. He was tied to a post and given eleven "stripes" on the bare back.

News of this settler-court reached England in 1725. It provoked no reexamination of Newfoundland affairs by officials, though the next commodore was instructed to investigate and reported back on the whipping and a case pertaining to property rights.[60] It was the intervention of Lord Vere Beauclerk, naval commodore in 1728, that brought the next change to the island. His report focused on Placentia, where he found it "impossible ... to settle who had a right to the plantations and who not." Gledhill had refused to appear before him to explain his claim to "most of the rooms and stages within the harbour," saying he was following instructions from governor Phillips. Access by fishing ships to "the most commodious harbour and the finest beach in the world" could be obtained only by hiring Gledhill's rooms. "Confusion" reigned. The fishery could not succeed "if the garrison continues upon the foot it now is." At St. John's, he found that the laws governing the fishery were also slighted. He heard that threats, rioting, and disorder prevailed in winter, owing to the lack of proper persons authorized to administer justice after the fishing ships and convoy left.[61] This deficiency had been pointed to repeatedly before.

But it was now pointed to by Lord Vere. His report was sent to the Council on Trade by Secretary of State Thomas Pelham-Holles, Duke of Newcastle, with a note saying that King George wondered if a garrison was required for the protection of his subjects "and the preservation of that settlement." The King was evidently unaware that to preserve the "settlement" had rarely been a concern of the Council on Trade. In response, the Council, after holding an inquiry and fretting over the question of land ownership in Newfoundland,[62] suggested that Gledhill be recalled and urged that the garrison be placed under the control of the commodore. As for the "unhappy people," these lived amidst assorted "miserys" — the rigor of the climate, barrenness of the soil, and a "state of anarchy." (This last having been created by British policy-makers, chief among them being the Council on Trade!) The Lords of Trade now said that the appointment of winter justices "might" abate the people's misery, though their real "opinion" was that the inhabitants should be "encouraged" to settle in Nova Scotia, where they could be "of some service to Your Majesty and to themselves."[63] It was 1728, and wholesale expulsion was still being recommended. Nor was this the last time that the removal of settlers from Newfoundland was considered an option open to the British government.

The suggestion was once again not acted on. Instead, the Council on Trade's opinion was referred to a committee of the Privy Council, and in April, 1729, a recommendation was made by that committee to appoint justices of the peace in Newfoundland.[64] The committee also noted that inhabitants held rooms either "under pretence of being entitled to them" by clause 7 of King William's Act, or having purchased them from the French. They thought the titles of all who claimed to own land should be examined. A "person skilled in the law" should accompany the next commodore to help with this inquiry. Such a person might also assist in "forming some regulations" for the better government of the inhabitants "during the winter season, so long as they shall continue there." The last phrase seems to suggest the continuance might well be brief.

But it was not to be brief, and a step was now taken that helped to ensure its longevity. At the end of May, 1729, the King gave a commission to Henry Osborn, captain of H.M.S. *Squirrel*, as "Governor and Commander in Chief" of Newfoundland. (This did not mean he was above the naval commodore; Lord Vere was back as commodore in 1729, and Osborn had to defer to him.)[65] Placentia was now removed from the government of Nova Scotia; Osborn was to be in charge of it and any other forts on the island. While there would be more trouble from Gledhill, his day was over; several of his rooms were stripped from him shortly after Osborn's arrival, and he was called home to answer for his conduct.[66] But the major innovation was legal, not military. In order to prevent "great irregularities, outrages, rapes, felonies, murders, and other heinous offences" committed in Newfoundland — words making the island sound like a new Gomorrah — and "to encourage Virtue,"[67] Osborn was authorized to appoint justices of the peace and "other necessary officers and ministers."[68] He proceeded to create six districts — the first time Newfoundland had been so broken down. In them he appointed seventeen justices and thirty constables.[69] He built several pairs of stocks, put up whipping posts, and authorized, through the St. John's justices, a levy on fish caught by both inhabitants and fishing ships to build a jail. A jail with a court house above it was "in a manner finished" by 1730.[70] In addition to its judicial functions, the court house would serve as a place of assembly for St. John'smen. Although his commission noted that wickedness in Newfoundland occurred "especially during the winter season," Osborn was not instructed to confine the justices' activities to that time of year, nor did he do so.[71] He was to ensure, however, that they did not obstruct the powers given to the admirals and convoy commanders in King William's Act; and they were so directed in a commission each was handed on being appointed.[72]

The institution of these new offices created a stir among the fishing admirals and merchants, the former of whom rushed to hold courts, belatedly attempting to discharge their long neglected duties. For their part, the merchants demanded that the justices serve only in winter and not intrude on the admirals' alleged powers.[73] A brief period of tension between admirals and magistrates ensued in Newfoundland. But it was soon made clear, on high authority,[74] that the judicial role of the admirals as defined in King William's Act was quite distinct from that of the justices. It was a limited role, though an important one. The admirals had no business meddling with general "breaches of the peace, and other criminal matters." There were also strong objections to Osborn's imposition of a levy on fish, especially in view of the declaration in the act that there was to be "free trade and traffick" in the fishery. Expert opinion was somewhat divided on the legality of the tax.[75] Both lawyers consulted agreed, however, that in certain circumstances, justices of the peace had the statutory right to raise levies. Thus the legal right to tax, though extremely limited, had arrived in Newfoundland. But one lawyer said that Osborn had "no power ... of imposing taxes in general without the consent of some Assembly of the people." The pointed remark did not find an immediate echo in the bosoms of the power brokers.

Osborn said that the "best" of the magistrates he appointed were "but mean people," but he did find them and, as directed, provide them[76] with Joseph Shaw's handbook, *The Practical Justice of Peace* (1728) to explain their functions. They were to act as if they were justices in England, enforcing "the Laws and Statutes of His Majesty's Kingdom of Great Britain."[77] They were duly sworn in, taking the required four oaths and making a declaration (after receiving communion according to "the usage of the Church of England") that "*I do* believe, That there is not any *Transubstantiation in the Sacrament of the Lord's Supper, or in the Elements of Bread and Wine, at or after the Consecration thereof.*"[78] There would be no "Papists" — or Dissenters —amidst their ranks. They were soon at work, licencing taverns, committing miscreants to the stocks, keeping an eye out for witches and sorcerers, and discharging the innumerable other duties that belonged to that office. Matthews has commented that "Probably by creating a permanent magistracy the Board of Trade did something to bring order to Newfoundland."[79] It is likely that the effects were far more profound and far-reaching than these words suggest. A mere glance through one of Shaw's handbooks for justices and constables (who had powers independent of the justices, including that of carrying before a justice anyone suspected of being a Roman Catholic)[80] will show what now had descended on Newfoundland — an entire apparatus of precedent, judgment, and enforcement touching virtually every aspect of community life except, as in England, "the Determination of Property."[81] Where there had been no law, or little law, there was now, comparatively speaking, law in abundance. At the level of parish law — in matters touching churches, roads, alehouses, inns, bawdyhouses,[82] drunkards, swearers, sabbath-breakers,[83] hawkers, apprentices, beggars, the poor, and much more — Newfoundland had changed radically. And while a justice had considerable power when acting alone, this was not all. Two justices acting together had different and well defined powers, as did three, four, five, and six.[84]

Justices were also empowered (by Osborn's 1729 commission from the King) to hold Quarter Sessions of the Peace, "according to the custom ... of England." The Quarter Sessions, presided over by two or more justices, was a court of limited criminal jurisdiction (it did not deal with capital crimes) which normally met, as is obvious, four times a year.[85] It could employ juries. It could receive presentments from the constables, on oath, "of all things within their Knowledge against the Peace."[86] Justices were preservers of the peace, and could interpret this mandate broadly. In Newfoundland they felt they could "present" grievances and anxieties to the governor. Two of the three St. John's justices made such a presentment[87] to governor George Clinton in 1731, pointing to various troubles, including the practice, just adopted, of shipping felons from Britain to Newfoundland.[88] This, they said, had resulted in five "most barbarous" murders. "We" (speaking for the population generally) "are a constitution not so capable of defending ourselves from such insults, as others of H.M. Plantations, which are under better regulations, and have men and money for defence and security therof at the publick charge." Clinton concurred with the justices, and dumping criminals on the island appears to have ceased at once. By the end of the 18th century the justices had become a major force in Newfoundland life.

Matthews took some solace from the fact that the new office of magistrate was filled mostly by merchants, thereby ensuring continued West Country influence in Newfoundland.[89] He was undoubtedly right in suspecting that merchant-justices would hardly be oblivious to the interests of their class in carrying out their official duties. Some complaints of this nature in fact were reported.[90] Yet a merchant behind his counter is not the same as a merchant holding court, sworn to "do equal Right to the Poor and Rich" and "not spare any one for any Gift or other Cause."[91] Becoming a justice of peace was a solemn undertaking. "Robes and furred gowns"[92] change the man wearing them. There were now forty-seven legally appointed local notables, in effect resident officials, in the various settlements. Not everyone would welcome their elevation, for to have a magistrate or constable next door is always an ambiguous if not distinctly uncomfortable experience, and the inhabitants were long used to living at arm's length from the law. But the justices and constables must have provided a degree of leadership and security. They would have strengthened residential life. And since the Quarter Sessions was a court where actions of justices out of Sessions could be appealed, the likelihood of continued tyranny by a merchant abusing his office was, while certainly not negligible, surely no greater than had been the case when admirals abused theirs.

In discussing Newfoundland, we now have to be conscious of a structure of law and ordinance operating, often invisibly, below the notice of most official documents, in effect at the level of the parish, though there were no parishes as strictly defined, and district. The structure was more than legal. Governors made use of the justices — they were at his command — in a number of administrative ways, for example in collecting statistics for the fishery and population. Prior to 1742 some governors tried to get the justices to collect manifests of cargoes from arriving ships. It was peculiar to have this kind of machinery in a "colony"[93] without a council, assembly, or year-round governor. (For there was no hint that Osborn was to stay in Newfoundland beyond the fishing season.) Yet it was there, a continuous, bottom-layer sub-government, regulating life, overlooking conditions in general, and offering a measure of protection for people high and low. The fact that it existed from 1729 and functioned in general satisfactorily[94] might account, to some extent, for the late arrival of democratic institutions on the island.

By the 1730s, the Newfoundland economy had diversified well beyond beyond codfish. Furring, never a major economic factor, might already have fallen into temporary decline. Less than £500 worth of furs were taken in 1729, down from £3,000 in 1718.[95] But the value would rise again. (Such figures were very rough estimates.) The hunt for furs went on. It drove men some distance into the interior, along the south coast, and especially to the north, bringing them inevitably into contact with the Beothuck. While the accounts of Guy's 1612 expedition to Trinity Bay show that trade had once been transacted between settlers and Beothuck, none was evident in the 1730s. Indians killed furriers, and furriers Indians.[96] The furriers' "constant cruel usage"[97] of the Beothuck was, in combination with other pressures, forcing the Indians northwards. They would soon be confined to an ever-diminishing space between encroaching English to the south and the French migratory fishermen to the north and west. Only ten leagues (about thirty miles) separated the English and French fisheries in the north in 1743.[98]

Furring was not the only intrusion on the Beothucks. A salmon fishery had sprung up in the early 1700s and its output, by contrast with furring, was expanding. A total of 710 tierces was exported in 1738, up from 199 in 1729.[99] This industry too took men to the north,[100] to the mouths of rivers to be netted, and up rivers into salmon-filled pools, natural and man-made.[101] As the ruthless netting cut back on the salmon population in one river, other streams were sought. In the 1730s salmon were being taken as far north as Dog Bay and Gander Bay. Netting the noble Exploits would not be far off. The Gander Bay fishermen must have gone inland to First, Second, and Third ponds, which are really only wide sections of the Gander River. We do not know which white man first saw Gander Lake, but not many years passed before it was seen, for it appears on 18th-century maps.[102] Gambo Pond is the thin, 20-mile long body of water that empties almost directly into Freshwater Bay. Here also salmon were netted at the river mouth. Fishermen would have explored the easily accessible pond, and so again found their way deep into the interior. They have done so as well by way of the Terra Nova River. Salmon fishermen, like the furriers, were in bloody conflict with the Beothuck, who depended heavily on the fish and possibly were dismayed to see the effects on the salmon supply of netting at the river mouths. The Indians stole nets, robbed other gear, killed, and broke down dams. They were in turn pursued and killed.[103] In January, 1758, a Beothuck girl of about nine years of age was captured by fur hunters in northern Newfoundland. The governor brought her "home," evidently as a curiosity.[104]

Sealing, destined to become one of Newfoundland's greatest and most distinctive industries, also emerged at this time. Once again this led fishermen into the northern bays and onto capes and offshore islands. In winter, sealing was commonly practised by setting nets in "passes" between islands, or between the mainland and rocks or islands. This was an intricate and difficult art.[105] In spring there was a simpler if more dangerous method, for whelping harp and hooded seals drifted south on the Arctic ice, and the ice could normally be depended on to come ashore north of, and in the general vicinity of, Cape Bonavista. (Though it did frequently come in in Trinity and Conception bays too, and sometimes farther south, at which periods seals would be taken all along the east coast.) Hunters could walk out on the ice, kill the animals, and drag them back to land, an occupation hard to match for sheer peril. Seal oil was exported to Poole in 1709.[106] In 1718 it was said that 200 men at Bonavista followed the "furring and seal oyl trades."[107] The following year Commander Ogle said that furring and sealing might even make a better "voyage" than cod fishing.[108] The abundant seals provided, not just pelts and oil, but nourishing and tasty food, especially important in spring when other supplies were often running low. In 1723 seal oil first appears in the reports by commodores; it was valued at the considerable sum of £6,025.[109] Thereafter, though subject to yearly fluctuations owing to the unpredictable ice and wind conditions, sealing statistics were reported, and the industry, as decades passed, gradually loomed larger in the life and economy of the island.[110]

But cod was still king. Following the post-Utrecht slump, the fishery in the 1730s and '40s prospered. The English migratory fishery, as Matthews and Handcock[111] show, was not now the ship fishery of old, which was characterized by merchants and smaller-scale shipowners sending or taking vessels out from various ports with shore- and boat-crews to favoured rooms on the Newfoundland coast. Though vestiges of this older style enterprise persisted well into the century, by-boat and bank fisheries largely replaced it. By the late 1740s masters of so-called fishing ships were either engaged in passenger traffic, bringing servants back and forth for planters and by-boatmen,[112] or else they were bank fishermen. In 1763 Governor Thomas Graves reported that fishing admirals in the various ports were "generally masters of bankers."[113] The bank fishery, carried out until the last decade of the 18th century not by residents but by migratory fishermen, had commenced on the southern English shore in 1714;[114] it quickly became a major component in the industry.[115]

Another change in the fishery was due to gradual mercantile consolidation and expansion. From the 1730s traders with "considerable fleets"[116] of ships were beginning to dominate fishing in certain areas, in a manner different in both method and scale from that of their ancestors. As the century wore on, and increasingly after 1750, West Country firms set up as fishing and supplying merchants at chosen locations on the island, with planters dependent on them, and numbers of servants, recruited in England and Ireland, directly employed by them, all providing mostly dried cod but also oil, salmon, and other products, including timber, for transport overseas in the firm's own ships. It was the setting up *on the island* that constituted the major change. In truth, it was a form of residency. The bigger firm's servants were installed not just in the immediate neighborhood of the premises but on gobbled up rooms in adjacent coves, and some coves farther off, in which the merchants built houses and stages. Some merchants in effect became major landowners.[117] (Or at least land*holders*, since though land was routinely leased, sold, and bequeathed in 18th-century Newfoundland, legal title was not yet established.) The home port for this newly shaped trade remained Poole or Dartmouth, which with some other English towns skimmed off most of the enormous profits,[118] though the take likely ended up in fewer hands than in the past. But at the Newfoundland end money was spent too. The lowly flake endured, but a more imposing architecture of wharves, storehouses, salt houses, lumber houses, forges, and other structures[119] to facilitate the collection of fish, distribution of supplies, and shipping appeared in larger "out-harbours":[120] Carbonear, Harbour Grace, Trinity, Placentia, St. Pierre (termed St. Peter's when in English hands), and, in time, more remote places. A detailed list of British premises at St. Pierre and Miquelon in 1763 discloses that eleven proprietors and firms owned a total of thirty-five houses, some obviously intended for factors or agents, but most humbler residences for the employees, i.e., fishermen and shoremen. The most costly structures were the stages "with conveniencies," valued at twice or three times the value of houses.[121] St. John's of course was a part of this development. But while it was still an important fishing town, its speciality was trading in fish rather than catching it. It was more a general entrepôt for passenger traffic, barter, smuggling, tavern keeping, and sale of merchandise.

Outside St. John's, the focus was more sharply on fishing. Surviving illustrations show how elaborate some outharbour mercantile premises were.[122] They were too expensive to be left untended after the fishing season ended. Relatives or junior partners in the firms were sent to Newfoundland in summer, and often to overwinter for there was much critical winter work to be done as well. Some stayed many years. A custom was soon in place, one that would endure into the 19th century, of a proprietor's son or nephew coming "out" to Newfoundland to supervise a fish business, returning "home" from time to time to enjoy the fruits of his labours, and ultimately retiring in his West Country mansion. Perhaps he would then get himself elected to office and hold forth on Newfoundland affairs. Irish merchants too ventured into this lucrative business, notably Richard Welsh of New Ross, a small port near Waterford, who was established at Placentia by the early 1750s, and likely before that. He founded what would become the Sweetman firm, a major establishment.[123] Liverpool and Glasgow were likewise drawn into the trade. A few Newfoundland born inhabitants — shortly to be called "Newfoundlanders"[124] — rose to be merchants as well.[125]

The merchant-driven 18th-century fishery became more expansive in nature. Competition led to the opening of fisheries in bays outside the traditional English shore, and to harbours, or indentations undeserving of the name of harbour, within the shore that had not previously been fully exploited. Where the merchants went, settlers and servants, many of whom ultimately became settlers, followed. As with the sealing industry, this commerce too led men north. Twillingate, soon to be the operational base of the Poole merchant John Slade, and Fogo were added to the regular reports by governors in 1738, but had been settled prior to that.[126] Both of course were well within the bounds of the French shore, on which the French had been given the right to catch and dry fish, though not an exclusive right. The main locus of French fishing activity on the coast was in any case west and north of Cape St. John, the promontory at the western extremity of Notre Dame Bay. It would not be long before the English intruded beyond that. English merchants also penetrated the western reaches of the south coast in the 1730s;[127] the fishery at Lapoile was reported on in 1740,[128] and there were settlers at Harbour le Cou, Boxey, St.

Jacques, and other places by 1763.[129] Cook found a well established Poole firm at Harbour Breton in 1765. The settlements that slowly took shape in the neighborhood of some of the more remote merchant premises were tiny. Most of the English and Irish population remained overwhelmingly on the Avalon, with Conception Bay having by far the largest concentration.[130] By 1750 the population of the whole island (excluding native peoples) was still under 10,000.[131] One cause of its more rapid growth thereafter — it stood at 16,000 in 1764[132] — was the increasingly residential nature of mercantile activity.

The number of residents was still small. Yet the colonial policy in place for Newfoundland ensured that the population would be watched, extensively commented on, and remorselessly counted — or at least said to be counted.[133] A distinction was drawn between summer residents and those overwintering. The former were evidently not regarded as part of the true population of the island; only the latter need cause anxiety among those whose objective was to keep the resident numbers low. We also get tallies of British fishing ships, by-boatmen, American ships, total quintals of cod exported, and various other economic statistics. Since the island was run as an extension of commerce, parts of the governors' reports somewhat resemble yearly ledgers, though to be fair, many of their remarks display considerable sensitivity above and beyond mere figures.

The statistics underscore one telling fact: the preponderance of servants. Their numbers fluctuated somewhat annually, but servants comprised 70% of the summer population of Newfoundland in 1753.[134] Thereafter the percentage declined, but it remained as high as 50% in 1775. This was likely much higher than in some adjacent colonial societies.[135] The life of an 18th-century servant in Newfoundland was undoubtedly laborious, for fishing is one of the hardest occupations on earth. "They labour very hard," one governor said of the planters, for "he that will not work, cannot live in this country."[136] We may take it the same was true of the planters' servants. The fishery was not now run on the shares system, as it had in Yonge's day, but on wages. Servants' wages varied somewhat from year to year — they were lower in peacetime than during war — but in the 1740s might range from £8 to £20 for the fishing season, depending on one's position in the crew.[137] These were high wages, and great numbers continued to flock to Newfoundland to earn them. It is not easy to divine, from sometimes contradictory governors' reports, what life was like for either servants or masters. One element found in both their lives was debt. By mid-century, supplying merchants (who often illegally "engrossed"[138] commodities from arriving traders, thereby gaining a monopoly enabling them to fix prices reportedly at 100 to 200% above cost, and sometimes higher),[139] had enmeshed Newfoundland by-boatmen and planters in a web of debt; these in turn frequently made debtors of their servants, who bought goods on credit, especially alcohol, from their employers before wages were due.[140] Passing debt on to servants was a means of keeping wage costs down, and of inducing them to remain in the country. But high indebtedness also led some servants to desert their masters and bolt to neighbouring outports where they were not known. Many fled to America. Still others turned to crime.

Indebtedness was common, but it was not universal. The high prices on merchandise had an inflationary effect on wages, driving those up as well. They had risen to between £10 and £25 by 1763.[141] It was of course possible for servants to spend all they earned on drink, and more than they earned, which compelled a longer stay in "bondage" than had been envisioned. But not all servants were drunkards. If a "sober industrious man" brought most of his necessaries in his chest and in general spent moderately, he could gain £20 in bills of exchange in four months.[142] He might even earn more, for some masters paid a premium on every thousand of fish caught. The servant could then well afford to return home in the fall. But he might still find reason to stay. In some regions of the island servants made money during winter by furring "on their own account."[143] A good furrier might make £15 to £30 for his winter's work.[144]

The evidence suggests that most English servants returned home at the end of their employment. The Irish were more inclined to stay. As a consequence, the number of Irish in the population had sharply increased by the mid-century. A 1753 count, likely distorted, had 2,683 Irish to the English 1,816.[145] Other reports likewise suggest the Irish were in the majority. Some thought was given to controlling the influx, for Irish servants, though essential for the fishery, were greatly feared by their (mostly English) masters. They were illiterate and numerous. Many were poor. After a time, it is possible that numbers of Irish servants were seldom paid any wages at all; in winter they might "engage themselves for only their provisions."[146] They were also, of course, Roman Catholics, and so belonged to a loathed and proscribed religion — the *only* proscribed religion in 18th century Newfoundland.[147] Many were also unilingual Irish speakers, which separated them even further from those who employed and exploited them.

Nor was the fishery the only means of entry to Newfoundland for the Irish. Others came as soldiers. And not just in the armies of the Mother Country.

In the 1740s, European nations found themselves once again at war. This time Newfoundland escaped invasion but was not unaffected. With the memory of earlier fiascoes doubtless in mind, the British government in 1740 authorized the rebuilding of Fort Frederick at Placentia and the construction of defences at St. John's, Ferryland, Trinity, and Carbonear.[148] On paper, this looked like high resolve. But the distance from resolve to action was great. Governor Thomas Smith, indeed, finding St. John's defenceless in 1741, built fortifications in the town, mounted cannon taken from the two ships under his command, and left behind a militia and a sizeable contingent of marines.[149] But fortifications toppled quickly from readiness to decay in Newfoundland, no doubt partly because no year-round governor was in place to prevent it. By 1743 it was reported that only Placentia was capable of defence, and it was too far from "the principal fishing places" to be of much use.[150] In 1744, when Anglo-French hostility broke out anew in North

America, the British bestirred themselves, and orders were again given to fortify Placentia, St. John's, Ferryland, and Carbonear, the last three with sodwork and palisadoes only, "to save time and expence." Trinity was to be defended "at as little charge as the nature of the place will admit." Lieutenant-governors were to be named for the forts at St. John's and Placentia.[151] Some of this was done. The intention was mainly to protect the migratory fishery, as Janzen notes;[152] but there was likely some thought given to defending the island generally. Yet as the war progressed and fighting took place elsewhere, Newfoundland tended to be over-looked. In 1746 and 1747 no governors were appointed; the island was given some show of protection from the fleet at Louisbourg (taken by the British in 1745). A governor was reinstated in 1748, as the combatants took a respite from war in the Treaty of Aix-la-Chapelle, and officials looked away from the drama of the battlefield to their more humdrum responsibilities. But war would soon break out again. A report on Newfoundland fortifications in 1748 revealed a fairly high state of preparation, though those at St. John's remained somewhat defective.[153]

St. John's had no soldiers in 1740, but by the mid-1750s it had a garrison of infantry and artillery numbering well over 100.[154] Placentia too had a garrison, and there were a few artillery men at Ferryland, Carbonear, and Trinity. At first blush, no doubt many found this comforting. Yet the 18th-century British soldier, under-paid and menacing, could be as dangerous to those he lived among as an Abenaki. Newfoundland residents were reminded of this soon after the inauguration of another judicial reform.

In 1750 Governor Francis Drake was authorized to appoint commissioners of oyer and terminer in Newfoundland to try capital offences, treason excepted.[155] This was a major innovation. To implement it required, not just the selection of commissioners, but impanelling a 24-man[156] grand jury to present indictments, and appointing a sheriff to execute the court's orders. Trial (or petty) juries, attended by a bailiff, would hear the evidence from sworn witnesses and return a verdict. Altogether, this was a considerable extension of Newfoundland's judicial estab-lishment. The grand jury, an institution which endured into the 20th century, was especially important, since, as we will see, it had functions beyond presenting indictments.[157] But that was its primary role. Initially, the power to deprive "of life or limb" was withheld pending review in London, but at Drake's request such power was granted, subject to his right to give reprieves until the King's pleasure was known. In 1751 he was told to grant such reprieves to all officers of British ships of war and trading vessels.[158] Court was held in late summer or fall, before the governor sailed for England.[159]

A brief summary of some early trials for capital offences sheds light on conditions in Newfoundland. The first was held on September 27, 1750. Lawrance Kneaves of co. Kilkenny, Ireland, a fisherman at Harbour Main, was charged with murdering John Kelly, a servant, by battering his skull with a stick and choking him. Both were "somewhat in liquor" at the time of the assault. The jury found

Kneaves guilty of manslaughter, whereupon he was sentenced, before being set at liberty, to be burnt "in the right hand with an hott iron marked with the letter R," and to forfeit his goods and chattels to pay court charges. In 1751 three soldiers from the St. John's garrison, Philip Coffey, Michael Ryan, and William Fielding, were indicted for the gang rape of a 17-year old girl named Elizabeth Melvin, who had gone into the woods with two other women near St. John's to pick strawberries. Two of the men "talk'd Irish together" prior to the rape. Coffey and Ryan were acquitted; Fielding was found guilty and sentenced to be hanged. The sentence was reprieved, and Fielding was later pardoned by the King.[160] At the same court, the Petty Harbour resident Edward Hoare — possibly English[161] — charged with break-in and theft, was sentenced to receive thirty-nine lashes on the bare back at the whipping post. Three others, including a thief from Waterford named Thomas Power and a woman who received stolen goods, were sentenced to transportation. In 1752, William Murphy, an Irish servant, murdered his fellow servant William Quinn at Fermeuse, following a fight in a stage while washing fish. Murphy could speak no English; an interpreter, Edward Cockerance, had to be called into court. Sentenced to be hanged, Murphy too was pardoned.[162] In the same year an English woman, Ann Coffin, was indicted for the murder of her apprentice house servant, Mildred Bevil. Bevil was Irish,[163] but Coffin had at various times called her "Indian bitch," "stinking Indian bitch," and "nasty Indian bitch," and said "it was no fine to murder an Indian." Vicious beatings over a long period, one with a set of tongs used in a fireplace, were testified to in court; but Coffin was found not guilty.[164]

As time passed, soldiers, many or most of whom were Irish,[165] continued to be charged with offences. Confinement in Newfoundland, well away from the North American war zone, might have been frustrating. It was doubtless also grating for uniformed men, accustomed to military command, to be disciplined by constables and justices.[166] Late in 1753, one soldier, private John Maddox, was sent to jail by magistrate William Keen, one of Newfoundland's richest men and a prominent office-holder,[167] allegedly for stealing three potatoes out of a garden. (Potatoes had been introduced to Newfoundland around 1750.) He evidently spent twenty days in jail before trial, and though no witness appeared to testify against him, was sentenced to twenty-one lashes. Maddox had been missing for fourteen days before his commanding officer, Capt. Christopher Aldridge, knew where he was. Aldridge complained that Keen had a habit of committing soldiers arbitrarily, keeping them from their duty for long periods.[168] There was now bad blood between Aldridge's company and local authority. In February, 1754, two of Aldridge's soldiers, Nicholas Hurly and Edmund McGuire — both Irish names[169] — assaulted a constable, John Worth, and his assistant, who were keeping night watch in St. John's. Worth was soundly beaten, and had to beg for his life. The soldiers were found guilty in the court of oyer and terminer in the fall. The commissioners petitioned the governor to remove the two soldiers from the island, and asked further that all soldiers "may be kept within the garrison as much as possible, and not permitted to go armed in the night season, as has often been practised to the terror of his Majesty's peaceable subjects."[170]

One reason given for the latter request was the grisly murder, on the night of September 9, 1754, of the elderly Keen by a group of no fewer than ten conspirators.[171] They broke into his house and carried off a chest said to contain his money; but they found no money in it. They entered the house again. McGuire and a man named Matthew Halluran (a variant of the Irish name Halleran) went to Keen's bedroom, attempted to smother him as he lay in bed, chopped him with a scythe, and finally killed him with the butt end of a musket. Four of the criminals were soldiers; at least three were from Aldridge's company. The others, mostly Irish, were from Freshwater Bay, just south of St. John's. At the head of these civilians were Robert and Eleanor Power. Eleanor Power, disguised as a man, was a leading player in the enterprise, for she said she knew where Keen's money was kept. Nine of the group were sentenced to death; the tenth, Nicholas Tobin, secured their conviction and saved his own life by turning King's evidence. McGuire, Halluran, and the two Powers were hanged immediately. McGuire's and Halluran's bodies were then hung in chains for public display. (There was "little or no thieving" in the ensuing months.)[172] The other sentences were reprieved until the King's pleasure was known. It was the most sensational murder in 18th-century Newfoundland.

Combustible and disaffected Irishmen and -women thus featured prominently, but by no means exclusively, in the annals of crime. Yet such records can give a distorted picture. Poverty no doubt breeds crime; it also breeds passivity. And maybe much more of the latter than the former. Besides, as already hinted, the Irish were needed, and so had their defenders. In 1752 a number of petitions from West Country merchants pointed out that the Irish in Newfoundland were "His Majesty's natural born subjects," had increased in number "no more than in proportion to the increase of Protestants," and had given, by their behaviour, no cause for official anxiety.[173] (Even though it was rumoured that twenty Irishmen had gone to Louisbourg in 1750 — it had been given back to the French at Aix-la-Chapelle — and sworn allegiance to Louis XV.) Such protests might not have been altogether sincere. The merchants had heard of plans for expanded government in Newfoundland, and wanted to head them off by suggesting there was no reason for change. Had the Irish seemed a real threat, Poole and Dartmouth might not have been so complacent. The Irish were now present in such numbers as to be, if not tolerated, at least grimly recognized as a fact of life. They were on the whole submissive, though not without incendiary feelings, as might be expected from any trampled-on people; and, despite an underlying loathing of their race and religion among "people of property,"[174] they were deemed to be useful.

Simmering Anglo-French hostility in North America again broke into open conflict in 1756 with the commencement of the Seven Years' War. The rumoured arrival of a strong French fleet at Louisbourg in 1757 caused a new flurry of fort repair and construction in Newfoundland, and a militia, under the command of the New England-born merchant Michael Gill, was created in St. John's. But the French held off. The West Country fishery, suffering from impressment, loss of ships to the enemy, scarcity of men willing to risk going overseas, and other wartime scourges, declined; but it didn't cease. With the French absent from the northern reaches of the island and the Treaty of Utrecht in abeyance, fishermen scrambled into rooms as far north as the Strait of Belle Isle. Some went beyond that. A New England vessel found "very commodious harbours & plenty of fish" north of the Strait.[175] Chateau Bay in Labrador was explored. It was thought to have "one of the finest harbours in the world." One ship went as far as Davis Inlet.[176] While the "Indians" (i.e., Inuit) were seen as violent, it was fancied that something profitable could be learned from them, for they knew "the art of killing whales."[177] In the parts of the island formerly occupied by the French were found "very convenient" rooms to carry on fishing and "much greater plenty of fish than [in] our harbours."[178] In 1759 Bristol merchants suggested that the British government "give encouragement to persons to make settlements" in the north, and there were English settlers at and near St. Julien's by 1762.[179]

Trade carried on by American shipping flourished during the war. America now vied with England and Ireland in supplying Newfoundland, bringing chiefly flour, bread, molasses, tobacco, lumber, cattle, sheep, swine, and rum. Dozens of distilleries in Massachusetts kept the rum flowing.[180] A list of importing vessels provided by the naval officer Nicholas Gill shows thirty-nine American ships arriving in St. John's between July 7 and October 21, 1760, carrying cargoes valued at nearly £18,000.[181] By the end of the war, this likely had more than quadrupled.[182] Outbound, they carried mostly fish, much of it "refuse fish," i.e., poorly cured and broken cod, taken first to America for packing in hogsheads and then reshipped for the slaves in the West Indies. But they also took some merchantable[183] fish to foreign markets. They arrived from, and went to, ports in Europe, America, the West Indies, and Canada. In St. John's, they traded with the resident dealers and factors, as did competing ships from Ireland (bringing beef, pork, butter, and linen), England, and elsewhere. While some sectors of the West Country fishery continued to thrive, Bideford had "decayed," Barnstaple had collapsed, Dartmouth was "declining,"[184] the Plymouth trade was dead;[185] but St. John's was, to all appearances, prospering.

This came to a temporary and sudden halt in 1762. Though Louisbourg, Montreal, and Quebec were now in English hands and the battle for North American supremacy effectively over, the war was not yet ended. In May, 1762, a squadron of five ships under the command of Charles-Henri-Louis d'Arsac de Ternay eluded the British blockade at Brest and headed for Newfoundland. Aboard the ships were 750 soldiers, including 161 Irishmen. The Irish, it was thought, would be joined by their countrymen in Newfoundland once the opportunity to fight the common enemy was provided. The objective of the expedition was "to cause as much harm as possible to the English," which meant not meeting the English in open battle, soldier against soldier, but, as in the past, attacking and pillaging a sparsely populated coastline known to be either undefended or incompetently defended. The squadron arrived off Bay Bulls on June 23, and raised British colours so as not to rouse the sleeping lions of that warlike community. They landed next day. The infantry, commanded by Col. Joseph-Louis-Bernard de Cléron d'Haussonville, marched to St. John's, where, meeting with nonexistent resistance, their assault succeeded. St. John's "fell" on June 27, having made no effort to stand. The garrison caved in at once. The militia had decayed to ineffectiveness; palisadoes, batteries, ramparts, and 24-pounders, which had been written about so often in dispatches, were useless. The "terror of the inhabitants"[186] at witnessing yet another French invasion was great, though it lessened somewhat no doubt when they saw no Indians, and perhaps picked up again, at least among Protestants, when they saw and heard the Irishmen. Among the invaders were four priests, one of them Irish, who said mass in the Anglican church.[187]

The French now sent the English garrison at St. John's and many Protestant inhabitants off to New England and proceeded with the business they were good at: pillaging and burning. Carbonear, Harbour Grace, and Trinity[188] were also occupied. The coast between Bay Bulls and Trinity was under their control for virtually the entire fishing season. Undoubtedly the French assault was less vicious than when they were assisted by Abenakis. Yet one estimate of the amount of damage caused was £1 million, part of this tabulation being the destruction of some 460 ships and boats. Salt was jettisoned. Fishing "utensils" — nets, killicks,[189] pews,[190] vats, tables, rope, oars, sails — were destroyed. Provisions and livestock were seized. Not for the first time the odour of frying horsemeat was sniffed by hungry settlers, who nonetheless did little or nothing to defend themselves, not even at Carbonear Island or Trinity, both of which had been prepared for defence at some cost to British taxpayers in 1760.[191] Many residents south of Bay Bulls found their way to Bois Island at the mouth of Ferryland harbour,[192] where a fort remained in fighting trim. The Irish sector of the population did not, it seems, distinguish itself, some Irish servants evidently either joining the French or plundering their masters.[193] The takeover by the French might have given licence to commit crime. A gang rape of a woman by Irishmen took place in July. (One of the rapists was hanged in November.)[194] Meanwhile, the razing of fishing premises proceeded apace. By the time the French left, the zone they occupied was strewn with wreckage and ashes.

The attack had not been anticipated by the British. Perhaps the half-remembered sub-colony had, at this point, been forgotten entirely by those whose duty it was, from time to time, to recall it to mind. News of the capture of St. John's reached Halifax on July 3. Lord Colvill, commander of naval forces in North America, seemed in no hurry to respond. Nova Scotian officials pressed him to stay and defend them, in case they too were attacked. Protecting them against an anticipated attack seemed to Nova Scotians more urgent than relieving an already invaded Newfoundland. Colvill finally left for Newfoundland on August 10, and did little of consequence when he got there. In New York, Jeffery Amherst, commander in chief of land forces, now got wind of Ternay's assault, and immediately dispatched his younger brother, Lieut.-Col. William Amherst, to drive the French out. He landed 1,500 troops at Torbay, just north of St. John's, on September 13. Two days later, having left close to 800 of his soldiers behind, Ternay skulked out of St. John's harbour with his squadron under cover of fog and darkness, slipping by Colvill who supposedly was blockading the Narrows but may have had his mind on his burdens back in Halifax.[195] The men Ternay abandoned in St. John's surrendered to Amherst on September 18. The island was back in British hands.

This was late in Newfoundland history. Even so, we have almost no indigenous literature[196] to convey the impact and provide a description of the French raid. But the lack of such a record should not conceal the reality and magnitude of the event. Yet again, Newfoundland society was assaulted, not superficially, but at its roots. What had been built, painstakingly, perhaps over many years, was ripped down or burnt. Boats, stages, flakes, cook rooms, warehouses — the architecture of the shoreline, on which men and women depended for their livelihood — lay in ruins, or nearly so. Such an event would have lent a despairing edge to life. If there had been pessimism before, it was deepened; bitterness would have been made more bitter. To rebuild once more must have taken reserves of courage and endurance. In the winter following the raid, there was considerable distress[197] in Newfoundland. Money was voted by Parliament for relief, and for passage of sixty-six poverty-stricken Irish to Waterford.[198]

Anger and dismay were not confined to common settlers. British merchants had by the 1760s invested heavily in Newfoundland. Following the war, they petitioned for an inquiry into the extent of their losses and demanded compensation.[199] On the list of losses they provided, one stands out: dwelling houses.[200] Merchants living in Poole and other cities now owned homes in Newfoundland, used by their relatives, agents, or servants. We have noted the Bristol merchants' call for encouragement of settlement in the north, a perhaps extraordinary action in view of the ancient mercantile hostility to inhabitancy. But as already noted, and as Matthews pointed out in his seminal work on Newfoundland, the merchants, far from being hostile to settlement now, were participants in it and dependent on it. (Which did not mean, however, that they necessarily wanted so many settlers that "colonization" would become inevitable.)[201] In 1759 Bristol merchants even suggested inaugurating a packet-boat service to carry mail between St. John's and New York, with a link also to Louisbourg. The British government might not yet be convinced of the value of permanent settlement; but merchants knew that settlers, in limited numbers, were needed to conduct "the British fishery."

Settlement they accepted; what they did not want was a radical change, or any change, in the age-old method of half-governing the island. After the Treaty of Paris was signed in February, 1763, the Council on Trade held another inquiry into Newfoundland affairs. Each city involved in extensive trading to the island was asked whether "the establishment of a compleat and perfect form of civil government" there "will, or will not, be for the advantage of the fishery and the navigation of this Kingdom."[202] The question as to whether such a government would benefit the *settlers* was not asked. Still, the request showed the germ of new thinking. Poole, Exeter, Bristol, Dartmouth, and Waterford said it would not be an advantage, with Exeter finding the whole notion of civil government "repugnant." Plymouth declined to answer, having "no ... trade" to Newfoundland. Glasgow and Cork, minor players, favoured civil government, while Belfast said it would support it "if no taxes, imposts, or restraints of any sort be laid on the trade or fishery" and if justice were administered with "all imaginable dispatch & the most moderate expence."[203] This was yes meaning no. One Poole merchant, George Milner, vigorously dissented from the dominant view of his colleagues in that town, but his letter was not enough to shift official opinion from the status quo. The merchants had had their fill of naval officers, justices, and commissioners. With perhaps a long peace stretching ahead, they wished to be left alone to make money. And so, for a time, they were.

Peace did lie ahead, but the terms of the Treaty of Paris, signed in February, 1763, were not favourable to the British merchants, who had hoped for France's exclusion from the Newfoundland fisheries. Instead, after much agonized negotiation,[204] the 13th article of the Treaty of Utrecht was confirmed (except for the sentence pertaining to Cape Breton and the islands in the Gulf of St. Lawrence, all returned to Britain). The French were back on the Petit Nord. Far from being punished for the humiliating and destructive raid in 1762, France was also ceded St. Pierre and Miquelon "to serve as a shelter to the French fishermen." The islands were ceded "in full right," though no forts were to be erected on them, nor any buildings but those "for the convenience of the fishery."[205] Rumours circulated that the Earl of Bute, chief architect of the peace, had accepted a bribe of £300,000 from France to secure her fishing rights off Newfoundland and get the islands.[206] After they were surveyed by James Cook, the islands were formally handed over to the French in July. St. Pierre and Miquelon, regarded by Britain as a compensation for the French loss of Cape Breton, would loom large in Newfoundland's future. Once given away, they would never be relinquished.

Chapter 6

Stirring Times: 1764-1800

WE ENTER THE PERIOD of two of the world's great political revolutions, or, to look at it another way, the age of Johnson, Hume, Paine, and Burke. Amidst this Enlightenment, Newfoundland begins to emerge from the shadows. Not politically. There is no Jefferson; no Sons of Liberty clamour against oppression. But "the drama of the sled and dory"[1] plays on, and we now see the actors more than fleetingly. Governors' reports are lengthier, parliamentary inquiry sheds light on the fishery, coastlines are charted, and printed literature — there's more of it — occasionally takes us close to conditions in the outharbours as well as in St. John's. Labrador, whose coast between the St. John River and Hudson Strait together with Anticosti and the Magdalen Islands was placed under the government of Newfoundland on October 7, 1763, emerges into the light of day, mainly through George Cartwright's writing.[2] Britain's enemies strike again, but internally peace reigns. At a time of rebellion and war, it was Newfoundland's lot to remain on the fringes of the main action, loyal and steadfast.

Yet events in the world beyond the headlands were so tumultuous that they had to affect Newfoundland. As they did, the population became more stable, more attached to the island, and as the century ended increased substantially; the migratory fishery from the West Country, though still a factor for much of the period, all but disappeared towards the end; a resident merchant class, whose presence was felt in earlier decades, grew in confidence and assumed a bigger role in the economy and society; the judicial system was overhauled; and the freedom to practise their religion was extended to Roman Catholics, who were of course overwhelmingly Irish or of Irish descent. It wasn't equality for the Irish, not fraternity either, but a degree of liberty came their way. Religion generally got a firmer footing. Coastlines opened up and closed to British and French fishermen, and to residents, depending on the vagaries of war and diplomacy. Micmacs too found new homes in Newfoundland, but the Beothuck were losing theirs. Commerce ebbed and flowed with the tides of war. As in the past, the British government was slow to respond to new realities in Newfoundland, though it did respond to some. Instead, it clung to a system of administration known to be defective; that is, if it is judged solely as a system of *colonial* administration. But when it is borne in mind that the major thrust of imperial policy, to squeeze the maximum profit and advantage out of the Newfoundland fishery, remained inexorably in place, then the system must be said to have functioned. It functioned well, or as well as the times permitted — for England.

Another reason for the slowness of change was that no demand for reform came from the island itself. No Newfoundlander in London agitated as boldly for new approaches to his homeland as Franklin did for America in 1774-5, though one such cautionary voice was raised in the 1780s. A revolution was not brewing in Newfoundland. It was safe to leave it hanging. Safe even to give France access to a huge part of it, or to use it as a bargaining chip with the Americans. British diplomats appeared to look on the island and fishery as a mere pawn to be bartered for some minor imperial advantage. But this appearance of disdain may be deceptive. Allowing the French access, even exclusive access, to parts of the Newfoundland coast was by no means at odds with the principal plank of British policy, i.e., holding permanent settlement down, maintaining a "free" fishery, and keeping the island as something far less than a real colony.

The customary official attitudes towards Newfoundland were reinforced in the mid-to late 1760s by a reactionary yet energetic governor, Hugh Palliser. The scion of an old landed English family, Palliser commanded ships while still in his twenties, tasted victory at Quebec in 1759, and was severely injured when an arms chest on a quarter deck exploded near him, leaving him "crippled and in pain in his left leg until his death."[3] An injury of this nature can leave a person deeply flawed, despite an apparent record of achievement. Such a man threw in the towel at a critical juncture in Newfoundland history — *the* critical juncture, the sellout of 1933.[4] There was no defect of will in Palliser, no instinct to doubt or hesitate. Appointed governor in 1764, he soon mastered, or thought he mastered, the complex problems of the sub-colony to which he'd been sent. He quickly saw a way to overcome them, a simple way that had but one flaw. It was totally impractical.

Palliser's solution to Newfoundland was to restore the old ship fishery, as regulated in King William's Act. That fishery, as he saw shortly after his arrival in the island, was now "dropt or excluded" (except for "a few bankers") since "almost all stages and ships rooms are become private property."[5] Most rooms were owned either by "monopolizers" (i.e., big merchants) or by encroaching inhabitants, the latter being "poor, idle ... and disorderly," "sloathfull miserable wretches"[6] — great numbers of them Irish wretches. This alienation of rooms appears to have blinded Palliser to the fact that, while the *ship* fishery had declined drastically, the *migratory* fishery from Britain was holding its own, given the severe impact of the late war. Most "monopolizers" were in effect British merchants who employed English or Irish servants and whose export of fish from Newfoundland directly benefited their home country. As for bankers, Palliser grossly mistook their significance. The bank fishery was on the rise — 222 British bankers would operate off Newfoundland by 1769.[7] And by-boatkeepers, who rented rooms from the inhabitants or found a means to secure their own, were still a major force in the fishery. In 1764 they numbered 281, and employed 2,903 men.[8] True, the total British catch of fish was below that of inhabitants in 1764, yet in five years this situation would be reversed.[9]

But Palliser was obsessed with rooms. To his dismay, some had been granted outright to settlers and merchants by previous governors. His predecessor Thomas Graves, for instance, had issued grants of abandoned rooms "to encourage new settlers."[10] It is a great rarity to read such words in a document from an 18th-century governor. James Webb, governor in 1760, had also granted land.[11] Palliser thought such grants illegal and, on their being brought to light, annulled them. (His successors made more of them.) The way the fishery was being carried on, he felt, held many perils for Britain. Too many men were staying behind after the fishing season and being transported to America, thereby reducing the Navy's available manpower. The resident population was far too large. Too many loose women were coming. (He countered this by giving notice, in 1764, that "no women are to be landed without security being first given for their good behaviour.")[12] Opportunities for expanding British trade were being lost. The way to advance "the true interest and security" of his country was "to restore the fishery to the state it ought to be,"[13] i.e., the ship fishery.

He proposed that certificates of ownership be demanded from occupiers of rooms. Rooms not held by such certificates would be declared available "to all British fishing ships." Clause 7 in King William's Act should be "further explain'd" to determine whether the "exclusive possessions" it authorized are "only for life" or "to be consider'd as real or personal estates." Nothing but a ship fishery should be allowed between Cape Bonavista and Point Riche, or on any other coast not in possession of England when the act was made. Any room lying unoccupied or unused for "one or two" fishing seasons would become available for the fishing ships. No man should become admiral of a harbour unless he was master of a true fishing ship and occupied a public room, not a hired one. And if any damage were done to a ships' room during the winter, "all the inhabitants of that place [should] be obliged to make good the damages," and until then the ship on arriving could "occupy and use any stage or room possess'd by any inhabitant." Palliser followed these proposals with nine more, aimed at "encouraging and obliging" men to return yearly to Britain.

Had authorities in London implemented all of these suggestions, we might have seen resistance of the kind that followed the Stamp Act in America. The British did try, belatedly and hopelessly, to forbid private ownership of land between Cape Bonavista and Point Riche, and Palliser acted on his own to publish some other of his notions as if they were, in fact, laws.[14] But he was not to get all he wanted. His initial reports were met with something approaching bewilderment in London. The Committee on Trade in 1765, after noting what a "melancholy Picture" Palliser presented of Newfoundland, stated that to return to the old ship fishery seemed a "very doubtful" proposition. That course of action was not only "attended perhaps with Circumstances of Injustice, if not of Inhumanity," but would also entail "a very great Expence to the Publick." Instead of making a recommendation, they left it to the King to decide whether "some more perfect and settled Plan of Government" should be established on the island, or whether "the Inhabitants should be removed."[15] The subtext here was: we expelled the Acadians in 1755 and 1758, so why not try it again? But with the American colonies on the verge of rebellion, George III likely didn't relish the thought of expelling 20,000 or so residents from Newfoundland. As for setting up a proper colonial government on the island, that was nowhere in sight. In the event, the King chose neither of the options offered to him.

After conducting yet another inquiry into the fishery in 1766, the Committee on Trade again equivocated, though the inclusion in their report of Palliser's suggestions for the reestablishment of the ship fishery was perhaps a tacit endorsement of that chimerical scheme. The King was merely told that the condition of Newfoundland required "the fullest Consideration."[16] But in truth the old ship fishery was outmoded. Palliser, whatever "consideration" he might give to it, couldn't bring it back, though his efforts undoubtedly had some impact.[17] As already noted, "fishing ships" now reported in official statistics were mostly passenger ships[18] (carrying servants) or bankers. Governor Molineux Shuldham's remark in 1772, that even the catch by bankers "bears but a small proportion to that caught ... along shore" by "those who are settled with one or two boats, in the many little harbours and coves of this island,"[19] was likely an underestimation of the bank fishery,[20] but Palliser's repudiation of the inhabitants — he calculated that nine-tenths were superfluous[21] — was just nonsensical. Removal of settlers, an observer said in 1773, would bring "to beggary a multitude" and cause "the destruction of the Newfoundland fishery."[22]

British policy during Palliser's comparatively long tenure as governor[23] was chiefly centered on French rights under the Treaty of Paris, which owing to the cession of St. Pierre and Miquelon were considerably enlarged over those granted at Utrecht.[24] There was now not just a concurrent fishery in the north, but a source of contention in the south. Palliser was told[25] that the rights of French fishermen on the treaty coast were not to be interfered with. Yet the French were to be kept within the limits defined in the treaty. Illicit trade with them was to be prevented. And the coast of Labrador was to be kept free of foreigners. None of this was easy to accomplish. The British had created a constant source of trouble and expense for themselves. An immediate outlay was for a bigger squadron to patrol the treaty coast, with ships assigned by the Admiralty to shorelines where vigilance was needed. It was needed. Once the treaty was signed, France moved with great speed to resettle St. Pierre and Miquelon and reestablish its fishery in the north. The tools of expansion were subsidy and aggressive diplomacy, and results were spectacular. In 1764 an estimated total of 12,853 men and 339 vessels (i.e., ships, not small fishing boats) prosecuted the French fishery, or engaged in trade connected with that fishery, in Newfoundland waters. Ninety-one of the ships and 5,315 men operated on the Petit Nord between Port au Choix and La Scie.[26] The numbers increased to 403 ships and 14,495 men in 1766, with 123 ships and 8,255 men in the north.[27]

In 1766 one French ship fished at Twillingate. Two years later, though overall numbers for the Petit Nord were down from the 1766 total, there were three French ships at Twillingate, one at Fogo, and two at Greenspond.[28] To the dismay of West Country merchants,[29] the French were pushing back east into parts of the treaty shore they had long abandoned, threatening English settlements. They even tried to fish in Bonavista harbour, which though strictly within the limit of the treaty shore was of course exclusively a British settlement. In 1772 they started building premises in Bonavista, and sent out eighteen boats a-fishing. Settlers threw fish caught by the French into the sea, tore down their tilt and partly-constructed stage, and drove the intruders out of the harbour; but the British government quickly intervened and allowed them to stay.[30] A French ship fished at Bonavista in 1774.[31] On the west coast, the French tried to argue that Point Riche was farther south than generally thought. Cape Ray was Point Riche, they said.[32] Moving the location of Point Riche would give them access to Bay of Islands, whose resources they knew well, with other rich fisheries. The island's nomenclature was to be adjusted to accommodate them. But Point Riche was to stay where it had always been.

Palliser tackled the work of overseeing and regulating this vast French enterprise with his accustomed vigour. In the north, he drove French trading vessels off the coast and seized boats built (illegally, as he thought) in Newfoundland. The French left stores of salt behind in the winter; he confiscated or destroyed as much of it as he could find. While the Treaty of Paris strictly limited military activity at St. Pierre and Miquelon, the French assembled a squadron there in 1764 with the intention of patrolling the treaty coast. Palliser warned the commodore, François-Jean-Baptiste L'Ollivier de Tronjoly, that such a step would violate English sovereignty over the island. The Frenchman backed down. He took other steps to stop warlike maneuvering by French ships. Just as the English suspected, St. Pierre and Miquelon became a center of clandestine trade for both the south coast inhabitants of Newfoundland ("almost all"[33] of them) and New England traders. Palliser put a stop to some of it by seizing American ships and, in July, 1765, by expelling from the island ten residents of St. Lawrence, Grand Bank, Fortune, Pass Island, and Long Harbour who had allegedly "fished for the French [and] traffick'd with them." He also confiscated the settlers' property and reserved it for ship fishermen.[34] The expulsions were intended as "severe examples" to prevent others from dealing with the French, but Palliser doubted the "savage & ungovernable inhabitants" would pay much heed to them.[35] They did not pay much heed to them. Illegal trade was going on at St. Pierre in 1772.[36] Fifty years later it was still going on. It continued after that. It was unstoppable.

French residents of St. Pierre and Miquelon also fished along the adjacent Newfoundland coastline; Palliser stopped that, or tried to. He reduced, but didn't end, the annual drain of men to America. To check illicit trade and other abuses, he appointed preventive officers in St. John's, Ferryland, and Placentia.[37] Another problem could not be dealt with by the customs. In 1765 about 150[38] Micmacs travelled from Cape Breton to join their former allies in St. Pierre, and proceeded from there to Bay d'Espoir, causing widespread terror among settlers. The situation seemed so serious that Palliser, though he departed as usual for England in the fall, left behind two warships to try and force the Indians back to Nova Scotia. They succeeded only in banishing some of them as far as Cape Ray.[39] In 1767 Cook found a tribe at St. George's Bay — they had dispersed throughout the region. This expansion of vigilance resulting from the entanglements caused mostly by the Treaty of Paris might have shown that "some more perfect and settled Plan of Government" was indeed required. But none was in the offing.

Palliser conceded that when he first arrived in Newfoundland he was "not aware of the great variety and intricacy of affairs here, respecting both the French and our own people."[40] He appears to have soon realized that Newfoundland, despite his efforts, could no longer be an exclusive resort for ship fishermen. But perhaps Labrador could. One of his early acts was to annul grants made by the governor of Quebec, James Murray, in Labrador, and to prohibit anyone from the American colonies, except whalers, from fishing there.[41] Both decrees, one of which landed him in court in England,[42] were overruled. Among other features of Labrador standing in the path of English commerce were the Inuit. Prior to 1763 Inuit had traded with the French both in Labrador and at the tip of Newfoundland's Northern Peninsula. Some knew a number of French words and phrases. Palliser put a stop to this trade and took a number of steps to placate the Inuit, who "partly out of stupidity & partly out of despair"[43] would come south to the Strait of Belle Isle not just to trade but to steal and kill to get what they were in need of, chiefly boats and tools. If the seal, salmon, cod, and whale fisheries were to expand northwards along the coast, as Palliser hoped, these people would have to be pacified. He issued an order in 1764, requiring "the most civil and friendly" treatment of the Inuit.[44] But the "Esquimeaux savages" were frightening people away. Palliser enlisted the help of Moravian missionaries, who had already tried, and failed, to establish contact with the Labrador Inuit in 1752.[45] The Moravian Jens Haven, a Danish carpenter, met Inuit at Quirpon in September, 1764, spoke to them in Inuktitut, and promised to return. He came back with three other missionaries in 1765. In August, with the Moravian Christian Drachart as interpreter, Palliser met the Inuit himself at Pitts Harbour, Labrador, and attempted to form an alliance of friendship and trade.[46] In case that didn't work, he also had a blockhouse built in Chateau Bay, manned with a garrison, to protect fishermen. (Soon after his term as governor it was judged useless and abandoned.) In the event, the progress of enterprise north was slow. The Moravians became established, but fear of the Inuit persisted, and with reason. A commentator in 1772 was still looking forward to the time when the Inuit "tempers" will be "improved" and they "will be reared up to a notion of industrious commerce."[47]

In August, 1765, while in Pitts Harbour, Palliser proclaimed a series of orders for the Labrador fishery. He now forbad, not just other British colonists, but inhabitants and by-boatkeepers of Newfoundland, to enter the Labrador fishery. Apart from American whalers, only ship fishermen coming annually from Great Britain were to fish in Labrador. All the rules in the "excellent" King William's Act were to apply in Labrador. No one except ship fishermen was to trade with the Inuit.[48] This was Palliser's doctrine in all its purity. Yet the attempt to prevent Newfoundland residents from fishing in an adjacent territory, one within the same government as they were under, was punitive and absurd. George Cartwright, after losing his salmon establishment on the Charles River owing to Palliser's rules, later pointed out to the Earl of Dartmouth, colonial secretary,[49] that the pursuit of seals in Labrador was "a winter and spring employment, [and] must be carried on by residents ... not by men carried out annually from Europe." As such, it required secure possession of rooms year to year. There was no analogy to the Newfoundland cod fishery. (Lord North made the point in the Commons.)[50] The same was true of the Labrador salmon fishery, Cartwright said. Trade with native people too could best be carried out "by making the sealing and salmon posts private property," which would induce men to settle among the Inuit and win their affection.[51] Even furring required "an exclusive right."[52] Cartwright's was not the only protest sent to London. Palliser's plan was discarded, though not before a bill incorporating its elements had been passed in the Commons. (It did not pass in the House of Lords.)[53] In 1773 governor Shuldham was authorized to tell seal and salmon fishermen in Labrador that their permanent establishments would be "protected." When Cartwright arrived late in Labrador, Shuldham had two fishing places reserved for him.[54] By 1774, when the coast of Labrador was, thanks partly to the confusion caused by Palliser's policies,[55] re-annexed to the government of Quebec, an annual migratory fishery from Newfoundland to Labrador had commenced.[56]

Palliser's one lasting contribution to Newfoundland was to encourage more work by the surveyor and mapmaker James Cook, though it was governor Graves who first recommended Cook to the Admiralty. Cook had been in Colvill's squadron in 1762, and had made charts of the harbours of Placentia, St. John's, Harbour Grace, and Carbonear[57] following the ousting of the French raiders. From 1763 to 1767, he carried out much more elaborate coastal surveys,[58] the purpose being partly to help enforce the terms of the Treaty of Paris,[59] some of which were of course geographical in nature. To combat inevitable French territorial claims and petty argument, exact cartographical knowledge was required. The Admiralty chose Cook to provide it. After finishing his 1763 survey of St. Pierre and Miquelon, Cook, directed by Graves, charted Noddy Bay, Quirpon, and Croque, at or near the tip of the Northern Peninsula, and Chateau Bay (York Harbour) in Labrador. In 1764, now under Palliser's command, he returned to the north and, beginning where he'd left off the previous year, moved south to Point Ferolle. That same year he sketched a map of Newfoundland, displaying the parts accurately drawn.[60] (The rest was severely misshaped.) In 1765 he charted from St. Lawrence on the south coast west to Bay d'Espoir; he continued west from this point in 1766, finishing at Cape Anguille. The west coast between Cape Anguille and Point Ferolle was completed in 1767. The product of this work was a series of exquisite maps, famous for their intricate detail and accuracy.[61] Those of the south and west coasts are especially impressive. While they were surveys intended, obviously, to be used mainly by shipping, Cook also mapped coastal topographical features such as brooks and hills, and supplied as well, in his manuscripts, written information of use to fishermen and merchants together with general remarks on landscape. He undertook some interior work in the course of his surveying, perhaps much more than we now realize.[62] His observations on coal deposits in Newfoundland and Cape Breton ("the coals might be thrown directly from the coal works themselves into the ships as they lie close to the shore") perhaps were intended to refer more to the latter island.[63] A ship and shovel will get one very little coal in Newfoundland. But he went up the Humber River into Deer Lake in September, 1767, in a journey lasting five days, and left a brief description of what he saw. There were still no settlers in Bay of Islands, though both Cook and Palliser, who visited the bay himself in 1764, saw much evidence of a prior European fishery. Palliser found French "dwelling houses" there, as well as "an infinite" number of discarded traps for furring. He concluded that the French had conducted a salmon fishery upriver as well as a cod fishery in the bay, and had overwintered.[64]

Cook's penetration of Deer Lake was not the only effort in the 1760s to explore the deep interior. In August, 1768, naval lieutenant John Cartwright, George Cartwright's brother, led an expedition up the Exploits as far as Red Indian Lake (termed Lieutenant's Lake), partly to gain knowledge of the Beothuck and try to establish contact with them but also to explore generally and see if it were practical to travel "across the body" of the island.[65] The expedition resulted in a sketch showing the Bay of Exploits, the Exploits River, some of that river's tributaries, and the eastern end of the lake, in fine detail.[66] This information was incorporated in two general maps of Newfoundland (1770; 1775), produced mostly from Cook's charts but also from those of his successor as surveyor of Newfoundland, Michael Lane.[67] The maps show Gander River and Gander Lake (and even the Northwest Gander), the Exploits River and part of Red Indian Lake, the Humber River and Deer Lake, and, perhaps most strikingly, Grand Lake, one of Newfoundland's most magnificent geographical features, fairly well drawn, with an enlarged Glover Island, and an oversized Little Grand Lake to the southeast. Most of the interior is blank, as might be expected. The interior of the Avalon Peninsula is blank. *All* the interior is blank on Cook's 1764 map. Yet by 1770 four of the greatest lakes on the island have made an appearance. The interior was becoming known to Europeans. The whole island and Labrador would soon become better known, for Cook's maps were put on sale both in England and Newfoundland.[68] One oddity of these maps was that the coasts most accurately drawn were the uninhabited, or least inhabited, shorelines. The more populous areas were still distorted. St. George's Bay and the empty Bay of Islands were far better depicted than Conception Bay.

In 1770 Conception Bay remained the island's dominant region, with the population overwhelmingly located on the west side, centered on Harbour Grace and Carbonear. Official statistics put the 1770 overwintering population of the Bay at 4,533. This was much larger than the population of St. John's, Petty Harbour, Quidi Vidi, and Torbay (taken together), and four times that of the Southern Shore between Renews and Witless Bay. All of Trinity and Bonavista bays had less than half the population of Conception Bay.[69] Economic statistics from 1770 (tons of train oil, amount of land cleared, etc.) tended to favour Conception Bay as well, though the St. John's region caught and exported more fish. But in 1775 there was more fish sent to market from Conception Bay than from any other district — St. John's was just behind — and 80% of it was caught by inhabitants.[70] The postwar period was one of expansion in Conception Bay as elsewhere. Harbour Grace in particular was a bustling center of mercantile activity, second only to St. John's.[71] But one cause of anxiety was the common one expressed time after time by governors, officials, and Church of England missionaries in the 18th century and later: the Irish. A large number of them (1,101 in 1770) were now settled permanently in Conception Bay, and many others came out annually as servants in the fishery. Despite the interdiction against it, Roman Catholicism had reared its head. Mass had already been celebrated at Harbour Grace. Undercover priests had been active elsewhere in the Bay. Some buildings where mass was said had been burnt,[72] perhaps out of fear that, were they left standing, they might contaminate the neighbourhood. This worry over the spread of a hated religion appears to have touched off a series of events in the early 1770s that illuminate to some extent the emerging society of Conception Bay.

Chiefly owing to the efforts of the Society for the Propagation of the Gospel in Foreign Parts (SPG), the Church of England had a presence in Newfoundland since the early 18th century.[73] In Governor Osborn's instructions in 1729, it was made the de facto established church in Newfoundland.[74] By the 1760s, Church missionaries had worked at St. John's, Bonavista, Placentia, and Trinity. Neither Harbour Grace nor Carbonear had been in a hurry to attract one. But in 1763-4 a church was built in Harbour Grace, and in 1765 one of the merchants there, George Davis, who was about to leave for England for the winter, was authorized to seek out a "protestant Minister" to occupy it. The minister he found was Laurence Coughlan, an Irishman and Irish-speaker who had converted from Roman Catholicism to Methodism in 1753 and soon afterwards became an itinerant preacher for John Wesley in England and Ireland.[75] In 1760 he preached in Waterford, the port of embarkation for most Irish servants going to Newfoundland, where he would likely have learned of conditions and opportunities on the island. The connection with Wesley ended in the mid-1760s, after Coughlan had himself ordained by a Greek orthodox bishop who had turned up in London. Wesley thought the unlearned Coughlan unworthy of ordination. There was also too much zeal and joy in Coughlan's brand of Methodism for Wesley's liking.

Coughlan sailed to Newfoundland in 1766, spent the summer there, and returned in the fall bearing a petition from the inhabitants of Harbour Grace, Carbonear, and "parts adjacent" to the SPG, asking that he be appointed missionary and given a stipend. They had gone to the expense of building a church, the petitioners said, "in order to prevent popery's gaining a footing in those parts, where so great a number of Roman Catholicks are employ'd."[76] The SPG duly appointed him, and he was ordained again, this time by the Bishop of Chester, in the spring of 1767, just prior to his departure for Harbour Grace. He now began a double life. As an SPG-sponsored priest, he for a time satisfied the orthodox. He opened a school and kept it open during his ministry. He preached to the Irish in their own language. Two more churches were built: one at Carbonear, and another at Black-head, ten miles to the north on what was called the North Shore. But Coughlan was also preaching house to house in the manner favoured by Wesley, hoping for an evangelical "awakening." In 1770[77] the revival began and spread *"like fire,"*[78] manifesting itself in public testimonies, deathbed conversions, and (according to Coughlan) a widespread reformation of morals. That it was an essence a Methodist revival is made clear by Coughlan's comments and subsequent events.

To have their minister convert Irish to the Church of England was doubtless what had, in part, been intended; to have him turn churchmen into Methodists was not. The faithful resisted, and their resistance became stronger when governor John Byron unwisely made Coughlan a justice, giving him considerable power over sabbath-breakers, swearers, and adulterers. He fought back and, being a zealot, fought hard; but in 1773 he was forced out. It is clear that Coughlan's appeal was to common people: servants, fishermen, fishermen's wives, "natives."[79] The "Gentry," i.e., merchants, magistrates, and "Gentlemen, so called," were his "Devil-like" "Enemies."[80] It is likely that the oppositional rhetoric in his preaching became more heated as efforts to oust him strengthened. In time it spilled over into the language, attitudes, and actions of his adherents. One of their letters to him in 1774-5,[81] after calling those who expelled him "Serpents" and "Scribes and Pharisees," noted with incredulity that the first sermon preached at Harbour Grace after his departure "ran on the Respect, Obedience and Homage that People ought to pay to Magistrates, &c." Coughlan's followers, though "poor" and "unworthy," saw themselves as "Rebels"[82] against the established religious order in the Bay. He not only "awakened" them, he radicalized them. When his successor as SPG missionary, James Balfour, tried to enter the chapel in Carbonear in 1775, the doors were shut against him, the people there insisting that they wanted "a Methodist, or Presbyterian" as their minister and that "the Meeting House was their own, and ... they would do with it what they pleased." If there were men to lead them, Balfour stated, "they would exactly resemble the Americans on the continent."[83] The comment is striking. While there is no indication in the letters to Coughlan from

Conception Bay that the antagonism he stirred up against the merchant class was economic and political as well as religious, it is hard to believe that such rancour could be confined to church affairs.[84] We perhaps see here the seeds of the Harbour Grace anti-truck protest and other agitation in the 1830s.[85]

Coughlan's congregation built the Blackhead church, big enough to hold 400 people, in less than fourteen days. The feat astonished him. "The people there in general are good Hatchet Men," he remarked, "few Carpenters in *Europe* ... are able to hew a Piece of Timber with those in *Newfoundland*." He marvelled at the variety of skills they possessed. A man "who could not read a Letter in a Book" would go into the woods, find timber, bring the timber out, build and rig a boat, and then go to sea in it. He commented: "they are People of a very bright Genius."[86] He drew no distinction between Irish and English in such statements. We might contrast his comments with those of Palliser and some other governors and observers. (No doubt they are coloured somewhat: it flatters a prophet to have his followers thought intelligent.) Noteworthy too is the distinction drawn by Coughlan between natives of the island and "*Europeans*, who come annually to fish."[87] "The People there" were not identical to those across the Atlantic. A new breed was emerging (though by "there" he meant Conception Bay, and not all of it; this was the only part of the island he knew well). The size of the congregation "contained" in his new church is also intriguing. The 400 people using it, or anticipated for it, would have come not just from Blackhead but from nearby coves: Broad Cove, Mulley's Cove, Adams Cove, and even farther afield. Little is known of the early history of these places. Settlement in Blackhead dates from 1708, when there were twenty-three people there, including nine servants.[88] By the 1770s the North Shore was starting to fill up. Soon a string of communities would be found along the cliffy coast between Old Perlican and Carbonear, with rough paths between them, making it possible for Coughlan's evangelical successors to create a real Methodist circuit.

If Conception Bay Methodists "exactly resemble[d]" Yankee rebels, St. John's merchants certainly did not, though there was trouble over customs duties that had about it a hint of American contrariness. Two customs officers were sent to Newfoundland in 1764, and a customs house was in effective operation two years later. The creation of such an office was in itself significant, since it seemed to imply that the island was to be considered, not just a fishery, but "a part of His Majesty's plantations in America," a concession which Matthews finds somewhat disappointing.[89] He needn't have worried; it was likely considered such merely for the collection of revenue. In any event, it was decided that vessels going there were to be treated as they would be in any other colony. Fees were duly imposed; and when they were not forthcoming, seizures were made. Both the collector and comptroller, as well as the naval officer, now had to be paid if one was to do business involved with shipping in St. John's. Not even fishing vessels were exempt. A contest arose between traders and customs house officers that didn't subside until the 1790s. The objections came not just from Dartmouth and Poole. In 1766 twenty-seven "principal merchants and traders of St. John's" (many of course with links to the West Country) protested, citing exorbitant fees and unwarranted delays.[90] More protests followed as, to bring about "equality" among the traders, fees were demanded in other ports.[91] St. John's merchants continued their resistance in 1770. The fishery had been free from time immemorial, they said, and they wondered under what authority the customs house had been set up. There were now forty signatures.[92] The years immediately before the outbreak of war with America were prosperous in Newfoundland, with large catches of fish and good prices. But much wants more. In 1772 merchants threatened to pay no duties, claiming the British had no legal right to impose a customs house on them. The only law that governed them, they argued, was King William's Act, which guaranteed a free fishery. Laws pertaining to "the plantations and colonies of America" did not "affect them as a fishery." They were talked out of active resistance by governor Shuldham, but in 1773 they "entered into an agreement" among themselves and flatly refused to pay the fees "unless compelled to it by law,"[93] maintaining their resistance even after a hearing at the Treasury in London had sided with the customs officials.[94] In 1774 customs duties and fees in Newfoundland were given parliamentary sanction.[95] Mercantile defiance in this instance might be thought to resemble American insurgency, but the resemblance was superficial. The views of St. John's traders appeared to be exactly like those of Dartmouth, purely mercenary. Yet their willingness to stand together and challenge a dictate from London was a hopeful sign. Though not apparent in this case, by 1775 St. John's merchants in fact thought of themselves as separate from the West Country. They petitioned on their own behalf, with Dartmouth and Teignmouth offering rebuttals.[96]

The British did not remove the customs house, but instead contrived to meet some objections to duties in a new act of Parliament "for the encouragement of the Fisheries,"[97] usually termed Palliser's Act, likely because it reflects so much of that governor's thinking.[98] The genesis of this act, which was given royal assent in May, 1775, lay in the lengthy parliamentary debates and hearings on the New England Trade and Fishery Prohibitory Bill[99] in February and March, under which New England colonists were prohibited from fishing on "the Banks of Newfoundland." With Americans driven off the banks, the British saw a chance to supply markets that would then be opened. But they would have to "encourage" the merchants to move quickly to fill the gap. That meant providing bounties. (To bankers only, though a subtext of reviving the old ship fishery was present in some clauses.) The act thus made sense, but aspects of it might be thought bizarre by someone unacquainted with the main drift of British policy towards Newfoundland. Many clauses in it pertained directly to the island and some had severe implications for Newfoundland residents; but the words "settler" and "inhabitant" were not mentioned in them (though "colony" and "plantation" did appear). It was conceded, however, that "great numbers" of people "remain in that country at the end of every fishing season," some of whom "turned robbers and pirates." It was "for remedy of which evil" that, in part, the new laws were enacted.

The first clause of the lengthy and complex act dealt with bounties, which were offered to British-built ships, owned by his Majesty's subjects residing in Great Britain, Ireland, Guernsey, Jersey, or the Isle of Man — shipowners living in Newfoundland were ineligible — of a specified tonnage and crew, employed in the bank fishery off Newfoundland. The ships were to be under "the same rules and restrictions" as were in King William's Act. Clause 2 specified that "any vessels" employed in the Newfoundland fishery could, on arrival from Britain, take any "vacant or void space whatever on any part of Newfoundland which is not then occupied or used for the said fishery," even if such spaces were not regarded as ships' rooms, and all such spaces were thereafter to be "taken to be ships rooms," whatever "custom or usage" might dictate. (So that if John Doe, resident, had used a room for thirty years but was no longer using it, it could be grabbed by the fishing ships and he couldn't get it back. The implication was, or seemed to be, that there were no normal property rights in Newfoundland.) It was also ordained that no delays to the operation of British ships engaged in the fishery were to be caused by the customs house in Newfoundland. Ships were simply to report on arrival and departure; a nominal fee was to be taken for each report, and no other charge.

King William's Act contained no clause that forbad leaving fishing servants in Newfoundland or transporting them elsewhere in North America, or that required their return to Britain. This defect was now addressed. Carrying men who'd been brought from Britain to be employed in the Newfoundland fishery as passengers to "any part of the continent of America," unless permitted by the governor, was outlawed under penalty of £200. Exemption from impressment, previously granted to seamen on ships or shore on "the continent of America," was withdrawn, to curb fishermen's desertions. To prevent men from remaining in Newfoundland, money "equal to the then current price of a man's passage home," but not to exceed forty shillings, was to be deducted from servants' wages to ensure their return. This money was to be paid to the master of a passage ship to bring the men back. Servants who went as passengers to Newfoundland "or any seaman or fisherman hired there" were included in this clause. As a further inducement to get servants to return, an employer was forbidden to pay or advance, either in liquor, money, or goods, more than half their wages; the balance was to be paid at the end of "every such man's covented time or service" in money or in bills of exchange payable in Great Britain or Ireland or in the country "to which such seaman or fisherman belongs" — i.e., "at their return home." Some regulations dealt with the behaviour and rights of servants. Servants who left their masters or refused to work would forfeit two days pay for each day of neglect. If they left their masters for five days without leave, they would forfeit all remaining wages, would be deemed deserters, arrested, imprisoned, and, if found guilty by a court of session, publicly whipped as vagrants and sent back to their country on passage ships. The first claim on an employer's fish and oil was to be for the payment of his servant's wages. (I.e., these had priority over other debts.)

Like King William's Act, which was not repealed, the legislation of 1775 was an effort to micromanage the Newfoundland fishery from afar. It was a refinement of the earlier act, and the purpose was more directly stated: not just to support the migratory fishery, mainly the bankers, but to secure the return of fishermen to England and in so doing inhibit the growth of a resident population. The extent to which West Country merchants "loathed" the act and "fought" to have it repealed has been exaggerated.[100] They were always against government intervention in the fishery except when they needed it, and they could be counted on to blame regulation for slowdowns in the trade caused by competition or wartime uncertainty. Poole traders had in fact begged the House of Commons for the kind of "Encouragement" the new act offered.[101] Merchants certainly raised no big objection to the bounties, the act's main ingredient, though it was hard at first to meet all the intricate qualifications. But in time bounties resulted in the expansion of the banker fleet, with the merchants duly cashing in. In 1788 no fewer than 130 ships were granted bounties.[102] The one substantial objection they raised to the bounty system in the act was that it applied only to ships navigated by "not less than fifteen men each." They wanted the number of men reduced, and they got what they wanted.[103] They objected to the provision giving the vice-admiralty court jurisdiction over wage disputes, and again they got their way. They said that limiting advances to employees to one-half their wages prevented employers from shipping "green men," i.e., inexperienced youngsters, since one-half the pittance these were paid would not cover the costs of clothing and necessities. Again, the clause was modified to suit them. They wanted the penalties increased for servants' neglect of work or absence without leave, and they were increased. It is true that some of their objections weren't listened to. Newfoundland traders and British merchants both opposed the clause empowering newcomers to seize unoccupied rooms, with the latter demanding "the right to hold their fishing rooms and habitations" on the island.[104] Dartmouth spokesman Arthur Holdsworth, a merchant and Member of Parliament, even proposed legisation that would vest occupiers of land there in their possessions "in fee simple."[105] The suggestion got nowhere. Holdsworth also proposed that only one-half of an employer's fish and oil be liable to the payment of servant' wages, but this too was not taken up. In the event, it turned out the relevant clause in the act was poorly thought through and could not always be legally enforced.[106] At least one other part of the act was seriously defective. The 40-shilling deduction clause, supposedly ensuring passage back to England or Ireland for servants, could be easily circumvented. Employers could make the deduction from wages without providing passage home, thereby leaving many servants stranded. A flabbergasted Matthews said the act "actually promoted settlement,"[107] but this is rather stated than proved. Official figures seem to show that the number of inhabitants actually fell between 1775 and 1784.[108] It picked up afterwards, but it is unclear whether the increase was related in any way to the operations of the act.

The act became law five weeks after the opening engagements of the American Revolution.[109] The immediate effect in Newfoundland was a food shortage, for the Second Continental Congress, meeting in May, 1775, banned exports to the island. While it was feared this would cause great distress, Newfoundland being dependent on America for most basic foodstuffs apart from fish and potatoes, governor Robert Duff later reported that local traders had managed to get supplies from other markets.[110] By midsummer any initial panic was over. "Great regularity and good order" prevailed in July; inhabitants as well as adventurers were "quiet and satisfied."[111] No effort was made to raise a local force to resist an attack. Recruiting parties, however, were at work, procuring 200 men for regiments in Quebec, as well as seventy-five seamen and carpenters also to be sent there. A further eighty-four were recruited for Samuel Graves' squadron at Boston.[112] More such recruitment went on in the years following. Weather, not war, caused the only damages in 1775. A windstorm in September brought enormous destruction. Boats, ships, and an estimated 300 men were lost. The sea, rising "to a height scarcely ever known before," wrecked fishing premises. Total losses were said to be at least £30,000.[113]

In instructions to governor John Montagu in 1776, the King seemed more concerned with appeasing the French than with defending Newfoundland. French fishermen, the instructions said, were being obstructed and molested on the Petit Nord "by means of sundry claims of our subjects to private property." Montagu was to prevent his Majesty's subjects from taking any possession whatever as private property "or from making any settlement" there. (Official statistics now listed over twenty British settlements on the Petit Nord, with a permanent population, including that of Bonavista, at above 700.)[114] In the south, residents of St. Pierre and Miquelon were to be permitted to cut lumber on the island of Newfoundland.[115] The British thought concessions like these would help keep the French out of the American conflict. But even as the proclamation granting the new liberty to residents of St. Pierre and Miquelon was being distributed, evidence of French complicity with the Americans was at hand. A recruiting officer sailing from Nova Scotia to Newfoundland, forced into St. Pierre on his passage, found an American privateer in port.[116] The French continued to pester the British government with complaints over the Petit Nord as their involvement with America deepened. Finally, in September, 1778, after it was made clear that France was in the war, boots and all, Montagu sent an armed force to St. Pierre. The governor, Le Baron De L'Esperance, surrendered as soon as he was told he could do so "with all the honours of war." The French inhabitants, numbering about 1,400, were expelled from the islands, and fishing premises, boats, and houses destroyed.[117] At last, there was some retaliation for the earlier French raids on Newfoundland settlements, though a wiser and more humane course might have been to occupy the island without wreaking the usual havoc.

The privateer encountered at St. Pierre was a sign of things to come. At the beginning of September, 1776, "the piratical cruizers of America," mainly fishing vessels fitted out for war, turned up to raid the banking fleet. They carried off two or three bankers and plundered about ten more. The harassment continued through the fall.[118] Montagu's small naval force, a part of which he left behind for the winter, seemed helpless against the American ships, which his captains had trouble finding, let alone seizing. He needed a larger squadron next year, he wrote, otherwise the bank fishery might be "wholly prevented."[119] He repeated the warning in 1777, when the attacks on bankers went on all summer. Two privateers even captured H.M.S. *Fox* of Montagu's squadron, a great humiliation.[120] American captains let it be known they were under orders from Congress "to take, burn, sink, or destroy" every English banker they could find, information that "greatly alarmed" the trade. But by October the plundering had stopped, and merchants had trouble finding ships to take their fish to market. Fears now grew of attacks on land as well as at sea. Burgoyne's surrender at Saratoga in October, it was thought, made an American invasion of Newfoundland "more probable."[121] Efforts to defend St. John's, where Fort Townshend was under construction, were speeded up, directed by military engineer Robert Pringle who commanded in the absence of the governor. Through neglect and incompetence, the St. John's garrison had dwindled to a small force of men "mostly old and unfit for duty," but by spring Pringle had about 250 ready in case of attack.[122] Instead of approaching St. John's, the Americans started raiding the outharbours. It is not clear how many they looted. Certain areas escaped; for instance, Fogo and the coastline near it were protected through the efforts of the merchant Jeremiah Coghlan.[123] But a St. Lawrence merchant's premises were plundered in May, 1778; in July Montagu reported that "different parts of the island" were being "daily attacked" and he feared "most of the outports will be destroyed."[124] A total of twenty-two ships were cut out[125] of various harbours over the summer; boats were burnt at sea, within sight of the coast around St. John's.[126] By August, the raiders had reached as far north as Sandwich Bay, Labrador, where the *Minerva* robbed George Cartwright of £14,000 worth of goods and provisions and carried off thirty-six of his seventy-three employees.[127] The ship also plundered Coghlan's posts in Labrador. Thoroughly dismayed, Montagu told colonial secretary George Germain that he was surprised that neither he nor any of the military command at St. John's "have any directions in what manner they are to proceed."[128] With an invasion expected and the coast and fishery under seige by a determined foe, British authorities still had the governor return home in the fall, leaving the defence of the island in the hands of junior military. War or no war, the key policy towards Newfoundland was not to be disturbed.

The privateers swarmed back early in 1779, and the mood of the inhabitants of St. John's was further darkened by a fire on May 15 that burnt thirty-five buildings — houses and merchants' stores — consuming much needed provisions.[129] But now, with France in the war, notice was taken of the threat to Newfoundland in the colonial office, and a supply of small arms and ammunition was sent for distribution to the outports, to be augmented with cannon from Placentia. Governor Richard Edwards (back for his second term in Newfoundland) oversaw careful preparations in and near St. John's against the anticipated assault. A volunteer force of 200 men was raised by November, to add to the garrison of 382. Sixty more soldiers were at Placentia, and two each at six major outharbours.[130] (But none in Conception Bay.) By early 1780, the number of privateers taken by British warships rose sharply. An American vessel attacking an outport might now expect resistance. One approached Mortier in the spring, but was beaten off with the loss of perhaps twenty men.[131]

In 1780 Germain warned Edwards that the French had assembled a formidable land and sea force at Brest, commanded by Arsac de Ternay, who had led the 1762 attack on St. John's. Gaining possession of Newfoundland, Germain said, could be one of the objects of the expedition.[132] The French squadron sailed in May. Newfoundland trembled. But no assault materialized. In September the American packet *Mercury*, en route to Holland, was taken off Newfoundland. Aboard her was Henry Laurens, who had been President of the Continental Congress in 1777-8. A bag of diplomatic papers was thrown overboard, but was retrieved, read by Edwards, and instantly forwarded to England, with Laurens as prisoner. Among the dispatches in the bag Edwards found evidence that the enemy "looks on Newfoundland with a jealous eye."[133] The volunteer force having dispersed, he gave orders, unauthorized in London, to raise an infantry corps of 300. This "Newfoundland Regiment" had almost reached its complement by November 15, though some recruiting was still underway in Placentia and Conception Bay.[134] Edwards left a detailed list of "winter instructions" for his soldiers, reminding them that taking shelter in the forts was a "last resource."[135] They had to march to meet the enemy. Roads — little more than paths, really — had to be guarded. Boats filled with rocks had to be kept in readiness to sink in Quidi Vidi Gut, through which invaders might try to pass. He had "authentick intelligence" that Newfoundland would be attacked in late fall or early next spring. He sailed for home October 28. The expected invasion didn't happen.

In 1781 Edwards' squadron captured an impressive total of seventeen privateers, yet this was perhaps but a small proportion of the "amazing number" around the coasts.[136] The effect of privateering on the migratory fishery was evidently to reduce it drastically, even though ships went to and from Newfoundland in convoy. The 1781 returns reveal the bank fishery[137] as almost insignificant, while the by-boatmen produced just one-quarter the amount of fish taken by inhabitants.[138] The 1782 returns show similar ratios, with the inhabitants slightly more dominant.[139] Privateering accounts only partly for the wartime decline of the British fishery. With America no longer supplying Newfoundland, prices of provisions and other commodities rose sharply, making by-boatkeeping precarious if not uneconomic. Some by-boatmen found it wiser to stay in Newfoundland, thinking that "planting [was] the only means of holding on."[140] Periodic shortages of supplies, high prices, and scarcity of paid work[141] evidently drove people out of the outports to America,[142] back to Britain, or to St. John's. Conception Bay may have been especially hard hit; its relative position in the Newfoundland economy seems to have fallen dramatically during the war.[143] But not all effects were bad. Food shortages were to some extent compensated for by an expansion of agriculture. Edwards remarked in 1779 on the "vast quantities" of "very fine" potatoes and other vegetables on the island.[144] After the war, one observer commented that the land around St. John's "is cleared, and under cultivation for a great distance from the town; great plenty of potatoes, barley, oats, &c. are grown." The "face of the country," he said, had changed radically.[145] To get wood for stages and flakes, a fisherman now had to go from two to three miles from the harbour.[146] Agriculture had doubtless changed the appearance of other places. As would happen in the Napoleonic wars, trade centered in St. John's expanded too. An observer in 1785 called attention to the "great number of new buildings" in the town.[147] Merchants filled, albeit temporarily, the gap created by the banishment of America from the British West Indies.[148] And since American competition was no longer a factor at home, they were much more in control of prices. The war created havoc in many outports, and nervousness everywhere. But "the capital"[149] was proved safe. Well might the St. John's merchants proclaim their gratitude to Edwards and loyalty to "His Majesty's Person and Government."[150]

His Majesty's government's view of Newfoundland was soon to be on exhibit once more. How that government could, in the light of its actions at war's end, continue to command loyalty on the island is perhaps not always easy to grasp. But Newfoundland had as yet no local patriotism, or at least none discernible in documents;[151] it still had no council or assembly around which such patriotism could take shape, no politics to stir it up, and no intelligentsia to articulate it, supposing it was felt. Merchants remained dominant, and though there had been signs among them of a local esprit de corps, most still had links to Dartmouth, Poole, and other ports at "home." To them, attachment to Britain *was* patriotism. Witnessing the success of the American Revolution, far from loosening Newfoundland's attachment to the "mother country," likely only made it stronger; and the bond of loyalty would, fatally, continue strong even into the 20th century, under conditions that would make even some Englishmen think it bizarre.

In the negotiations over the articles of peace with America and France in 1782-3, Britain had no worries about troublesome repercussions in Newfoundland. It could cut and patch as it liked. And it did. The Treaty of Versailles was signed on September 3, 1783. It gave the Americans access to the Grand Bank "and all the other banks of Newfoundland." Though they were denied the right to dry and cure fish on the island, they were also given liberty to take "fish of every kind on such part of the coast as British fishermen shall use." They could land and cure fish in unsettled parts of Labrador. France too was welcomed back. St. Pierre and Miquelon were again ceded "in full right," but without the restrictions named in the Treaty of Paris. This meant French warships could be brought into the fishing zone with impunity. And they were. France renounced its right to fish between Cape Bonavista and Cape St. John, where it had virtually no fishery anyway, and as compensation was permitted to extend its fishing limit south of Point Riche as far as Cape Ray. The entire west coast of Newfoundland was now part of the French shore. In a Declaration appended to the treaty, George III further undertook to "take the most positive measures" to prevent his subjects "from interrupting in any manner by their competition" the fishery of the French "during the temporary exercise of it which is granted to them." George's subjects were not to interrupt the French even by *competition*. The rights granted were evidently intended to be exclusive, though the word "exclusive" wasn't used. The Declaration, as an English official later put it, was "an indirect surrender of a right which it would have been too invidious to have conceded more expressly."[152] In order to give the French the freedom they needed to fish, the Declaration said, the King would "cause the fixed settlements" formed there "to be removed." He would also order that the French fishermen were not to be "incommoded" in cutting wood needed for repair of "scaffolds," huts, and fishing vessels.[153] These were astonishing concessions, especially in view of France's active participation with the Americans in the revolutionary war. The English were later inclined to explain them by noting that their country in 1783 was in economic depression.

But even these concessions were deemed insufficient. Shortly after the articles of peace were signed, the French asked that colonists at St. Pierre and Miquelon be given leave to cut wood in Newfoundland. This was granted at once.[154] Steps were soon taken to implement British undertakings in the treaty. In 1784 governor John Campbell issued a lengthy proclamation outlining French rights and ordering that "fixed settlements" on the coast between Cape St. John and Cape Ray be removed "without loss of time." Anyone disobeying his instructions would "answer the contrary at their peril."[155] In 1785-6, the French drove British fishermen out of Sops Arm, Holm Point (near Sops Arm), Noddy Bay, Hawkes Bay, St. George's Bay, River of Ponds, Port Saunders, Codroy, and the Humber River. John Dennis's salmon establishment at St. George's Bay, including his house, was burnt.[156] Thomas Spelt had built "houses and other conveniences" for himself and his family at Noddy Bay, and "had liv'd there & enjoy'd the same for 12 years." He "wished to remain there in the winter." His room was "demanded from him by the French."[157] Netlam Tory from Poole was forced out of Sops Arm, where he had been established for twenty-four years. French marines landed with drawn swords, cutlasses, pistols, and bayonets, overwhelming the fishermen, who declined to take up arms with their dipnets and prong handles. In addition to his fishery at Sops Arm, Tory had fishing establishments at Englee and St. Lunaire, employed seven or eight winter crews furring and sealing in White Bay, and had more crews on the coast of Labrador. All was lost or disrupted.[158] No protection was offered by the British governor. On the contrary, the French were told that "every means" would be used to effect "the removal of the English settlers."[159] After a Dartmouth merchant, having taken legal advice, defiantly sent a crew to Hare Bay in 1787, the British cabinet hesitated, and governor John Elliott was told it would be "very improper" to use any "force" against him.[160] Parliament was asked to intervene. In May, 1788, an act of Parliament[161] empowered the King to instruct the Newfoundland governor to remove stages, flakes, train vats, "or other Works whatever" together with "all Ships, Vessels, and Boats" from the Treaty coast and "to compel any of His Majesty's Subjects to depart from thence." Thus force was authorized.[162] Notices embodying these orders were immediately posted in Newfoundland.[163] And so the cod and other fish along a vast stretch of the Newfoundland shore were handed over. (But the British were to retain some control of the salmon fishery, which they belatedly realized was often conducted some miles up rivers, hence was an internal as well as coastal activity.)[164]

As for the "English" shore, the postwar period was one of renewal and anxiety. The British government considered again how to extract profit from this half-colony. The first consideration was trade. Now that the Americans were foreigners, would they be allowed to resume their trade with Newfoundland, even using British bottoms? This was a vital question to residents, since American foodstuffs were not only cheaper than most supplies from overseas and often greatly superior in quality, but of course closer to home and hence more accessible. When bread and flour arrived in St. John's from Philadelphia in the summer of 1784, prices immediately fell 30%.[165] Dartmouth merchants responded to the threat posed by cheaper goods from the U.S. by pressing for a total prohibition on American imports, with Holdsworth heading the lobby.[166] Poole quickly joined the parade of avarice.[167] Here was West Country greed at its ugliest. Dartmouth was already on record as claiming American supplies were of critical importance to the fishery.[168] And England, herself liable to food shortages, was no dependable supplier. The merchants even fought against giving the Newfoundland governor a discretionary power to issue import licences to ships in case of necessity. They had heard some such scheme was afoot. What did a little hunger in Newfoundland matter alongside the prosperity of "the trade"? The case for a more open trade with America was put in London by the St. John's naval officer[169] Archibald Buchanan, who argued in 1784 that provisions and other merchandise should be supplied without restraint, from wherever they could "be got cheapest."[170] Cutting the Americans out would result in rising prices for provisions and falling prices for fish. It was by the fishermen's labour alone, he said, that "the trade of Newfoundland exists"; therefore their interest "is to be attended to in preference to that of all others." Precisely how the colonial authorities reacted to this idea has not been recorded. Apparently not warmly. An act of Parliament in 1785 forbad the importation of all goods and commodities into Newfoundland from the U.S., with the exception of bread, flour, and livestock, which could be imported only under licence granted to British-built and British-owned ships; the licences were to be issued by customs officials in Britain or Ireland.[171] The system naturally proved cumbersome. Another act soon had to be passed giving the governor of Newfoundland authorization to licence the import of bread, flour, livestock, and corn from America "in case of Necessity," but "for the then ensuing season only." He still had to use British-built and British-owned ships.[172] By the end of the decade, about a quarter of Newfoundland's supplies of bread and flour were coming from America.[173] Some other merchandise was entering legally as well, with much more doubtless being brought in by smugglers. But Newfoundland was then largely a captive market for British suppliers.

"Scarce and dear"[174] provisions could well have provoked a crisis in St. John's in the immediate aftermath of the war, for the winter population rose quickly, possibly as a consequence of new liberty given to Catholics. Grenadian Catholics had been permitted to vote and sit in their Assembly in 1765. The Quebec Act of 1774 had granted freedom of religion to French Canadian Catholics. It was now Newfoundland's turn. The prohibition against the Catholic religion was quietly lifted in instructions to governor Edwards in 1779,[175] and in July, 1784, a priest, the Franciscan James Louis O'Donel, arrived in St. John's from Ireland.[176] To the dismay of some English merchants,[177] a chapel[178] was soon under construction. FitzGerald says it was "little more than a barn-like structure" and was called "the Chapel of St. Louis."[179] O'Donel could speak Irish as well as English, as he had to if he was to communicate with servants in the Newfoundland fishery. Accompanying him was another Franciscan, Patrick Phelan, who was sent to Harbour Grace. A third priest, Edmund Burke, went to Placentia the next year. On October 28, 1784, governor Campbell issued an order to justices of the peace: they were "to allow all persons Inhabiting this Island, to have full liberty of Conscience, and the Free Exercise of all such modes of Religious worship as are not prohibited by law, provided they be contented with a quiet and peaceable enjoyment of the same, not giving offence or scandal to Government." This is said to be "a sign of a new era" in Newfoundland,[180] and no doubt it was, though the proviso at the end offered some room for exercise of the normal bigotries. It was, in fact, one governor's dictate; later governors could decree otherwise,[181] except that they couldn't take back the right to practise the religion, which derived from London. Roman Catholicism might be permitted, but that is some distance from being accepted. Catholics could still hold no public office, not even that of constable. And they were still subject to public vilification. George III's son Prince William Henry, later William IV, serving as naval surrogate in Newfoundland in 1786, threw an iron file at O'Donel and injured him in the shoulder.[182]

Irish servants did not now need to return home to make their Easter Duty.[183] That could partly explain the presence in St. John's at the end of 1784 of about 500 unemployed men, many of them arrivals from the outharbours.[184] They were of "the lower class of people," i.e., Irish, and they were "reduced to the greatest distress." The "chief magistrate" and "principal inhabitants" of the city were alarmed, fearing their lives and properties were at risk.[185] Major John Elford, the lieutenant-governor of St. John's — he served as such, in the absence of the governor, from 1783 to 1790 — solved the problem by introducing able-bodied relief: men were dispensed food from the military stores as payment for work cutting wood.[186] As a result, "no bad effects" were felt over the winter. But the problem would be an enduring one. The winter population of St. John's was estimated at 4,000 in 1785.[187] From 1786 to 1787, according to one calculation, the population of the whole island jumped by 6,400.[188] Servants were staying in the country, and many came to the city at the end of the fishing season to board and perhaps try to find work. Despite efforts to keep their numbers in check, they would keep coming. They were termed "dieters." Proclamations against harbouring them would soon become a regular feature of life on the island.

England was worried about the rising population. The bedrock government policy towards Newfoundland, namely, "to discourage plantation, and fix the seat of trade in Europe,"[189] might be failing. A new clause in the 1786 amendment of the fishery laws demanded that every master of ships receiving bounties "make oath" that he brought back the number of men he took out.[190] But dieters stayed on. In 1787 governor John Elliott ordered the number of public houses[191] in St. John's reduced from twenty-four to twelve. Merchants immediately protested, saying that planters and boatkeepers would be unable to find lodgings when they came to the town in fall to transact their business, and that servants awaiting ships to Britain and Ireland would have to stay under the flakes.[192] Elliott declined to act; he would have to receive His Majesty's command for so doing. Two years later, governor Mark Milbanke forbad seamen or fishermen to winter in St. John's unless they were regularly hired as servants. Outport magistrates were not to encourage men to come to St. John's, but instead were "to oblige them" to return to Britain or Ireland on the passage ships.[193] No statute or instruction gave the governor power to expel, as well he knew, but he acted as if he had one. Milbanke suggested that governors be given such a power,[194] and a 1792 bill was duly presented to the House of Commons authorizing the expulsion of any unemployed "Seaman or Fisherman" who was not native to the island, had no child there, and was unmarried.[195] (It was not enacted.) Governors had already been authorized to curb the building of houses; Campbell and Elliott had pulled down some, and had published proclamations against building homes and making gardens below the "upper street or path" (i.e., what would become Duckworth Street).[196] Building *above* the street was apparently in order, but even there the King had ordered that no possession of land as private property was to be taken and no "right of property whatsoever acknowledged." But buidings in place were to be left standing, unless they were on "ancient fishing rooms" or were "nuisances" to the fishery.[197] Milbanke, given essentially the same instructions,[198] acted with greater force. In October, 1789, he issued a proclamation stating that he would not suffer "any" buildings to be erected "in and about" St. John's that were not needed in the fishery. Existing erections or fences that were nuisances to the fishery he would have removed. Anyone keeping dieters would, on conviction, be sent off the island and their houses would be "taken down and removed." Constables were to visit the different quarters of the town once a month in winter to demand information about who was living in the houses. Magistrates were not to allow any buildings to be erected in winter, except for the fishery, without permission in writing from the governor.[199]

The severity of the proclamation bespeaks uneasiness. After rebounding strongly in the mid- to late-1780s, with huge catches in 1787-8, the migratory sector of the fishery shortly commenced a decline that — if the West Country merchants are to be believed — caused a "great many" bankruptcies and huge losses among the still solvent.[200] The bounty-driven British fishery, in combination with an increased effort by inhabitants, had produced by official count 950,000 quintals of cod in 1788. The catch glutted a market that was, after all, open to other exporters. Not war, scarcity, or administrative encumbrance caused the decline in 1789-93, but competition from the French and Norwegians, with America looming as yet another dreaded rival.[201] Nearly one-third of the fish caught in 1788 could not find buyers.[202] The boom was followed by, not a bust, but a gradual, then considerable falling off. The number of bankers going out in 1789 was still substantial, but down[203] from the previous year (though the catch was still very high). By-boat-keeping fell off too. By early 1790 Dartmouth was complaining to government of the "great decline of the trade"; it would be lost altogether, they said, unless all acts of Parliament relating to the fishery passed after that of King William were repealed.[204] Exeter, Topsham, and Teignmouth followed with similar murmurs. From 1789 to 1793 the number of British bankers off Newfoundland went from 153 to 63. Two years later, bankers owned by residents outnumbered those from overseas. As the crisis in the migratory fishery deepened, the output of inhabitant fishermen also declined, but then levelled off. By 1793, the inhabitant fishery was dominant; by 1800, assisted by a war that showed no signs of ending, it had effectively supplanted the fishery from the West Country. (Though a small migratory effort persisted into the next century.)

West Country wrath in the early 1790s was directed at the judicial and administrative machinery in Newfoundland that had, in their eyes, impeded their fishery. That didn't mean they were against all such impediments; only those that prevented them from making money. The barriers preventing ready entry of U.S. foodstuffs into Newfoundland, for instance, they approved of. The customs house was again railed against, as were several clauses of Palliser's Act, though not the ones offering bounties. The merchants hearkened back King William of blessed memory. No further laws beyond his, passed in 1699, were needed to secure the British fishery, they said. What seemed to enrage them beyond all else was yet another court that had been created in 1789 by governor Milbanke. A man somewhat resembling Palliser in temperament, Milbanke found, or said he found, on his arrival in Newfoundland that the court system was "standing still."[205] Fishing admirals, being most of the time at sea in bankers, were unavailable to hear disputes over rooms. Courts of session, he said, felt a want of legal authority, took too long to decide disputes over wages, and had been intimidated by merchants. Governors, who once themselves (illegally in his view) sat as judges, had stopped doing so after Richard Edwards' judicial authority had been challenged in 1780.[206] The governor's surrogates had kept on holding court after the governor himself had ceased, but learned in 1788, when one of their decisions was appealed in England, that they had no legal right to sit as judges either.[207] The vice-admiralty court, which had intruded beyond maritime questions into civil cases, was irregular and arbitrary, "more like an inquisition that a court." The commissioners of oyer and terminer indeed functioned, but many considered even that court illegal, since King William's Act directed that capital crimes were to be tried not in Newfoundland but in England. For that reason, some prominent men declined to sit as commissioners, fearing repercussions. Altogether, to Milbanke there was hardly a properly functioning court in the island, certainly none of civil jurisdiction (the sessions being mainly a criminal court, and the commissioners of oyer and terminer exclusively so). Milbanke read in his commission and instructions that he had "power and authority to constitute and appoint judges, and in cases requisite commissioners of oyer and terminer for the hearing and determining of all criminal causes (treason excepted.)"[208] He took the first eight words to mean that he could appoint as many judges as he liked and for whatever purpose struck his fancy, and proceeded to appoint four judges to sit in a "court of common pleas" to try civil causes. The court met in September, 1789, and to Milbanke's delight promptly decided thirty cases. The eight words, of course, applied to the court of oyer and terminer only; he had not been given carte blanche to appoint judges. Angry petitions were immediately raised against the innovation, but the law officers of the Crown ruled at once that Milbanke's action was "not founded in any authority legally."[209] The court of common pleas would not meet again in Newfoundland.

Yet he had made a point, and it was one that had to be taken up. Over the next three years, the legal system of Newfoundland was reformed. The law officers in 1790 recommended the establishment of a "court of civil jurisdiction" on the island, to be presided over by an English barrister of not less than five years' standing. A court of that name was established by act of Parliament in May, 1791,[210] and duly conducted proceedings in the island. A year later, again by statute,[211] and against the bitter opposition of British merchants, the court was reconstituted as "The Supreme Court of Judicature of the Island of Newfoundland," with both criminal and civil jurisdiction. It was to be headed by a chief justice, assisted by two assessors and "such Clerks and Ministerial Officers as the Chief Justice shall think proper to appoint." All were to be paid salaries in lieu of fees or other "Emoluments." The supreme court was to hold plea of all crimes and misdemeanours "in the same Manner as Plea is holden" in England. It could proceed "in a summary Way" in civil causes, which were to be tried "according to the law of England, as far as the same can be applied to Suits and Complaints" arising in Newfoundland. The act also authorized the governor, with the advice of the chief justice, to institute surrogate courts, which could hear cases of a civil nature "in different Parts of the Island of Newfoundland." They were inferior to the supreme court, to which they were required to refer "Matters of Difficulty." Decisions of the surrogate could be appealed to the supreme court. A surrogate was to be assisted by a justice of the peace as assessor, but he could hold court without one. The vice-admiralty court could try maritime causes and "Causes of the Revenue" (i.e., those relating to customs), but not disputes over seamen's wages. Those disputes, together with "all Offences" committed by "any Hirer or Employer" against seamen or fishermen, were to be tried in sessions court. No other court but the four named could hold plea of any suit of a civil nature. Thus ended the fishing admirals' part in the legal history of Newfoundland. The court of oyer and terminer, obviously no longer needed, could still be called into session.[212] The act did not specify that the supreme court was to sit year-round, nor was it formally authorized to do so until 1798.[213] The law officers had noted "the peculiar policy of this kingdom with respect to the territory[214] of Newfoundland, which has always been directed at the discouragement of ... subjects ... establishing themselves in that island," and had recommended that the court meet from June 1 to December 1.[215] In 1792 it met only in September and October. Britain was still far from accepting Newfoundland as a permanent colony.

The first chief justice of Newfoundland was John Reeves, an Oxford-educated barrister of the Middle Temple.[216] It was Reeves who, having gone to Newfoundland as chief judge in the court of civil jurisdiction in 1791, recommended the establishment of a court with wider powers, since "in a country where no attorney is to be found ... the distinctions in forms of actions [are] incomprehensible."[217] Reeves was the first man of parts outside government, the first thinker, to get an intellectual grasp of Newfoundland. His reports in 1791[218] discussed the nature of litigation on the island, the class structure of merchants, boatkeepers, and servants, and the need for reform. The population, he wrote, has "increased so much in number, as to compose a society," one requiring "more attention, and looking after, than it has yet received from the government at home." He suggested that Newfoundland be granted a "legislative power" to make "bye laws, and regulations for the interior government, and police of the place." Once made, the bylaws should be proclaimed, then registered in the supreme court. This would give them "force." The Committee on Trade could revoke or alter them. It seemed preposterous to Reeves that such regulations should be imposed from afar, by persons "who have never seen a distant country." Those persons could only lay down "principles to be pursued." To "enter into the detail of particulars" required what he termed a "local legislature." It would advise, not control, the governor and consist of not more than twenty-three persons drawn from different sectors of the community. There was no suggestion that these were to be elected; they were evidently to be named by the governor. Reeves was no radical reformer. Neither was his suggestion to raise revenue by a system of quit rents intended as a prelude to "colonization." So far from promoting that end, Reeves had in mind a plan for securing the return of seamen "which will more completely execute the favorite policy of preventing settlement and colonization than any that has yet been attempted."

After presiding over the new court in 1792, he returned to England and in 1793 gave evidence to a parliamentary committee studying the Newfoundland trade.[219] He rejected the self-serving opinions of Dartmouth merchants Peter Ougier and William Newman, who had, he said, "been too much listened to." In opposition to their views, he argued for permanent courts in Newfoundland, courts that would, in the absence of the chief justice and surrogates, "determine Causes of any Sort or Kind." He interjected a note of realism into the discussion of land tenure in Newfoundland, pointing out that people in the outports, "being removed from the Eye of Government ... make Inclosures, and carve for themselves almost as they pleased." As for population, the topic of so much anxiety in government, he said that even if it were 50,000, as some had stated, inhabitants were "thinly scattered" in distant harbours "and have little Knowledge, or Connection with one another, to unite them." Anyone thinking they might have a "Mischievous Tendency" could lay their fears to rest. Merchants who had clamoured against permanent government allegedly to keep the population down were actually "adding to the Number of Residents every Year," he said. They wanted the governor out of the way for their own end, which was "to go on without Inspection or Controul." But the people now needed "something more of a resident Government." The British fear of turning Newfoundland into a colony had meant that the island had been abandoned "to be inhabited by any one who chooses," and "the consequence has been, that New-foundland has been peopled behind your Back."

More was yet to come. In 1795 Reeves published his *History of the Government of the Island of Newfoundland*, a book based on research in the files of the Committee of Trade in London. It was a study of the development of the island's "constitution," if such a term can be used of what Reeves, in another context, called its "very partial and slender code of laws."[220] Having recently listened to the whining rhetoric of fish merchants, Reeves was prepared to offer a theory of Newfoundland history. He saw it as comprising "struggles and vicissitudes" between "two contending interests": "The *planters* and *inhabitants* on the one hand, who, being settled there, needed the protection of a government and police, with the administration of justice: and the *adventurers* and *merchants* on the other; who, originally carrying on the fishery from this country, and visiting that island only for the season, needed no such protection for themselves, and had various reasons for preventing its being afforded to the others."[221] Though oversimplified, the idea had much to commend it. Reeves' book was the careful work of a legal scholar. It would, however, be made the foundation of much shrill colonial rhetoric in the next century, as Reeves himself was quietly passing his final years as a rich bachelor, possibly astonished at the fuss he'd inadvertently caused. His "struggles" and "vicissitudes" were meant as a theoretical formulation. Some of his interpreters would turn them into real scraps and bloody noses.

The parliamentary inquiry of 1793 made nothing happen, for war with France had broken out shortly after the execution of Louis XVI in January, and Newfoundland was soon relegated once again to the back porch. St. Pierre and Miquelon were seized in May; "complete evacuation" of the 1,200 residents was ordered a year later.[222] Governor Richard King was told to "lose no time" in dislodging the French from whatever other parts of Newfoundland they "may reside in or resort to."[223] Attention turned once again to defending the island. By late 1793 the military engineer Thomas Skinner had raised a volunteer corps of four companies to support the small detachment of the King's Own Regiment doing garrison duty in St. John's. When it was rumoured in 1794 that the King's Own were to be sent to Canada or Nova Scotia, St. John's merchants protested, pointing to the "inadequacy" of local defences. This "Colony," they said, was "of more importance to His Majesty, than any other possession in North America."[224] This looks suspiciously like pride in Newfoundland, though expressed in a roundabout way. Such feeling was rare prior to the nineteenth century. Perhaps it was a by-product of anxiety. Recruitment for a Nova Scotian regiment was taking place in a meagrely defended Newfoundland, while it looked as if the King's Own would be shipped off; as this was happening, men were deserting from the King's ships. The island seemed frightfully exposed. Impressment did nothing to ease the tension. In October, a press gang from H.M.S. *Boston* succeeded in pressing eight men from the number "idling about" in St. John's. Lieut. Richard Lowry, accompanying a few of the men back into the town to collect wages and clothes, was stopped by "sundry persons armed with bludgeons"; the men were freed and Lowry was killed. "Great disquiet and alarm" succeeded in the town. Grand jurors feared a riot would break out if an attempt was made to rescue those charged with the murder, a riot that the small number of military on hand would be unable to quell. The jurors asked governor James Wallace to delay his departure from England. But justice, if such it was, was swift. Two men, both with Irish names, were sentenced to death for the murder on October 30, and were hanged, dissected, and anatomized next day.[225] A "hot press" was still in operation a year later.[226]

The King now ordered that a regiment of 600 men be raised in Newfoundland. Over 400 of these were soon in arms. By late 1795, defences were somewhat in order; the respectable number of 844 infantry and artillery awaited the French onslaught.[227] But the French showed no warlike intentions until early September, 1796, when a squadron of ten ships appeared and hovered off St. John's. Wallace declared martial law and placed an embargo on trade. A boom was put in place across the Narrows. Three fire ships were made ready. But instead of attacking St. John's, the French landed "about 60" men in Bay Bulls, burnt the houses, stores, flakes, and boats, pressed some men, placed sentries around the harbour to prevent counterattack, captured justice John Dingle, who had earlier boasted that Bay Bulls was "free from disturbance, riot or seditious discourses,"[228] and, after occupying the outport for less than a week, took to their ships.[229] The fleet did some more pillaging in St. Pierre and Labrador. The raid on Bay Bulls was to be the final display of French military valour on the island.

But the war continued. As it did, trade declined. Getting fish to market was dangerous enough; finding markets was just as uncertain. By 1797 export of dried codfish was down by 50% from what it had been in 1794.[230] With most European markets shut, Portugal, which remained open, was quickly glutted in 1797, leaving nearly 110,000 quintals of unsold fish in Newfoundland.[231] Prospects for 1798 were no better. The effects of this downturn were felt at once. The acts encouraging servants to return "home" and the proclamations against dieters were by now largely ignored. Crossing the Atlantic was perilous, and there were in any case no passage ships to carry men back. The population climbed, to about 30,000 by century's end. With the fishery in disarray, the numbers of unemployed rose. The prohibition[232] against carrying passengers to America was still in force, but many[233] people still made their way to the continent. Jobless men congregated in St. John's, their presence adding to the general anxieties of the day, for the period 1794-1800 was one of disturbance and trepidation in Newfoundland, as it was in England.[234] Governor William Waldegrave[235] faced one insurrection in 1797, when a mutiny broke out among the foretopmen of H.M.S. *Latona* in St. John's.[236] It was put down fast, but Waldegrave feared the mutineers had sown sedition on land as well. In May, 1799, long before the governor's arrival, a letter signed by six unemployed men, but representing the protest of sixty to seventy, reached the commander of the island's forces. At least five of the six were Irish or of Irish descent. The men wanted to be allowed to leave the island and seek work elsewhere in North America. This was "the only resource" they had left.[237] The letter, which was seen as menacing, caused a stir in the town, but the needs of the men were addressed, if not answered, by discussion at a public meeting in June. The crisis passed. Yet another commotion, this one nearly an uprising, occurred in April, 1800, among sympathizers of the United Irishmen[238] in the Newfoundland regiment.[239] A plot supposedly aimed at the armed takeover of St. John's was blown; five of the ringleaders were hanged at once, and seven more sent to Halifax "to be further dealt with." The oaths of the United Irishmen were allegedly taken by large numbers both within and outside the regiment. On the Southern Shore, they were said to be taken "almost to a man." This turmoil too subsided, partly through the intervention of O'Donel, now a bishop, who later boasted of his role in bringing "the maddened scum of the people to cool reflection."[240] The effort to transport failed Irish schemes to Newfoundland

and try and make a success of them there might be noted. It would be writ large in the 19th century.

While no spirit of rebellion was to appear among those above "the maddened scum," neither was there abject submissiveness. The St. John's merchants in the 1790s grew assertive, perhaps sensing their new power in the changed circumstances of the fishery. On being asked, by chief justice Richard Routh, for their opinion on a possible duty on West Indian rum "for the purpose of defraying the internal expenses of the island," they vehemently opposed it. They wanted no "species of taxes" introduced "while the present laws of this island continue in force."[241] They went further, expressing some resentment that, since Newfoundland "is not viewed by government as a colony," they "are not even allowed to build or repair our houses." (It is intriguing that they would know what British policy was, evidently resent it, but not try to change it.) Furthermore, they said, in view of the "rapid population" of the island, the "poorer part of the natives" should be permitted more leeway in cultivating the soil. Given the context of sub-colonial Newfoundland, these were not seen as meek sentiments. Waldegrave was much taken aback. He picked up "an insolent idea of independence" among the merchants, which would, he predicted, "some day, shew itself more forcibly."[242] But against all his instincts, he was obliged to consult them. He also had the good sense to heed the advice of the four St. John's magistrates, who cautioned him, at some length,[243] against enforcing his stern proclamations against dieters and home building. "I shall lose no time in profiting by your suggestions, & fulfilling your wishes," he told them.[244] By 1800 the governor, even one inclined to be a martinet, could not rule in isolation. But "colonization," as it was understood in contemporary terminology, was still far off and a "resident fishery," now permanently in place, was still viewed with some consternation. Before departing for good in 1799, Waldegrave suggested a way to obstruct such a fishery. "Could half the inhabitants of this island be sent either to Nova Scotia or Upper Canada," he said, "it would be, by no means, an undesirable measure."[245] The century ended with notions of expulsion still lingering in the British brain.

Chapter 7

Prologue to Politics: 1801-32

POLITICAL REFORM was a late arrival in Newfoundland.[1] One reason for this, as already hinted, was that while the island had no politics prior to the early 1800s, it did have government. Peculiar and amphibious as that government was at the top, at the bottom it was the sort of administration that would have been found in a coastal English county, comprising justices, constables, courts of session, a grand jury, a sheriff and deputy sheriffs, customs officers and their deputies, and other minor officials. Not only did this machinery of government exist. It had existed for a long time. In the larger centers, people no doubt were used to it and accepted it; in out-of-the-way places, it rarely intruded into daily life. In neither case was there a demand for change. There were no direct taxes, unless the Greenwich Hospital duty of sixpence per month from fishermen and seamen is termed a tax. This too made the system palatable. It might be thought that it was mostly a judicial establishment and that the executive part of government remained primitive, but in the 18th and early 19th centuries the two branches were not rigidly separated. The role of justices had always been partly administrative. They sometimes thought of themselves as presiding over districts, as if they were mayors.[2] Naval surrogates in Newfoundland held court but were also executive officers under the governor. (From the 1790s civilian surrogates were also appointed.) In effect, while at the beginning of the 19th century the governor came to the island for only a few months a year, and sometimes less than that, a year-round civil government, complex and adaptable,[3] was in place. It was government in which the people didn't participate (apart from their role on grand juries); it was visited upon them, arriving from London, or, in the form of naval surrogates, from St. John's. The mental habit of viewing it thus, as something imposed from without, likely died hard, if indeed it did die.

The chief omission in the government was, of course, in the legislative branch. An assembly and council were still missing. The British withheld these, imagining that once the Napoleonic Wars ended the old migratory fishery might be restored. After they stopped thinking that, they still withheld them. Withholding them became as much custom as policy. But this deficiency didn't mean the people were deprived of certain basic constitutional rights. Habeas corpus, trial by jury, the right to petition Parliament and the Crown, and the right to appeal supreme court decisions to the Privy Council were available to them, with other freedoms, some of which they didn't know they had. Nor did the lack of a legislature mean the people had no means of reaching and influencing the governor. The grand jury, recognized by governors and judges, and indeed by Parliament,[4] as "the organ of the community,"[5] made presentments on matters unrelated to crime.[6] So did the justices. On occasion the grand jury, or the magistrates[7] in concert, acted as unofficial councils for the governor.[8] They were no substitute for a legislature, but they fulfilled some of its functions. At times the grand jury assumed wide-ranging power. In 1818 it was asked by Conception Bay magistrates to approve a scheme for raising a poor rate; the jury turned it down as "the plan proposed is opening a road to direct taxation."[9] The grand jury and magistrates played big roles in the hands-on, day-to-day regulation of St. John's.[10]

The point is, the reform movement in Newfoundland did not create government, legislative or otherwise. It aimed to substitute one form of government for another, and prior to 1832 it met with resistance, not just from lawmakers and colonial administrators in London, but from a privileged and well entrenched cadre of officials on the island, Protestant local notables, whose interests were best served by carrying on in the old ways. These men already had a modicum of power, and were naturally reluctant to see that power diminished, or its possible augmentation curtailed, by sharing it with others.

We might add that in a fashion, indirectly, through Parliament, Newfoundland could be said — and was said[11] — to have had legislative government. Prior to 1832 the island was represented in the Commons as, say, Birmingham was, for that city had no direct representation there until the passing of the Reform Bill. In the parlance of the day, both were "virtually" represented. British parliamentarians were not slow to enact legislation for Newfoundland when they thought it expedient to do so. After 1775 they legislated often, more than is realized. Apart from separate acts on the courts and fishery, the island found its way into bills dealing, for instance, with the warehousing of goods in North America and the West Indies,[12] or with rum exports into Canada. Parliamentarians by no means thought themselves unqualified to regulate the rebuilding of St. John's after a fire; they specified the minimum widths of streets, pointed precisely to where new "Cross Streets"[13] should be made, and even decided the location of coopers' shops.[14] As the new century began, one statute was of direct benefit to the local fish trade. Enacted in June, 1801, it provided bounties of three shillings per quintal "or Hundred Weight" on "any salted or pickled Salmon, or salted dry Cod Fish" imported from Newfoundland or Labrador into Britain.[15] The bounties remained in effect until 1810.

In the light of this act and, as we will shortly see, some later ones, it was hard to picture the imperial Parliament as oppressors of Newfoundland. Yet reform, if it is to proceed, needs villains in office. In late 18th- and early 19th-century Newfoundland these were in short supply. This too meant change would occur slowly. The governors were certainly autocrats, but they tended to be decent, well-meaning men whose imperial bark was often far worse than their bite. It would be misreading the period to dismiss them as obtuse reactionaries, while portraying the reformers as full of virtue. The reform movement was not a contest with evil but, in part, a struggle for power. (Which is not to say there were no abuses to correct.) It was Waldegrave, not a reform-minded merchant, priest, or doctor, who inaugurated a "Committee for the relief of the poor" to collect money from residents of St. John's for distribution to the needy; over the winter of 1797-8 close to 300 people, over half of them children, were given relief from this source, to which Waldegrave himself contributed generously.[16] James Gambier (governor, 1802-04) proposed "a plan for charity schools,[17] wherein the children of the poor may be taught to read, and be instructed in the Christian religion."[18] Having proposed the plan, he "effected the establishment" of one such school.[19] Gambier also took the bold step of leasing twenty small portions of land for agriculture in the vicinity of St. John's. In 1803 he was so exasperated by certain aspects of administering Newfoundland that, like Reeves, he suggested, to no avail, the need for some resident "legislative power" on the island.[20] But back in London, Lord Liverpool affirmed the "ancient policy" must stand. The "established maxim" was that Newfoundland should never be considered a colony. This was changing, he said, the place had indeed become "a sort of colony." But "it is proper to counteract this tendency as long as possible," while making occasional concessions "to prevent tumult & disorder among the people ... who are in general of a very low and a very bad description."[21]

Gambier's successor, Erasmus Gower, organized a Society for Improving the Condition of the Poor, under whose auspices a schoolhouse was built which in the fall of 1804 had about 150 children, divided by gender into "schools of industry," taught by a master and mistress. Reading was taught, but in addition the boys learned how to knit twine and make nets, while the girls were trained "in carding and spinning wool and knitting stockings, mitts &c."[22] Gower extended the practice of leasing land to provide not only more ground for growing vegetables but also building lots "in the rear of the flakes at the distance of two hundred yards from the water."[23] The harbour front, he noted, was "crowded" with public houses, retail shops, and dwelling houses, many occupied by "artificers" unconnected with "the trade and fishery." The St. John's population had diversified. Carpenters, masons, coopers — there were forty-three coopers' shops by 1820[24] — tailors, cabinet-makers, shoemakers, sailmakers, and other tradesmen were now factors in the life of the town.[25] Room had to be made available for them to build on. Both Gower and Gambier chafed against the petty restrictions on buildings and property they were directed to enforce, and Gower occasionally declined to follow his instructions. He had been given directions, similar to those handed to Elliot and Milbanke, to forbid the erection of buildings unconnected with the fishery within 200 yards[26] of the high water mark in St. John's; but he found it "impossible" to act on the letter of this instruction, which implied that the bustling town of St. John's was "a mere fishing station," and recommended that the order be amended. He had also been told "not to allow any possession as private property to be taken of, or any right of property whatever acknowledged in" land even beyond the distance of 200 yards

— again, a directive similar to that given governors in the 1780s. Gower commented tartly that there was not a single "settled harbour" in Newfoundland in which lands were not held contrary to that clause; hence "I have not thought it expedient to carry this instruction into effect." Near the end of his tenure as governor, he suggested that restrictions on property rights should "be rescinded, or so altered as to recognize the existing customs." While declining to recommend the appointment of a council, though he knew such a body was found "universally" in other colonies, he said the governor should be allowed to call the "civil, judicial, or revenue officers" before him to hear their "opinion on questions of importance."[27] But Gower's suggestions for changes, like Gambier's, were resisted in the colonial office. "The professed object" of policy towards Newfoundland, it was noted, "has hitherto been" to encourage the migratory fishery and "to prevent His Majesty's Subjects who may from time to time reside in Newfoundland, from forming themselves into a colony." That was why there were to be no property rights there.[28] The hoary policy was again left, at least notionally,[29] in place.

Gower's successors, John Holloway (1807-10) and John Thomas Duckworth (1810-12), especially the latter, were much more willing than he to enforce the prohibition against building houses and enclosing land, and residents during their terms had to go cap-in-hand to the governor's secretary if they wished to shingle a house, extend a porch, or erect a chimney. Numerous applications of this nature were rejected. "Tranquility" might reside in St. John's, as the governors often noted on their arrival in summer; Freedom, at least in the sphere of property, did not. Yet enclosing land and building houses went on, often in winter during the governor's absence. In 1807, by official count, there were 3,671 "private houses" in Newfoundland; in 1813 the number stood at 4,444.[30] The pressure from a growing community for more land for private use was irresistible.

Two events in 1807-8 signalled a new era in Newfoundland. The first was the establishment of a newspaper — fifty-five years after one had appeared in Halifax. The veteran printer and newspaper proprietor John Ryan,[31] a Rhode Island Loyalist, came to St. John's from New Brunswick in 1806. Gower, who fancied — wrongly, though governors would not learn this until 1814[32] — that he had the power to control the press, gave him permission to set up a printing shop and newspaper, provided he submit each number of the paper to the magistrates and omit "any matter which, in their opinion or the opinion of the Governor ... may tend to disturb the peace of His Majesty's Subjects."[33] The following year Holloway laid down even more severe conditions.[34] Ryan submitted. The first number of the *Royal Gazette and Newfoundland Advertiser*, published by Ryan and his son Michael, appeared on or about August 27, 1807. It displayed the royal coat-of-arms on the masthead, its motto was "Fear God: Honor the King," and the prospectus promised that its columns would never "offend the Ear of delicacy or distress the heart of Sensibility" nor "be occupied by party controversy." The paper was a single sheet, folded to form four pages. It appeared every Thursday, and was delivered around

St. John's by a carrier. Its contents were notices and proclamations from government offices, mercantile advertisements, news from British and foreign papers, parliamentary and congressional proceedings, and local news. The back page had anecdotes, short essays, and sometimes a "Poet's corner." Editorial comment was rare in the early years; local news was brief. Altogether, it had far more to do with merchandise than politics. Holloway could sleep soundly. Yet the appearance of a newspaper in St. John's was of great importance, since it provided an organ for public debate[35] and alerted the city's population to developments in neighbouring colonies. It was readily apparent from even the bland *Royal Gazette* how far the island lagged behind the Canadas, Nova Scotia, and Prince Edward Island in terms of the progress of representative institutions. Many who had never felt the need for a local legislature might now see reasons for having one. In addition, one newspaper engenders others. Granted, the new birth was not immediate. But when it came, it was outside the governor's direct control. The printing of the *Newfoundland Mercantile Journal* in 1815 marked the beginning a free press in Newfoundland.

In 1808 another event of some consequence is to be noted: the arrival in St. John's of the Scottish physician William Carson.[36] Carson was a complex and secretive man, and in the absence of a memoir or private papers, much about his life prior to 1808 — he was nearly thirty-eight when he landed — remains unclear. He was a student in Edinburgh University's faculty of medicine in 1787-90 but sat no examinations for the M.D. degree and consequently of course did not graduate. Before coming to Newfoundland, he worked as a surgeon in Birmingham for fourteen years. That city had a large and progressive medical establishment; Carson was not prominent in it. In a published list of twenty physicians and surgeons in Birmingham drawn up in 1806, "W. Carson" occurs far down — seventeenth.[37] He now had a wife, Sarah Giles, and a large family. He decided to emigrate. Did he choose a place where nobody knew him? Throughout his career in Newfoundland, he called himself William Carson, M.D. While too much emphasis can be placed on this, it surely offers some kind of clue to Carson's character. He was gifted. Perhaps he'd been slighted by lesser men with degrees, or thought himself somehow diminished by being in their company. Perhaps he felt he really had earned the degree, and that an obstacle not of his making, one he couldn't overcome, a tyrannical professor, an unnoticed regulation, had denied him his just rights. Some deep anger rankled within him, together with a hunger for respect, wealth, and influence. He carried all this to Newfoundland, together with other intellectual baggage derived from what he termed "the study of politics." In this study, the great advocate of liberal reform, Charles James Fox, had been his "guide."[38]

We lose sight of him for two years, during which he began his medical practice and no doubt studied the odd community he'd decided to make his home.[39] St. John's was a place smelling of fish, presided over by a part-time benevolent despot, and with an official population of 5,421, two-thirds of whom were Irish.[40] The economy was dominated by merchants; an astute observer would have sensed their rising power and pretensions. They had by now formed a Society of Merchants. In the period 1807-12, under the leadership of the Irish Protestant James MacBraire,[41] this Society, meeting at a "Merchants' Hall," became increasingly vocal both to the governor and departments of the British government. Their principal concern, naturally, was profit. We find them pressing for increased bounties on cod, for countervailing duties on American produce, and for other advantages.[42] They were not as prone to squawking about the threatened "ruin" of trade as their Poole predecessors, but sometimes they did just that. Yet their themes were often more general. Being "eye witnesses, to the distresses of the people,"[43] they saw it as a "principal duty" to "communicate" to the governor "all necessary information ... and all occurrences [he] should be acquainted with."[44] For example, they proposed insertions in the revised judicature act of 1809 (in which the coast of Labrador from the St. John River to Hudson Strait, together with Anticosti — but not the Magdalen Islands — were re-annexed to Newfoundland),[45] and demanded an investigation into Thomas Tremlett's conduct as chief justice, persisting until due notice of their complaints was taken in London. Tremlett was transferred to Prince Edward Island.[46] They also kept an eye on the high sheriff and other officers. They "conceived it to be their duty" to "expose every attempt of men in office to tyran[n]ize," and to defend "the rights secured to them by the laws and constitution of their country."[47] (Their country being Britain.) Holloway and Duckworth were conciliatory in their dealings with the merchants. They could hardly be otherwise. In 1811 Duckworth called them before him and, with Tremlett present, read aloud the minutes of the official inquiry into the chief justice's activities, conducted in London.[48] This must have surprised even the most Whiggish merchants, for here in effect was the governor reporting to them.

Yet the merchants were as subject to the petty restrictions on buildings and property as the humblest fisherman. They were men of substance, doing business on the crowded St. John's waterfront. To have to beg a naval governor, here today and gone tomorrow, if they could build a shed or extend a wharf was mortifying. MacBraire himself was forbidden to build and repair houses.[49] In the report made to Duckworth in 1810 on structures raised since Holloway's departure, sheriff John Bland noted that ten had been built with "no permission," and of these, eight were put up by merchants.[50] The merchants were not only building unauthorized structures; they were encroaching on the nine[51] or so remaining ships' rooms in the harbour — precious frontage, no longer used for fishing.[52] The rooms had in fact become commons, and merchants and fishermen made use of them without fee for building boats, storing lumber, and other purposes. In 1810 the colonial authorities considered charging quit rents on whatever encroachments had been made on those rooms.[53] Duckworth, with an entourage of officials, perambulated the rooms that summer, spotting encroachments, and stirring up, among the merchants, not just resentment but defiance.[54] Judging the rooms "altogether useless" ("it is long since any Ships have arrived to claim them"), he recommended that they be leased "and the rents applied to various public uses in St. John's."[55] This was accepted, likely because the British thought it would reduce the annual Parliamentary grant to the island, which had risen to a hefty sum.[56] In May, 1811, an act of Parliament[57] took away "the public use" of six named ships' rooms in St. John's, and made it "lawful for the same to be granted, let, and possessed as private Property, in like manner as any other Portions of Land in *Newfoundland* may be." The craftiness of the last phrase will be noted. Yet despite this deliberate ambiguity, the act might well have been seen as a step forward, since it permitted the building of "Dwelling Houses" within 200 yards of the high water mark, the traditional boundary of land reserved for the fishery, and at least did not deny that private property existed. It might even be interpreted as meaning that it did exist. In September Duckworth proceeded to offer building lots to the public on thirty-year leases, the total projected income being about £1,600 per year.[58] To compensate for the loss of the rooms, an area at the western end of the harbour was set aside for the use of fishing ships, should they ever return.[59]

Instead of being welcomed, the act of Parliament provoked opposition. On November 7, 1811, two weeks after Duckworth's departure for England, a public meeting of "Merchants and principal Inhabitants" was held in the Merchants' Hall. It had been preceded by correspondence with the sheriff[60] and grand jury in late October, and the meeting was chaired by the foreman of the grand jury, Alexander Boucher, a merchant. After the meeting opened, this prior correspondence was read. The mover of the motion to read it was Carson. Two months earlier, Duckworth had told him that the "considerable enclosure of ground" he had made — presumably meaning he had fenced it — on the outskirts of the town would have to be removed, since the King's instruction forbad "the occupation of land in this country." Carson rushed to explain how the land he occupied had come into his hands; Duckworth allowed him to stay on it, but noted that he could only hold the new enclosure "during the pleasure of the governor for the time being."[61] He could not actually own it. This display of curtly worded officiousness likely stung Carson, whose temperament could not easily suffer rebuke. And he was always sensitive about land. In any case, now, in the company of merchants, he took his first small step as a public agitator in Newfoundland. After some hesitant debate, the meeting approved an address to the Prince Regent which Carson, with two others, had drawn up. The address cited various grievances. The laws under which the island was governed were of "ancient date" and "inapplicable to existing circumstances." The petitioners had been "surprised" by the statute on ships' rooms. (The word "surprised" was objected to by the merchant Stephen Knight. The act hadn't surprised him, he said. But it was allowed to stand.) The leases on the ships' rooms could be sold on terms "so exorbitant and unprecedented" only because residents had been previously prevented from building and repairing houses, an "impolitic and we humbly conceive unnecessary restriction." (An objection to "unnecessary" went unheeded.) The address went on to note the deficiencies of St. John's: narrow, unlit streets, isolation in winter "owing to the severity of our climate" (what the Prince could do about that wasn't specified), danger from fire, no "Public establishment for the education of our Youth" (though the schools of industry as well as private schools, humble in character, were operating), no "Market-place," and no "legal provision for the Poor." Another act of Parliament was called for that would "establish a Police" with the power to receive the rents from the ships' rooms and use the money to carry out needed improvements. Seven men were chosen — by ballot, though there was some reluctance over this — to form the projected "Board of Police." Six were merchants, one of them Knight, who had objected to more than one part of the address, and at one point said he thought the whole proceeding premature; the seventh was Carson. The British M.P.s who should receive copies of the address were named; the address was to be printed in three London papers.[62]

No allusion was made to the need for a legislature. The minutes of the meeting also show that the petitioners did not intend "censure upon the Government." Loyalty was proclaimed. These were essentially mild transactions. Even so, a controversy followed — the first sign of something resembling partisan conflict in Newfoundland — in which Knight bitterly challenged some parts of the published minutes, and appears to have withdrawn altogether from the process now undertaken. He was answered, harshly, by a trio: Carson, MacBraire, and another merchant, George Richard Robinson.[63] So there was not, even now, unanimity on the side of reform, limited as that reform was, among the merchants. Still, as far as can be seen, the majority did favour it.

The proceedings would accomplish nothing by way of immediate gains, though they did provoke yet another reexamination of the laws pertaining to Newfoundland.[64] But the meeting and address were big events in the small seaport of St. John's. Mild though it was, this was organized political protest, something previously unheard of. Much of Carson's life thereafter was devoted to nurturing such protest. Before an official response to the address had been received, he published a short tract (author: William Carson, M.D.) entitled *A Letter to the Members of Parliament of the United Kingdom* (1812), in which he asserted that the act of 1811 had not only "surprised," but "alarmed," the inhabitants of St. John's, who judged it irreconcileable to a "love of justice, and of liberty." This was certainly taking the protest to a higher plane than what the merchants intended. Carson's pamphlet also tried "to expose the evil genius that has hitherto blasted the fortunes of this Country." Drawing on Reeves' book, he described the history of Newfoundland as one of misrepresentation and oppression by West Country merchants, charged the governors with "ignorance," pomposity, and illegal, arbitrary behaviour, and denounced the naval surrogates as ignorant "of the most common principles of law and justice." He transformed Reeves' unemotional legal analysis into a fierce rhetoric of blame. The enemies of reform were now publicly identified; the battle lines could be drawn. Carson narrowly escaped a libel charge for some of his more extreme comments.[65] But parts of the tract, for instance his account of the scenery and resource potential of Newfoundland (not just fish, but agriculture — a major emphasis throughout Carson's life — and mining as well),[66] were not written in high dudgeon. The genuine note in Carson was, simply, a belief in Newfoundland. He thought the island capable of supporting a large and prosperous population. It had been "completely neglected" by Britain, while "many feeble, puny, and rickety settlements [were] graced with a resident government, and colonial assembly," but if it were now granted a proper constitution, progress would follow. In a second tract, published in 1813, he declared himself convinced of "the capability of Newfoundland to become a pastoral and agricultural country," and called for "a civil resident Governor, and a Legislative Assembly." If governors and other officers continued to slight the people of Newfoundland, he said, "admiration will be converted into contempt, affection to animosity, and submission to revolt."[67] The incendiary last phrase need not be taken as a mere flourish. As later events would make plain, Carson had in him some of the makings of a revolutionary, tempered as they were by lingering attachment, often stated and perhaps genuinely felt, to constitutional principle.

Revolution would remain only an idea in Carson's mind. The times were not ripe for it. Nor were they ripe even for reform, which also thrives best in periods of hardship and uncertainty. By 1811 the Newfoundland economy had entered a period of expansion, brought on mostly by the reopening of the Spanish market for salt cod, on exceedingly favourable terms, two years earlier.[68] With both fish prices and servants' wages rising, the boom attracted a flood of immigrants, some from England and Jersey but many more from Ireland. By an 1804 statute,[69] vessels to Newfoundland had been exempted from the provisions of an act of Parliament of the previous year regulating transport of passengers from the United Kingdom. In effect, all restrictions on travel to the island were dropped until 1816.[70] The number of Irish "passengers" rose steadily during the first decade of the century, but remained at less than 1,000 in 1810.[71] From 1811 to 1815 the annual intake went from 1,200 to nearly 6,000, an increase made possible by a flourishing passenger trade between St. John's and Waterford, in which the Irish-born merchant Patrick Morris was a conspicuous figure.[72] A large number of these new arrivals, who included farmers,[73] craftsmen, clerks, and shopkeepers as well as labourers, stayed on, fleeing one colonial system only to find themselves in another. It is likely that they were of a less tractable cast of mind from the earlier Irish, for the memory of the failed United Irishmen's rebellion was fresh, and Ireland had been brought more thoroughly under the British yoke in the Act of Union of 1801. The Irish flooded into the capital and places close to it. In 1815 it was estimated that there were fewer than 2,500 Protestants in St. John's, but more than 7,500 Catholics.[74] To judge by numbers of people alone, it had many qualities of an Irish town. (The Irish influence wasn't so evident when it came to owning property and holding office, but in this too there was more than a little resemblance to the homeland!) In Petty Harbour and Torbay the Irish were now in the majority, as they were on the Southern Shore and in St. Mary's Bay, Placentia, St. Lawrence, Mortier,[75] Burin, and Tilting; although a minority, they numbered close to 3,000 in Conception Bay.[76] Almost half the population of the island, estimated at "not less than 70,000" in 1814, was now Irish.[77]

The response of the English Protestant establishment to the volatile and growing Irish Catholic component in the population was complex. It was marked characteristically by fearful vigilance, though perhaps not without some trace of tolerant feelings.[78] Officials worried about some kind of "faction" existing among these "loose & vagrant people, without order or principle."[79] Efforts of Catholics in education were deliberately counteracted by government support to the schools of industry.[80] Scrupulous attention was paid to excluding Catholics from holding office under the government.[81] (But they did serve on juries.) Incoming Irish women were monitored in case they were of low character. A careful eye was kept on the activities of Irish priests, and warnings about "Romish" zeal in proselytizing among Protestants were sounded in dispatches. Renegade priests[82] who might gather a following among the "low Irish" and stir up sedition were watched with special care. The typical wariness in the governor's approach to the Irish Catholic clergy was, however, balanced by his shrewd sense of their utility to him. O'Donel and his two successors in the Catholic episcopate, Patrick Lambert (bishop, 1807-16) and Thomas Scallan (bishop, 1816-29) were perceived as useful in keeping their priests and people in order. No great effort of manipulation was required. The last two were as likely as O'Donel to think of parts of their flock as "scum," and all saw it as their duty to promote "Loyalty, Peace and Good Order among His Majesty's Subjects here."[83] And in fact an illusive "good order," cloaking the power structure, mostly prevailed. O'Donel would have shown his utility even if he hadn't been directly bought off, but the British gave him a "pension" of £50 a year in 1805, and in 1814 increased the payment to Lambert. Scallan was denied the boon.[84] As an additional inducement to loyalty, the Catholic church was conceded certain benefits. Land was made available for chapels. In 1811 Catholics were allowed to bury their dead.[85]

Fear of Catholic "ascendancy"[86] in Newfoundland as more Irish arrived inspired the governors to renewed efforts in support of the Church of England. Governors referred continually to the "Established Church," so whether or not this title had a legal foundation,[87] they thought such a church existed, and in this case the thought alone counted. They shielded Anglicanism and encouraged its expansion in a number of ways. They assisted in recruiting clergy in England for outharbour parishes, and urged on the colonial secretary and Archbishop of Canterbury the importance of increasing the number of Anglican priests on the island. Otherwise, Holloway feared a Catholic "triumph over our established church."[88] They paid, sometimes out of their own pockets but more substantially out of public revenues, in support of building Anglican churches and manses. Donations for such projects were also expected from the inhabitants, but the government's share of expenses was often considerable.[89] Such use of public money was routine. No one objected to it, not even, until much later, the Irish, who must have thought the Church of England "established" too. In addition, ways were found to supplement the stipends paid to priests by the S.P.G., either through salaried appointments as surrogate or (in St. John's) magistrate, or directly from public funds.[90] Lay readers in outports without a minister were also paid salaries by the governors.[91] These efforts were endorsed by the British government, which in 1805, for instance, authorized spending £700 towards the construction of a new house for the Anglican minister in St. John's, and in 1811, in order to encourage priests to remain longer in Newfoundland, approved the addition of £100 to the annual salary of S.P.G. missionaries who had worked on the island for ten years.[92] In these ways, an alliance between church and state was effectively created. At the same time as a governor was contributing heavily to the Anglicans, he might let it be known, say, to those setting up a benevolent society among the Irish that in such an initiative "all national and religious dictinctions should be carefully avoided, as tending to prevent that union of heart and general co-operation among his Majesty's subjects."[93] This might not be hypocrisy. The deepest prejudice can lurk under such unexamined platitudes. And given the typical attitudes of the times, perhaps none of this is surprising. If "profound anti-Catholicism" characterized the American revolutionaries,[94] it would be pervasive too in Newfoundland officialdom, though perhaps given more piquancy in the latter case by the addition of the normal English distaste for Irishmen.

While many Irish congregated in St. John's, others drifted into remote regions where, out of sight of officials, they could not only fish but clear ground and perhaps start small farms. They settled among the Methodists on the North Shore of Conception Bay, in places such as Gussets' Cove where the land looked tillable; some went to the Cape Shore, the Alpine-like coast south of Placentia, where there were however fertile chinks between the hills; the Careen family founded the agricultural outport of Point Lance,[95] in the southwestern extremity of the Avalon peninsula. Most would spend their lives in safe obscurity. But the hostility felt towards them among the island's governing establishment meant they were all vulnerable. A few (it is not clear how many) would feel the long arm of the law.

An example of the kind of tyranny possible under the government of Newfoundland in 1813-14 is provided by an episode involving Irish settlers on Bell Island, which now had a population of close to 300, two-thirds of them Catholics.[96] In 1813 the deputy sheriff of Conception Bay, John Mayne, was directed by Richard Keats[97] (governor, 1813-16) to go to the island to investigate alleged encroachments by one Sweeney and to forbid all such encroachments and enclosures, except for small gardens to raise vegetables. Mayne reported in November that on finding James Sweeney, a man unconnected with the fishery, had "enclosed more than he would be able to cultivate in two hundred years," he ordered him to confine himself within certain boundaries "which I conceive sufficient to raise vegetables enough for the consumption of a family." Sweeney, Mayne wrote, was "a single man, and has no body to provide for but himself." When Mayne returned the following year, he found that Sweeney had expanded his holdings "considerably" to about forty or fifty acres. Acting on orders from Keats and naval surrogate David Buchan, Mayne "levelled to the ground" a house and other buildings occupied by Sweeney, and "demolished" as well a building owned by another would-be farmer, Owen Kelly, who had made an enclosure of ten to twelve acres. His intention was to create "a lasting example" for the people. Sheriff Bland, sent by Keats to investigate the incident, ordered that no further erections be made, that Sweeney's and Kelly's crops, when grown, be disposed of, and that the land the two men said they possessed be abandoned. This likely meant the destruction of fences, though Sweeney's was constructed in such a way as to constitute "a task for Hercules to remove it." Bland's report to Keats on Sweeney's "fancied estate" was full of derisive humour. The "old man" had come from Ireland "ten or eleven years ago and laid his plan for raising an estate." He had then sent for his three sons, who were now employed away from home as servants in the fishery. Sweeney "has hardly five words of English, and is perfectly unintelligible to me," said Bland.[98]

Many aspects of the incident remain obscure, and the likelihood that Sweeney and Kelly had displayed uncommon greed cannot be overlooked. The hunger for land was not easily satisfied among people inured to an overcrowded homeland, where they were perhaps "dependent on a potato-patch for economic and physical survival."[99] Yet in the Newfoundland outports there was far less regulation of hinterland property than in St. John's. (Sweeney's and Kelly's enclosures evidently did not include fishing rooms.) Those who wanted unclaimed land normally just took it.[100] Besides, Keats had been given permission to allow enclosures for farming, and by late 1813, in the vicinity of St. John's, had in fact leased 110 pieces of property up to four acres in size.[101] He would later claim that the availabilty of leases was partly responsible for the great influx of Irish in 1815.[102]

All told, the arbitrariness of the proceeding is evident, as is the cruelty. While it was occurring, the law officers in London were again pondering the legality of the governor's control of property in Newfoundland. If the question of a governor's right to remove a person from his possessions had been referred to them, they noted, they would have wished to be told the particular law by which he is "invested with such power."[103] The Sweeney-Kelly incident, at its essence, displays abuse of power. It can be taken as symbolizing much about Newfoundland society in 1814, for in it we see representatives of a scorned underclass pitted against a dominant and arrogant elite. Reform feeds on such episodes. But this one would pass without notice by vigilant citizens, though Keats testified that St. John's was now "a place easily agitated."[104] It even slipped by Carson, whose nose was as keen as a bloodhound's for official transgressions. Six years later it would be reenacted with far different consequences, both immediate and long-term.

We will shortly see how closely the reform movement and Irish-Newfoundland aspiration were wedded. It was in many respects a moving story. It was, in part, a struggle against prejudice and exclusion. It was an assault by the powerless on an elite. But it had its ugly side, for it featured violence, hatred, and division too. It wouldn't be long before many sensible people, Protestant and Catholic, looked back to the early decades of the century as a period of peace and mutual help. As the Irish in Newfoundland start insisting on their rights and, not long after, begin their climb to political power, it is to be noted that in the world of the early 19th century they were not the only ones with cause for complaint. The aboriginal peoples of Newfoundland and the territory of Labrador rarely entered officials' consciousness (though some honest effort was directed at saving the Beothuck). Native-born Newfoundlanders were marginalized in the power structure too. Conditions in some of the remote outports of whatever faith were primitive and, on the French shore, lawless. You didn't have to be Irish to learn that life could be nasty, brutish, and short. They had no monopoly on injustice. And, as we will see, to dump Ireland's grievances onto a colony with its own set of problems — which, in part, was what happened — was not just a complicating, but an inhibiting, factor in its development. Further muddling the story of the Irish in Newfoundland was the fact that, while they fought for and won a higher rank in society, not all the Irish would be welcome on the ascent. It would not only be the English who viewed Irish insurgency with alarm, but some of their own unjustly ostracized compatriots.

* * *

The total Newfoundland catch of cod in 1813 exceeded that of any year since 1788.[105] During the following summer tradesmen in St. John's were observed abandoning their normal avocations to take to the boats. In Burin a committee formed to attract an Anglican missionary stated that £300 per year could be counted on for his support from local sources.[106] They eyes of the trade, however, were on Europe and the Duke of Wellington. As the merchants knew, the prosperity now being enjoyed by all hands was due, in no small measure, to the exclusion of the two traditional competitors, the French and, following the outbreak of the War of 1812, the Americans, from the Newfoundland fishery. In November, 1813, anticipating the end of war, St. John's merchants signed a petition asking that neither the French nor Americans be restored to their fishing rights along the coast on the return of peace.[107] The arguments they presented, especially against the French, were telling. Since the French had been driven from the north and west coasts, they pointed out, the "British" fishery there had been prosecuted with vigour: "Dwelling houses, substantial stages and stores would soon rise up in that quarter of the island, were it certain that the builders would at the return of peace be allowed to retain their property." It was, in fact, a critical point in Newfoundland history, one in which the lack of an assembly is strongly felt. An assembly would have given legitimacy and legal force to the views which now, expressed by merchants, could be dismissed as embodying only a narrow interest. Keats forwarded the petition to

London, adding his own support.[108] Neither representation was effective, and soon after the peace treaties (1814-15) with France, and that with America in 1814, the Newfoundland fishery was once more international in character. As if readmitting them were not in itself an act of singular obtuseness, the French were restored to their right of fishing, not as defined at Utrecht or in the Treaty of Paris of 1763, but instead "upon the footing in which it stood in 1792."[109] The evident intention was to return to them the exclusive right they had, to all appearances, won in the treaty and declaration of 1783. St. Pierre and Miquelon were again handed over. It took a little longer to let the Americans back, but in a convention of 1818 their rights were extended by granting them permission, not just to fish along the south coast from Ramea islands west to Cape Ray (sometimes termed the "American shore"), on the west coast,[110] and on the coast of Labrador, but to dry and cure fish on unsettled parts of the south coast (again west of Ramea). Once these parts were "settled," however, it would not be lawful for them to dry and cure fish there without the agreement of "inhabitants, proprietors, or possessors of the ground."[111] These last phrases appeared to imply that private property rights existed on the island.[112] Otherwise, the concerns of inhabitants were ignored. In 1819 Parliament passed an act[113] giving the King power to make regulations to enforce the convention with America. This made it lawful for American fishermen to enter any harbours in British North America for shelter, repairing damages, purchasing wood, and obtaining water. Outside treaty shores, no foreigner was to fish, cure, or dry fish of any kind within three "Marine Miles" of the coast.

Late in 1814 Newfoundland dried cod entering Spain was subjected to "rapid and enormous tariff increases."[114] The boom showed signs of ending. Fish had been scarce along some coasts in 1814, and while "a spirit of adventure" had driven wages to "an immoderate and unprecedented pitch" — they had quadrupled since 1811 — prices in the foreign markets were dropping. Uncommonly large advances had been made in servants' wages, and many planters were ruined. In turn, merchants lost their supplies.[115] In the spring of 1815, the wages offered were considerably lower than in the previous year, and by March very few servants had been hired. Boatloads from Ireland kept coming. There was unrest among Irish labourers in St. John's that didn't subside until June. They exchanged oaths, as was their habit in times of distress, but to what purpose was not clear to uneasy officials. Chief justice Caesar Colclough, a Wexford man, doubted if plans were afoot among his "wild, foolish and headstrong" countrymen "against the government of the country." MacBraire and Lambert were active in suppressing such rioting as occurred.[116] By late 1815 the economy had worsened. Nervous creditors demanded payment of debts with "unexpected urgency," and between the settling of accounts in late October and mid-December there were around 700 writs issued and nearly forty insolvencies. A grim sign of what lay ahead was a fire in St. John's on February 12, 1816, in which 120 houses were destroyed and many more damaged.[117] Among the houses burned were several built by merchants on the ships' room called

Admiral's Beach, which had been made accessible to lessees by the 1811 act of Parliament. Eleven of the chastened owners were soon petitioning for an abatement of rent and lamenting the "unfavourable change" in the trade and fishery.[118] Newfoundland had started on a slide into a serious postwar depression that would be a catalyst for change in the economy and society. But Keats said there was no "immediate necessity" for altering the laws relating to Newfoundland. "I would on no account," he stated, "propose any departure from the old system."[119]

The Newfoundland economy was in fact more diversified than ever before, owing to the emergence of a herring fishery on the south coast and a big expansion of sealing to the north of St. John's. The herring fishery in Fortune Bay had attracted merchants and settlers from the 1790s, in which decade also men began taking seals in spring from large boats and schooners.[120] This sea-going hunt quickly became the dominant mode in the industry. In 1799, 40,000 seals were taken in Conception Bay alone.[121] Between 1811 and 1816 the average seal kill was nearly 130,000. There was a drastic falling-off in 1817, but it rose to 165,000 the next year.[122] Here, then, were new supports for the economy when codfish failed to come inshore or the markets dried up. But life still depended heavily on cod. 1816 to '18 were years of declining trade and faltering hope. Once war ended, Newfoundland saltfish merchants faced not only higher duties in Spain and elsewhere in Europe, but also increased competition, principally from the newly subsidized French fishery.[123] Higher duties meant increased prices to the consumer, which in turn meant lower demand. This forced the exporter to keep his prices down at a time when the costs of catching, curing, and shipping fish were likely rising. In 1816, following a summer of reduced catches, poor weather for drying fish, yet another "vast emigration"[124] from Ireland, and high unemployment, the average price for fish sold in the European market, after subtracting the cost of freight and insurance, amounted to approximately 18% less per quintal than the price paid to Newfoundland suppliers. So, at any rate, a select committee of the House of Commons was told.[125] Bankruptcies and a general contraction of trade followed. As merchants collapsed, those dependent on them — planters, tradesmen, shopkeepers — followed them into insolvency.

The *Royal Gazette* and *Mercantile Journal* of 1816-18 provide a dismal record of insolvencies, dissolutions of partnerships, notices from merchants quitting the fishery or withdrawing from business in outports, notices of sheriff's sales, and other bleak testimonials of failure. Only the auctioneers seemed to thrive. One observer noted that by February, 1817, when the crisis was far from over, no fewer than 100 shopkeepers had been ruined in St. John's alone. He estimated that "not five" of the remaining shopkeepers in the town were "perfectly solvent."[126]

The winter of 1816-17, one of the coldest remembered by inhabitants, was also one of the hungriest. Francis Pickmore (governor, 1816-18) had come to the island in September with £10,000 relief for the victims of the February fire. Before his departure in November, he earmarked some of the money to pay return passages of 1,000 of the numerous destitute poor in St. John's back to Ireland;[127] but this was a small response to an approaching tide of misery. In the months that followed provisions had to be doled out with great caution by committees of inhabitants to about 2,000[128] paupers in the town, while measures were put in place to billet and feed nearly 1,000 more homeless men, mostly Irish, who had found no productive work in the summer fishery.[129] (The population of St. John's was now about 12,000.)[130] Although an "armed association" was formed in St. John's to protect property, and unusual vigilance was maintained by civil authorities and the trade elsewhere on the island, sporadic looting of merchants' warehouses and vessels broke out in a number of communities.[131] A brig sailing from Halifax to St. John's, carrying bread and flour, put in at Bay Bulls and was seized "by the almost starving inhabitants."[132] At one point an "armed mob" was on a rampage in St. John's.[133] Organized Carbonear and Harbour Grace "rioters" demanded, and got, access to merchants' provisions, "on pain of plundering of the stores."[134]

Sealing in the spring of 1817 was crippled by lack of provisions and by the actions of hungry rioters who obstructed the outfitting of vessels; the summer cod fishery was poor. Yet another grim winter came, during which Pickmore, the first governor to be instructed — in 1817 —to live year-round in Newfoundland, perished. More fires in St. John's could only have deepened the gloom. In November, two major fires, widely thought to have been deliberately set, destroyed stores of winter provisions and left 2,000 homeless.[135] Demands for relief were received from Burin and Bonavista.[136] Merchants in Harbour Grace started a fund to send indigent Irish back home.[137] The distress, felt keenly in the capital, was again by no means confined to it. Gradually, as the number of immigrants dropped off and outmigration to the U.S. and neighbouring colonies removed part of what was said to be the excess population, the crisis appeared to diminish, though mercantile gloom and pleas to aid the distressed, or to keep distressed outporters away from the capital,[138] continued to feature in official correspondence until 1822.

Economic woes led to calls for changes in the island's government and spurred a newspaper debate[139] about its future prospects. For their part, St. John's merchants in 1817 demanded "a permanently established government in this place," which in fact they got when Pickmore was told to overwinter. But they evidently wanted more than just a full-time governor. The "established government," they said, should have "power to enact such local regulations as are necessary for the well being and good order" of the community. As to its "precise mode," they did not presume to say what this should be. They asked colonial secretary Henry Bathurst to send one or more commissioners to the island to investigate conditions there, after which the commissioners would propose "what description of government may be best adapted to our particular circumstances."[140] They didn't press for an assembly or council, only for further study. Skepticism about the value of an assembly was widely felt. It is not hard to see why. No one welcomed the prospect of direct taxation. And democracy could, as hinted earlier, allow the underclasses into the power structure, together with their populist spokesmen. Sheriff Bland mocked assemblies as "mere burlesques," desired only by "needy and contentious spirits."[141] Many in the trade likely shared his view. It seemed clear that what had caused the depression in Newfoundland was not a lack of democratic institutions, but collapsing markets overseas and subsidized competition. How can a "*local legislature*," a critic inquired, "influence the price of fish in a foreign market?"[142] This was a hard question to answer. In a sense, the whole history of Newfoundland would hang on it. Carson was active, behind the scenes[143] and in public, in these discussions, arguing that the causes of Newfoundland's downturn lay in "the peculiarity of our laws and government." Laws and governments could be changed. Amidst the gloom of 1817-18, he stoutly maintained that, provided those changes were made, the island could become a sufficient and comfortable home for its "despised and insulted people."[144]

In view of the £10,000 from London and the postwar relief effort generally, the last phrase might well have seemed just empty rhetoric. Yet an incident now occurred that, to many, validated it. In 1818 the Cupids fisherman James Landrigan,[145] a first-generation Newfoundlander of Irish descent, contracted a debt of over £13 with a supplier operating in Conception Bay. The following year an action for debt was brought against him in the surrogate court of Harbour Grace, and a decision given in favour of the merchant, with costs. The surrogate was the Church of England priest F.H. Carrington. Judgment was by default, since Landrigan did not appear. A constable proceeded to Cupids and attached Landrigan's property. He tried to take possession of the fisherman's house but was prevented from doing so by Landrigan's wife, Sarah, who threatened "to blow his brains out." On July 5, 1820, another surrogate court, sitting at nearby Port de Grave, summoned Landrigan to appear before it. Two surrogates presided this time: Buchan, commander of H.M.S. *Grasshopper*, who had figured in the Sweeney-Kelly affair, and another priest, John Leigh. Landrigan declined to come to court, saying "he had no shoe to his foot and was nearly naked, and was ashamed to appear before gentlemen." On being told by a constable that a party of marines would come to get him, Landrigan replied that he wished them "a damn good time of it." The court issued a special warrant to arrest him, and he was taken into custody that same day. The warrant charged him with contempt of court and resisting arrest. The next morning Leigh (with Buchan concurring) sentenced him to receive thirty-six lashes on his bare back and ordered that possession of his property be taken "this day," which meant the immediate eviction of his wife and four young children. Landrigan was tied to the shores[146] of a flake, and the boatswain's mate of the *Grasshopper* inflicted fourteen lashes with a cat-o'-nine-tails, opening deep gashes, whereupon the fisherman, who was an epileptic, fainted. The attending surgeon, seeing that Landrigan was "much convulsed," presumably with a seizure, asked that the punishment stop, and it did. A day later the same court met in Harbour Main, and an Irish fisherman Philip Butler, another debtor, was sentenced to receive thirty-six lashes for contempt. He was given twelve. When Butler's wife refused to vacate her home, which she claimed was her own property, the door was broken down and she and her children were evicted.

The treatment of Butler and Landrigan aroused deep outrage, particularly, for reasons that didn't need to be spoken, among the Irish. In early November, the two fishermen, prompted by a reform party which now included not only Carson but Morris, William Dawe of Exeter, who had landed from Liverpool in 1816 and set up as "Attorney & Solicitor,"[147] and Lewis Kelly Ryan, son of John Ryan and editor of a reform journal, the *Newfoundland Sentinel*, made the daring move of taking out actions of trespass for assault and false imprisonment against Buchan and Leigh in the supreme court. Both claimed damages, Butler £500, Landrigan £1,500. On the bench was a young chief justice, Francis Forbes,[148] who stated that the cases hinged on the question of whether surrogate courts had the right to punish for contempt. In his view, they did have that right. The jury in each case accordingly returned a verdict for the defendants, though not without expressing "abhorrence" at the "unmerciful and cruel punishment" given to Landrigan. Forbes, too, rebuked Leigh and Buchan for "a mode of proceeding which disuse had rendered obsolete in England; and which in every view of the present case, was particularly harsh and uncalled for." At the close of Landrigan's case, the fisherman gave notice of appeal to the Privy Council.[149] A few days later, Leigh's attorney told the court that "great misrepresentation" had led to the punishment of Landrigan, and that Leigh intended to buy back the room at Cupids and restore it to the fisherman and his family.[150] Landrigan was soon restored to his possessions. He lived to a ripe old age.

Court actions to recover small debts were normal, as were attachments of property; Carson himself resorted to litigation frequently to recover debts as low as £2-3.[151] And in 1820 there was still nothing highly abnormal about the whipping of civilians.[152] But Butler and Landrigan were not pickpockets or vagrants but poor fishermen in debt, one a sick man, both booted off their land after summary conviction by a court already pointed to by reformers as a throwback to quarterdeck justice. Altogether, as Dawe perceived, "the moment was too favorable to be lost." The whipped fishermen became symbols. Losing in court only added to their symbolic value. On November 14 a public meeting in St. John's passed resolutions expressing a determination to pursue legal and constitutional means "to have *the law repealed* which it appears sanctions such arbitrary proceedings in the Surrogates," which could only be viewed with "*abhorrence* and *detestation*." A petition to the King was soon in circulation which linked the Butler and Landrigan incidents to other grievances, including the lack of a "superintending legislature in the Island." "We labor under the want of that representative organ of expression which is the boast of the British constitution," the petitioners said.[153] It was the first time a petition from Newfoundland had made this demand. (If that is the right word. The petition said also: "it is not the want of a local legislature of which we have principally to complain; it is the state of such laws as have been made for us," a complaint that could of course be answered without the creation of an assembly.) Around 180 signed the document, which reached England early in 1821, together with governor Charles Hamilton's point by point rebuttal. Dawe went to England in March to press the petitioners' case with the government and Parliament.[154]

Hamilton said that "it does not appear that any of the principal merchants [in St. John's] have given their sanction to the petition,"[155] and this seems to have been the case. The signatories were predominantly Irish.[156] The "principal merchants" had rarely had trouble making their voices heard, if not always heeded; it was the stifled Irish who saw the assembly as a way to join the chorus. Not that the names lacked respectablity. Some of the Irish were now rising merchants, and there were in any case a number of solid Protestant names on the petition. It could hardly be ignored. In March, Bathurst told Hamilton that the King "has under consideration how far the altered state of Newfoundland requires some alteration of the existing laws with respect to it." But Hamilton was to "discourage all expectation" of an "independent legislature," since the "particular evils" complained of, even if correctly stated, were not due to the absence of one[157] — a valid counter to most points raised in the petition. But in a subsequent dispatch Bathurst said that "the surrogates should in future be cautioned against inflicting corporal punishment" in cases similar to those involving Butler and Landrigan. The proper punishment was confinement.[158] That point at least was conceded.

The St. John's reformers' response to the incident at Cupids was to a degree rhetorical and staged. Not so the response in Conception Bay, where the authority and standing of surrogates were likely further undermined by the affair. The rule of law there may have fallen, at least temporarily, into disrepute; though perhaps, as illustrated by Landrigan's initial refusal to cooperate with the court, a tradition of resistance was already entrenched. A constable sent to execute a court order, in an expulsion similar to Butler's and Landrigan's, was shot at in Brigus early in 1822, compelling one of Hamilton's captains, a surrogate, to send in the marines.[159] Libellous placards against the surrogate later appeared in Harbour Grace. The Brigus incident was serious enough to be reported to London.[160] As we will see, ten years later there was a near uprising in Harbour Grace, though directed at merchants rather than government officials. This was as close as the island would come to a Boston Tea Party. But the rebellious spirit exhibited in it did not spread. Reform in Newfoundland would proceed, as in the Butler-Landrigan affair, incrementally. The old autocratic system would topple, but slowly, only after a succession of mostly non-violent buffets from without, and some as well from within the system.

The most serious challenge from within[161] came from chief justice Forbes, a Bermudian who arrived in Newfoundland in 1817 and left in 1822. His early life is obscure, but he may well have travelled to the U.S. as a youngster and there sniffed Yankee liberty. In any event, he was a London-educated barrister of liberal instinct and some sensitivity to colonial aspiration. His years in Newfoundland saw the rigorous testing of many of the assumptions, regulations, and informal structures that had grown up on the island — in sum, "the peculiarity of the local government," as Forbes phrased it[162] — against the principles of the English law and constitution, for the judge's guiding principle was that "the law of England is the law of Newfoundland."[163] Governor Hamilton found one of his orders checked almost immediately after his arrival in 1818, in a case relating to the payment of the Greenwich Hospital duty.[164] The following year sheriff Bland found himself in court, charged with forcible entry into a building in St. John's used by citizens to house a fire engine. Bland had been acting on the governor's orders, but Forbes stated that if he had entered property where the Crown did not have title "he is a Trespasser, however high the orders under which he may act," and even if the Crown had title, Bland might still be "liable to a criminal prosecution" if he entered "with force, and without the solemnity of lawful proceeding."[165] The rule of law applied to high and low. This was Forbes's message. It was not one governors and sheriffs were used to hearing. In 1819 he took a more important step. In the King v. Kough and Houston (August 23), a case centered on an official attempt, instigated by Hamilton, to reclaim land near Fort William that had been in private hands for sixty years, Forbes examined British constitutional documents — he read many of them in Reeves' *History* — and concluded that the legal right to own property in Newfoundland had already been conceded. He found for the defendants.[166] It was a big moment in Newfoundland history.

Fearing the loss of more critical cases in Forbes's court, Hamilton asked London to appoint a law officer in Newfoundland to defend the Crown's interests; an attorney general was duly sent.[167] But in 1820 the governor was to be dismayed by an even more stunning decision. Jennings and Long v. Hunt and Beard (October 18-19) was an action provoked by the decision of surrogate Hercules Robinson in Sandwich Bay, Labrador. Robinson was a ship's captain who had enforced regulations for the salmon fishery proclaimed by the governor. The plaintiffs' nets had been removed by order of the surrogate, whereupon they appealed. The surrogate, Forbes noted, "had received the orders of his commander in chief, which he merely obeyed as a subordinate officer, without question as to their legal authority." But the judge questioned the legality of Hamilton's proclamation, affirming he had no legislative authority to issue it; hence it was in effect illegal. The surrogate "mistook that for law, which was not law, so for that his judgment was erroneous." This judgment, obviously of general application, undermined in a single stroke the informal gubernatorial system of ruling Newfoundland. Governors could no longer simply issue orders and expect to be obeyed; the orders had to be grounded in a statute, or at any rate in law. The surrogate's case was supported in court by "a bundle of orders and other acts of the local government" stretching back at least as far as Palliser, from which, Forbes noted, "I am to infer that a legislative authority in this government, unknown to the laws of England, but claimed under a prescriptive exercise in Newfoundland, is now for the first time sought to be established in this Court." This seemed to him "so dangerous an innovation" that he took some time to respond to it and reject it. Reeves had indeed suggested that the supreme court might function as a quasi-legislature. But Forbes would have none of it. A court was only that, a court. Legislative authority had to be sought elsewhere.[168]

In another case (Trimingham & Co. v. Gaskin, August 21, 1821) of striking significance, the military had its day in court. The defendant was a soldier in the artillery who fired on a merchant ship, the *St. Vincent*, passing through the St. John's Narrows. All ships leaving the harbour were required to obtain a pass from the governor; this was a means of ensuring that port charges were paid. If they didn't have a pass, they would be fired on, compelled to heave to, and required to pay charges, together with the cost of shot and powder. In the case of the *St. Vincent*, charges had been paid, but in the copy of the pass in the hands of the soldier, she was described as a brigantine, not a brig, whereupon, perhaps being pedantic in matters of naval nomenclature, he promptly fired off a cannon. Merchants had long been angered by the practice of firing on ships. In 1815 a vessel leaving for Valencia with cargo was struck by a ball from Fort William and forced to put back for repairs. Damages were estimated at £600. Forbes now effectively ended the practice. "I know of no principle in the common law," he said, "which sanctions such a mode of bringing offenders to justice."[169] Hamilton was obliged to ask the military commander to desist from firing on vessels until details of the case could be laid before authorities in London. But the law officers of the Crown sided with Forbes. Seeing military force thus constrained could not help but be noticed by the inhabitants.[170] The governor was both a military[171] and civil officer. The garrison was a symbol of his power and of British power, as were the men-of-war. And more than a symbol. They were there to be deployed, not just against foreign enemies but against unruly inhabitants at times of crisis. In 1820 there were about 700 troops in St. John's. The number would fall to 150 by 1833, not a large contingent but, as events would show, by no means ineffective. Newfoundland was occupied territory and would remain such until the withdrawal of the garrison in 1870.

During Forbes's term as chief justice, all eyes were on the supreme court and the judicial system generally. With fairness installed at the top, lower courts could be scrutinized for nepotism and arbitrary judgments. Dawe ended up serving a six-day jail term for persistently questioning the jurisdiction of a court of oyer and terminer, a relic of former days which governors persisted in convening.[172] Such bravado was applauded, even if it centered on an abstruse point of law. Forbes had given a licence to such fearless probing. Yet despite his reformist instincts, on his return to London in 1822 the judge, who served briefly as consultant in the colonial office, argued against creating an assembly in Newfoundland. It is striking that someone as nonpartisan and fair-minded as he was would so argue. The points he made are worth noting. He had no doubt that some "local power" to make bylaws and regulations for "the towns and populous parts of the colony" was needed. The "fact of a large body of people collected together" sufficiently justified that. But in

Newfoundland the different settlements "are disjointed and remote from each other, and can only communicate by water." People were "scattered about the colony in small societies."[173] He implied there were no (or few) shared interests from place to place, so no body to legislate generally was called for. If one were, legislative business would necessarily be conducted in winter, when "both sea and land are impassable." Again, the great bulk of inhabitants "have never expressed any wish to have a local legislature." St. John's alone had petitioned, he noted, and it contained not more than a tenth of the population. Only "a few hundred" there had expressed a desire to have an assembly. "It may therefore be fairly inferred from the silence of the other inhabitants," he said, "that the desire is not generally felt in Newfoundland." And in St. John's itself "the principal merchants" were decidedly against "a local parliament."[174] All told, even if a legislature were practicable, which he doubted, and unanimously sought by the Newfoundland people, which it clearly wasn't, Forbes said that no case has been made to show that such a body "would be at all useful to the island."

Forbes was wrong to say only St. John's had petitioned for an assembly; Ferryland district had as well.[175] But most of his arguments had some merit. Newfoundland from Notre Dame Bay to Fortune Bay was still, as he saw, a collection of disparate settlements, some of which might be still as connected to Poole as to St. John's, which is to say, likely not very connected to either. Horizons in most places were narrow; perhaps they had even narrowed from earlier days. W.E. Cormack, a young St. John'sman of Scottish descent and upbringing, visited Bonaventure[176] in Trinity Bay in 1822, prior to undertaking his celebrated walk across the island. His brief description focused on the economy. About a dozen fishing families culivated only a few potatoes and some other vegetables. All other provisions, clothing, and fishing gear were imported ("from Europe and else-where") and supplied by Trinity Bay merchants, who in return took and exported the fish and oil. The image he provides is of a functioning economy, but one where the merchant was not just a supplier but a buffer between the labouring inhabitants and the outside world. The inhabitants weren't able to give him "any information" about the interior, not having strayed far "from the salt water." The "whole population of Newfoundland," Cormack wrote, "may be viewed as similarly circumstanced with those of Bonaventure."[177]

If that community was, to some degree, a little world onto itself, which is what Cormack appeared to be suggesting, it could well be imagined that the French shore was even more so. But that might not have been the case. Cormack visited parts of the French shore too in 1822, finding a considerable settlement at Sandy Point,[178] where the economy was based on salmon and fur. Most of the parents in the twenty European families, he noted, were from England or Jersey. But a Micmac population was present as well. There were four resident-owned (and -built) schooners in the community, "in which most of the male inhabitants make one voyage annually, either to Halifax, Nova Scotia, or to St. John's." Some bartered their produce "with trading vessels from Canada or New Brunswick, or with the vessels of any other country that may come to the coast, receiving provisions and West Indian produce." Sandy Point wasn't the only settlement Cormack visited. He also found seven or eight families at "the Barasways";[179] these too had their own schooner and carried their produce to St. John's or Halifax. Farther south, at the Great and Little Codroy Rivers, were twelve or fourteen families. He mentions other inhabitants in Bonne Bay and Bay of Islands to the north (neither of which places he visited) and gives some notion of settlement on what he calls the "American portion of Newfoundland," i.e., between Ramea and Cape Ray. Here, then, was a Newfoundland coast very different, at least in some parts, from the old English and Irish shore, apparently more in touch with the world, closer to North America. The population on the west coast would for obvious reasons remain low, but it would grow, for the French needed some residents — they themselves could not legally overwinter — to look after their fishing establishments, and where they didn't have or want such establishments a few Anglophone livyers would put down roots. In time, some Frenchmen and Gaelic-speaking Scottish Highlanders from Nova Scotia would as well. The French shore would gradually assume something of an international character and by the 1860s would differ strikingly from the earlier settled parts of the island.

Besides these coasts, Labrador remained a distant and obscure wilderness, hardly comprehensible let alone governable. There was as yet no collectivity that an assembly could be said to represent. Even Carson conceded that the inhabitants did not blend "into a distinctive national character" but rather preserved differences inherited from their place of origin.[180] Another reform-minded pamphleteer, in 1823, gave credence to the view that "in its present condition" the colony was "not susceptible" of representative government.[181] Coast to coast cleavages and conflicts would in fact become too apparent in the decades ahead. As we will see, the Assembly, when it came, after a promising start did little to heal, and before long only exacerbated, the divisions already forming, or formed, within Newfoundland society. An argument could be made for Forbes's view that what Newfoundland required was not an assembly but "something of a parochial character to attend to ... little local concerns." Hamilton by 1822 had reached a similar conclusion.[182] So had a controvertist in the local press.[183]

Yet a colony — and nation, if such it was to be — needed an assembly as an instrument of progress, an affirmation of growing independence and responsibility, a forum for legitimate political contest, and a symbol of the people's democratic life. For all the anticipated difficulties, it might have been just as well to bring it in in 1822 or '23 as ten years later.

After yet another winter of distress and scarcity, 1822 brought an "unproductive" fishery and more groans from the grand jury in St. John's about pervasive "poverty and want."[184] Reports were received of "the dark and melancholy condition" of Protestants along the northeast coast; Catholics, we might well imagine, were as badly off, if not worse. Twillingate, Moreton's Harbour, and Exploits Burnt

Island were all hard pressed, though the population in each was growing. Exploits Burnt Island[185] already had 175 people.[186] It was not until 1823 that a good fishery brought an end, short-lived though it was, to the postwar depression. Yet even in 1822 an optimisitic feeling was afoot in some quarters. There was talk of roadbuilding, though Hamilton commented on the unfitness of roads "even a mile out of St. John's" and noted the frequent impediments of bogs and ponds.[187] But plans for roads between Placentia and St. John's, and between Conception Bay and St. Mary's Bay, were studied, the latter course being favoured because Lieut. Valentine Munbee, on Hamilton's orders,[188] trekked between Holyrood and Salmonier River in the summer and drew attention to the shortness of the route. An estimate was made of the cost of building this road.[189] A renewed interest in minerals[190] and the interior[191] also sprang up, and again this was connected with an exploratory walk. Cormack, who had studied mineralogy at Edinburgh University, started from Random Bar, the spit connecting Random Island to the mainland, in Trinity Bay on September 5 and emerged at Flat Bay on November 2. He was accompanied on the entire route by a Micmac guide, Joseph Sylvester, and on the last sixty miles by another Micmac named Gabriel. A short account of this journey, with a map, was published two years later[192] and afterwards expanded into a book. The southern interior, for Cormack kept well to the south, was thus partially unveiled, together with (as noted above) the unfamiliar coast between St. George's Bay and Bay d'Espoir. Cormack didn't substantiate claims being made that the interior was more suited to agriculture than the seacoast,[193] but he offered some hope for cattle raising, especially in the west. He also found "well-stocked farms" in St. George's Bay, which had "the most extensive tract of good soil any where on the coast of Newfoundland."[194] He provided as well tantalizing, and exaggerated, reports on coal deposits.

One of Cormack's purposes was to locate and study the Beothuck Indians. He found none, though he encountered a Mountaineer (Innu) from Labrador, James John, and his Micmac wife on Meelpaeg Lake and, later, a number of other Micmacs, now the true possessors of the interior. It was clear to Cormack that the Micmacs routinely traversed the island between Bay d'Espoir and St. George's Bay on known routes. The rocky and boggy interior was as familiar to them as the eastern coast was to the English and Irish. The Beothucks, meanwhile, were on a rapid path to extinction. Buchan had found about seventy-five of them on Red Indian Lake in 1811, and had tried valiantly to save them. Through bad luck and the fear and cruelty of the Indians, his effort failed.[195] A bloody episode in 1819 led to the capture of a woman, Demasduit, who was taken to St. John's. She died of tuberculosis in 1820, while Buchan was bringing her back to her people. When Cormack went looking for them in 1822, perhaps fewer than twenty Beothuck were left alive. He made another fruitless search in 1827, commencing this time at the mouth of the Exploits. Two other expeditions in 1828, carried out by Indians "of the Canadian and Mountaineer tribes,"[196] failed to find them. In 1829 the last known Beothuck, a woman named Shanadithit, died in St. John's. The killer again was tuberculosis. Taking Beothuck to the capital had proved as fatal as letting them be.

Cormack's 1822 trek and the curiosity about minerals and Beothucks that inspired it were signs of a modest intellectual awakening taking place, mostly in St. John's. This was occurring even during the postwar depression but accelerated after it. Residents were aware of "the rapid progress of the polite arts among us."[197] Such remarks reflect an amelioration of life at some levels of society. A public hospital had opened in 1814. A postal service (but not an official post office) was in place. Horse races were popular. Clubs formed. A few professionals with elevated tastes and pretensions, of whom Carson was one, had made their appearance and had an influence. By the 1820s, amateur theatre was a regular feature of life in the capital, and Harbour Grace had a "play house" by 1824. Plays were critiqued in the press. Local printers were active. Poetry reared its head. Although Carson's two political pamphlets were printed in Greenock, the lengthy pamphlet on Butler and Landrigan, *A Report of Certain Proceedings of the Inhabitants of the Town of St. John* (1821), was printed in St. John's. But most pamphlets of the 1820s were published in London. Three or four were by the garrulous Morris, prominent during and immediately after the Butler-Landrigan fracas as chairman of the committee of inhabitants pressing for reform.[198] One didn't need to live in Newfoundland long to write a book about it. The literary naval lieutenant Edward Chappell, after a brief encounter, wrote *Voyage of his Majesty's Ship Rosamond to Newfoundland and the Southern Coast of Labrador* (1818), filled with snobbery and lies. The priest L.A. Anspach's *History of the Island of Newfoundland* (1818) was of a different order entirely. It was a pioneering work with particularly important chapters on the fisheries and inhabitants. A "St. John's Library" was in existence for a time, and British monthlies, newspapers, and books were available. Forbes and the Irishman Patrick Kough[199] set about establishing a book club in St. John's in 1820. Carbonear had one by 1827. Efforts to improve education continued, with public schools by the 1820s already beginning to assume a denominational character.[200] Private schools also operated. Mrs. McCauley's "Young Ladies' Seminary" was underway in 1813. To all appearances, illiteracy was on the decline.[201] In 1820 there were four newspapers in St. John's, a fifth was projected, and one was announced for Harbour Grace.[202] One of the St. John's papers, the *Public Ledger*, calls for particular notice. It was founded in 1820 by Alexander Haire and Henry Winton,[203] the latter an immigrant from Devon who established himself as a stationer, bookseller, and bookbinder. From 1823 Winton was sole owner and editor of the paper, which was to play a leading role in the life of the island in the decades ahead.

In August, 1822, a public meeting was called in St. John's to discuss the state of the colony, a committee was struck, and a memorial was soon on its way to London.[204] The memorial stressed the need for "a local government," "a civil government," "a government formed on the basis of the constitution of England."

Oddly, the words "assembly" and "legislature" were not used. Perhaps the committee thought an assembly was alluded to by inference.[205] But there might have been differences of opinion among members about the kind of "local government" that was required. In 1823 the printed draft *Bill for the better Administration of Justice in Newfoundland*[206] was circulated in St. John's. It made no mention of a legislature but instead proposed the annual election of "a committee" to regulate the capital, to be chosen at a public meeting called by the governor. Bathurst told Hamilton that the British government would not "press the adoption of such clauses," but intended "merely to offer them" as the only practical "expedient," given the state of the "colony,"[207] a tepid endorsement.

Such opposition as there was to this and other parts of the bill among reformers quickly dissipated. They would accept, for now, municipal government, which was, after all, "civil" or "local" government, i.e., what they had asked for. The stream of comments that flowed to Bathurst included, significantly, objections by the Roman Catholic clergy and laity of St. John's to the section of the draft bill dealing with marriages.[208] The right of Catholic priests to solemnize marriage, recognized since the practice of their religion had been permitted, was confirmed in a Newfoundland Marriage Act in 1817. (Though not without protest from Dissenting clergy, who saw in it a tendency "to establish popery.")[209] Now, in the proposed new bill, they were to be granted this right only when it was not convenient to have a Church of England priest perform the ceremony. This would mean that Catholic priests would not be able to marry their parishioners in, say, St. John's or Harbour Grace. The petition against the bill in October, 1823, addressed to governor Hamilton, was the first organized protest by Roman Catholics in Newfoundland. With nearly 600 signatures, it represented a powerful interest. It coincided with the arrival in St. John's of the Irish Franciscan, Michael Anthony Fleming.[210]

In June, 1824, three acts[211] of Parliament were passed that are said to constitute Britain's "recognition" of Newfoundland's "colonial status." In the acts "the last vestiges of the age-old policy were swept away." So it is claimed. The "colony had triumphed."[212] It is true that Newfoundland was *called* a colony in the acts, and they did represent advances on various fronts. But if being a colony meant that Newfoundland was to be permitted to regulate its own internal affairs, then the "recognition" was minimal. There was to be no assembly. His Majesty could, however, create "Bodies Corporate and Politic, for the Government of any Town or Towns" in Newfoundland, and the "Bodies" could make bylaws for "regulating the Police" of the towns, for preventing and abating "nuisances,"[213] and for prevention of fires. The narrow jurisdiction of these municipal bodies was thus carefully spelled out. They could also impose "reasonable and moderate Rates and Assessments" upon inhabitants and householders to carry the stated "Purposes" into effect. The reference to elections was dropped. The corporations were to comprise "such Persons as to His Majesty shall seem meet," meaning they were to be appointed. All this amounted to only a slight relinquishment of power by the colonial office. Britain would still legislate for Newfoundland in most matters, internal and external, and until the corporations were established, would of course continue to legislate for all. Nothing in the legislation said that the corporations were to be set up; it was simply made "lawful" for them to be set up. The process through which they were to come into existence was left undefined. This was in keeping with Bathurst's earlier statement that the British would not "press" this reform. Yet they expected that the corporations would, in time, appear. A "Mayor" is mentioned in one of the acts.

Some parts of the acts have an antique air about them. One paragraph requiring that "no Ballast, Stones or any Thing else hurtful or injurious" be thrown from ships into harbours was almost identical to an order issued by John Guy! Another clause forbad anyone to "shoot" his net "upon the Net or Sean of any other Person," another venerable provision. But as a direct consequence of the Butler-Landrigan affair, the surrogates were replaced by a system of circuit courts. These would function in three districts, the boundaries of which would be determined by the governor. Each court was to be presided over by either the chief judge or one of two assistant judges, all of whom were to be qualified barristers. This renovation, which became effective in 1826, was widely trumpeted, at least initially, as a major reform. As for the question of property, any doubts in that quarter were removed. The governor was given power to sell "all" remaining ships' rooms and to grant "waste and unoccupied Lands." The clerk of the supreme court would function as a registrar of deeds to record the granting, devising,[214] conveyancing, and mortgaging of "any Lands or Tenements." Roman Catholic objections to the draft bill's suggested regulation on marriage were answered, though Methodists remained unsatisfied with the final wording.[215]

Clauses in one of the acts returned to fishing rights in Newfoundland. No "Alien or Stranger" could take bait or fish in Newfoundland waters, apart from those having treaty rights, i.e., the French and Americans. The King was again authorized, as he had been in a 1788 act, to order the governor to remove stages, flakes, and other works built by his subjects on the French shore, together with their ships and boats. Anyone refusing to leave could be compelled to go. The fine for refusing to leave was £50 sterling. One clause stated who exactly had the right to take, cure, and dry fish in Newfoundland. All subjects of his Majesty residing in the United Kingdom or in "any" of his "Colonies, Plantations or Dominions" had that right. They had "the Freedom of fishing and taking Bait" anywhere in Newfoundland (the French were momentarily forgotten) and had as well "Liberty to go on shore on any vacant or unoccupied Part" of the island or Labrador to cure and dry their fish and make oil, as well as to cut wood, make stages, build ships, boats, and other necessaries. This was not altogether a new regulation, though it removed all possible ambiguities from prior laws.[216] Bermudians, once denied access to Newfoundland to cure and dry fish, now were granted it, along with Nova Scotians and all other colonials.

There may be something in the claim that the 1824 acts gave Newfoundland "colonial status," but the British in effect retained firm control. He who is prepared to give away the shop thinks he runs it; does run it.

At one stage in the drafting of the new legislation, an appointed council "with certain legislative powers" was envisaged.[217] Its role, at first to be mainly confined to regulating St. John's, "would be extended further" if it proved effective. The colonial office withdrew the proposal at the last minute owing to the intervention of Morris and Dawe, who were in London representing the inhabitants.[218] But when the new governor, Thomas Cochrane, arrived in St. John's in October, 1825, he carried orders to appoint a council "to advise and assist the Government" and immediately proceeded to have one sworn in.[219] It comprised chief justice R.A. Tucker, the two new assistant judges, and Lieut.-Col. T.K. Burke, commander of military forces in Newfoundland, a Roman Catholic. Burke was unable to take all fourteen oaths demanded of councillors, one of which, the Test Act, in force until 1828, required him to abjure transubstantiation, but he could and did take the oath of allegiance, and Cochrane thought that sufficient.[220] He was, however, overruled by Bathurst in London, and Burke was not summoned and never did sit on the council. This episode further aggravated Catholic discontent. Cochrane later suggested bishop Scallan might be named a councillor; this was again vetoed.[221] Yet the appointment of a council was obviously an improvement in the system of government, bringing it more in line with those in other colonies.

Early in 1826 Cochrane also tried to introduce municipal government in St. John's, in accordance with requirements in the new statute. Public meetings were held in February, March, and May. A controversy erupted. Petitions reaching the colonial office disclosed sharp divisions in the population, centering mainly on taxes. One opinion, supported by a majority at the May meeting, resisted taxing only "Inhabitants and Householders," as specified in the 1824 act. They favoured a tax on the rental value of houses, thereby forcing absentee landlords to pay up as well. Merchants and others were fiercely opposed to such a measure and begged Cochrane to canvass public opinion more fully before forwarding the suggestion to London.[222] They seemed to think a majority of citizens would oppose direct taxation for any purpose. (The shrewd John Bland had noted that direct taxes were regarded as "obnoxious" in Newfoundland.)[223] In the event, Cochrane decided that further public meetings would disturb "the subsisting harmony,"[224] and by late 1826 the project of a St. John's corporation was dropped. James Stephen, counsel in the colonial office, was taken aback by the failure, since, he said, the corporation had been approved by the inhabitants' "deputies" as the act was being drawn up, "if indeed it was not introduced at their desire." In view of what had happened, he suggested his Majesty might establish "a legislative council for the internal government of this colony," with "some mixture ... of members elected by the people."[225] Given Stephen's considerable influence, a legislative assembly, in principle much favoured by him,[226] could not be far off.

In 1826 Cochrane had more to occupy him than reorganizing government, for by then Newfoundland had fallen back into another serious depression caused by a combination of continuing high tariffs in Spain — precipitating a further decline in imports and reduction in prices[227] — increased Norwegian competition in that market, and poor fisheries at home. These were conditions no local authority could alter. All it could do was offer relief to those affected. Cochrane loved the trappings of high office, but one of his main jobs was overseeing the distribution of relief. He carried this out, however, with a certain aplomb and, it appears, not entirely without compassion, though he was inclined to blame distressed inhabitants for extravagant living and admonished the clergy to teach them "frugal habits."[228] As reports of distress reached him, he re-introduced the system of able-bodied relief, putting the needy to work building roads, repairing streets, and other tasks. In the winter of 1825-6, Bonavista and Tilting were in desperate straits; the governor had to send a warship to Fogo Island to stop people from breaking into merchants' stores. Some thought was given to sending troops to Harbour Grace. Cochrane spent £2,100 on relief, a tidy sum, but £200 less than the annual cost of his "colonial vessel," on which he and the judges could coast in style through the outports, and just one-half his salary.[229] Hardship, though not on the scale of 1825-6, persisted in ensuing winters. To the consternation of London, the expenses of running the Newfoundland government were rising sharply, with Cochrane himself adding to the costs by living, or trying to live, as a grandee. The governor's spending had to be curtailed, but he eventually carried through his plan to upgrade the path to Portugal Cove into a proper road and built as well a hugely expensive residence for himself to make living in "that dreary country,"[230] as he termed Newfoundland, a trifle more palatable. His elegant "Government House" remains the home of the lieutenant-governor to this day. The road to Portugal Cove, upgraded through poor relief, was important insofar as it permitted quicker communication between St. John's and Conception Bay towns. A "Union Packet Boat" operated from Portugal Cove in 1828.[231] Travel to and from Harbour Grace by carriage and packet boat soon became a regular feature of 19th century life.

By 1827 the cost to the British Treasury of maintaining Newfoundland was thought to be "so burthensome" that a decision was made to cut Cochrane's salary by £1,200.[232] The parliamentary grant for salaries more than doubled from 1823 to 1827, rising to £12,461.[233] Meanwhile, rents from leases of public land declined. Net proceeds from duties rose slightly between 1819 and 1828, but far below the rate of increase in the costs of government.[234] Most customs house revenue derived from duties on alcohol; other merchandise "necessary for the British fisheries" (including food, clothing, implements, and boats) was exempt.[235] The path of financing the colony by placing an ad valorem duty on almost all imports, and of increasing that on alcohol, was considered. A plan to that effect in 1827,[236] in the midst of depression, sent panic through the Newfoundland trade. Petitions against it arrived in London from the St. John's Chamber of Commerce (which had replaced the old Society of Merchants), and from Harbour Grace, King's Cove, Aquafort, and Port de Grave.[237] But Cochrane's bosses made it clear that "the Colony would have to pay its own expenses."[238] Various schemes to impose local levies for the public hospital and other purposes had been proposed over the years, but most collapsed quickly owing to the lack of constitutional authority. Forbes even doubted that the Greenwich Hospital duty could legally be collected in Newfoundland. Altogether, the prospects for the Treasury were gloomy. British colonial policy might have changed somewhat since the 18th century, but profit and loss were never far from sight. The objective "to rule the colonies on the cheap, to get the most out of them for the least,"[239] essentially remained in place. As the bills rolled in, and Cochrane sent other proposals requiring not just approval and extra expense but parliamentary action, the idea of an assembly was greeted with less than the accustomed hostility among colonial officials. By October, 1828, Stephen was noting that on "every" topic connected with Newfoundland "the want of an internal legislature is continually felt." He suggested that the 1829 Newfoundland bill (the 1824 acts were in force for five years) make provision for one.[240] Internal British government constraints as much as pressure from Newfoundland led in time to the granting of the boon.

But pressure in the colony mounted as the time for bringing in the new bill approached. It is hard to say which of the forces now moulding public opinion was strongest. It could simply be that the assembly was an idea whose time had come,[241] or at least was rapidly approaching. Carson and Morris had drummed the many advantages, economic and otherwise, accruing from a legislature into people's heads, and even Winton, skeptical by nature, supported it. As already hinted, a progressive outlook had spread throughout the community. That outlook was shaped in part by news from overseas, for the late 1820s brought some liberal sentiment to the fore in England, such as that leading to the repeal of the Test and Corporation acts[242] in 1828. An assembly was, over time, seen by many as a natural step forward in the evolution of the island, one thinking people would favour. Some nativist feeling was afoot; this too fueled, though probably not by much, the desire for local government.[243] It was also perceived, in both England and Newfoundland, that critical parts of the 1824 laws had proved to be defective. The corporation for St. John's had been discarded. Attorney general James Simms said that the system of circuit judges was "a total failure" and should be replaced by ten sedentary district courts.[244] A clause in the fisheries act could place the livelihood of fishermen and planters in jeopardy in the prime weeks of summer.[245] It dawned on people that London was not able to legislate for Newfoundland.[246] The decisive influence, however, was likely that of the merchants, whose natural aversion to an assembly was overcome by their greater fear of increased duties imposed by London. Winton in the *Ledger* kept telling them the duties were coming. The only check to the "evils" that would result, and the only way to prevent the duties from rising further, he said, was an assembly, which would of course, at least in theory, control all taxation, direct and indirect, apart from imperial duties. No doubt the merchants thought they in turn could control such an assembly. In public meetings at St. John's and Harbour Grace in December, 1828, protests against additional duties took precedence over calls for a legislature, though both initiatives were supported at each meeting, and petitions were forwarded to London on both subjects.[247] The merchants were, at last, onside with reformers. But it was self-interest rather then idealistic argument that drew them there. Not that self-interest necessarily equated with excessive greed. Trade was now at a low ebb, as was illustrated by the 1829 bankruptcy of the Poole firm Spurrier, headquartered at Burin but with premises elsewhere in Placentia Bay.[248] Another big merchant, Danson of Harbour Grace, with premises also at Holyrood and Bay de Verde, followed shortly into insolvency.[249] These were major happenings in the colony. As noted earlier, collapsing merchant houses dragged many down with them. Sometimes people even deposited their savings with merchants. These would be lost in the general ruin.

Despite the petitioning, and despite arguments on Newfoundland's behalf presented in the Commons by Robinson, now M.P. for Worcester, the British government in 1829 balked, choosing merely to extend the existing laws until the end of 1832.[250] "We have not attained even to the *dignity* of a corrupt and rotten borough in England," Winton snarled.[251] The notion of a parliament in Newfoundland struck some Britishers as comical. If the "cod-fishers" get representative government, said a *Quarterly* reviewer, "we shall next hear of the liberated negroes of Sierre Leone."[252] William Cobbett too had a poke at the "miserable" colony.[253] Such remarks, published and commented on in St. John's, no doubt stiffened the resolve to pursue an assembly. But by mid-1829 another issue, Catholic rights, was at the forefront in the colony. Daniel O'Connell's election to a Commons seat in Ireland had precipitated reform of laws relating to Catholics. In April the Catholic Relief Bill passed third reading in Parliament and received royal assent (whereupon it of course became an Act). The news reached Newfoundland in early May. Catholics were overjoyed. In Harbour Grace the "glorious epoch" was marked by a "tremendous" bonfire, while "the streets were paraded by a band of music, playing beautiful and delightful airs."[254] But the bliss was premature. In December it was learned that the act, on a legal technicality, would not apply to Newfoundland.[255] It wouldn't have taken a great deal of effort for the British to remove the technicality, but in fact they didn't do so until 1832.[256] (A local legislature would have been able to extend the Relief Act to Newfoundland inhabitants, as that of P.E.I. did for Catholics there in 1830.)[257] Here, then, at the end of yet another poor fishing season, was one more source of anger, protest meetings — there were two in St. John's in December[258] — and petitions — one with 700 signatures was prepared in January.[259] In choosing a word to describe relations between Catholics and Protestants in Newfoundland, Cochrane picked "tranquility" over "harmony." He added: "a small spark would excite a flame not easily subdued."[260]

There was now one more reason to fear that spark. In 1827 bishop Scallan, suffering from a liver condition, asked Rome to appoint a coadjutor to help in the administration of the church and to have the right of succession. He recommended three possible candidates, in order of merit: Fleming was first, James Sinnott second, and Timothy Browne,[261] an Augustinian priest who had been in Newfoundland more than fifteen years, third. He preferred Fleming because he was not only "learned" and "graced with the highest morals," but was "more prudent than the others."[262] It was a fateful moment in the history, not only of the Catholic church in Newfoundland, but of the colony itself. In the event, Catholics soon had a new hand at the tiller. Fleming was consecrated as Bishop of Carpasia in late October, 1829; the ailing Scallan died the following May. Now in command, Fleming sent his own petition on the Relief Act's application to Newfoundland. He asked for this on his own behalf but also for "forty thousand of his Majesty's faithful and loyal subjects."[263] The Bishop of Carpasia already talked as if he were an elected politician with a constituency.

In 1830 and 1831 agitation on both fronts, religious and political, was kept up. Another petition to the King went from St. John's in September, 1830, provoking, unexpectedly, a long editorial in the *Royal Gazette* warning that "we are not yet ready" for representative government. Given the power of merchants, the editorial (doubtless conveying Cochrane's sentiments) stated, "there would be *no* freedom of election" in Newfoundland.[264] Such statements had become eccentric. Calls for an assembly now emerged from places outside the two chief towns. Placentia[265] petitioned; so did Carbonear,[266] Brigus,[267] Port de Grave,[268] Western Bay,[269] and Old Perlican.[270] There had been feeling against a legislature in some outports; people feared it would be dominated by St. John's. The opposition faded. Some residual hostile opinion from within the old bureaucracy and from Poole, which still had economic links with Newfoundland, was swept aside.[271] In July, 1831, Robinson told the Commons, which was being asked to appropriate over £11,000 to defray the charge of Newfoundland's civil establishment, that he had been instructed by the inhabitants to say that once a legislature was granted "they would never ask that House for another farthing." He was told that the British government was "most anxious" to give Newfoundland colonists "more direct control over their affairs than they at present enjoyed."[272] Such remarks were eagerly seized on and reported. Late in 1831 big meetings were held again in Harbour Grace and St. John's; at the latter, a motion was passed pointing to the "absolute necessity of obtaining a Legislature" and noting that a sufficient revenue for the island could be raised "without being made burthensome to the people."[273] The words bespoke confidence. The dawn of a new day was imminent.

A few clouds from Conception Bay threatened stormy weather.[274] As hinted earlier, a mutinous disposition already existed there, for reasons not well understood. In 1827 the merchants, householders, "and other respectable inhabitants" of Harbour Grace and Carbonear had called attention to the "very dangerous state of the public peace" and begged to have a "military force" permanently stationed in the district.[275] A "considerable part of the lower orders," they said, exhibited a "spirit of insubordination to, and defiance of the laws," which manifested itself in depradations on property, "almost daily" insults to individuals, and opposition to civil authority. Their request was denied.[276] But events would soon show their worries were not without foundation. In June, 1830, a brawl at a merchant's premises in Carbonear grew into a riot involving 6-700 men. A "blood-thirsty and villainous scene" (to quote Winton) ensued.[277] One of the brawlers was thought to have been the instigator of an earlier riot in Brigus. January, 1831, brought another fracas, this time at Harbour Grace. About eighty "painted or masked" ruffians surrounded a house at which a dance was in progress; most then entered and besmirched the partygoers with "blubbered mops."[278] Yet another outrage by a "lawless mob" in Harbour Grace took place in May.[279] A group of "shoremen and servants" employed by the insolvent merchant Danson demanded payment of "their several shares and wages." When the trustees declined, the men, despising any legal remedy, went to Danson's stores and rolled 100 casks of oil into the street. They relinquished the oil only on being promised payment that evening.

Summer brought a "remarkably bad"[280] cod fishery. The unusually cold winter that followed was one of great misery, sickness, and deprivation, complicated further by the threat of cholera. On January 9, 1832, in an astonishing display of solidarity as well as numbers, some 2,000 or more[281] fishermen and shoremen met on Saddle Hill, between Carbonear and Harbour Grace, to consider ways "of getting clear of truck — the ensuing spring."[282] They met again on February 9. Their objective was "to compel their Merchants and Employers to adopt a different mode of dealing with them from that which had heretofore constantly prevailed." So Tucker, administering the government in Cochrane's absence, phrased it.[283] He thought the new "mode" was to apply to the cod fishery; i.e., that it was to govern prices paid by merchants for fish, and by fishermen for supplies. The first posted advertisement for the gathering seemed to suggest this, for it called on fishermen "to shake off the yoke they have so long and unjustly (tho' patiently) borne." A general antipathy to what the men called the "truck system"[284] was certainly in evidence after the meeting in January, when they paraded through Harbour Grace "with flags and colours, upon one of which was 'Down with all Truck.'" But the assemblies likely had more to do with the approaching seal fishery. As magistrate John Stark said, the men "would not proceed to the ice, unless the merchants agreed to give them all cash for their seals."[285] The merchants were evidently trying to force men to take "truck" (i.e., goods) for their shares of the seal catch, and the men were demanding the "liberty to dispose of [their seals] how or in what manner they please, after paying any debt they may owe the owners of the vessel or supplier." So a "fisherman" from Carbonear explained the root of the affair.[286] The "great and growing evil"[287] of truck was being extended to sealing, and the sealers resisted.[288]

Merchants were summoned to the meetings to learn the men's decrees. Carbonear firms fell into line at once, but the Harbour Grace company of Thomas Ridley declined to take part in the meetings and refused to meet the demands. On February 18 about 130[289] men attacked Ridley's schooner *Perseverance*, in port, with hatchets and saws, and damaged masts, rigging, and spars in an evident attempt to prevent her from going sealing. They rendered her "pretty nearly a complete wreck."[290] A week later, Tucker issue a proclamation offering a reward of £100 for information leading to the arrest and conviction of the offenders and a free pardon to those involved in the ransacking who were willing to betray their accomplices. He declared such meetings as those on Saddle Hill "Unconstitutional and Illegal." The proclamations were torn down in Harbour Grace, and the sealers proceeded, despite the presence of magistrates and constables, to force the desired "mode" of payment on shipowners in both towns.[291] By March 20, the sealers had "put to sea and quietness [was] again restored."[292] In effect, this was a sealers' strike, and the sealers won, through sheer force of numbers and not a little violence and intimidation. In August, as if by punishment from above, a fire in Harbour Grace destroyed nearly 100 buildings and left 600 homeless. The Ridley establishment was among those burnt. If it was a divine visitation, it was not clear whose side divinity was on.

To one 20th-century observer, the strikers exhibited "sophistication" and "dedication." The strike was a sign that "The plebeian population was vibrant and active."[293] It struck Winton, now the most influential journalist in the colony, somewhat differently. He was deeply shocked by the goings-on in Harbour Grace and railed against "the rabble of Conception Bay" in the *Ledger*.[294] Yet for a decade he had in effect advocated a process through which such "rabble" might get a say in the government of the colony. If this was a worry, he soon had another one at hand. The *Ledger* had long been a friend of Catholic emancipation, but in 1831 that issue, as it pertained to Newfoundland, was becoming entangled with O'Connell's political moves back in England and Ireland. To Winton, "the Liberator" was a troubling and divisive figure. "We are no very great admirer of Mr. O'Connell," he said in April.[295] The comment is judiciously phrased. Winton's view likely differed little from the normal opinion of O'Connell among the English establishment, where the great Dan was seen as "Agitator, Demagogue, and Jesuit."[296] But among the Newfoundland Irish O'Connell had many friends, one of whom was Fleming. Throughout 1831 a sizeable fund was raised locally for the national "tribute," being collected for O'Connell in Ireland; the money and a piece of plate with an inscription noting the Irishman's effort "in the cause of freedom" were sent overseas. Part of the collection was raised in the Catholic chapel.[297] The bishop gave £20.[298] In March, 1832, Fleming delivered a eulogy of O'Connell at a meeting of the Benevolent Irish Society. O'Connell, he said, was to be compared with Scotland's William Wallace. He had enemies, but so did the "distinguished characters" of other nations "who endeavoured to light up the spirit of freedom and independence" He was the "regenerator of his degraded country," and "every nation over the globe" would cheer him "in his glorious career."[299] Here were Fleming's true colours, his militant Irishness, on full display. The canting (as Winton would have seen it) about freedom, as well as the phrase "degraded country,"[300] would have made a sensitive and proud Englishman, and such the *Ledger*'s editor was, sit up and take notice. What else was Fleming hinting had "degraded" Ireland but English rule? Who else had denied her freedom but English kings? Fleming had gone far, and would shortly go further, on a dangerous political road.

In March also Newfoundland got the longed for news. It was to be granted representative government. In the evening of April 2 St. John's was illuminated. Next day Carson, somewhat hastily, announced his candidacy for an Assembly seat.[301] In August, once Parliament acted,[302] Cochrane arrived back in St. John's with a new commission and detailed instructions for setting up the representative regime.[303] There would be a six-man Council[304] on which the chief justice, attorney general, other officers of the government, and the soldier turned farmer, William Haly, would sit. (The Relief Act now having been extended to Newfoundland, a Catholic could sit on the Council; yet there was still something offensive in the oaths councillors had to take, and Fleming soon made his objections to them known. In the event, the British government was in no hurry to put Catholics there.)[305] All laws had to be passed by the Council as well as by the Assembly; thus the Council had legislative as well as undefined executive functions. (But until 1842 it is properly called simply the Council, not executive council or legislative council.) The governor could "suspend any of the Members of [the] Council from sitting, voting or assisting therein" — a power, as would soon be pointed out, "inconsistent with the free exercise of any legislative function."[306] He could also adjourn, prorogue, or dissolve the Assembly, and as well had "a negative voice in the making and passing" of laws, which meant his assent was required. The power to reserve[307] a bill was not given him. All laws had to be sent to the King for "approbation or disallowance." No time limit for such approbation or disallowance was set. In theory the King could disallow a piece of legislation ten years or more after it had passed. Parliament placed one severe limitation on the fiscal powers of the Assembly. The duties collected in the colony (as noted earlier, no direct taxation existed) were to be spent with the "advice and consent" of the Assembly, except for a sum not exceeding £6,500, which was to be reserved for the maintenance and support of the governor and other high officials. This clause in the statute would be repealed when the Assembly made adequate provision for the civil list. The British wanted no repetition of the pre-revolutionary American experience, in which governors had to go as beggars to assemblies for their salaries.

The "General Assembly" would comprise fifteen members elected from nine districts, St. John's having three members, Conception Bay four, and Placentia and St. Mary's (one district) two. The districts covered the coast between Cape St. John in the north and Bonne Bay,[308] an arm of Hermitage Bay, in the south. The remaining coasts, including all the French shore, were to be unrepresented. (This didn't mean they were outside Cochrane's government. His commission gave him authority over the whole island, together with the coast of Labrador as redefined in an imperial act of 1825.)[309] The franchise was considered generous for the time. It of course excluded women. Every man twenty-one and over who had occupied a house for at least one year "as owner or tenant thereof," who was "of sound understanding," who was a British subject by birth (or who had been lawfully naturalized), and who had never been convicted of any "infamous crime," could vote in the district in which his house was located. One didn't need to own property of a certain value to vote, or pay rent at a set rate, as in Upper and Lower Canada.[310] Nor were there property qualifications for members. A qualified voter who had been resident for two years could stand for election.[311]

The election was called for early November. The campaign was peaceful enough, apart from a chilling series of incidents in St. John's, where five candidates stood for the three seats. At the center of the controversy was John Kent, an Irish-born commission agent who was Morris's nephew and suitor of Fleming's sister Johanna. (He married her in 1834.)[312] In 1832 he was in his mid-twenties. He had played a minor role in Newfoundland affairs up to then, but in September he offered himself to the electors, stating in his advertisement that "Our Constitution has as yet only half developed itself." In a nominated Council "irresponsible to the people," he said, "oligarchical principles must prevail." The "people" had the task of "prostrating" those principles. And so "I present myself to you."[313] Winton was the sort of man who responded to such presumption. On September 7, he cautioned voters not to select for the Assembly "inflated schoolboys, or superannuated old men," a clear allusion to Kent and, though Winton later denied this, to Carson. Kent, who was singularly thin-skinned — he once formally protested to the governor when he wasn't addressed as "Esquire"[314] — responded furiously, in the *Newfoundlander*,[315] saying "an odour of prejudice" emanated from Winton. He added that there was "a party here ... who, if I were an imbecile, would elect me." To this, Winton, on September 14, wondered if Kent "be not on the verge of becoming a fit subject for a lunatic asylum." In a circular issued a day later, Kent accused Winton of having "an uncompromising hatred to Irishmen and Catholics."[316] On September 18 Winton, in a long editorial, inquired about the "party" that would elect an "imbecile" to the Assembly. "What! does this man possess an influence sufficiently powerful to command the return of an *idiot* to our local Parliament!" This was "a barefaced insult, not only to the Protestants, but to every respectable Catholic in this district!" But to what influence was Kent alluding? "Sure we are that the Right Rev. the Bishop at the head of the Church of which Mr. K. is a member will not tolerate such conduct, nor permit it to be tolerated by any of his respectable clergy." If Kent did indeed have the influence he boasted of, he was "a highly dangerous political character." If he didn't, "as we verily believe to be the case," he was "a political *impostor*."

This, by bringing Fleming into the picture, though not by name, was ratcheting the dispute to another level. Yet the remark was such that a moderate man would have let it pass by. Fleming didn't. On September 20, in the *Newfoundlander*, he objected to "the unwarrantable and unjustifiable manner" in which "my name" had been brought before the public. Winton, he said, being unable to meet Kent in fair argument, "turns on me [!] the tide of his personal hostility." He and his clergy stood accused, by inference, of having "highly dangerous political principles." It was the "old cant" of "priestly influence" surfacing once more. Why shouldn't he have the same right as Winton of expressing "political opinions"? Fleming proceeded to name the three St. John's candidates he supported: Kent, Carson, and William Thomas, a Protestant merchant. Alongside his name at the end of the letter was the bishop's insignia of the cross.

And so the cross of Christ was dragged into St. John's politics. This was an extraordinary event — unique in Newfoundland history. Winton was appalled. It might be thought that this was a time for him to back off, for he was capable of cautious and measured responses, and the stakes on this occasion were high. But the bishop had gone too far. In an open letter to Fleming on September 21, Winton accused him of "as gross and wilful a misrepresentation of our sentiments as the mind of a Jesuit could possibly conceive." To "affix the emblem of the cross"[317] to further his views "in a mere trumpery contested election squabble!" Fleming had turned his back on the respectable inhabitants, Catholic and Protestant, and "thrown [him]self upon the rabble." FitzGerald has commented that Winton's "logic" in this response to Fleming is "mystifying."[318] But this is to misunderstand the strength of Winton's feeling against the use of the cross in a political campaign, which to him was sacrilege.

By now the "squabble" had turned into something more, a local sensation. Catholic anger was aroused. Meetings were called in St. John's, Harbour Grace, Carbonear, and Brigus to support Fleming and denounce Winton. The editor was pilloried in print as a liar and coward. The latter charge, made by James Kent, John Kent's brother, was tantamount to a challenge to a duel.[319] The *Ledger* was termed the "Orange Press." Placards appeared on walls in St. John's, pronouncing Winton's doom. Events would show that Kent was no imbecile or impostor (though he was no statesman either; rather, a gifted opportunist). And there was indeed a party in St. John's that would elect him. That "party" was led by Fleming, who took the earliest tally to the hustings and was the first to cast a "plumper" for the young Irishman.[320] Kent topped the poll, with Thomas coming second. Carson, who had unwisely engaged in a vicious spat with the Anglican archdeacon Edward Wix prior to the election, was narrowly defeated by Kough, who was a Catholic and a great friend of Scallan's but wasn't in Fleming's good graces. The conservative lawyer William Bickford Row, the fifth candidate in St. John's, withdrew early in the polling.[321] Utterly disgusted, Winton dismissed Kent as a "mischievous, infatuated boy," Fleming's "impudent protegé," who had "emerged from behind the bar of a tap-house in some obscure part of Ireland," while Fleming held "not a much higher or more exalted office." He called for narrowing the franchise "to a very great degree" and for the introduction of balloting.[322]

Outside St. John's the politicking was decidedly less fractious. At a Harbour Grace meeting in late September, 1832, a list of pledges was approved to present to prospective candidates. As members of the Assembly, the candidates were: to practice "the most rigid economy" in spending public funds; "strenuously" to oppose any tax that might injure the fisheries or agriculture, or "bear exclusively upon the poor"; to procure an act which would cause the balance of servants' wages "TO BE PAID IN CASH"; to oppose any bill "to alter the customary mode" of payment in the seal fishery; to prevent public offices from being filled by other than "NATIVES, or residents of *long standing*" in the colony; and to accept no paid office in the government while serving in the House. Four names were then chosen as "most worthy" of nomination, and a committee was struck to approach each to see if he would accept and sign the pledges.[323] Extracting pledges in this manner shows once again the strength of popular feeling in Harbour Grace. The sealers' strike and pledges, considered together, reflect an understanding of grassroots democratic process,[324] unusual for its time. The strike in particular is a reminder that the "lower orders" of people always had a trump to play in the hard game, about to commence, of Newfoundland politics, i.e., protest en masse. A century later, in St. John's, the trump would be played with such force that the house of cards, so long prayed for, would collapse.

But this is to look far ahead. 1832 was a fateful year. A House of Assembly was elected, but with the election the seed of ethnic and sectarian hatred took root. The next fifty years would show into what fertile ground it had fallen.

Chapter 8

"A Transatlantic Tipperary": 1833-43

AMIDST CONSIDERABLE FANFARE, the Assembly began its deliberations in St. John's, in a hotel owned by Mrs. Mary Travers, on January 1, 1833. Governor Cochrane briefed the members on the financial position of the colony and pointed to matters that needed their attention. Owing to the failure of the potato crop in 1832 and a falling off in fish exports,[1] distress was widespread outside the capital, begetting anxious petitions, warnings about imminent famine, and reports of misery and destitution. One aspect of the economy was ominous. Total cod production was decreasing, even as the population was growing.[2] It had been usual in literature about Newfoundland to describe the cod supply as "inexhaustible," but in fact cod was a limited resource, abundant one year and scarce the next. In these conditions, more workers and greater effort did not spell higher production.[3] Succeeding years would make this truth only more apparent. Not by cod alone could this country thrive. Nor could the seal fishery always be counted on. From the earliest days of the legislature MHAs recognized the need for "an auxiliary to our fisheries" to support the rising population.[4] This "auxiliary," it was often said, but not by all, was agriculture, and potatoes had now indeed become a staple foodstuff. Yet the delicate potato is susceptible to frost and appears to be particularly disease-prone in Newfoundland. Reliance on fish and potatoes, regular fare in a Newfoundland household along the old English shore, was perilous. Hunger was never far off in the homes of 19th-century fishing families. 1832-3 was but one interlude in a long drama that featured want as much as, or more than, plenty.

In 1833 the governor and magistrates were compelled to send out relief, though reluctant to do so, fearing that "to listen to [the] supplications of one year, only insures their repetition in the next."[5] The dole normally consisted of one-third of a pound of bread per day "to each person where parties have fish of their own," and one-half pound per day "to those who have no fish."[6] Molasses was provided as well. Bonavista and its vicinity, Trinity, Bay Bulls, Brigus, and the North Shore of Conception Bay were places causing particular anxiety. In spring, instances of starvation were reported from Placentia Bay.[7] Desperate people ate their seed potatoes, so that new supplies had to be provided by the government. Cochrane said that "with a few trifling exceptions," at the end of the winter there wasn't a district in the island "with a particle of food left, or means to purchase it."[8] Conditions improved somewhat in the winter of 1833-4, but more complaints about far-reaching distress were sounded the following spring. Reformers' boasts about the capacity of Newfoundland to provide a decent life for its people were put to the test immediately on the Assembly's inauguration. To anyone recalling them, the boasts must have seemed empty and absurd.

Cochrane pressed the Assembly for action on the prevailing poverty, but MHAs at first seemed only too willing to leave such an apparently insoluble problem to him and the Council. Some of the Assembly's earliest deliberations centered on constitutional questions and members' privileges. They flatly rejected a proposal, emanating from Goderich in the colonial office in London and supported by Cochrane, whereby the Council and Assembly would unite in an amalgamated legislature. This, MHAs said, was "not in accordance with the principles of the British constitution."[9] Wary of the Crown's anticipated encroachments on their rights, they debated whether or not to appoint, at once, the Assembly's officers, i.e., the clerk, sergeant-at-arms, and messenger.[10] Introduced on January 1, the question was still being debated in July, and would remain a bone of contention for years. Should a government contractor be admitted as a member of the House? They pondered this too, with an eye on Kough, despised by Fleming as a mere "carpenter"[11] but in fact a man of substance and courage. Kough's allegedly unfair electioneering was petitioned against by Carson, who withdrew his protest when he learned it might cost him money to proceed with it.[12] It had no merit in any case. Peter Brown,[13] an Irish-born Harbour Grace merchant, demanded that a computation be made of "the number of each religious creed, with the names and religious creeds of the different public officers of this Colony."[14] He also wanted to change the name of the island to Clarence Island. But useful work was done even in the first couple of sessions. The first act passed by the Newfoundland legislature was "An Act to provide for the performance of Quarantine and more effectually to provide against the introduction of Infectious or Contagious Diseases, and the spreading thereof in this Island."[15] This was intended mainly to combat cholera. A number of acts were designed to prevent or limit damages by fire in St. John's and Harbour Grace; a Nuisances' Act provided "a remedy for the disgracefully dirty and neglected state of all the towns & settlements in the colony";[16] and a revised Marriage Act restored the right to celebrate marriage to Methodist and other dissenting clergy. Nor were these all. Some acts, it is true, proved defective and had to be amended quickly, but this might have been expected in any new attempt at parliamentary democracy. There were combustible elements in it — chiefly Brown and Kent — but the Assembly was at least functioning, and might even be said to be working well.

Trouble arrived early, and it was not of the Assembly's making. Instead it came from members of the old bureaucracy who were still unwilling to accept the new regime. In late February the MHAs passed a revenue bill, placing additional levies on so-called "luxury" items, namely wines and liquor, already subject to imperial duties collected by local customs. To the astonishment of many, the Council rejected it. The vote there was split two-to-two, other members being absent; this nonetheless spelled defeat. Opposition was led by chief justice Tucker, the Council president,[17] a man with a greatly inflated notion of his capacities. He made no effort to disguise his belief that an Assembly was out of place amidst "an uneducated people."[18] On the bill's substance, he argued that since the merchandise in question was already subject to duties imposed by Parliament, it could not be taxed again by a colonial assembly. A bill that imposed such duties was "repugnant" to the imperial act. So he said. He had the support of attorney general Simms, who voted with him. The judge's longwinded arguments were published in the local press, then sent to London, where they were deemed at once to be "decidedly wrong."[19] Having gone overseas to defend his views, Tucker was told "he will no longer hold the office of chief justice."[20] The colonial secretary, Stanley, wouldn't see him. Humiliated, he attacked Cochrane in letters to Stanley and threatened to publish a vindication of his actions, with accounts of the governor's extravagances.[22] His letters possibly damaged Cochrane's reputation.[22] In the event, the legislature enacted the disputed bill, but the revenue from the increased duties was insufficient to meet demand. Early in 1834 the Assembly and Council separately petitioned London for a grant to make up a shortfall.[23] The Council's petition was worded sharply, reminding the "parent state" of the "disastrous consequences" of giving foreigners and other colonials access to the Newfoundland fisheries. The "exclusive" rights of France were pointedly noted. In essence, Newfoundland was "a mere fishing station," the Council said. The fishery was its sole source of wealth. Yet inhabitants had to face competition from other fishing nations on their own shores and were forbidden to fish on a valuable part of the coast. It was unfair that the whole burden of the civil government should fall on them. The implication was that Newfoundland residents were paying for botched British policies.

This was not the only bad news Cochrane had to send home early in 1834. He had made a blunder the previous year by recommending the MHA Thomas for appointment to the Council, thereby causing a vacancy in a St. John's seat.[24] This opened the door to Carson who, as he aged, seemed to grow not less extreme, as is normal, but much more so. Denied an elective role in public affairs, in mid-1833 he, with some others,[25] started a newspaper, the *Newfoundland Patriot*, which would in time become a major force in the colony. Under his editorship, which did not last long,[26] it quickly plunged into shrill oppositional rhetoric. But his interest in journalism was slight; politics, even more than medicine, was now his game. The St. John's by-election on December 2 was fiercely contested. Opposing Carson was the Irish merchant Timothy Hogan, a liberal-minded Catholic who had, however, once embarrassed Fleming in front of Bishop Scallan.[27] Fleming threw his support and that of his priests behind Carson, though the doctor was by now widely known, not without reason, for his "crude scepticism."[28] Hogan defied both clerical intimidation and the threat of economic boycott until the first day of polling when, no doubt recognizing the hopelessness of his candidacy, he withdrew. He later felt obliged to make a public apology to the bishop, who was offended at Hogan's hint of episcopal interference in the election.[29] Had Hogan not apologized, it was said, grass would grow in front of his shop door.

The days following Carson's victory were uneasy. Mobs broke the windows in the *Ledger*'s office — Winton had backed Hogan — and hauled the door off its hinges at the *Times*, another paper of conservative bent.[30] Undeterred, Winton continued his assault on Fleming and his clergy, declaring the priesthood to be "the greatest political nuisance with which this country can be cursed," and calling again for the restriction of the franchise to "much more narrow limits."[31] In mid-December, his premises were again assailed, as were Hogan's. The true *"ruffianly offender"* instigating the attacks, Winton wrote, was Fleming.[32] Winton and his family were in bed on December 22 when their front windows were smashed.[33] On Christmas Eve the assaults continued. Next day a crowd assembled on Water Street, where Winton lived, and approached his house as evening drew on. Someone delivered a speech; the crowd grew bigger. Magistrates and constables soon appeared on the scene but could not prevent the further stoning of Winton's property. The military was summoned. Eighty men from the garrison, with fixed bayonets, formed a protective line before Winton's house, then marched up and down the street in an effort to "clear" it. The riot act was "repeatedly" read. In time, as people dispersed, the soldiers withdrew, leaving sentries behind; but they returned when the crowd reassembled. The street was again "partially cleared." The rioters were not fired on by the soldiers, but rough treatment was doubtless handed out, a few were jailed, and it was later alleged that some were bayoneted.[34] Fr. Edward Troy,[35] one of Fleming's close confidants, appeared and exhorted some of the men to return to their homes. By 10 p.m. quiet was restored.[36]

Use of the garrison in this fashion should have taught Fleming a lesson, one that would be delivered more forcibly to his successor in 1861. That didn't happen. Cochrane summoned the bishop on Boxing Day, at which meeting, Fleming reported in the *Newfoundlander*,[37] he was assured that calling out the military "was an act in which [Cochrane] had no participation whatever." He said Cochrane had also expressed his "disapprobation" of those who "prostituted the Press" and told him "minute investigation" of the incident would follow. Fleming likely distorted what Cochrane said, though the governor was quite capable of ambiguous, self-serving utterance and might well have employed it on this occasion. But James Crowdy, the colonial secretary,[38] immediately wrote to Fleming and contradicted his account of the conversation. Cochrane had been consulted on using the military, and had authorized it. Fleming had "entirely misconceived" what the governor said.[39] This letter found its way into print. It came close to calling Fleming a liar, which Cochrane, along with Kough, Winton, Hogan, and others in fact thought he was. (He was a master of evasion, a quality which makes it treacherous to place much reliance on his statements.)[40] Meanwhile, a public meeting on December 27, chaired by Carson and attended by Kent, Morris, and other prominent Catholics, protested the "despotic attempt to infringe upon our liberties" by the introduction of "a large military force," and expressed "the grateful and heartfelt thanks of the inhabitants of St. John's" (they spoke for all) to Fleming for "calming an incensed multitude, maddened by insult and outrage."[41] The protest was forwarded to Cochrane, with a request for a judicial inquiry. He promptly said no. The magistrates, he wrote, had acted properly in calling out the soldiers, who for their part had behaved "with great forbearance and moderation."[42] By June, 1834, the full tale of woe, political, economic, and ecclesiastical, had reached the colonial office, and Cochrane learned that he would be replaced as governor.

It had not taken long for Newfoundland politics to veer, if not totally off course, then into very contrary winds. The infant Assembly was under assault from two directions: from the Council, where the entrenched elite obstructed it, and from Fleming, who gave signs of wanting to hijack it. But the extent of opposition from the Council can be exaggerated. After Tucker's bizarre intervention, that body evinced no particular hostility towards the Assembly until 1837, when the Assembly itself provoked it. The real source of trouble was Fleming. It is hard to take the measure of "that incendiary priest."[43] His writings show that his motives as an ecclesiastic, to judge him first in that capacity, went beyond simply strengthening his church, tending the flock, and seeking converts. (Not that he neglected those.) He was a consolidator of clerical control over the church and people, and a flamboyant empire builder. Catholicism under him didn't run and hide its head, but strode through the marketplace, bold and irascible. But his ambition was not simply to swell the ranks and open more churches and schools. It didn't take him long to conceive a project to symbolize the anticipated Catholic hegemony: the building of a great cathedral in St. John's, one that would tower over the city, "a temple superior to any other in the island — a temple at once beautiful and spacious."[44] There was something prideful and impractical in this aspiration. But he succeeded, and let Ireland know he succeeded, for he went there often. Obtaining Irish approval was important to him. One hundred and fifty years after his death, the Cathedral (later Basilica) of St. John the Baptist remains the most imposing building on the island.

The same energy and singlemindedness were evident in his politicking. It would not have been unreasonable for any observer to conclude that Protestants had too much power in Newfoundland in the mid-1830s, had held it for too long, and were loath to share it with Catholics. Fleming certainly was aware of it. There was still no Catholic on the Council or bench, none in the major offices under the government. The governor, attorney general, solicitor general, collector and sub-collectors of customs, colonial secretary, colonial treasurer, surveyor general, clerks and registrars in the courts, stipendiary magistrates, coroners, and sheriff were Protestant. Catholics, Fleming wrote, "see every shilling raised by heavy taxation upon the industry of a Catholic people expended upon Protestant officials to the entire & complete exclusion of Catholics."[45] This was an exaggeration,[46] but it was his style to "exaggerate" to make a point. The point was a valid one.

Protestants still clung tenaciously to their privileges and positions. Any rumoured promotion or retirement within the bureaucracy sent aspirants scrambling for the vacancy thus created. Without insiders' knowledge, Catholics would hardly know to apply. Fleming was a man who responded emotionally to perceived inequity, and whose mode of correcting it was through protest and action rather than persuasion and argument, though, as hinted, he could at times be as slippery as the most cunning politico. What he was trying to do, in conceiving or encouraging a takeover of the Assembly, was, in part, to force Protestants to share public offices, and hence influence in society, with Catholics, who were, after all, 50% of the population.[47]

But this is to put the best possible interpretation on his actions. His aims went beyond sharing simply on denominational lines. He wasn't content to have just any member of his congregation rise to prominence and influence; in fact, he was suspicious of some who did. Nor did he want the support of every Catholic who tried to support him. It had to be a Catholic of a certain type, someone reliable who would serve his ends. A Waterford rather than a Wexford Catholic. A Catholic who needed him, rather than one who didn't. A native-born, allegedly freethinking Catholic like the physician Joseph Shea,[48] who had studied abroad and returned to marry a Protestant, Carson's daughter Margaret,[49] or men like Hogan and Edward Kielley[50] who moved on easy terms with the elite, or Eliza Boulton, who was not only in another "heterogeneous" marriage but dared to challenge him on matters such as purification of women after childbirth,[51] were outside the pale. Shea made a number of attempts to make peace with Fleming, all to no avail. The bishop was puritannical and, in matters of doctrine, severe. To win his favour as a political candidate, a Catholic had to toe two lines, his and the Church's. Otherwise, even though he viewed Protestants as "heretics" and would sometimes, in a public manner that must have given offence, boast about the number he converted from "error" to the "true faith," he preferred, at least initially, to support someone like Thomas who was probably perceived as tractable. (This was not the only occasion when he made a public show of supporting Protestants.)[52] Fleming not only sharpened division between Catholics and Protestants, but caused, and made little or no effort to mend,[53] a bitter cleavage within his own church.

He seems also to have carried a full load of Irish grievance with him across the Atlantic. What he saw, or thought he saw, in Newfoundland evidently convinced him that he had landed in another Ireland, and that his was the only way for the Catholic congregation, or rather the portion of it he favoured, to take its rightful place in the colony. A glance through some correspondence of the period, especially Cochrane's private papers,[54] or Wix's published journal,[55] could give the impression that, if Fleming thought this, he wasn't far off the mark. Anti-"popish" hatred existed in the new world as in the old; and we have seen how the Irish were treated in Newfoundland prior to the 1830s — and how their religion was treated, not just prior to 1784, but after. Fleming was particularly enraged by the big financial and institutional support given by the government to the Church of England, while he had to be content with the reinstated pittance, as he saw it, of £75 per year. His petition to the King in 1835 contrasted the salaries and comforts of the St. John's Anglican clergy with his and his priests' embarrassments.[56] He felt personally demeaned by such discrimination, and refused to accept it, indeed mounted an O'Connellite resistance to it. He was the first Catholic bishop in Newfoundland whom the British couldn't control. This is hardly surprising when we consider that the Pope couldn't control him either.

Cochrane said Fleming and his associates wanted "political ascendancy,"[57] but of course this would be impossible as long as the Council and bureaucracy remained Protestant, and as long as the secretary of state in the colonial department, through his agent the governor, remained ultimately at the helm. But to gain influence or control in the Assembly would still represent a considerable accession of power. Behind all Fleming's protests and manipulations, there lurked a hunger for power that was incongruous in a cleric. FitzGerald says that the bishop's "unstated agenda" was "the creation of a Catholic community unencumbered by Protestant or British intermeddling"; McCann states that "Fundamentally, he stood for the integrity of the Catholic religion."[58] But the "Catholic community" Fleming built wasn't one for all Catholics, just for those who bent the knee to him. As for his wishing to create a "community" that was not cumbered with British and Protestant intermeddling, he likely would have found it easier to create one if he hadn't bulled his way into secular politics. It is too much to ask that a prelate who seeks, directly or through his delegates, political power, and uses questionable methods to obtain it, should not be "meddled" with by those in charge of the government. Did he stand for the "integrity" of the Catholic religion? It is likely that he stood rather for its paramountcy, with him deciding what was the "Catholic religion" and what was not.

While Fleming is normally thought of in the context of St. John's, his influence penetrated far beyond that town, for he travelled widely and at one point petitioned the British government for a stipend to support a coastal vessel for him and his priests. The numerous Irish priests he recruited, for instance James Duffy,[59] appointed to Ferryland parish as assistant to (and watchdog over) Timothy Browne, were of his temperament and kept his flame burning.[60] But in more remote places where many Catholics were perhaps of an older vintage than those in the capital or often just out of touch with events, there was possibly less upset. Wix pointedly noted that Placentia Bay Catholics were of "a character very different" from those "misled" by the new priests in St. John's.[61]

* * *

With Carson on board, the Newfoundland ship of state headed into more stormy waters. On the reopening of the House in 1834, he ran for speaker, but was defeated by Thomas Bennett, the member for Fogo. The so-called reformers were now a sizeable minority in the Assembly. Opposing them were men not easy to classify as a group, nor did they always vote as a group;[62] but perhaps it is fair to say as a generalization that they represented established mercantile interests.[63] They were mostly Protestant. For convenience, we might call these "parties" reformers (or liberals) and conservatives,[64] though this is rather a convention of historians than an accurate summation of what the two groups actually were. To term some of Carson's actions and Fleming's manipulations liberal is to stretch the word's meaning beyond recognition. Fleming in fact despised Catholic liberals and would mock the word "liberal" in communicating with Rome.[65] But he'd tell the colonial secretary that he supported liberals, knowing that was what one of Melbourne's ministers might like to hear.[66] The "conservatives" for their part were not incapable of supporting initiatives which, to modern ears, sound somewhat progressive. In any event, the House was divided so. Carson immediately set about trying to get three members disqualified, for an assortment of reasons, mostly bogus. When this failed, in March, 1834, a petition was prepared calling for the dissolution of the Assembly and a new election. The only object, Cochrane wrote of the petitions' promoters, was "to procure an accession of strength to their cause."[67] The petition was signed by about 2,000; third on the list was Fleming. Cochrane refused to dissolve the House, which continued to pass legislation of value, including a Road Act, a Lighthouse Act, and a Savings Bank Act. A savings bank opened in St. John's in 1834. Two acts dealt with social issues: one for the protection of illegitimate children ("hitherto ... a great burthen on public charity")[68] and another for the support of deserted wives and children.[69] One dealt with convicts.[70] A banished convict who was found at large was to be kept at hard labour, and in addition "sentenced to be once, twice or thrice publicly or privately whipped." (But women were not to be whipped.) Anyone convicted of a crime for which the law of England prescribed imprisonment and hard labour could be sent, wearing "an Iron Clog, or other Shackle," to work on the roads and streets.

As if the colony didn't already possess a sufficient number of "great" men, another had by now stepped into the limelight. This was the English trained barrister H.J. Boulton,[71] who succeeded Tucker as chief justice late in 1833, coming to Newfoundland after a stormy period, ending in dismissal, as attorney general of Upper Canada. He was decisive, brilliant, and independent, with a strong disposition to tinker and question. An inveterate rule-maker, he tried to renovate the Council to bring its operations in line with the Legislative Council of Upper Canada. In his effort, he was stopped in his tracks.[72] Another of his early actions was to change certain procedures in the supreme court, including the method of impanelling juries. His new system evidently made it easier for lawyers to challenge and strike off names of jurors regarded as prejudicial.[73] The Irish thought the innovation had the effect of discriminating against them, and likely, in the course of time, it did. The composition of juries was to be a major issue in Newfoundland until the 1840s. From the cases that came before Boulton in January, 1834, it is not hard to see why. Forty prisoners were in the St. John's jail, thirteen charged with murder.

The forty were "almost exclusively Roman Catholics."[74] One of those convicted of murder and sentenced to death was "a poor ignorant half Indian" from Labrador named Hackett, who happened to be visited in jail by Fleming after being sentenced to death. Fleming stumbled on information that suggested Hackett was innocent. This information was communicated to the sheriff, who was in charge of prisoners, a mere twenty-four hours before the execution. On investigating, Boulton too saw reason to believe that Hackett was wrongly accused. The man ultimately received the King's pardon. In the course of his investigation, Boulton rebuked Fleming for his priests' normal inattention to prisoners in the jail, to which the bishop "made some allusion to their not being paid."[75] Fleming may well have resented Boulton's censure. And his nature was such that resentment, once formed, was not easily eradicated. He came to the conclusion that Boulton was a bigot and partisan.

Some of the remaining seven murder cases raised intricate points of law. One of the most troubling was that of Peter Downey and Patrick Malone, Harbour Grace labourers, who were convicted of killing schoolmaster Robert Crocker Bray, his child, and a female servant. They were sentenced to death; Downey was executed. To Cochrane's surprise, Malone's sentence was respited, and the crown lawyers later recommended he be pardoned. Downey's and Malone's joint petition[76] to the King, from prison, on January 5 was sent initially to Boulton, who spurned it. The petition presented a long catalogue of reasons why their arraignment, trial, conviction, and sentence were "utterly illegal." Some were founded on Boulton's new rules for the supreme court. Fleming forwarded the petition to O'Connell, who sent it to the secretary of state for the colonies. Fleming wanted one or all of the Newfoundland judges unseated. He recommended that one Ronan be appointed, who was a friend of both O'Connell and "poor Ireland."[77] This was enough to make him qualified to sit on the bench in Newfoundland. Considerable feeling was stirred up by Downey's execution. His body, hanging in chains in Harbour Grace, was cut down one night and deposited at the door of William Stirling, a justice and surgeon.[78] The action indicates the continuance of "plebeian" anger against established authority in Conception Bay, soon to manifest itself in more spectacular fashion.

But the greatest commotion was stirred up by the fate of Catherine Snow, whose husband John, a planter living near Port de Grave, was killed by Catherine's lover, Tobias Mandeville. Mandeville had implicated his servant, Arthur Spring, in the crime as well. All three were sentenced to death, and on January 13 the two men were hanged.[79] Snow was found, by a jury of matrons,[80] to be pregnant, and her sentence was respited until the court reopened in summer. She was a Catholic, and in the course of her imprisonment priests visited her, including Troy, who became convinced she was innocent. He made frantic, but late, efforts to save her. A memorial to Boulton and the two assistant judges dated July 14, 1834, got up by Troy but signed by nearly 300, asked that her case be laid before the British government for review. The memorial pointed out that she had eight children, and that she had already suffered "a close imprisonment" for nearly a year, together with "harrowing of feeling." Boulton replied, not unmercifully, that the court would meet on July 18, and he was willing to hear legal evidence in her favour. Troy responded by asking for a new trial. A further memorial, to Cochrane, signed by Troy and two other priests, claimed there was "very slight evidence" against her, and again asked for referral to London. No answer to this was received. Snow was hanged on July 21.[81] She had also been sentenced to be dissected and anatomized. Though worried about the "public excitement," district surgeon[82] Kielley reported next day that he had carried out the sentence on her body. He did so indoors at the jail where no proper facilities for such existed. Had he performed it in the open yard, "exposed to public gaze, *violent prejudices*, hot weather and immense swarms of pests ... I will venture to say even my life would be destroyed."[83] Troy charged that the execution had been carried out "two hours earlier than usual." He published a full account of his efforts on behalf of Snow, with copies of memorials and responses, in the *Patriot*.[84] Then either he or John Valentine Nugent,[85] a radical Irish schoolteacher recruited by Fleming in 1833, commenced a series of vicious attacks on Cochrane, under the pseudonym "Junius," in the same paper.[86]

Boulton was now firmly in the enemy camp, his situation being complicated by his wife Eliza, who as a Catholic was privy to what was said over the altar on Sundays. She evidently got an earful, which she duly reported.[87] When the new governor, Henry Prescott, was sworn in in early November, he found himself in a divided community, with Boulton and Winton the targets of intense hatred, both partisan and religious — if these two were not one and the same. The attacks on Winton in the *Patriot* displayed a mounting ferocity, though both men were thought to be in danger. A conciliator by nature, Prescott tried to "allay party feeling" by dropping a libel case brought by Cochrane against Troy and maintaining "habits of civility" with Fleming;[88] but this had little effect. It didn't take Prescott long to conclude that the bishop was "illiterate and vulgar,"[89] a harsh judgment, suggestive in that it came from a normally moderate man. By December Fleming had received a severe letter of chastisement from Rome for turning the Catholic chapel in St. John's into "a political clubhouse."[90] Even this didn't daunt him. It might have made matters worse, for Winton, with some glee, was soon reporting, wrongly, that Fleming had been summoned to Rome.[91] He called this "one of the greatest blessings" that God could bestow on the colony. As for the "would be dictator" Boulton (so termed in the *Patriot*)[92] when the Assembly opened in January, 1835, Carson took aim at him, first, by demanding official documents relating to the court, among them records of convictions and names of jurors, and then, in February, by moving for a select committee to inquire into the administration of justice. The committee was voted down,[93] but this was but a temporary setback in what would be a determined assault on the judge. Adding to the heady political mix of early 1835 was agitation over a proposed increase in duties, for London had made it clear that no further assistance could be expected from that quarter. (In fact, a grant-in-aid of £5,000 was made in 1835.) A public meeting in St. John's in February, with Carson in the chair, railed against the prospect of new taxes. The colony's increased expenditure, it was stated, served only to provide "extravagant salaries for useless officers."[94] Petitions against more taxation reached the House, along with others pointing to areas where expenditure was needed.[95] But an act taxing many food-stuffs (but not molasses) and placing a 2½% ad valorem duty on much merchandise (excluding wines and liquor, already taxed, as well as salt and fishing gear) was passed in April.[96] With it the colony's financial difficulties came to a temporary halt.

The political atmosphere of 1835 was darkened by tyranny and menace. (An instance, perhaps, of what McCann, in a whitewashing phrase, terms "extra-parliamentary activity.")[97] The *Ledger* was now banned — by Fleming[98] — from Catholic households. The names of the "seven" Catholics who supported it were posted in the chapel yard in January; the congregation was ordered to have no dealings with them, on pain of excommunication. (Troy had commenced the boycotting of uncooperative shopkeepers in 1833.)[99] They included "dirty" Michael McLean Little, a trader who stood his ground, but by March fancied he stood alone.[100] He was not, in fact, someone to push around. In time, his persistent complaints against Fleming and the priests reached London and Rome. Other offending subscribers to Winton's paper were obliged to disclaim their support for it in the pages of the *Patriot*.[101] The like of this had never been seen in Newfoundland. Meanwhile, the *Patriot* kept up its attacks on Boulton. In May it went too far, in a brief paragraph under the heading "*Stick a pin here!*"[102] This stated that Boulton, on the reopening of the central circuit court, had lectured jurors "on the very great benefits which *hanging* the people confers on society." On May 18, the editor of the paper, R.J. Parsons, was summoned to the court to answer to a charge of contempt. A week later Boulton found him guilty and sentenced him to three months in jail. He also had to pay a fine of £50 and stand committed until it was paid.[103] The sentencing caused an uproar. A constitutional society was formed, and threats to tear down the court house and jail were received. Prescott put the military on alert.

As this was progressing, an equally grim piece of news arrived from Harbour Grace. In a February dispatch Prescott expressed concern about Winton, who he thought was in real peril. The editor's railing against "the unceasing efforts ... of the Roman Catholic Priesthood ... to assume a political domination over both the Government and the people" had not abated a jot.[104] At least one of his fulminations in February, 1835, a piece of ridicule directed at the Presentation Order of nuns who'd been brought by Fleming to St. John's in 1833 to establish a girls' school, was outrageous, though he had the grace to apologize immediately for it.[105] On the day following the insult, a preparatory meeting of "all classes" of Catholics, those who had been denounced by Fleming as well as his adherents, was called to consider condemning Winton's behaviour. Priests did not attend. It was a real opportunity for reconciliation between the warring elements in the church. When Fleming heard of the meeting, he spoke after mass to his congregation, saying he needed no help from the likes of Kough, Hogan, and Joseph Shea, who had failed to support him before. He would defend the nuns himself. He spoke "very violently." On the following Sunday, the priests saying mass turned to the people and asked if any of those who'd been named by Fleming were present; if so, the ceremony could not proceed. A priest made it clear on succeeding Sundays that those who had been denounced were in fact excommunicated by Fleming's fiat.[106] Excommunication was the Catholic church's strongest punishment. It excluded the erring sinner from participation in the spiritual life of the church. More than that, the excommunicated were to be shunned even in secular matters. To the believer, it was a terrifying weapon.

It did not, of course, worry Winton, who on May 12 alluded to the priest Duffy as "*a Rev. and well-known* scoundrel." On May 19 he was in Carbonear, and in the late afternoon was travelling on horseback towards Harbour Grace, in company with William Churchward, master of the brig *Hazard*, who was on foot. Winton was armed with a pistol. While descending Saddle Hill, the two were attacked by a group of about five men with faces disguised by ochre.[107] Winton had no time to use his pistol. He was struck on his head by a stone, a blow that opened a large wound, and felled from his horse. More blows on the head followed, while Churchward was bustled into the woods to prevent his attempting a rescue. Winton's ears were then stuffed with mud and gravel. One of his attackers opened a clasp-knife, cut two pieces from his right ear, and cut off the left one. A piece of his cheek was also cut off. He survived, but despite an immediate inquiry by the Harbour Grace grand jury and a large reward (ultimately rising to £1,500) offered by the government and merchants, the assailants were never identified.[108] Winton attributed the attack to the malice of priests, but it is possible that its cause lay farther back, in his writings on the Conception Bay "rabble" in 1830-32. However, it was widely believed at the time that Catholics were responsible. The new colonial secretary in London, Glenelg, who was shocked by the incident, concluded that Winton had been the victim of "religious fanaticism."[109] According to Prescott, the mutilation was "a matter of open triumph and rejoicing to the Catholics of low degree, even female servants and children expressing the greatest satisfaction."[110] Assistant judge Edward Brenton detected much "chuckling" over Winton's fate in Harbour Grace too.[111] Proclamations offering the reward were speedily torn from walls, and a joyful ballad about "Croppy[112] Winton" was soon in circulation. The *Patriot*, in an editorial likely written from jail by Parsons, didn't countenance the mutilation but said that "if ever mercy was deservedly extended to crime — this case above all others demands it."[113]

Parsons' incarceration and the excision of Winton's ears further split the Newfoundland community. A petition against Boulton, who had gone to England on leave, was presented to Prescott on June 29 for forwarding to the King. It was "said to be signed" by 5,000 inhabitants of St. John's.[114] O'Connell received a copy and presented it to the Commons. In London Boulton defended himself against the allegations in the petition, and desperately sought employment in Upper Canada, the West Indies, and even Ceylon. Conservative opinion, meanwhile, rallied around Winton. Prescott wanted both Fleming and Boulton removed from Newfoundland, and even went so far as to suggest a replacement for the former, namely Browne, whom Fleming disliked and distrusted. (The feeling was warmly reciprocated.)[115] But the colony would not be rid of the judge and bishop so easily. Boulton was back in St. John's in late October. Fleming was installed there for life. Politics was now effectively derailed into sectarianism.

It was actually a time when the greatest vigilance in public affairs was called for. The devolution of authority to St. John's from London in the 1820s and '30s had, as we have seen, a number of causes, but one cause was doubtless the falling off in importance of Newfoundland as an imperial possession.[116] This didn't necessarily place it in peril. Britain would still look after Newfoundland, as she would any of her colonies. But the island, not being the economic asset it once was, had slipped down on the scale of priorities. This meant, for instance, that pressure on Spain and Portugal to reduce duties on Newfoundland fish, or at least not to increase them, might still be applied, but perhaps not with the same urgency or speed as in the past, when moguls of the migratory fishery were beating on the door of the colonial office. The St. John's Chamber of Commerce petitioned the home government in May, 1834, asking for intervention to cause a reduction in Spanish tariffs.[117] In June, the Chamber learned that the Portuguese market, "the main stay of their fisheries," was threatened as well, for the new government in Portugal had adopted a policy of "equalizing" duties on all imported fish, thereby reducing those on Newfoundland's competitors but not on Newfoundland's. They again asked for intervention.[118] By November no answer had been received to the May petition, and the Chamber petitioned a third time, pointing to high duties in Naples as well as Spain, and adding that a military subsidy duty had recently been placed on fish at Oporto in Portugal, in contravention of the treaty between Britain and Portugal in 1810.[119] Finally, in February, 1835, the MP Robinson was asked to intercede, and British officials bestirred themselves in March, wondering if it might be "proper" to make a representation to the Portuguese government on the alleged violation of the treaty.[120] In January, 1836, the Chamber was back with another petition, centering on Portugal but listing other impediments to the trade.[121] Again in 1837 they petitioned against increased duties in the Portuguese market.[122] In 1838 the British minister at Lisbon, Baron Howard de Walden, told Palmerston in the foreign office that it was useless to make such a protest, though he had "on several occasions" done so in the past. He suggested that fish be brought into Portugal by "contraband trade."[123] In 1840 the Chamber noted in a letter to the colonial office that their "repeated exertions" to get reduced duties had failed.[124] The stream of petitions and the tardy response to them indicate both the crucial importance of low fish duties to Newfoundland and the exporters' hazardous distance from the levers of power. The merchants suspected that Britain's failure to act on one matter, Portugal's "equalizing" policy, was due to considerations "by which the Empire at large has derived benefits." If so, they asked for "compensation." As these vital transactions were in progress, the Newfoundland state was semi-paralyzed by ethnic wrangling.

The French meanwhile were pursuing their fisheries in the north and south, safe from effective scrutiny, for Britain withdrew the naval squadron from Newfoundland soon after the introduction of circuit courts. The French shore "question" was kept well in the background in London during the 1820s and early '30s; opinion within the British government was that earlier diplomacy had conceded the exclusive right of fishing to France.[125] On the local scene, the St. John's Chamber of Commerce had sent a vessel to fish on the Petit Nord in 1830, but the ship was driven off by a French frigate.[126] Crews heading north had to bypass fishing grounds they had grown used to during the Napoleonic Wars and resort instead to Labrador. On their way north in the spring, they would land and plunder the French possessions. The French fishermen left their equipment in the hands of English caretakers in some coves, but these caretakers, Cochrane said in 1834, likely "participate in the plunder or connive at it on the part of others."[127] In 1834, weary of receiving complaints from the French, he proposed that their fishermen be allowed to leave behind "a small boats crew" to overwinter in every port they occupied. This recommendation, if accepted, might well have changed the course of Newfoundland history. It was rejected.[128] In June, 1834, the French shore was raised in the Commons, and internal government deliberations recommenced in London, leading to a decision by the crown lawyers in 1835: "we are of opinion that the subjects of France have the exclusive right of fishery" between Cape St. John and Cape Ray.[129] As we will see, this was far from being the end of the story. A new era of diplomacy on the tortured issue would shortly begin. But there was no strong probability that it would turn in Newfoundland's favour. Good relations with France were "deemed more important than the welfare of a small colony."[130] This is something to bear in mind in discussing the imperial connection with Newfoundland. Keeping up membership in the European club to which England belonged often meant leaving codfish in the dustbin outside the door.

Newfoundland politicians were unaware of these potentially momentous discussions about the colony's west and north coasts. But they did notice developments in Fortune Bay, from which reports were received in 1835 that the fishermen of St. Pierre were destroying caplin stocks in an effort to get bait for the large French banking fleet. They were doing this by "sweeping" the coves with seines. Nor was this the only worry. The French had introduced a new piece of technology, the bultow,[131] regarded as damaging to "mother fish,"[132] and they were illegally cutting wood on shore in Newfoundland. Inhabitants in Fortune Bay feared being driven out of their homes, or at least said they feared it. They could well have been trying to deny the French direct access to bait and wood in order to force them to buy it.[133] The Assembly appointed a select committee to investigate. A petition was sent to London requesting an intervention by the British government and restoration of the naval force.[134] In July, Palmerston agreed that action by the navy "to apply a remedy" was called for,[135] and a sloop, the *Racer*, was duly sent from Halifax. The captain found more than 200 fishing vessels operating out of St. Pierre, employing over 3,000 men.[136] The St. John's Chamber of Commerce, whose president in 1836 was Charles Fox Bennett, the speaker's brother and a rising businessman — and, three decades later, as an old man, leader in the battle against confederation with Canada — estimated that the French fishery in the north was at least four times as large as that in the south. Policing this immense industry would never be easy. The Newfoundland government lacked the resources to do it, and in any case when the legislature passed an Act in 1836 to deny "Aliens" access to Fortune Bay and adjacent places to cut wood and procure bait, it was disallowed by Britain as an intrusion on the prerogatives of the King and Parliament.[137] But no matter what was done in Parliament or the Assembly, the fact was that the French were already being integrated into the economy of the south coast. St. Pierre needed bait, game, and wood, and Newfoundland fishermen supplied them. The fishermen in turn smuggled tea, sugar, brandy, clothing, and much more from St. Pierre. When captain Thomas Bennett of H.M.S. *Rainbow* arrived at St. Pierre in April, 1836, he found eleven Newfoundland boats there trading.[138] Smuggling, he said, went on all along the south coast. Despite the tenor of the Fortune Bay petition, the existence of the French undoubtedly ameliorated life on a coastline far removed, not indeed geographically, but mentally, from St. John's.

This was not the only illegal activity from which fishermen benefited. Pillaging wrecked vessels helped as well.[139] (There was still no lighthouse on the south coast.) Ships from Halifax, Quebec, and elsewhere brought liquor, flour, bread, and clothing to exchange for fish, while American traders were active on the west coast. The growth of population in and beyond Fortune Bay was now "most rapid,"[140] so much so that the Assembly sought to create a new district, Hermitage Bay, stretching from Jerseyman's Harbour, near Harbour Breton, to Bonne Bay on the west coast.[141] The act was disallowed, as the envisaged district encroached on the coast north of Cape Ray and would raise "inconvenient and embarrassing" questions from France.[142] (The settlers on the west coast would have to remain, for the time being, "officially unknown.")[143] But in the census of 1836 the twenty-eight settlements between Bonne Bay, in the south, and Cape Ray were placed in the district of Fortune Bay, thereby acquiring official existence of a sort.[144] In 1836 as well a sub-collector of customs was sent to Lapoile.

1836 was an election year. Prompted by Prescott, the British government suggested to the Assembly that the election be put off until 1840.[145] The proposal was not warmly received. In April MHAs asked Prescott for dissolution at the end of the session, and the governor replied that it was not his intention to convene the present House again.[146] Sectarian feelings had abated slightly towards the end of 1835, possibly owing to distraction caused by an outbreak of smallpox in and near St. John's. This begot "great horror" among the people. At Prescott's request, the young physician Henry Hunt Stabb vaccinated children and some adults, but vaccination too was dreaded.[147] Catholic sensitivities soon brought attention back to courts and politics. The priest James Duffy now took center stage. In January, 1835, while in St. Mary's, part of Ferryland parish, he had been the instigator in the burning of a fish flake owned by Slade, Elson and Co., whose resident agent was the Protestant MHA and justice of the peace John Wills Martin. The flake prevented ready access to the new church Duffy had built near the beach. After much delay, he was arrested in Fermeuse, where he lived, and charged. This was in early November; he entered into recognizances to appear at the next session of the supreme court. Simms then drew up a warrant, and had it signed by Boulton, for the arrest of eight men in St. Mary's. In December two constables went to the outport to apprehend the men; violence and threats drove them away. With Duffy's trial thought to be imminent, Catholics in Harbour Grace and Carbonear sent petitions to the supreme court — "a Protestant tribunal" — asking that he be allowed to select a Catholic to represent him.[148] (All lawyers in Newfoundland were Protestant.) The court severely reprimanded the bearers of the petitions, among whom were Morris and Kent, for trying to interfere with its proceedings. Duffy's trial was again put off. Boulton became the object of more Catholic rancour. At a public meeting in St. John's in January, 1836, a committee was appointed to draw up a petition against him, a version of which appeared in the *Patriot* of February 2. Another meeting on February 8, this time of "respectable" inhabitants, approved a counter-petition in the form of an address to Glenelg, pointing to Boulton's "integrity, ability, and character."[149] The counter-petition reached London before the petition. War had resumed.

In February yet another incident exacerbated tension in St. John's. A Catholic soldier named John Neaven, well known to the Irish, died on February 2. He had earlier been an object of pity as having allegedly been cuckolded by Lieut.-Col. William Sall, commander of the garrison.[150] On the day of his funeral, a Catholic crowd assembled and offered to assist in carrying the coffin. The small party of soldiers conducting the burial consented, but at a certain point the men with the coffin decided to alter course and take a longer route to the cemetery. Anticipating trouble, the lieutenant in charge ordered the soldiers to fix bayonets, took back the coffin, and proceeded, not to the cemetery, but to Fort Townshend to receive further orders. The crowd followed. The commanding officer at the fort called out the entire force available to him, and "gave orders to load with ball." At this point a priest, James Murphy, intervened, and quiet was soon restored. This was the second dangerous skirmish, or near skirmish, between troops and a Catholic crowd in St. John's. Fleming reacted angrily, publishing a letter in the *Patriot* to give his version of events and demanding an investigation. He was aware, he said, that Prescott was "surrounded" by advisors "interested to asperse the character of the people" and "to defame the Priesthood."[151]

The priesthood, especially one member of it, Duffy, was in fact much on Prescott's mind. He awaited a ship of war to enforce the law at St. Mary's. It arrived May 1. On May 6 he closed the Assembly, where, amidst some important measures, especially one establishing non-denominational school boards and providing funding to schools of all religions,[152] debate had dragged on over a contentious press bill aimed at the *Patriot*. Prescott made it clear in his speech on closing the House that he would send troops to St. Mary's. The following day he issued a proclamation demanding the surrender of the eight men. Fleming, for it was he, not Kent or Carson, who was now the leading opponent of the government, capitulated. On May 10, in a pastoral letter, he told the men to come to St. John's and give themselves up, which they promptly did. It was a striking illustration of his power. He had only to say the word and his will was done. His pastoral letter was defiant, calling the plan to send soldiers to St. Mary's "silly mockery" whose real object was "coercion of the people."[153] (Defending "the people" had become a big part of his rhetoric.) Prescott, greatly relieved, reported his victory to London, and shortly afterwards supported Fleming's request for land to build his new church. Many such grants had been made to the Protestants, he said, and "on a principle of impartiality" the Catholics should get theirs.[154] Fleming was making headway on his grand design.

Meanwhile, the petition to the King and Parliament against Boulton was gathering signatures. It was forwarded in July, with an astounding 8,864 names, all of which, said Nugent, in an accompanying letter, were genuine.[155] On receiving a copy from Prescott, Boulton pronounced it "utterly devoid of truth" and "impertinently expressed."[156] The petition was quickly dismissed by the colonial office.[157] Fleming went overseas, cheered on by Winton: "May we never see him more!"[158] An election was called for November. As it approached, it became clear that the system of school boards instituted by the legislature would not work. Catholics and Protestants were now too far apart to implement it. In St. John's, the Anglican priest Carrington couldn't get Troy to go to a meeting.[159] In Harbour Grace, the board divided on the question of using the King James version of the *Bible*.[160] There was trouble elsewhere. Winton, who was led, uncharacteristically, to express theological objections to Roman Catholicism by the issue, said the only practical view was "that the Protestant part of the community must educate their children, and the Roman Catholic part of it must educate theirs."[161] Ultimately this was the course Newfoundland would follow. The question further soured an already poisonous mood as the election came closer.

Polling began in Harbour Grace on November 1. It immediately descended into riot. Soon after the poll opened at 10 a.m., supporters of the two "tory" candidates, Thomas Ridley and Robert Prowse, the latter a Port de Grave merchant and father of the historian, were set upon, beaten, and driven from the hustings by "a brutal and ruffianly mob,"[162] mostly from Carbonear. The local magistrates and constables, fearful and of course outnumbered, were powerless. Twenty "tory" supporters were injured, some seriously. Next day Prowse and Ridley retired from the fray and on November 3 the returning officer, R.J. Pinsent, declared the four reform candidates elected.[163] Somewhat feeble attempts over the next two weeks to discover and arrest ringleaders among the rioters were resisted. The normal veil of secrecy fell over Conception Bay. One malefactor who was fingered, the cooper Roger Thomey, seized in Carbonear, was "rescued" before the deputy sheriff could get him to Harbour Grace. (He was later apprehended.) Informers' houses, including that of the Carbonear merchant Simon Levi, a Jew, were attacked and invaded.[164] Forty-eight frightened Harbour Grace householders petitioned Prescott for "an efficient and permanent force," i.e., soldiers, to protect their lives and property.[165]

With the election in progress, though not yet commenced in St. John's, Prescott called the Council together on November 9 to discuss events in Conception Bay. On looking over the documents laid before him, Boulton saw that the writ calling the Conception Bay election did not bear the great seal of the island. In his view, it was invalid. Other writs also lacked the seal. The Council adjourned until the following day, to give members time to consider this bolt from the blue. When it met, Boulton gave his written opinion: the King's writ without the seal "is no writ at all."[166] The normally sensible attorney general, Simms, agreed. Prescott in the meantime had learned, or at at any rate was told, that the writs issued for the 1832 election and for intervening by-elections also bore no seals. The legality of all enactments of the Newfoundland legislature were called into question. He decided to write to London for advice and to let the elections proceed.

Fleming was still out of town, but Troy and other priests ably filled the breach. The St. John's election began on December 14. At Sunday mass the previous day, Troy ordered two of the "Orange Catholics" (also termed "mad dogs")[167] out of the church and called down "the curse of Jesus Christ" on such as "oppose us the Church, and who trample on the cross!!"[168] When one of the "mad dogs," Michael Scanlan, stood up and asked what he had done to justify eviction, Troy tore off his vestments and headed in his direction.[169] But Scanlan, his wife Eleanor, and his daughter were roughly hustled out of church, principally through the agency of one Patrick Brawders, labourer, who referred to Eleanor as a "strumpet" and the daughter as a "faggot." The expulsion was witnessed by Joseph Shea's young brother Ambrose, destined to play a large role in Newfoundland history.[170] Such behaviour was characteristic of Troy, who was enacting what he thought Fleming wanted. He also denied the last rites to "mad dogs," refused their children baptism in the home, even in inclement weather, and would not attend burials.[171] Such denials, frightening to most Catholics, could only further inflame passions already sufficiently aroused. Military aid had been asked for, and the soldiers put under arms, on November 10, when a mob beseiged an evening meeting of "tories" and beat the windows out of their committee room. As on similar occasions in the past, the riot ended only when a priest turned up to calm the incensed crowd. On the morning of the 14th, as the candidates were nominated — Kough, James J. Grieve, a Scot "deeply interested in our Trade and Fisheries,"[172] and the native-born merchant Nicholas Gill vs. Carson, Kent, and Morris — the scene around the hustings became disorderly, some of the 140 special constables were assaulted, and the riot act was read. Soldiers were summoned at close of day[173] in anticipation of more violence, and spread out on patrols. They remained on duty on the 15th when, as polling began and news of threats and beatings spread through the town, Kough, Grieve, and Gill withdrew under protest. To add to the general tumult, five Catholic priests, including Troy, were on the hustings, along with men from neighbouring outports and Carbonear, evidently brought in to intimidate supporters of the "tories." On the resignation of the conservative trio, the victors' supporters paraded through the streets, shouting "Down with the tories!" and "Down with the mad dogs."[174] It was clear as results came in from other districts that the reformers had won, or been handed, a decisive victory. Morris won in Ferryland as well as St. John's; Nugent and Patrick Doyle, the latter a native Newfoundlander, took Placentia and St. Mary's. The reformers had at least nine of the fifteen seats,[175] and in all likelihood ten, once Morris decided on the one he would vacate. John Shea, another of Joseph's brothers and editor of the *Newfoundlander*, won in Burin. His political views were unknown, but his paper was pledged to uphold "liberal principles," so presumably he'd fall into line.[176] On November 19, the *Newfoundland Patriot* printed the U.S. Declaration of Independence. It was not clear why, since reformers, even when threatening violence, as they were sometimes wont to do,[177] pledged allegiance to the monarch and to the British constitution; but a declaration of some sort seemed called for. 1836 did not bring a revolution, nor did reformers often claim it did. When they later defined what had happened, they called it "the overthrow of an undue Mercantile Ascendancy."[178]

Boulton had fled to London again in the summer of 1836 to press his case for a position that had opened up in Upper Canada, one much below the rank of judge. "I have fallen among thieves & been grievously beaten," he told the colonial office. He was snubbed and sent back to St. John's.[179] At the opening of the supreme court in late November, he told the grand jury of their duty to institute a "rigid investigation" into the election turmoils. Trials soon began; with all eyes on them, they lasted into the new year.[180] All those charged, whether from Conception Bay or St. John's, were tried in the capital before Boulton and the two assistant judges. Doyle and Morris (both J.P.s), Kent, Carson, Troy and another priest, Patrick Ward, with twelve more, found themselves in court, charged with unlawful assembly. Morris, who was often excitable when delivering one of his interminable speeches, had allegedly threatened political opponents with death at the rally in question, which took place in October. This was testified to in a sworn statement, but was denied by other witnesses. Only one of the eighteen, Patrick Power, was found guilty; he was fined. Brawders pleaded guilty to assault for his effort in assisting Troy and was fined £25.[181] (Simms said his motive in pleading guilty was "to prevent the whole circumstance of the case being publicly exposed.")[182] Thomas Shortall, "alone identified as one of the mob" stoning the "tory" committee room, was sentenced to six months in jail.[183] William Ryan was found guilty, fined, and sent to jail for a month for striking C.F. Bennett, a J.P., on the head on the 14th. James Mackey had spit in the face of a special constable. He too was fined. But others involved in the St. John's fracas got off, and Boulton complained that the petty juries, which had strong Catholic representation,[184] acquitted many "without any intelligible ground being assignable for such a result." He attributed this to "strong party feeling."[185] For the leaders of the Harbour Grace riots, a special jury[186] was called. Among those charged were Robert Pack (another J.P.) and James Power, two of the elected members. They were found not guilty. But Thomey, William Saunders, and William Harding were found guilty of making a riot, and were sentenced to prison for twelve months.[187] The men went to jail in St. John's on January 5; by March they were being termed "Glorious Martyrs."[188] A stream of petitions flowed to the King, including one each from the prisoners themselves.[189] Troy started saying mass in prison for them the day after their sentence commenced. He had to be watched. Authorities suspected he was smuggling in liquor.[190]

In January, both Fleming and Prescott faced what must have been unpleasant assignments, though in carrying them out the former perhaps displayed greater aplomb. Fleming, still overseas, responded at length to five charges against him drawn up in the colonial office in London. His letter to Glenelg gilded many lilies.[191] Parts of it were immediately sent to those he mentioned or accused, and the comments of these men were by no means flattering to the bishop. In effect, Fleming's political actions in Newfoundland were subjected to a government inquiry. But there was no snaring him. Protests sent to Rome had no effect. Fleming spent five months in Rome in 1837, and when he left Pope Gregory XVI gave him, not a rebuke, but a special jubilee to carry home.[192] Stephen in the colonial office realized the futility of appealing to Rome. "I suspect," he wrote, "that the Pope secretly enjoys the power of keeping a whole English colony in a ferment which His Holiness alone can quell." Even in the 19th century, he added, England cannot "entirely shake off its dependence ... on the Papal power."[193]

In the meantime, Glenelg, trusting too much in Boulton's judgment, had directed Prescott to issue "fresh writs" for another general election.[194] Prescott had the grim task of declaring the 1836 elections "void and of no effect," which in the light of a subsequent opinion of the crown lawyers was a preposterous development.[195] Each of the successful candidates received a letter stating the writs were invalid. Not surprisingly, this was met by outrage and disbelief. Many, including Troy, suspected a "trick," which of course it wasn't; but it didn't reflect well on either the competence of officials employed by the governor or the judgment of Boulton, Simms, and even Glenelg. The anger of members was justified. A petition to London in February, signed by close to 1,800 residents of St. John's, placed the "plot" in a historical context, with the inhabitants and the British government (which "at all times exhibited their anxious desire to protect the people") pictured as, from time immemorial, arrayed against the oppressors, the "Merchants and Adventurers." Reeves' *History* was the supporting text. The two parties in contemporary Newfoundland were continuations of those envisaged by Reeves. Though "there existed not the slightest indication of disorder" in the recent elections, "coercion and intimidation" had been practised on the supporters of "liberal principles" — a counterattack that comes close to outright deception — and there was much evidence that the informality of the writs pointed to "a conspiracy against the liberties of the people." The Assembly of 1832 did not represent "the wishes of the people"; that of 1836 did. The aim of Council and executive, representing the merchants, was to get "dominion" over the Assembly.[196] No reference was made to the role of the Catholic clergy in the elections.

Opinion was already starting to turn against the experiment of representative government, with Winton in the lead, calling for the withdrawal of the Assembly and its replacement by "Governor and Council."[197] It will be noted how early this line of thinking began. And it began in Newfoundland, not in London, where the idea of abolishing the Assembly was dismissed out of hand.[198] Nor did Prescott, in the darkest days of 1837 and '38, lose faith in the legislature as constituted. It was the "respectable" inhabitants of the colony who were losing faith. Instead of trying to defeat the opposing team, people were beginning to think the game, though barely started, should be called off. Such feeling intensified after the election in May, which resulted in an even stronger "reform" House than the earlier one. "The colony is not yet ripe for free institutions," Winton said, "not yet sufficiently emancipated from ignorance and thraldom."[199] But in fact there was no ruckus in St. John's or Harbour Grace this time. Had there been any sign of it, additional troops would have been sent from Halifax. Carson, Kent, and Morris in St. John's[200] and four Conception Bay reformers were returned unopposed. The conservative lawyer Row was elected in Fortune Bay, but in the event declined to take his seat. H.A. Emerson, the solicitor general, won in Bonavista, but he was heavily in debt and though conservative in outlook could not be counted on as an opposition figure. Through a kind of cowardice, or a feeling that Newfoundland politics was too dirty for men of civility and substance to engage in, or a sense that defeat was inevitable, the "tories" retired from the fray. It wasn't a "wave of popular feeling" that "swept" the reformers into the Assembly.[201] Kent, Carson, and their colleagues, and in the background Fleming, had the Assembly passed to them. And having handed it over, merchants would soon complain they were not represented in it!

The reformers' day had dawned at last. The House met on July 3 and unanimously chose Carson as speaker, a powerful position in the representative system. It need not be doubted that his combative instincts, not to mention his private interests, were behind many of the initiatives in the new Assembly.

Prescott's speech on opening day was conciliatory, but members defiantly appointed their own officers, immediately bringing them into collision with the governor and colonial office, and proceeded to other aggressive acts. Nugent, who was again elected, with Doyle, in Placentia and St. Mary's, and Morris at once assumed a conspicuous position. Morris rose on July 3 and gave notice that in a few weeks he would move for a committee of the whole House to inquire into the administration of justice. There would be no respite for Boulton, who had unluckily clashed with Carson and, perhaps even more dangerously, with Carson's son Samuel, another doctor, in two court actions in May. In one of these, William Carson v. John McCoubrey, the latter editor of the *Times*, Boulton told the jury that the phrase "mad Dr. Carson" was not a libel.[202] In the other, a case of defamation of character brought by the younger Carson against Kielley, who was Boulton's family doctor and friend, the chief justice strongly rebuked both Carsons in open court. (Carson *père* appeared as a witness.) Although Samuel Carson had brought the action, Boulton gave him to understand that he was lucky not to be hanged.[203] In June another petition against Boulton was being taken up in the Catholic chapel in St. John's, following a public meeting in the church yard.[204] The day after Morris's statement in the House about the administration of justice, Nugent demanded documents pertaining to criminal cases over the past two years, all election writs issued since 1832, depositions regarding Martin's alleged poisoning of a public well, and information about the arrest of a Protestant clergyman named William Nisbet, charged with "an unnatural crime."[205] He also wanted information about charges brought against Troy, Duffy, and Ward.[206] (The Duffy case had at last come to trial in May; he was found not guilty.)[207] Once they got a share of power, the Catholic Irish knew how to exercise it. Through the summer and fall of 1837, they took steps to consolidate and expand it. Their confidence grew in July when Prescott, acting on orders from London, released the three martyrs. They had served only half their sentence.[208]

With the hothouse about to get even hotter, it is well to recall that outside the capital life went on, though not untouched by the political battles at the center. Slow improvement — two steps forward, one back, sometimes two back — was the order of the day, as it was to be for most of Newfoundland's history until the 1930s. A few years of good fisheries were followed by one, or ones, of scarcity, climaxing in winters on the dole. The economy was not diverse enough to perform otherwise. Yet change was occurring. Government policy now encouraged agriculture, and it progressed, especially near St. John's, but slowly. Oats and barley were tried, without much success. Potatoes and hay remained the main crops. Those who couldn't afford to buy lots of land were allowed to rent them, with rent remitted for the first two years. In 1837 grants were made of some 2,000 acres. Much more was occupied by squatters. All those given grants had to swear that they intended "to settle and cultivate the same."[209] Despite all this, a deep skepticism persisted about the island's agricultural potential. Road building, which of course facilitated agriculture, had begun in earnest, and would get a decided boost in the reformers' House. By the mid- to late-1830s roads were either a-building or projected from St. John's to adjacent communities, around the head of Conception Bay, down the Southern Shore, across the peninsula from Carbonear to Heart's Content, between Holyrood and Placentia (linking Colinet and Salmonier), and from Trinity to Catalina and King's Cove. The main idea was to connect bays rather than encircle the coasts. Regular government-subsidized coastal service was not yet envisaged, but packet-boats were now in place, not just from Portugal Cove to Harbour Grace but between other centers in Conception Bay. In 1835-6, for instance, James Hodge had a "foursail" boat plying from Kelligrews, Brigus, and Port de Grave. She operated through the winter, weather permitting, and if it didn't permit, letters would be carried by land "by a careful person." This was one of at least three packets in Conception Bay.[210] In 1837 a copper-fastened 30-ton cutter named the *Æeriel* operated between Brigus and Portugal Cove. She had "a separate cabin amidships for the Ladies." In the same year the packet *Nora Creina* plied between Portugal Cove and Carbonear.[211] Moving overland and along the coast was getting slightly easier. New lighthouses at Cape Spear (the light was first exhibited on September 1, 1836) and Harbour Grace Island (from December 21, 1837), to add to the one at Fort Amherst, on the Narrows, also made coastal travel safer. As for education, the boards established by the Assembly, as already indicated, were impeded by sectarianism. Carson had tried to get a public classical academy established in 1834, but Peter Brown led the charge against it, fearing it would benefit St. John's pupils only. The middle classes were forced to send their children out of the country for advanced instruction, hire tutors, or make use of private schools of uncertain quality such as Nugent's in St. John's or William Gilmour's in Carbonear. At the elementary level, the Newfoundland School Society, founded in 1824 by the Low-Churchman Samuel Codner, in 1836 was operating thirty-eight schools in which about 2,500 were receiving instruction. Seventeen settlements, some with school rooms standing empty, pressed the Society to send teachers.[212] Fleming was of course driving Catholic education forward. As for science, it raised its head too. In Carbonear, the naturalist Philip Henry Gosse had completed, and beautifully illustrated, his study of Newfoundland entomology by the mid-'30s.[213] He bought his first microscope at an auction in Harbour Grace. It was perhaps through him that the youthful Philip Tocque acquired an interest in science,[214] later reflected in a number of publications, including one on oceanography. In 1837 money was voted by the House to defray the costs of a geological survey of the island. And Joseph Templeman, a clerk in Prescott's office, carried out impressive meteorological studies in St. John's from 1834 on.[215]

This progress was modest, to be sure, but progress nonetheless. Yet Newfoundland had already begun to export its middle class, even the native-born. Politics was partly to blame. Gosse left Carbonear in 1835 because the "social state" there "pulsated with Ireland's," and Newfoundland "was becoming a very unpleasant place to live in." "Flaming accounts" of the fertility of the soil in Upper Canada were now circulating; Gosse and some of his friends went there.[216] Joseph Shea was driven out by Fleming's remorseless persecution in 1837; his brother John left the same year. Timothy Hogan left. The 56-year old attorney general, Simms, after living on the island twenty-seven years, found that his income of £700 p.a. was insufficient to educate his children, who had to be sent to England for their schooling. In 1837 he asked to be transferred to another colony on a higher salary.[217] Templeman and his wife wanted to get out, as did Henry Simms, another denounced Catholic in St. John's. Part of Boulton's dissatisfaction sprang from concern for his large family. He found Newfoundland good for his children's physical health, but for little else. As events would show, they soon had their chance to savour milder climes.

The Assembly in August, 1837, renewed its assault on Boulton when Morris moved for his committee of the whole House to inquire into the administration of justice. His speech, on the 25th, was ordered to be printed. Occupying fifty-seven pages, the pamphlet listed nine "grounds" of complaint against the chief judge, including the charge that he exhibited "strong party prejudices" on the bench, leading to judgments that were "unjust, arbitrary, and illegal."[218] One complaint related to a case,[219] tried November 20, 1835, in which Boulton sorted out, at least to his own satisfaction, the relationships among three parties: the fishing servant hired on wages, the planter who hired him, and the merchant who supplied the planter and received the fish and oil. Boulton ruled that the servant whose labour produced the fish and oil had no claim on the supplying merchant for his wages. It was the planter who employed the servant, not the merchant.[220] This decision, widely trumpeted as overturning established customs in the fishery, was a grudge of long standing against Boulton, for it seemed to display an indifference towards ordinary workmen. It occupied a large part of Morris's speech, but his fierce objections at bottom were merely rhetorical. Morris did not have the knowledge or skill to tackle this or any other legal question. Fleming had made the charge too, and Boulton spent some tedious hours in September responding to it. But there was no way to respond to it that would ever satisfy his enemies. (Boulton's successor, J.G.H. Bourne, upheld the decision.)

In October the House, having narrowed the scope of their inquiry to the administration of justice in the supreme court, i.e., focusing it on Boulton, came to the conclusion that the "discontent and dissatisfaction" with Boulton was well founded, and that "his continuance in office would be inconsistent with the public good — the maintenance of public tranquility." A petition embodying this decision and asking for his removal was drafted. The House proceeded to appoint three delegates, Carson, Morris, and Nugent, to go to London to lay "the prayer of the people" for the judge's removal at the foot of the throne, on which Queen Victoria was now sitting. This led Boulton to instigate an action for damages of £2,000 against Morris, Kent, and Nugent, which in turn led to a petition from the Assembly to London complaining that the action breached its privileges.[221] Sheriff Benjamin Garrett, another long-time target of reformers' venom, accused in the Assembly of packing juries, initiated an action against Morris too. For good measure, he proceeded against Parsons as well, for printing Morris's libellous statements in the *Patriot*. Garrett was awarded damages in both cases. Morris got off comparatively lightly, the jury responding with compassion when they were told (by Morris's lawyer!) that the MHA was "half mad."[222] Though its agricultural produce was sparse, Newfoundland had been highly productive of litigation and petitions since the early 1820s. The output was about to pick up. Aware that the attacks against him were "unwearied," Boulton decided to head for England yet again. (As did Fleming, who was active there in the campaign to oust him.) The judge was supported in a petition to the Queen in December, signed by about 1,000 merchants, traders, and other inhabitants of St. John's, which repeated Winton's charges about "priestly tyranny" but stopped just short of asking for a change in the system of government. Boulton's removal, the petitioners said, would be "a loss not easily repaired."[223] The St. John's Chamber of Commerce endorsed the petition and sent it off under a separate cover.[224] Various other respectable citizens presented supporting documents as well.

The Assembly's guns were not aimed only at Boulton and Garrett. This was a belligerent House. (Which is not to say that all its actions were wrong-headed.) It sorely tried Prescott's patience over the appointment of its officers and resisted attempts at conciliation from London. It also tackled the Council, which it naturally came to see, and not without cause, as the bastion of Protestant and mercantile privilege. In October, 1837, late in the session, conflict erupted between the two branches of the legislature over money bills. The Assembly sent up a supply bill[225] comprising the full expenditure proposed for the year in a single appropriation. Included were large expenditures in a road bill that the Council had already rejected. The Council rejected the supply bill. The Assembly then removed the appropriation for roads and sent up a revised road bill, which the Council passed, though parts of it were considered objectionable. Then the Assembly sent up a bill covering remaining expenditures, including a large outlay for the contingencies[226] of the legislature. The Council demanded the right to consider and reject individual grants in the bill; this was denied. Undoubtedly guided by Carson,[227] MHAs maintained they alone had the power to appropriate public funds; the Council could only rubberstamp their decisions. Nothing in documents creating the legislature had limited the Council in this way, or given the Assembly this power. Councillors fought back, though conceding that the Assembly alone should have the power to initiate money bills, and otherwise signalling a willingness to compromise. Apart from theoretical considerations, the MHAs were allocating money in what seemed to Council members a shamelessly partisan fashion, paying off their friends, punishing opponents, and lining their own pockets. (Carson's rival Kielley, for instance, had his salary and responsibilities reduced in the proposed supply bill.)

There had been friction over money bills in the previous legislature, but it had not stalled proceedings. Now the Assembly would brook no interference, and when Prescott closed the session in November supplies had not been voted. This was serious, for the winter ahead looked as if it might be another lean and hungry one. And so it turned out to be. News of "the greatest distress, amounting almost to starvation" came from Harbour Grace in December, followed quickly by similar grim reports from Trinity, Port de Grave, New Harbour, Grates Cove, and other places.[228] Prescott could spend money only through the method of warrants, which meant he had to limit such expenditure to absolute necessities.

Once the supply bill failed, both the Council and Assembly drafted protests to the Queen.[229] The Assembly's begged her to "regenerate" the Council by separating its executive and legislative functions, presumably by making two councils, and by giving the legislative part of it a "representative principle," which must have meant bringing in Catholics and members from outside St. John's. Judges should be forbidden to sit on either council. These were sensible suggestions. If they couldn't be carried out, the address said, the two branches of the legislature should be amalgamated, according to the principles laid down by Goderich in 1832. This would allow officers of the Crown to sit with representatives of the people and "together consider the exigencies of the country." It was an afterthought, perhaps. But the Assembly's last proposal would return to haunt it.[230]

The address was delivered to Glenelg in London by Carson and Nugent in January, 1838.[231] This was not the only mail they carried. They had with them the charges against Boulton, addresses relating to the fisheries and agriculture, and a host of instructions, one relating to the nearly total exclusion of Catholics from public offices.[232] With these they had a number of accusations against Prescott, most utterly without foundation.[233] The address on fisheries, in essence a prayer for bounties, also insisted that the rights of the French between Cape St. John and Cape Ray were, properly considered, concurrent only. The latter point, here perhaps just a flourish, in fact now coincided with the official view of the British government which, after much agonized internal debate, decided in 1838 that notwithstanding the "practice" since 1783 of regarding the French rights as exclusive, no right to an exclusive fishery had ever been "specifically recognised" in an act of Parliament or other official document.[234] But the main object of the Newfoundland delegation was to drive out Boulton, whom Carson on departing had pilloried as a despot "who ought never to have been permitted to contaminate our shores." He made this remark in an address to the householders of Newfoundland, in which he appeared to take credit for all improvements since his arrival in 1808. "Your Liberties have been achieved," he told them.[235] Now that the Assembly was in the reformers' hands, the notion of progress from tyranny to freedom under their aegis was a favorite theme. Without bloodshed, said the *Patriot* in March, 1838, reformers had taken the colony "from absolute despotism to unalloyed freedom."[236]

The "despot" Boulton's fate was placed in the hands of the judicial committee of the Privy Council. Glenelg referred the address on the fishery to the Committee of the Council for Trade, which promptly turned down the request for bounties.[237] To the address on agriculture, which complained of the high cost of crown lands in Newfoundland, Glenelg answered that such "waste lands" should be sold at auction to the highest bidder.[238] On the conflict between the Council and Assembly over supplies, the Queen offered her mediation. The Council had the right to exercise "freely and fearlessly" the right to reject an appropriation bill,[239] her Majesty decided, but in the case in question did not make a "judicious exercise" of that right. The amount voted by the Assembly for contingencies was indeed large, but not so large as to justify the Council's charge that the money was directed "to the personal advantage" of MHAs. If such "selfish misappropriation" did occur, the Council might refer the parties involved to the "tribunal of public opinion," where the "censure of society at large" would be felt. In politics, her Majesty implied, it didn't pay to be too fastidious. On the whole, she was of opinion that if a supply bill substantially corresponding to the one previously thrown out were to be sent up again, it "ought not to be rejected."[240] When the House of Assembly reopened in June, Prescott brought the good news of this conciliatory plan. The House immediately sent to the Council a supply bill almost identical to the one rejected in 1837. It passed by a vote of 4-3, with the three dissenters vehemently opposed.[241] Conflict between the two bodies continued throughout the new session.

* * *

During the spring of 1838, rumours about the delegation's accomplishments trickled back to the colony: Glenelg thought highly of the road bill; the unofficial delegate Fleming, though again under investigation by Rome, had received good news about the land he wanted for his cathedral;[242] Nugent had a two-hour conversation with Lord Durham, who was about to leave for British North America to take up his duties as governor general and make recommendations for its future;[243] and London was said to have caved in on the question of the Assembly's right to select its own officers.[244] There was some headway reported on the French shore. Nugent and Carson had even been presented to the Queen.[245] As for the Council, Glenelg implemented the Assembly's suggestion to exclude the chief justice from it, and seemed inclined as well to split it into legislative and executive branches. (But he didn't do this.) For the reformers, every prospect seemed pleasing. But there were signs of division within their front ranks. Brown, always wary of St. John's dominion over the outports, was giving indications of doing his own thinking, and the *Patriot* broke with Carson, terming him an "imbecile."[246] The doctor, Parsons wrote, "was never a sincere advocate of the religious, social or political rights of the great Body of the People," i.e., the Irish. (Which was true enough, but Parsons' own sincerity as a promoter of the Irish was highly questionable.) But the transatlantic journey gave Carson new ideas, or strengthened old ones. An "essay" by him in May, 1838, responding to the rebellions of 1837 in

Upper and Lower Canada, envisaged bringing together all six British continental possessions "under one general Government" as "The United British Colonies of North America."[247] This was as a prelude to the time when "separation" between the colonies and mother country "must" take place. It was perhaps the earliest intimation in Newfoundland that the colony might be united with Prince Edward Island, New Brunswick, Nova Scotia, and the Canadas.[248] Carson did not, however, see the constitutions of neighbouring colonies as analagous to Newfoundland's. The model for Newfoundland's system of government was Britain. The King (or Queen), Lords, and Commons were analagous to Governor, Council, and Assembly; it followed that the Assembly's powers resembled those of the Commons. He had always held this view, and he explained it again in a letter published in July.[249] Glenelg seemed to support it too, in his dispatch conveying the Queen's mediation between Council and Assembly. He said: "The Constitution of the Legislature of Newfoundland is avowedly modelled on that of the Imperial Legislature."[250] Stated thus blandly, the proposition seemed harmless enough. But given the political atmosphere of St. John's in the late 1830s, it was dangerous, for the House of Commons had one power that was too tempting for the radicalized Assembly to pass by: the power to commit for contempt.

An occasion now arose to test the boasted analogy. One of the objects of reformers' derision was the surgeon Kielley, who although a Catholic was a friend of Boulton, Winton, and other prominent Protestants. He had long enjoyed the patronage of the governors, and had his name on all three lists of nominees for the St. John's "tory" candidates in the 1836 election. Although of Irish descent, he was a native Newfoundlander. This too might well have been a mark against him. Nativism was now in the air, and it did not mesh well with transported Irish chauvinism. The newly-arrived, semi-genteel Irish tended to look down on the natives. Fleming would permit none of that lesser breed in the priesthood; only Irishmen[251] were worthy of serving as priests in the diocese of Carpasia. In a notorious sermon to sealers in March, 1836, he linked "two or three natives" with the "knot of bad Irishmen" trying to put him down.[252] Nugent, as we will soon see, sneered at natives. Kent too, though he might say otherwise, possibly thought them inferior.[253]

In late July, 1838, Kent attacked Kielley in the Assembly, alluding to him as a sycophant and questioning whether he strictly performed the duties of the many medical offices "the Executive lavished upon him."[254] The two men met on the street on August 6. Kent called Kielley a "cormorant and robber of the poor," and Kielley responded by terming Kent a "lying puppy" and threatening to "pull his nose." Perhaps unused to hearing such a vigorous retort to his insults, Kent ran off to the Assembly and claimed his privileges as an MHA had been violated. After examining three witnesses, including Kent, MHAs determined that the speaker should issue a warrant to bring Kielley to the bar of the House. Carson issued the warrant, and the arrest was made by the sergeant-at-arms, Thomas Beck, and the messenger, David Walsh. Walsh later admitted he used "a little force" to get Kielley out of his home. Kielley remained in Beck's custody until the following day,[255] when, with "considerable excitement" spreading through the town, he was brought before the Assembly and asked to account for his conduct. He said the dispute with Kent was a private quarrel, and otherwise "justified his conduct." Carson did not interrupt him, or permit others to do so. But according to Winton,[256] when Kielley asked to bring witnesses he was stopped by Carson, who said the House had decided there had been a breach of privileges; Kielley could call no witnesses and would not be permitted to enter into particulars. Kielley at one point angrily termed Kent "a liar and a coward." (He apologized for this outburst in a letter to Carson next day.) He was ordered to withdraw, and was put in Beck's custody until further orders. This meant being confined to Beck's house. The following day, Kent moved to have him jailed until he made an apology in a form dictated by the House. (Demanding consent to an already drafted apology was a tactic of the priests.) A crowd in the gallery cheered, but Brown, to his credit, wondered about the justice of committing someone to jail without a trial. It was decided, by a 7-3 vote, to postpone Kent's motion for a day.[257] On August 9 Brown proposed that Kielley, on being brought to the House, apologize in these words: "I exceedingly regret that I have been guilty of any act or expression which has been considered by your honourable House to be a gross breach of its privileges" — upon which he was to be reprimanded by the speaker and discharged, after paying all (unspecified) expenses. Kent supported this more moderate approach.[258] Kielley was again brought to the House. The apology was put in his hands. On his asking for what "alleged offence" he was being asked to apologize, he was instantly stopped by Carson and others and told to answer "yes" or "no." Only that. Would he or would he not make the required apology? He asked for permission to withdraw for a few moments, which was granted. On his return, he tried again to ask what offence he had committed. He was again stopped by Carson and others. He was to say "yes" or "no" as to making or signing the apology, and "nothing more."[259] He declined to make the apology, whereupon Kent brought back his motion of the 8th, which passed. Carson issued warrants to the sheriff, Garrett, and the jailer, committing Kielley to the common jail, where he spent the night.

This was already an extraordinary proceeding. But much more was to follow. On the 10th, Kielley was brought before acting assistant judge and former auction-eer George Lilly[260] on a writ of habeas corpus.[261] Lilly decided the process by which he was held prisoner was "void" and ordered him released. Garrett then let him go. "Will the house hesitate in purifying itself from this foul indignity?" Parsons asked in the *Patriot* on the 11th; adding, in one of his most foolish sentences, "In the name of the people we call upon it to pursue the authors of this outrage to the death if needs be!" Carson that same day issued an order to Garrett to deliver Kielley to the House. Garrett reported what had happened on the 10th. The Assembly then resolved itself into a committee of the whole on privileges and, after due deliberation, ordered the arrest of Lilly and Garrett, and the re-arrest of Kielley. Beck, with a reinforcement of Assembly employees, went looking for the trio of privilege-vio-lators. He could not find Kielley, who was hiding out in Winton's house,[262] having seen enough of the inside of a jail. But Garrett and Lilly were taken into custody. Lilly resisted, and was dragged from his chambers in the court house and locked in the speaker's room downstairs, during which process he injured his left hand. After spending a half hour incarcerated there, he and Garrett, accompanied by a large crowd who had come out to see that rare phenomenon, the arrest of a sheriff, not to mention the even rarer one, the arrest of a supreme court judge, were led through the streets to Beck's house, where they were held until the 13th.[263] The Assembly had asserted its dominion. MHAs had already intruded into the executive functions of the governor by appointing its officers and through other actions. They had tried to monopolize legislative power by restricting the Council's jurisdiction to non-monetary items. The Kielley business showed them entering the judicial sphere.

On the 13th Prescott announced he would prorogue the House.[264] Despite efforts by MHAs to stay in session, he did so that day, whereupon the judge and sheriff were released. The immediate crisis was over. On the 13th also Lilly delivered his judgment on Kielley's imprisonment, in which he lucidly dismissed the Assembly's claim to the right to commit. The House had not been given that right, nor did it need it, since "the laws of the land are open to them as to every other body." If the power of summary committal assumed by the Assembly were legal, he wrote, then "such a power is of all others the most liable to be so abused as to render the liberties of all who dwell in this portion of the British dominions dependent on as frail a tenure as those of the subjects of the most despotic government in the world."[265] The judgment, which was quickly printed,[266] hit home, for it seemed to many that the MHAs had indeed behaved as arrogant despots in the Kielley affair.

As a naval surgeon, Kielley had been through bloody battles while Kent was a boy adding sums. He struck back. On August 20 Prescott reopened the House. On entering the speaker's room shortly before resuming business, Carson was served with a writ on behalf of Kielley, claiming assault and false imprisonment and setting damages at £3,000. Similar writs were served on other members, including Kent and Brown, on the messenger Walsh, whom Kielley tried to have arrested, and on Beck. On being handed the writ, Carson reacted with apparent nonchalance, but he was likely very frightened. As a (latterly unwilling) proprietor, he had "displayed the *white feather*" more than once in suits against the *Patriot*, labouring "most indefatigably to clear himself out of any scrape which was likely to affect his purse."[267] To lose this case might ruin him. Kielley's writ, sued out by his lawyer Bryan Robinson, was discussed in the House, and some thought was given to arresting Robinson as well. But caution suggested otherwise, and MHAs contented themselves with passing fourteen resolutions designed mainly to try to protect themselves from financial losses.[268] One resolution noted that, having jailed Kielley, Lilly, and Garrett, "it is not prudent, nor expedient, or necessary again to resort to the exercise of such extreme power." This was the dog with its tail between its legs.

Winton's analysis of the affair was scornful. While "incessantly brawling about *liberty*," he wrote, these "ultra-reformers" confirmed "the belief that they ardently aspire after supreme dominion" and that "they are the most unappeasable, incorrigible TYRANTS under the sun!" He added: "no man's personal liberty is safe. How can it be, when even our Judges may be dragged from the judicial bench and subjected to every indignity!" He called for the "total abolition" of the "charter" that had set up the Assembly.[269] The Harbour Grace *Star* echoed his sentiments, saying of those who sent Kielley to jail, "These are the gentlemen who abhor oppression, who all along have been declaiming against our *arbitrary* Fishing Admirals, our *despotic* Governors, our *tyrannical* Judges, our *absolute* Surrogates, our *grinding* and *exactious* Merchants and *snarling* Officials."[270] It was a point well made.

To add to the feelings of disgust and rage in "respectable" circles, news of Boulton's dismissal reached St. John's immediately after the Kielley fracas. The judicial committee of the Privy Council had reported on July 5.[271] The committee found no evidence to support the Assembly's imputation of "any corrupt motive or intentional deviation from his duty as a judge." In the light of this verdict, it hardly seems just for a modern historian to condemn Boulton for "persistent miscarriage and perversion of justice."[272] The "language and conduct" adopted towards the judge, the committee said, were unjust and disrespectful. Nevertheless, in "some" transactions he displayed "indiscretion" and he had "permitted himself to participate" in the "strong feelings" agitating the colony. It was therefore "inexpedient" for him to continue as chief justice of Newfoundland. Boulton protested, to no avail. His career, not just in Newfoundland, but in the service of the British government, was over. Open rejoicing, including the singing of the Te Deum, greeted the news in the Catholic chapel, though Eliza Boulton confronted the priests and created a scene in the churchyard that moved many.[273] But the reform party was exultant. If Lilly was to be credited, the Assembly might not have the power to commit — this in fact was a long way from being finally decided — but the reformers had undoubted influence in high places, for they had brought Boulton down, forcing even the colonial secretary Glenelg to bend to their wishes, as he had bent in the quarrel with the Council, and was weakly bending to Fleming[274] even as Winton condemned the "depraving process of concession" he engaged in. That process, Winton wrote, with "its correlative, arrogant pretension, which has occupied Ireland for 45 years, was, in Newfoundland, completed in less than the same number of months, and Newfoundland is already a *transatlantic Tipperary*."[275] "Where is all this *humbug* to end!" he exclaimed. When would Glenelg learn the baneful consequences of collaborating with "the factious revolutionary demagogues in this colony"?[276] The use of the word "revolutionary" was provocative. Winton accused the St. John's reformers of being in sympathy, even collusion, with the Canadian rebels. On the outbreak of the 1837 rebellions, the *Patriot* had editorialized: "may the God of Battle ensure the patriots success — and that speedily!"[277] It was a sentence the *Ledger* would not quickly let the public forget.

The expulsion of Boulton and incarceration of Kielley, Lilly, and Garrett aroused new antipathy, not just towards the reform party, but towards the system of government. The Assembly found itself under renewed attack. It sent off three more addresses to the Queen in October, two just before prorogation on the 25th. One of these answered accusations of disloyalty, for the charges of colluding with rebels had reached London. They also reached Liverpool, where, in September, merchants submitted a petition expressing "apprehension and alarm" over developments in the colony and demanding that "additional troops" be sent there. They referred to the Kielley affair and pointed to the "necessity" of investigating the nature of the elective franchise.[278] Similar addresses from Poole and Bristol, and a second from Liverpool, followed quickly,[279] all reminders that English merchants and investors still had a strong interest in the Newfoundland trade. In December two petitions in support of the Assembly were got up by the reform party. Both called for "a commission" of inquiry into the government and condition of the colony.[280] The St. John's Chamber of Commerce now took their protest one step higher. In a published petition to the Queen, it fiercely denounced the Roman Catholic priesthood for seizing control of the Assembly. All but one or two MHAs, the Chamber said, "were persons possessing but little property, hardly any education, and no standing in Society." They were selected "solely because they would be passive tools in the hands of the Priesthood." No one "possessing the education and the feelings of a gentleman" would enter the Assembly "to be associated with the individuals he would there meet." Given the nature of the franchise, there was no hope that any future election would change the make-up of the House. There had been prosperity and happiness in Newfoundland until, "in an evil hour," a representative system was "inflicted upon us." Among the grievances listed were the mistreatment of Kielley and removal of Boulton. The Chamber concluded by praying for "an immediate abolition of the present Colonial Legislature" and its replacement by a governor and enlarged council, the council to be appointed by the British government.[281]

This was a bombshell. It was the first public call by a body of prominent citizens, perhaps the most prominent, for the withdrawal of representative government. Its publication in St. John's in late December coincided with the supreme court judgment in the case of Kielley v. Carson, presided over by the new chief justice, Bourne, another Protestant English barrister with a Catholic wife, but a man whose leanings made him generally more acceptable to reformers. The decision went against Kielley, with Lilly, however, registering a cogent dissent.[282] Kielley immediately appealed to the judicial committee of the Privy Council, to which the question had already been referred by the colonial office in London. The anxiously awaited supreme court decision was greeted with some satisfaction by Carson, who stated in the *Newfoundlander* that the Assembly at its next session would take note of John Sinclair, the forwarder of the Chamber's petition to the Queen.[283] Sinclair, a prominent merchant, was the president of the Chamber and a member of Council. Carson's letter was a thinly veiled threat, and was recognized as such. But before the House opened, Prescott, in April, 1839, published the crown lawyers' view of the question, which was that the Assembly "has not the power of commitment."[284] Prescott's action may have kept Sinclair out of jail.

The Chamber's petition was received in the colonial office in January, 1839, and caused some dismay. Stephen asked: "Is it possible seriously to entertain such a question" as the "subversion" of the Assembly? He answered: "I apprehend not."[285] But the views of men such as Sinclair, Robert Job, Thomas Bennett, Ewen Stabb, and John Butler Bulley, together with the eight other signatories, had to be weighed carefully. Their petition was followed, moreover, by one from the merchants, traders, and shipowners of Conception Bay, likewise calling for the abolition of the legislature, and by three others (from the merchants of Torquay, Dartmouth, and Teignmouth) with the same objective in mind. In March Liverpool came back with a third address, requesting a "commission" to inquire into the constitution of the Assembly.[286] The sheer bulk of the petitions, seventeen in number, made an impression. The House of Lords took due note of the commotion.[287] In July, the Commons ordered that the petitions be printed. All signs pointed to deep trouble in Newfoundland. As one pamphleteer pointed out, the calls for an investigating "commission" came from both supporters and opponents of the Assembly. In his view, "some alteration" in Newfoundland's constitution was "indispensable."[288] It was not an unreasonable opinion. Supposing the foundations of politics in a democratic society to be compromise, fair and open debate, and respect for adversaries, then Newfoundland in 1839 was not a functioning democracy. One party had retreated into an armed camp, flinging complaint-laden petitions out into the world, pleading the "hopelessness" of securing fairness from a constituency blindly subservient to the priests.[289] The other, triumphant and arrogant, hungry for power, driven by a sense of grievance rooted as much in Irish grudges as in Newfoundland history, was edging its way towards tyranny. The experiment of representative government was not working. But it would take some more time for the colonial office to accept this. Having created the legislature, Stephen was reluctant to shut it down, and hoped that the savage sectarianism in Newfoundland would in time subside. One constitutional "alteration" was indeed officially proposed in 1839, namely that in Lord Durham's *Report*. He wanted Newfoundland brought under the projected British North American federal union. No one took this seriously. "We want no federal Government," Winton growled.[290]

Religious and political differences "are the bane of our peace," Prescott told the House as it closed late in 1838. "They destroy the delights of social intercourse, and impede every effort for the public good."[291] It was a grim comment on the first six years of democracy in Newfoundland. But outside St. John's and the two large Conception Bay towns, in places where there was less government, or even no government, there was, it seems, less discontent. A detailed report from the west coast of the island in 1838 noted that the population of Sandy Point and nearby "hamlets" in St. George's Bay stood at 400. They had no magistrate presiding over them, no clergy or customs officer; they were "all uneducated," with about fifty able to read and write. Yet they formed "a thriving community in possession of more comforts than any similar class I have met with around the shores of this island." So said Capt. J. Polkinghorne of H.M.S. *Crocodile.*[292] The settlers in the Bay lived by fishing salmon, herring, and cod, and by "great industry and thrifty habits" had cleared land as pasturage for cattle and sheep. Pigs and poultry were also abundant. About 100 more people lived at the mouth of the Great and Little Codroy rivers — north of Cape Ray, and so also within the French shore. This population of 500 was of varied origin. There were French from Cape Breton, St. Pierre, and France, some from England, Ireland, Scotland, and Guernsey, some from other parts of Newfoundland, one from New York, and a great many who were "born here." Polkinghorne didn't mention the Micmacs, but they were present as well. All seemed to coexist without undue friction. There was less ethnic variety in more recently and sparsely settled places to the north, where the English were dominant; but "the banks of the Humber" (with a population of seventy-four) and many coves on the coast north of Bay of Islands were now inhabited. French fishermen, who came to Bay of Islands and other parts of the coast in summer, did not "molest" the settlers, at least according to the captain. The only potentially warlike incident occurred when Polkinghorne saw a French flag flying over an establishment in St. George's Bay. He sent an officer ashore to take it down. Nobody stopped him.

The Cambridge-educated J.B. Jukes, who came to Newfoundland in May, 1839, to begin a geological survey and stayed until November, 1840, confirmed Polkinghorne's view of society on the west coast. "All nations" there, Jukes wrote, "live comfortably and peaceably together."[293] The only "want" he heard of in St. George's Bay ("the most inviting part of Newfoundland") was a wish for schools. The people on the south side of the bay were "more agricultural" than other inhabitants of the island. One spot "seemed a little paradise." In the vicinity of Crabbes River people were "all happy, comfortable, and independent," the sole complaint being a lack of books. Jukes found[294] some coal near Grand Lake and some more upriver at Barachois Brook in St. George's Bay, but when he got to the mouth of the Codroy River, also rumoured to have a coal formation, he had difficulty finding a Micmac guide to lead him to it. An Englishman named Gale had "strictly charged" the Indians to give no information about the location of the coal. He and other English settlers feared "that mines would be established, and that thus the neighbourhood would be regularly settled, and not only their trade and authority interfered with, but taxes and customs opposed." Jukes was regarded with "great suspicion" as a "Government agent." This is a reminder, if any were needed, that parts of Newfoundland, far from welcoming the intrusion of government, were glad to live without it. When Jukes got to Lapoile he again found "happy" people, though a customs officer now lived there. Government had arrived. The officer's presence, however, did not altogether prevent the practices of plundering wrecked vessels and smuggling. At St. Pierre Jukes found a number of schooners "from the neighbouring shores," loading French wines, spirits, and groceries. They "probably," he noted gently, intended to smuggle them into English settlements. As for relations between French and English on the south coast, despite the men-of-war on patrol "a tolerably good understanding" existed between the "lower orders of each nation, who probably find their account[295] in it." But Jukes did find evidence of the fostering hand of government on some eastern coastlines. Having had to suffer through so much thick brush and deep bog to carry out his geological work, he was always happy to come upon roads, and there were quite a number now made or under construction. The best one, he said, was the sixteen-mile road between Carbonear and Brigus. He found bridges too. He took the packet boat in Conception Bay. He called attention to the Harbour Grace lighthouse. Jukes even heard of a Bonavista Bay man who lived exclusively by farming, "entirely independent of the fishery," all the more remarkable in that he lived on an offshore island. The western side of Conception Bay, he said, had most of the comforts and conveniences of civilized life."[296] So, of course, did the capital city. He passed a pleasant winter in St. John's, partying, sleighing, viewing amateur theatre, and giving lectures on geology.

As for the practical results of his survey, they were not such as to start a gold rush or any other rush. He found gypsum, lime, plenty of stone for building materials, and, as indicated, some sign of coal. He visited Bell Island but didn't spot the iron ore there, which may not speak well for his ability to see what was in front of his nose. He didn't go far into the interior, although he was the first to describe Grand Lake,[297] which by 1839 was well known to Micmacs and other settlers; he also took a boat some distance up the Upper Humber, and went inland at the head of Freshwater Bay.[298] He didn't reach either Red Indian Lake or Gander Lake. There was plenty of exploring left for Alexander Murray and J.P. Howley in the later decades of the century, when the Geological Survey of Newfoundland, ably assisted by Micmac guides, carried on its important work.

Not even a geologist could avoid politics. In St. John's Jukes gave lectures in a hall that had previously been used only for meetings of the "Catholic party." "Some persons would not enter it," he noted. There was "a very considerable bitterness of party spirit" in Newfoundland, "but what the cause may be no one seems able to tell." His remarks convey the depth of animosity into which politics had fallen.[299] In his final months as colonial secretary, Glenelg had tried to reduce the rancour by appeasing Fleming, but the fretting bishop was not easily appeased, not even by the gift of land to build his cathedral. As already suggested, he did not respond well even to direct orders from Rome. When he was told in 1838 to deprive Troy of "all spiritual authority," he sent the priest to Merasheen Island in Placentia Bay — where there were people over whom the priest had spiritual authority.[300] Early in 1839 Prescott told Glenelg that he could see little hope of reconciliation with Fleming. If his resignation would help matters, Glenelg could have it. Prescott, one of the ablest of 19th-century governors, was becoming weary of presiding over the distracted colony. McLean Little confirmed his view of the bishop. "Dr. Fleming in 1835 is Dr. Fleming in 1839," he wrote.[301] But there was reason for worry outside the ecclesiastical sphere. The winter and spring of 1838-9 brought more demands for relief, so many that Prescott overspent the sum voted for such assistance by the Assembly.[302] If no easy solutions were at hand in the government of Newfoundland, neither were there any in the economy. Nor did conflict with the Assembly show signs of ending. Having showed its muscle in the Kielley affair, the House in May expelled Power, the Conception Bay MHA and a Catholic, for accepting an office under the Crown. Prescott had appointed him stipendiary magistrate. But the governor refused the Assembly's request for a by-election writ, and the crown lawyers soon declared the House had acted "contrary to law."[303] Power was entitled to retain his seat. This was but one point of friction. The long 1839 session was productive of little good and much hard feeling. The two branches of the legislature couldn't even agree on a relief bill, though again it was clear one would be needed for the coming winter.

Yet in July, in a lengthy report to the new colonial secretary, Normanby, Prescott argued against the abolition of the legislature. While acknowledging "the outrageous violence" of the Assembly in the Kielley affair, he said that "in the midst of contention, animosity and jealousy" Newfoundland had "advanced" in some important areas. He did not believe the "trade and industry" to be in a state of "progressive or permanent decay" and there was no "just cause" for fear over "security of property." Prescott recommended a number of reforms: increasing the number of districts (as had been legislated in the disallowed bill of 1834), which he thought would bring more Protestant members into the House, and extending the area represented to Cape Ray; creating a property qualification for representatives to keep fishermen, attracted by the stipend of £1 per day (up to a total of £42) that MHAs had voted themselves, out of the Assembly; some tinkering with the structure of the Council, should it be decided to divide it into executive and legislative branches (which in principle he opposed); and other small changes.[304] Stephen was delighted with his evenhanded report, as was Henry Labouchere, now under-secretary in the colonial office. Labouchere had no doubt the Assembly was "a rude & illiterate body," but it had inflicted no "positive injury" on the community apart from its use of the power of committal.[305] Prescott's report took the edge off the arguments for radical change coming in from merchants and their lobbyists in London. It appears to have convinced Normanby[306] and his successor in 1839, Lord John Russell, that for the moment there was no need to ask Parliament to enact any changes in Newfoundland's constitution, not even the modest ones Prescott suggested. The governor was asked if the changes he had in mind could be effected without recourse to Parliament. In other words, could they be introduced by local legislation. He quickly saw the absurdity of this. The power to prevent his measures from being adopted, he pointed out, was held by the very ones, i.e., members of the House, "against whose ascendancy [they were] intended to operate."[307] That being so, remedial action from that quarter was extremely unlikely.

Unsettling news from "the oldest colony" kept arriving. In December Prescott sent Russell a lengthy printed address from the Assembly to the Queen, together with his own comments on it. A party that had accomplished the "overthrow of an undue Mercantile Ascendancy," and conducted its reform agenda through a number of sessions in a House without opposition, might have been expected to present Her Majesty now with a recital of accomplishments. But the document was a litany of grievances. The "difficulties and embarrassments" facing MHAs were "hourly increasing." They complained of animosity towards them in the executive government, of mercantile enmity, of a lack of cooperation from the assistant judges and the attorney general, of attacks by the press, of obstruction and abuse of the Assembly's privileges by the Council —of having to struggle against "a tide of hostility and opposition." The "march of Reform" had not been slowed by them, but by their numerous enemies. The "Mercantile Party" — themselves complaining of the tyranny imposed by the reformers — had "succeeded" in "cramping the genius" of the people and "impeding" the development of the country. The House looked to her Majesty to solve this myriad of problems by adopting such reform of the Council as would "most tend to produce a harmonious working with the Assembly for the public good."[308] Even the conciliators in the colonial office could see the significance of this address, filled as it was with half-truths and shirking of responsibility. The reformers had stirred up so much enmity in society that the Assembly they controlled wasn't functioning. By the MHAs' own admission, elective government was breaking down. Russell waited until March, 1840, to respond to this and yet another moaning address from the Assembly.[309] Her Majesty's opinion, he told Prescott, was that the Council had not exceeded the constitutional powers vested in it. There was no basis for the charge that it had impeded public business or deprived the Assembly of its rights. The British government still held the view that the differences between Council and Assembly were transitory, and that some forbearance on the part of MHAs "will ensure them the respect of those classes which they now admit to be indisposed towards them." If that didn't happen, "it will be necessary to examine more deeply into the source of the evil, with a view to ascertain why, in Newfoundland, a system of free [government] should have failed in producing its natural happy results." Should the existing constitution be thought unfitted for the island, the "system of representation" would be "remodelled" and the franchise changed to "secure the participation of those portions of the community who are at present excluded from it."[310] It was the first intimation from London that drastic change might be imminent. Colonial officials were prepared to wait a while longer to see if good government could be restored in Newfoundland. But their patience was running out.

The March dispatch[311] had the effect of bringing MHAs at least temporarily to their senses, and when the House closed at the end of April, 1840, a supply bill as well as a revenue bill[312] had been passed. In an effort to secure tranquillity, Prescott early in 1840 took two steps, neither of which displayed his usual circumspection. The Council, acting in its legislative capacity, had refused to pass the Assembly's contingency bill, which meant that none of the officers or others entitled to stipends had been paid. Nor had the equivalent bill been passed the previous year. Two days before the House closed, Carson, to whom his pay of £200 p.a. as speaker was now no small consideration, asked Prescott on behalf of the Assembly to issue warrants to defray the contingent expenses of the legislature for both 1839 and 1840. Prescott of course refused.[313] On April 30, Carson wrote the governor and begged for his money. He was experiencing "great pecuniary inconvenience."[314] Prescott again refused. But on May 5, with the legislature no longer sitting, Carson and seven other MHAs, including the fisherman Edward Dwyer and the Dildo constable Thomas Fitzgibbon Moore, again approached Prescott, asking that he authorize payment of the parts of the contingency bills that had not been objected to, which of course included the speaker's stipend. Acting with the advice of the Council — in its executive capacity — Prescott issued the necessary warrants. The "most irregular proceeding" was noted in the colonial office and the hint was given to the governor that his "reasons" for acting as he did would be required.[315] The incident revealed both Carson's and other members' willingness, despite their fiercely declared purpose of adhering to constitutional practice, to step outside such practice when it suited them. Less than a year before they had denounced the governor for defraying modest but unvoted expenditures for the poor.[316] Prescott's other doubtful action in the spring of 1840 was to nominate Morris as councillor and colonial treasurer. London confirmed the appointments in May.[317] Morris addressed a farewell letter to the St. John's electors, commenting bitterly on his relationship with Carson, and moved up the ladder.[318] Once an ostentatiously wealthy man, his fortunes, as Prescott knew, had declined, and he had given evidence of erratic behaviour. Fleming's unwillingness to act as one of his sureties should have given a hint of what was to come.[319] Stephen in London noted at one point that there were "grounds for suspicion" of Morris's "pecuniary trustworthiness," but he didn't act on them.[320] On his death in 1849, it was found that Morris had robbed the treasury of some £6,600. His legacy to his family was destitution and disgrace.

Shortly after noon on May 15, 1840, five years almost to the day after the assault on Winton, one of his employees named Herman Lott was attacked near Saddle Hill by four men disguised by means of black crepe over their faces. Lott had a sword-stick and managed to wound one man in the face. He was dragged into the woods and beaten; clay was stuffed into his ears and mouth, whereupon "portions of both ears [were] removed evidently by a sharp cutting instrument."[321] The attackers also stole some money Lott had in his pockets. A reward of £300 was offered for disclosure of the assailants' identity, and an investigation was carried out. As was normal in Harbour Grace, it led nowhere. The outrage itself was only slightly more shocking than the episode that apparently provoked it. Late one night the previous February Lott had been kidnapped in St. John's, blindfolded, and led to a house where he was closely questioned about activities in Winton's home and printing shop.[322] Following the lengthy interrogation, he was warned not to divulge "one word" of what transpired, for there was a "Ribbon Society"[323] in Newfoundland "equally as terrible as ever it was in Ireland." He was again led blindfolded through the streets, and released. Lott at once reported what had happened to the St. John's magistrates. With the help of a constable, he tried to identify the house to which he'd been taken, and decided that the likely one was the home of the Assembly doorkeeper, John Delaney, Troy's brother-in-law. The constable initially was refused admission to the house, but when magistrates P.W. Carter and Charles Simms turned up, Delaney let them in with Lott, who could not make a positive identification. But he remained convinced he had found the right house. News of this affair reached the Assembly, where Nugent, now a dominant figure, angrily defended the doorkeeper and evidently termed Lott "a drunken young scoundrel."[324] The House appointed a committee to investigate, with Nugent as chairman, and the magistrates were summoned to give evidence. Nugent later tried to get the House to reduce their salaries as punishment. Simms and Carter, the former, as Nugent would learn, by no means a man to meddle with, claimed the committee was "an interference with the duties of the magistracy."[325] They were prepared, they said, to have their conduct undergo "a rigid inquiry" before the supreme court or elsewhere. Prescott ordered no such inquiry, though he might well have done so in what seemed a clear case of intimidation of magistrates. But he did refuse the House's request for copies of depositions. For its part, the colonial office viewed the "barbarous" assault on Lott with "indignation."[326] Stephen noted that Prescott hadn't denied the charges brought against the Assembly by the magistrates. The House's conduct, if Simms and Carter were to be believed, was, he said, "exceedingly absurd, if not oppressive."

The officials were soon to hear more gloomy tidings. The elevation of Morris meant a by-election had to be called in St. John's. Prescott called it. Polling was set to begin May 20. In an effort to conciliate Catholics, he appointed Beck, who had arrested Kielley and Lilly, as returning officer. Events at first unfolded peacefully. James Douglas, the former part-owner of the *Patriot* and a Scottish

Presbyterian, was nominated as the "liberal" candidate. He had tried to get elected in 1836 in Bonavista Bay. Conspicuous among his supporters were Kent, Nugent, Carson, and Laurence O'Brien, this last an Irish merchant from Waterford known for his hard dealings and reputedly unpopular with the "lower orders."[327] Parsons of the *Patriot* supported Douglas as well. In another display of senseless aloofness, the "conservative" party nominated no one. As support mounted behind Douglas, Fleming decided it was time for action. He had stayed out of the political arena long enough. A few days before the poll opened, for reasons perhaps needing no deep inquiry to discover, he concluded that O'Brien was a more acceptable nominee, and the merchant was persuaded, or ordered, to run. Kent immediately defected to O'Brien, as did Nugent. Fleming's support for O'Brien was announced over the altar, at first by his priests, then by the prelate himself, who addressed his constituency not just in church but in front of his Palace (as the bishop's residence was called). On polling day the priests appeared on the hustings, urging support for O'Brien. They stayed there throughout the election, letting it be known, as Prescott reported, that the honour of "their holy religion" was at stake, as well as that of their bishop. Even Parsons denounced their intervention as "unpardonable."[328] As days passed, excitement grew, for the election was close. "Respectable" Catholics came out to support Douglas, and with them, in time, Protestant conservatives as well, though quite a number were turned away by Beck on the advice of Nugent, who as O'Brien's attorney was on hand, with priests, in the polling room.[329] Attacks on special constables were reported. On May 25, Prescott received a protest from Douglas's supporters, calling his attention to the "gross outrage and violence" directed at them from the party "headed ... by the Catholic Priests." Carson's name was third on the list.[330] Prescott alerted the military, but didn't call them out until May 28. The poll remained open another ten days. When it finally closed, O'Brien had won by eight votes. Fleming had triumphed once again. "I hold his continuance here," Prescott wrote home in June, to be "utterly incompatible with the peace and prosperity of the colony." No governor could obliterate "religious jealousy and hatred" while he remained.[331] Lord John Russell suggested to the foreign office that another effort be made to remove him.[332] A strong protest should be sent to Rome. One was sent. The Pope got angry. In November, Cardinal Giacomo Fransconi, prefect of the Propaganda, wrote to Fleming and summoned him to Rome. Had he gone, the British minister Thomas Aubin reported, he likely would "never" be permitted to return.[333] But he didn't go. He "claimed never to have received this letter," writes his biographer Lahey.[334] It would take more wiles than were at the disposal of the Cardinal prefect of Propaganda to corner this old fox.

The by-election appeared to show that the allegedly profound historical and philosophical differences between "liberals" and "conservatives" were skin deep. Talk of "mercantile" and "popular" policies in Newfoundland now seemed little more than hot air. What politics was chiefly about was religion, or, to refine it even further, about who got Fleming's support and who didn't. One day a merchant might get it, another day a pauper. It was perilous to divine which way the sainted man would turn. In the wake of Douglas's defeat, a bewildered Parsons tried to puzzle out the meaning of the tory-liberal alliance that had backed him. It seemed to Parsons that he had witnessed "the long wished-for amalgamation of the Mercantile party with the Liberal Interest." This was important because "it united the great capitalists of the country with a people who were taught hitherto to regard them as their enemies."[335] He asked: "What kind of a creature shall be ushered forth as the fruit of the union"?[336] In fact, the "fruit" of the by-election was an unexpected one. At some point during the campaign Nugent made a fateful error. In a speech he referred scathingly, apparently to some of Douglas's supporters, as "copper-coloured natives in their native woods."[337] It is not clear exactly what he meant by this, and indeed he denied he said it.[338] But he made some such remark. Perhaps he was hinting Newfoundlanders were half-breeds; certainly that they were deficient and primitive. The remark stung.

It provoked the formation of the Newfoundland Natives' Society.[339] Within a month of the election, the society in St. John's had a membership of nearly 300, and it was said that branch associations were springing up in Conception Bay. "This is a new era in our local nomenclature," Parsons, who was a Newfoundlander, wrote in the *Patriot*.[340] Because the committee in charge of a bulding called the Factory (which gave employment to the poor) would make a room available only under demeaning conditions, while the Benevolent Irish Society refused outright to let it use the Orphan Asylum school, the Natives' Society held its first quarterly meeting on September 12 in John Ryan's fish store. About 200-300 attended. "This night," Parsons said in a fiery speech, "we proclaim ourselves a people — we proclaim our nationality, and we shall fail to do our duty, if henceforth we do not make that nationality to be respected."[341] At the meeting a motto ("Union and Philanthropy") and a flag were displayed. The complex flag bore an elaborate device around which was a wreath "composed of the rose, thistle and shamrock, denoting the stock from which the Newfoundlander derives his origin." A twenty-five member committee of management, including an executive, was already in place. The first president, Kielley, stated the society's purposes, which included "co-operating with the peaceable, orderly, respectable and well-disposed inhabitants of this Island" — this sounds very much like a backhanded slap at the rowdy Irish —as well as promoting the interests of "our fellow countrymen." The "Rules, Regulations, and Bylaws" of the Society made it clear that membership was confined to "the Natives of Newfoundland exclusively."[342] The organization was now, to all appearances, firmly established. It would be a factor in local society, and a means of drawing Newfoundlanders into public life, until the mid-1840s. It was always more Protestant than Catholic but its overwhelmingly "respectable" membership spanned both religions. It seems to have been a genuine effort by reasonable men to escape the hateful transatlantic legacy that had so embittered life on the island, and to claim for the native-born a place in the power structure. In practice, this meant trying to wrest control of the country's political institutions from the priests' party, a fact that the priests and Irish were not slow to discover. By September, 1840, the society was being preached against over the Catholic altar.[343]

Events would soon show that the priests were not easily dislodged. Increasingly under attack as a weak, temporizing governor,[344] Prescott, having blundered on various fronts, soon had an opportunity to blunder again. One of the Conception Bay MHAs, Anthony Godfrey, died in June. The governor called a by-election, to take place between October 25 and December 8. The two candidates were James Prendergast, born in Harbour Grace, a businessman, and Edmund Hanrahan, a native of Carbonear. Both were Catholic and supposedly "liberal," though Prendergast had the support of the leading Harbour Grace merchants William Punton, John Munn, and Ridley. The priests, however, supported Hanrahan. The returning officer, Pinsent, opened the poll in Harbour Grace on November 9, and the next day magistrate Thomas Danson reported that Hanrahan was in the lead and all was well.[345] All would stay well as long as Hanrahan's lead held. It didn't. By November 13, when the polling ended at Harbour Grace, Prendergast had overtaken him, but only slightly. A week later at Brigus he was ahead by 200, but Harbour Main, being Catholic, brought this back to 60. Carbonear and the area north of it (the North Shore) were still to be polled. Pinsent now headed for Western Bay on the North Shore, intending to return to Carbonear to complete the polling. On November 30 members of Prendergast's party, trying to pass through Carbonear to Western Bay, were severely beaten by Hanrahan's supporters. The magistrates, unable to preserve "the public tranquillity," asked Prescott to send a military force from St. John's. He refused. On December 1-3, polling took place at Western Bay. Some initial skirmishing was put down, but on the 2nd about 80-100 voters from Lower Island Cove, backers of Prendergast, were driven away by twenty men armed with sticks. Prendergast's lead dropped to 48. The magistrates again asked for military protection. Prescott called the Council together on December 5, although he needed no approval from them to send troops. The Council advised him that, considering the season of the year and the imminent closing of the poll, sending soldiers was "impracticable." The polling at Carbonear was set for December 7-8. On the 8th, evidently because the priests' party feared the election was lost,[346] a wholesale riot broke out and in the early afternoon, well before the scheduled termination of 4:00 p.m., Pinsent closed the poll. (Prendergast was still narrowly ahead, but no winner was declared.) Despite the presence of magistrates and constables, Hanrahan's men now made a "general attack" with pickets and stones on those of Prendergast. Ridley was hit from behind on the head with a heavy stick and was seriously injured, as was Punton. Many others were bloodied. At night, with Carbonear "in possession of an infuriated mob," two houses were burnt, one only "partially," many others had their windows smashed, and guns were fired. Four men and two women were shot at and injured. Pandemonium reigned. On the night of December 9,[347] fearing an assault by rioters from Carbonear, Harbour Grace men armed themselves with sealing guns and stood guard until morning. Carbonear, said the magistrates, was "without the pale of the law."[348]

On the 9th Prescott at last agreed to send troops, and 100 soldiers were dispatched, arriving on the 12th. Order was soon restored, and magistrates and constables started rounding up rioters. Within a week thirty-four warrants were issued. Court work stretched well into 1841, though as in the past few convictions resulted. Prescott argued that the events showed the necessity of putting a permanent military force in Conception Bay, but he was abruptly told this would not be done; he was also rebuked for his failure to send troops on the 5th.[349] On learning of the riots, officials in London threw up their hands. Stephen said that at Carbonear "the elective franchise is in the hands of the Irish colonists," a "herd of wild people" who "approach the savage much more nearly than the civilized state," and who were as little qualified for voting "as so many Malays would be."[350] The priests had been very active in the Hanrahan campaign, but while "walking among the assembled multitude" had recommended peace and exerted themselves on occasion to repress brawling. This, said Prescott, was like a man who sets fire to a house, then tries to extinguish the flames. He blamed Fleming for permitting his clergy to take part in such a "degrading" contest.[351] Stephen saw "no proof" that Fleming was directly answerable for the riots, yet he thought, with Prescott, that both the bishop and the priests bore responsibility for what happened.

Prescott reopened the legislature on January 2, 1841. In his address he pointed out that a new election law was needed to preserve the peace and secure the undisturbed exercise of the franchise. If in the two chief districts "elections can only be carried on under protection of bayonets," the "inevitable inference" must be that "the island is unfit for a representative system" and "not duly prepared for conducting its own affairs."[352] He had not in fact reached that conclusion[353] — he was a man of great patience. But he had his fill of governing Newfoundland, and on January 12 asked to be relieved.[354] 1841 would in the natural course of things bring another election, but Prescott let it be known that unless the electoral law he had proposed were passed, he would issue no new writs. No effort of persuasion by him had any effect. The legislative session proceeded with as much if not more acrimony between Assembly and Council, and not without some trepidation in the House owing to the news from overseas that the appeal in Kielley v. Carson had been heard by the judicial committee. When MHAs presented a petition asking for the division of the Council into executive and legislative branches, they were tartly informed that her Majesty's government would have to consider "several other questions" before getting to that one.[355] On April 2 a dispatch was sent to Prescott, informing him that a select committee of the House of Commons had been appointed to inquire into Newfoundland affairs. His presence would be required in London.[356] The Assembly closed in late April. As if to illustrate the crisis in Newfoundland's elective system, the legislature had passed no supply bill, road bill, land bill, education bill, or electoral bill. Parsons commented that MHAs had exhibited not just "inefficiency" but "madness."[357] (He was smarting from having lost his position as House printer to the new Catholic paper under Nugent's control, the *Newfoundland Vindicator*.) Legislators had, however, passed a revenue bill, to expire the following June, so public funds would be available for the governor or administrator to spend by warrants. The House had now run its four-year term.[358] Prescott, fulfilling his earlier threat, would not take the responsibility of calling another election under existing laws. He left for England on May 24. Delegations from the Council and Assembly set off too, and a number of other would-be witnesses, including Herman Lott. The hearings would be long over when they arrived.

Stephen was at last convinced of "the existence of a great and crying evil in Newfoundland."[359] So was the British government, which took the step many had been asking for. It "determined[360] to suspend the constitution of the island."[361] The permanent withdrawal of the legislature was not seriously contemplated, though it was made clear that "under circumstances of more urgent necessity than at present exist" even that drastic action might be taken.[362] Yet suspension was serious enough. Elective government, while not without turmoil, had worked in other colonies — too well in America! Yet Newfoundland appeared to be unable to govern itself. The normal colonial constitutional structure had not functioned there. What had brought the island to this juncture? What was to be done with it?

In the House of Commons committee hearings in May, with all Newfoundland's dirty linen on display, special attention was paid to Fleming and his priests. The evidence presented on religious matters was riveting, and in the case of Joseph Shea, summoned from Wigan (near Manchester) to testify, deeply moving.[363] Lord Stanley, soon to be colonial secretary, the young Gladstone, and O'Connell were some of the committee members. A few seemed genuinely appalled by the goings on in Newfoundland. Besides Shea, Thomas Holdsworth Brooking[364] could not have failed to make an impression. He had lived in Newfoundland from 1806 to 1830, and had been active in the campaign for representative government. He had also visited the colony in 1831 and 1835. His firm, Robinson and Brooking — his partner was the Worcester MP — had remained active in the Newfoundland trade and fishery, and in 1841 had premises in St. John's, Trinity Bay, and Bonavista Bay. In short, he was a big merchant. He now claimed that the constitution granted to Newfoundland in 1832 "has failed in every particular." Society was "perfectly distracted" through sectarianism. His own effort to make peace with Fleming had miscarried owing to Fleming's rudeness. When O'Connell tried to get him to enumerate Catholic grievances, he retorted: "The grievances were on the other side; the Roman-catholic priest party wanted to get possession of the House of Assembly ... to govern the island through the administration of the Roman-catholic bishop." His firm, he said, was withdrawing a portion of its capital from the island because of "political distractions." The extensive suffrage in Newfoundland had brought

about "tyranny." There was no cure for the "evils" except "abolishing the legislature." He wanted no legislative authority left in the island, unless it were vested in
a governor and extended council who could bring in measures to be later confirmed
in England. He would do away with the "principle of election" in the colony.

In Brooking's testimony and that of Robert Job and Ewen Stabb, both merchants, and even Shea, the son of a merchant, the questioners might have picked
up something more than hostility to Catholic insurgency, namely a skepticism about
the possibility of developing Newfoundland's resources. It was a fishing station
and nothing more, said Shea. Stabb said the same. All four questioned the value of
roads. The usefulness of roads, perhaps understandably, was not clear to one and
all, since no one lived, or wanted to live, in the interior and boat travel was obviously
the more efficient means of transport for a small and scattered coastal population.
What was more, heavy expenditure on roads led inevitably to increases in taxes.
Tax increases, i.e., increased duties, fell first on importers of merchandise. The
merchants had supported a local legislature in 1831-2 because the power to tax
remained in Britain and so was out of their hands at a time when the "home"
government seemed much disposed to use it. Ten years later it was still out of their
hands, and was being used, not always sensibly, by a party hostile to them, one
partly made up of men of little or no property. Men "with no stake in the country,"
as they were fond of putting it, and worse than that, some not far above the rank of
paupers, were picking their pockets. This accounts to some extent, perhaps even
more than their loathing for priestly rule, for the merchants' changed attitude
towards legislative government.

The Catholic MP Charles Langdale, questioning the artillery captain and
Catholic convert Henry Geary, wondered if mercantile opposition to roads was due
to the access those roads gave to cultivable land. Increased home production, he
hinted, would threaten the interests of those who supplied provision to the island.
Geary replied "There is no doubt of it." Some truth may lie in this — the charge
had previously been made by reformers — yet the merchants' attitude to agricultural development was ambiguous. They had called on Britain in 1817 to promote
the cultivation of the soil.[365] They too were trying their hands at farming. Their
names were prominent among the founders of the Agricultural Society in 1842.
Still, the Council's opinion in 1834 to the effect that agriculture "can never subsist
as an independent branch of national industry"[366] likely expressed the merchants'
real view. They could see for themselves what the rocky, acidic soil would produce.
As it turned out, any doubts they had were well founded, as Carson, who lost a lot
of money in agricultural pursuits, was now finding to his dismay.

The House of Commons committee ended its hearings on May 18.[367] Three
days later in St. John's, a procession, with the bishop and two priests in the rear,
made its way through the streets to the cathedral site, where Fleming laid the
foundation stone of his great edifice. Banners bore the images of the Virgin, the
Pope, the Queen, St. Patrick, St. John, the Redeemer, and Daniel O'Connell.[368] This

could not have been thought the happiest of harbingers for the future. Winton said that one of the bands attending, that stationed between the Queen and O'Connell, struck up the merry air of "Go to the d——-l and shake yersilf, and when ye come back behave yersilf," adding: "But how DARE Dr. Fleming insult this community with these exhibitions!"[369] His bad temper continued through the summer. But the news of Melbourne's electoral defeat by the conservatives under Peel in July greatly cheered him, as it must have dampened any plan of a return to politicking by Fleming, for O'Connell, though reelected, was now shunted well into the wings. To add to the good news, a governor was on his way. Like a holiday, a new governor was always better in anticipation than in actuality. Sir John Harvey, lately dismissed as governor of New Brunswick, arrived in September, 1841. He was greeted on the Ordnance wharf by Fleming and his priests, amidst various other dignitaries. In their address of welcome, the bishop and clergy assured him they had never failed to urge upon the Catholic people "respect for the laws, and submission to the constituted authorities." He responded warmly to this rewriting of history. When the Natives' Society alluded vaguely to past troubles, Harvey said "it may be wise to throw the mantle of oblivion" over them.[370] He would not be the last to try to gloss over events in early 19th-century Newfoundland. Later historians would make a habit of it.

Harvey was less a conciliator than a glutton for applause. But such a governor, rather than a disciplinarian or man of principle, might have been just what the colony needed in 1841-2. Harvey went to work and soon, by illegally granting funds out of the disputed supply bill,[371] something for which he had precedent in Prescott's earlier dubious action, he had Carson and other out-of-work MHAs on side. He let two rioters out of jail in Harbour Grace, but kept a reduced detachment of soldiers there over the winter, thereby satisfying both the unruly elements in the area and those terrified of them. In October he gave £5 to Fleming towards building the cathedral. The amount, which in fact he could ill afford since he was heavily in debt, was so small that it could hardly offend Protestants, and yet not so insignificant as to constitute an insult to Catholics. By arts like these, Harvey soothed the frayed tempers of the colonials. Winton kept a wary eye on him. Even that stern figure warmed slightly towards the close of 1841, and we find him, astonishingly, praising Fleming's efforts in the temperance movement. But in December he pointedly noted Prescott's "great error," which was to attempt to conciliate the "*soi-disant* 'Liberal'" party by such efforts as the unwise appointments given to Morris. The efforts had backfired, Prescott in the end being despised for "his want of firmness."[372] It was a not-so-veiled warning to the new governor.

Harvey might wish to cast a veil over recent problems, but Stanley and his officials wouldn't. They searched for a solution. In his questions to Brooking at the House of Commons committee Stanley had already given indications of what the answer might be.[373] Late in 1841 he told Harvey that "half the trouble" in governing small colonies arose from feuds and jealousies over privileges between the two branches of the legislature. He thought the union of the two in one chamber might be preferable, and he asked Harvey, who had already lengthily delivered his views on possible constitutional change, for his advice on the "practicability" of such an amalgamation of the Council and Assembly in Newfoundland. His idea was that the proportion of nominees to elected members would be 2:3.[374] Stanley thought this was a means of getting "the two great classes" of the community, "the commercial and resident class," to "act and re-act upon each other" without either getting a monopoly. He had doubtless learned much of the conflicting roles of these "classes" in the letters sent by the House of Assembly delegates,[375] who were in London during the summer and persisted in spouting Reeves' *History* as if it were gospel. How far this idea of "class" conflict might go towards explaining New-foundland society in 1841 might be debated. The "liberal" Parsons had earlier rejected out of hand the depiction of merchants as belonging to a non-resident class and as the opponents of the "poor man."[376] E.M. Archibald, a shrewd lawyer, made essentially the same points to Stanley.[377] The St. John's Chamber of Commerce bitterly refuted the reformers' claims, saying that what was the case in "ancient times" was no longer valid; the merchants were now resident on the island and knew "their interests to be identified with those of the other inhabitants." They were not slow to point out to Stanley the "true cause" of dissension in Newfoundland, i.e., Fleming's and his priests' "co-ercive interference" with "the political rights of the people." Villainizing merchants, the Chamber said, was a way for the reform party, which had inflicted "disgrace" on the colony in the House of Assembly, to deflect attention away from real source of trouble.[378] The *Newfoundlander*, a paper of liberal principles, similarly repudiated the idea that "there are separate interests in this community — the Trade on the one hand, and the Planters and Fishermen on the other."[379] So did Winton in the *Ledger*. In 1842 he commented specifically on Stanley's analysis, and dismissed it as one of the "popular fallacies" imposed on the British government, and on Harvey, by the reform party.[380] And yet the testimony before the House of Commons committee indicated that the reformers' claims were not entirely unfounded.

By March, 1842, Stanley had his mind firmly made up. Against Stephen's advice, he would bring in an amalgamated legislature. The concept was not new. As indicated earlier, Goderich was much taken with it, though the nominated part of the legislature in his scheme was small — only three members. Similar structures were being tried or planned in British Guiana and New South Wales. But these were at early stages of colonial development. Guiana had not progressed far beyond a slave colony, and New South Wales still retained something of its character as a convict farm. By contrast, Newfoundland was already used to being called Britain's oldest colony. Other British North American possessions were moving towards responsible government, and indeed Parsons was busily promoting the idea in the *Patriot* as a solution for Newfoundland. Amalgamation was a step backward to a more primitive system, one more easily controlled from above.

News of imminent change soon circulated in Newfoundland. Morris, who was asked for his views by Harvey, said that if the generous and liberal constitution conferred by George IV had not answered expectations, "the fault does not lie in the constitution."[381] Where the fault lay he didn't say. A protest meeting of St. John's Catholics in St. John's resulted in a petition, forwarded by Harvey in early April. The signers demanded "to be permitted to enjoy, uninterruptedly, that Constitution to which they are attached, and which alone, is suited to the exigencies of the Colony."[382] But there was remarkably little protest. Stanley's draft bill was in print in Newfoundland before the end of June.[383] Leading off the Commons debate on July 23, O'Connell presented a petition from the four-man 1841 Assembly delegation, which included Kent. An amalgamated assembly with ten appointed but voting members would, the delegates said, "neutralize the influence of the people, and make a mockery of representative government." It would create "an irresponsible Colonial Oligarchy in St. John's."[384] O'Connell fiercely attacked the bill. Britain was rewarding the colonists' loyalty, he said, "by trampling on them and taking away their constitution." The people were being persecuted "because the majority of them were Roman Catholics." He read a letter from Fleming, dated June 25, 1842, in which the bishop blamed the Council and "the official party here, who are leagued with the merchants" for the difficulties in Newfoundland. "Every measure ever recommended by the Secretary of State, or by the governor," Fleming said, "was ever sure, without one solitary exception, to be adopted by the Assembly." The letter from Fleming must have surprised Stanley. The two had met in London. Fleming "had admitted to him that, although the facts were exaggerated, there was some truth in the charges that had been made" against the Catholic clergy, Stanley said in his reply to O'Connell.[385] He solemnly declared that his bill was not directed against Catholics. And he rejected O'Connell's plea that a decision be postponed until the next session of Parliament. Debate on the bill resumed on August 5. On the 6th an attempt to have it "engrossed this day three months," which would have defeated it, failed. The House divided at least twelve times on the bill. It received royal assent on August 12.[386]

Stanley sent Harvey detailed instructions in September.[387] A plan to impose a property qualification on voters, which O'Connell had objected to, was dropped, but the required period of residence was raised to two years. A member, however, had to have either £100 p.a. or property of £500. That took care of fishermen-MHAs; it almost took care of Nugent. It was now made clear that a man qualifying as a member could run in any district (this had not been specified in the 1832 regulations). Elections were to be held simultaneously and to be of limited duration. An Executive Council was to be created. The appointed "Legislative Council" (in fact no body of that name had existed previously) was abolished as a distinct branch of the legislature; its members were to sit and vote in the Assembly "as fully in all respects as the elected Members." But they were never to constitute more than two-fifths of the total number of the Assembly thus created. Her Majesty could restrain the Assembly from appropriating "any Part of the public Revenue" in cases where she had not recommended, or been asked for, such grants. The clause presumably meant that there would be consultation with the governor prior to the introduction of money bills. Undoubtedly this was intended as a formality. It was nonetheless a restraint. No such clause was in the previous constitution. The new constitution would not continue beyond September 1, 1846, "unless Parliament shall otherwise order."

And so the "bastard system of government," as Winton later styled it,[388] came into being. Harvey, who relished making appointments, had already suggested the composition of an Executive Council, taking into consideration what he thought were the various interests of the community. He had on his preliminary list Carson, Kent, and the Catholic (but Halifax-born) merchant James Tobin, who had boldly and successfully applied for a position as councillor in 1840. The "native" interests, Harvey said ludicrously, would be represented by Carson and Kent.[389] Native-born Newfoundlanders were in fact excluded. Nor were any named when he finally called the Executive Council together in October. Despite reservations expressed by Stanley, Carson remained in place. Morris was included, Kent and Tobin omitted. Both would be appointed members of the new Assembly. And so Kent joined the "oligarchy" he had so recently denounced. As with Morris before him, his scorn for oligarchies did not prevent him, should occasion arise, from becoming an oligarch himself. With Winton balefully looking on, Harvey brought reformers and Catholics into the government. He did not altogether forget natives. He made Doyle stipendiary magistrate in St. John's, bringing a protest from sixty-seven petitioners.[390] Doyle seemed surprised to get the post. "I am not at all acquainted with the duties of the office," he openly declared on taking his place on the bench in a sessions court.[391]

A general election was called for mid-December. As it approached, the *Newfoundlander* turned savagely against the reform party. The paper was now under the direction of the brothers William and Ambrose Shea, the latter a prominent nativist. It was Ambrose who by November was likely writing the editorials. The reformers, he wrote, "stand charged before the Country as the chief destroyers of the Constitution we possessed." They had "filched from the people their privileges and liberties." They were "unauthorised intruders" in Newfoundland, an "unprincipled faction, who seek the extinction of liberty of thought and action, and claim for themselves a position in the colony to which they have no natural and defensible right."[392] This was kept up. Nugent struck back in his new paper, the *Indicator* (the *Vindicator* had been driven under by libel suits), charging that nativists were enemies of the Irish, but Shea would have none of it.[393] Nugent, a skilled and tough arguer, had met his match. An election was now going to be fought on true "liberal and enlightened principles," wrote Shea. The conduct of the reformers, he said on December 8, is falsely termed "Liberalism." They were "pests and marauders." If they had power, they would be "the vilest ... despots under the sun."

In St. John's the merchants Walter Grieve and Charles Fox Bennett, together with Kough, opposed Carson, O'Brien, and Nugent. The conservatives polled well, but lost. It was, said Shea, a "sickening" result.[394] Nugent won despite, or perhaps because of, a humiliating pre-election incident. As hinted earlier, Nugent had made dangerous enemies of the St. John's stipendiary magistrates Carter and Simms; both won libel suits against him in 1842. In Simms' case the award was £150.[395] Nugent couldn't pay. Simms held his fire until the late evening of Saturday, December 10, when Nugent was returning home from a meeting of all St. John's candidates, which had been marked by "the utmost harmony," at least according to Harvey.[396] He then ordered Nugent's arrest for non-payment of the damages. Nugent spent Saturday night, all day Sunday, and Sunday night in the common jail. It was sweet revenge. Grieve, Bennett, and Kough immediately disclaimed any involvement in the affair, and even offered a "handsome contribution" towards the sum needed for Nugent's release. But the aid was declined. Catholics paid the bill, and amidst great jubilation Nugent on Monday was escorted to his home in a "triumphal car." A congratulatory letter was presented to him by natives (but not the Natives' Society). "I have always loved the native character of Newfoundlanders," he replied. His victory at the polls in 1843, however, was to be his last.

In Conception Bay, with soldiers on the spot, proceedings were at first peaceful. But the troops had to be dispatched to Spaniard's Bay and Port de Grave, where rioting broke out.[397] Carbonear, however, was quiet. Ridley, Munn, Prendergast, and Hanrahan were returned, a result very pleasing to the conservatives. Parsons, who ran in Trinity Bay and was now back in the anti-merchant camp, was defeated by Richard Barnes,[398] prominent in the Natives' Society and a young man of brilliant promise. The president of the Society, Robert Carter,[399] P.W. Carter's brother, was elected in Bonavista. (He had been the MHA for Ferryland, and the only native Newfoundlander, in the first House.) Winton, drawn at last into active politics, ran in Burin, and suffered defeat at the hands of one Clement Benning.

The legislature that met in January, 1843, had more Protestants than Catholics, more conservatives than reformers, and many more non-natives than natives. It also had five more elected representatives than appointees. Within the appointed rump were three Catholics. The tenor of the Assembly was quickly tested when a feeble Carson, on January 16, ran for the speaker's chair. He was defeated by Crowdy, by a vote of 12-9. The following day Carson, seconded by Kent, moved that Robert R. Wakeham, a Newfoundlander who had been appointed clerk of the House in 1837, be reappointed to the position. The motion was lost. The Nova Scotian Archibald was then made clerk, by a vote of 12-11. Carter and Barnes voted against Wakeham and for Archibald, an irony not lost on the Irish members.[400] A meeting of natives soon afterwards condemned the two MHAs for their treatment of

Wakeham.[401] The incident shows the discomfort of Newfoundlanders as they tried to find their place in the snakepit of colonial politics. But the true meaning of these incidents was, first, that the Irish-dominated reform party had lost control of the House, and second, that elective government had been substantially diluted.

The reformers slipped further in February, when Carson died. He would be replaced by Parsons in a by-election, but Parsons, though nominally a reformer, was a man of doubtful allegiance. A few days before he died, it was reported that Carson intended to sail for London at the first opportunity to petition against the election of Crowdy as speaker. He viewed that as "a gross violation of the first principles of the British constitution."[402] Some said his death was hastened by bad news from England. The judicial committee of the Privy Council had decided against him (and others) in the appeal of Kielley v. Carson, thereby limiting the powers of all colonial assemblies. Opponents of the reform party might now breathe easy, while those named as defendants in the case were sent scrambling to protect their assets. Kielley's triumph and Carson's death mark a convenient point to end this act of the unfolding Newfoundland drama.

Chapter 9

Epilogue

THE FOOTPATHS AND BYWAYS of Newfoundland's past join together and head towards the crossroads of our history, which is 1933, the year the legislature voted itself out of existence and with it the country's independence. Following 1843 the paths would take many turns. It is too gross an exaggeration to say that after that year Newfoundland could go only one way, towards the surrender 90 years later, for some critical choices lay ahead, along with many triumphs and achievements. Representative government would be restored, responsible government installed; the Canadian wolf would be spurned, the French driven off the Petit Nord. The Bell Island mine would open. The railway would be built. Richard Squires would put the hum on the Humber. Newfoundland would have its day — days — in the sun.

Yet as we look forward from 1843, in the far distance, across bogs of conflict and economic depression, through thickets of tangled diplomacy, 1933 looms. The struggles and vicissitudes of the early 19th century give a foreboding of what is to come. We already hear calls for commissions of inquiry in the 1840s, and there would indeed be such commissions in the next century, one of which, under Lord Amulree, decided Newfoundland's future. The constitution of the colony was suspended by the British government in 1841; it would be suspended again for a much longer period in 1934, and the debates in the House of Commons over the two crises are similar.[1] Reactionary calls after 1836 for rule by governor and council would be answered a century later when governor David Murray Anderson and six British-appointed commissioners took the elected MHAs' place at the cabinet table. Distaste for politics, which set in shortly after elective politics began, remained a powerful undercurrent of Newfoundland history. The Chamber of Commerce begged for relief from "political depravity" in 1838. In the 1920s and '30s many merchants and respectable inhabitants likewise demanded a holiday from politics; and they got it. In all of this there are links between the early decades of the 19th century and 1933, and beyond that, since everything afterwards was, in a way, anticlimax, to the world we know.

After two centuries without politics but not of course without government, Newfoundland in the 1830s got government through politics, and the experience was bitter. Fleming, his priests, and the new Irish bear much of the responsibility for the coarsening of political life. Fiona MacCarthy notes that by 1800 "conspiracy and fear, treachery and double-dealing were habits of mind that had governed Ireland for centuries."[2] Those "habits of mind," that fear and paranoia, and the shame that sprung from centuries of ignominy and failure, were transported to

Newfoundland and put to use. Here, after all, was another Ireland, with the "people" in bondage as in the homeland. This time the Irish and their leaders would not wait to be given their rightful place in the society. They would take it, and quickly. They would rule, as they should rule back home. The path of moderation was shunned. There were to be no half measures. They hadn't worked before. Nor would they now.

But Newfoundland was not another Ireland. It was a British North American fishing colony. The population that had settled before the Irish influx of the early 19th century had its own "habits of mind." There were strong bonds of loyalty and economic links to England. There was a rooted bureaucracy. There were laws, institutions, ways of proceeding. Injustices too, certainly, but before the period of Irish insurgency some of these were being addressed. To try to make this half-awake colonial society, where the practice of self-government was in its infancy, into a surrogate Irish state, to make it into something it could never be, a compensation for failure back home, was to wrench it out of shape. It is true that the movement under Fleming gave the Irish, new and old, a keener awareness of their rights than they had before his advent, and that some good — many would argue a great deal of good — came of it. But at what cost? During Fleming's episcopacy sectarian hatred flourished as it never had before, poisoning every corner of society, even at times the courts. And it did not die with his death in 1850. Far from it. Blood would be shed, and not just from blows by fists and pickets, before it began to subside. It lingered well into the 20th century. There would be public jeers flung at "papists" and Jesuits as late as the 1990s. If Newfoundland didn't turn into a transatlantic Ulster, it was no thanks to Fleming and his priests.

As for the "tory" party — the merchants, officials, lawyers, and their supporters in the press — they must share the blame for the debacle of the 1830s and early '40s. They threw in the towel too fast in the struggle with Fleming and his followers. They thought the game of politics would be, if not genteel, then manageable, and that gentlemen would naturally win. But it was a hard game, for to the Irish the stakes were high and they were sick of losing. They were prepared to fight dirty. They did fight dirty. Yet in 1837 the merchants could have sent an opposition to the Assembly from the outlying Protestant districts they had won the previous year. They might even have elected a member or two in Conception Bay. As O'Connell indicated in the Commons, a small number of conservatives would have had "great influence" in a House of only fifteen members.[3] If Row had taken his seat in 1837 and made common cause with Emerson, who on occasion, even alone, showed some mettle, the "tories" in a rump of two members would have made a difference. Their almost total withdrawal from the scene gave the Irish party a free hand, which in turn led to excesses and the discrediting of the Assembly. Instead of fighting in the arena that had been granted them, the "men of property and education"[4] stepped outside the ropes, deciding instead to try and undermine the British government's confidence in the Assembly through petitions and lobbying. They wouldn't play, but demanded that the rules be changed. British officials had more faith in Newfoundland's constitution than most of the leading "tory" inhabitants. In time they lost it.

The assemblies in America were genuine forums for democratic action. They were part of the structure of government and society from the early stages of American colonial history. Citizens came to count on them for the defence of their rights, to value them, make use of them. By the mid-18th century they had become threads in the fabric of life. A recent scholar has shown, for instance, the vital role of the assemblies in shaping the Declaration of Independence, which was as much the end product of a collective democratic process as the production of a small group of men charged with drafting a document.[5] This kind of consultative government was foreign to Newfoundland. It came late. It didn't have the hoar of ages on it in 1832. There was no widespread allegiance to it. Until the 1820s hardly anyone had even asked for it, for people were wary of taxes and in any case were used to another kind of administration. A long period of nurturing peace and accomplishment might have secured that respect without which elective government can hardly function, but with which it can survive hard times. Instead, the experience quickly soured. The exaggerated hopes that had been raised by those who promoted the representative system were seen as shallow, and it led, not to prosperity, but to division and hatred. Elective government had barely raised its head before that head was bloodied. The years 1832-43 were far from being the end of the story of Newfoundland democratic self-rule, but they offered very shaky groundwork for the building of a nation.

Endnotes

Notes to Chapter 1

[1]See Gwen Schultz, *Ice Age Lost* (Garden City, N.Y., Anchor Press, 1974), pp. 62-4.

[2]James Tuck, "Maritime Archaic Tradition," *ENL*, vol. 3, p. 465.

[3]Tuck writes of their "demise" in Newfoundland but says his "thread of evidence" connects them with Labrador Indians of the historic period, presumably Innu (*Ibid.*). In *Newfoundland and Labrador Prehistory* (Ottawa: National Museum of Man, 1976), p. 64, Tuck wrote, on the basis of "new" archaeological evidence: "maybe [the Beothuck] were descendants of the Maritime Archaic people." A "direct link" between the Beothuck of the island of Newfoundland and the Maritime Archaic "cannot be demonstrated," writes Priscilla Renouf, in "Palaeoeskimo Seal Hunters at Port au Choix, Northwestern Newfoundland," *NS*, 9, 2 (1993), p. 186. She notes there is "no evidence of Indian occupation of the island of Newfoundland" from 1200 B.C. to 0 A.D. (p.c.) Ralph Pastore, in *Shanawdithit's People: The Archaeology of the Beothuks* (St. John's: Atlantic Archaeology Ltd., [1992]), p. 2, says "we cannot trace Beothuk ancestry directly back to the Maritime Archaic people."

[4]See Bryan C. Hood, "The Maritime Archaic Indians of Labrador: Investigating Prehistoric Social Organization," *NS*, 9, 2 (1993): 167-72. Renouf says "There is currently no evidence of what the superstructure was" (p.c.).

[5]Robert McGhee, *Ancient People of the Arctic* (Vancouver: UBC Press, 1996), p. 189.

[6]Tuck, *Newfoundland and Labrador Prehistory*, p. 39.

[7]Tuck, "Maritime Archaic Tradition," p. 465.

[8]For an illustration, see Peter Neary and P. O'Flaherty, *Part of the Main: An Illustrated History of Newfoundland and Labrador* (St. John's: Breakwater, 1983), p. 14.

[9]Hood, "Maritime Archaic Indians," p. 170. The use of such dwellings, says Renouf, "could have been only once a year or so" (p.c.).

[10]Renouf thinks "extinction" is an overused concept in Newfoundland archaeology. She says the early peoples, instead of dying off, shifted to other places. See her paper, "Prehistory of Newfoundland Hunter-Gatherers: Extinctions or Adaptations?" *World Archaeology*, 30, 3 (1999): 403-20.

[11]Renouf (p.c.).

[12]Plate 8 in McGhee, *Ancient People*. The maskette was found on Devon Island, located north of Baffin Island (McGhee, p.c.).

[13]Plate 2, *Ibid.*, gives information about how the later Palaeo-eskimo (known as Dorset) dressed; a notable feature is the high, three-sided collar.

[14]*Ibid.*, pp. 37-40

[15]*Ibid.*, p. 102. Evidence for this transfer is "tenuous," says Ingeborg Marshall, *A History and Ethnography of the Beothuk* (Montreal & Kingston: McGill-Queen's Univ. Press, 1996), p. 261.

[16]Renouf, "Palaeoeskimo Seal Hunters," p. 188.

[17]*Ibid.*, p. 197.

[18]The approximate dates for the earlier groups are: Palaeo-eskimo, 1000-800 B.C. (Labrador only); Groswater Palaeo-eskimo, 800-100 B.C. (Labrador), 800 B.C.-100 A.D. (Newfoundland).

[19]See McGhee, *Ancient People*, pp. 116-7, passim; Tuck, *Newfoundland and Labrador Prehistory*, p. 91; Renouf, "Palaeoeskimo Seal Hunters," p. 189. Renouf seems to favour the view that the Groswater Palaeo-eskimos were "ancestral to the later Dorset."

[20]McGhee, *Ancient People*, p. 135.

[21]Pastore, *Shanawdithit's People*, p. 3.

[22]"Like the earlier Paleoeskimos, they hunted seals, but did so in larger groups, from more permanent sites" (Renouf, p.c.).

[23]Renouf (p.c.)

[24]But on the "considerable ... variability in house form" at one Dorset site, see Renouf, "Palaeoeskimo Seal Hunters," p. 201.

[25]McGhee, *Ancient People*, p. 136.

[26]See Pastore, *Shanawithit's People*, p. 10.

[27]*Ibid.*, p. 9.

[28]*Ibid.*

[29]McGhee, *Ancient People*, p. 152, quoting William E. Taylor Jr.

[30]Pastore, *Shanawithit's People*, p. 10.

[31]Marshall, *History and Ethnography*, p. 261. But McGhee says "large-scale killing has rarely been a part of warfare among peoples living in small societies" (*Ancient People*, p. 226). Renouf says there is "no evidence" of such fighting. (p.c.)

[32]See Tuck, *Newfoundland and Labrador Prehistory*, p. 66, for photographs of prehistoric Indian arrowheads.

[33]By the 16th century, their range extended to the Strait of Belle Isle and (seasonally) northern Newfoundland. Pastore says they may have encountered Europeans in the Strait "as early as 1500 or 1501" ("The Sixteenth Century: Aboriginal Peoples and European Contact," in Buckner, Phillip A., and John G. Reid, eds., *The Atlantic Region to Confederation: A History* [Toronto: Univ. of Toronto Press, 1994], p. 23). See also Martijn, Charles A., RA on Marshall, *History and Ethnography*, in *NS*, 12, 2 (1996), pp. 115, 118.

[34]Renouf (p.c.).

[35]McGhee, *Ancient People*, p. 195.

[36]Meaning before contact with the Europeans.

[37]See Pastore, "Sixteenth Century," p. 24.

[38]Martijn, RA on Marshall, *History and Ethnography*, pp. 108-9; see also Pastore, *Shanawdithit's People*, p. 12.

[39]For a discussion touching on this, see Martijn, RA on Marshall, *History and Ethnography*, pp. 108-14; also Martijn, "An Eastern Micmac Domain of Islands," in *Actes du Vingtième Congrès des Algonquinistes* (Ottawa: Carleton Univ., 1989), pp. 208-16. But see Ralph Pastore, *Newfoundland Micmacs: A History of their Traditional Life* ([St. John's], Newfoundland Historical Society, 1978), p. 10. Renouf says "there is no concrete evidence" of this early Micmac contact with Newfoundland (p.c.).

[40]All three are "possible candidates," says Stuart Brown, "Norse Discovery," *ENL*, vol. 4, p. 103. Others, including Tuck, favour the Beothuck (*Newfoundland and Labrador Prehistory*, p. 62). For a longer discussion, see Helge Ingstad, *Westward to Vinland* (Toronto: Macmillan, 1969), pp. 78-82. I assume that the accounts of Vinland in the Norse *Sagas* apply generally to Newfoundland, i.e., that Vinland is Newfoundland. Robert McGhee, in *Canada Rediscovered* ([Ottawa], Canadian Museum of Civilization, 1991), p. 48, says northern Newfoundland is "the most likely geographical area" for Vinland. But this is a much debated question; other interpretations are possible.

[41]*The Vinland Sagas*, trans. Magnus Magnusson and Hermann Pálsson (London: Penguin, 1965), p. 53.

[42]They were known as knarrir or hafskip. See McGhee, *Canada Rediscovered*, p. 43, and Birgitta Wallace, "L'Anse aux Meadows: Gateway to Vinland," *Acta Archaeologica*, 61 (1990): 167.

[43]*Vinland Sagas*, p. 55.

[44]*Ibid.*, p. 57. A troublesome point to those who identify Vinland with Newfoundland; see Alan Macpherson's comment in his essay, "Pre-Columbian Discoveries and Exploration of North America," in *North American Exploration*, vol. 1, ed. John Logan Allen (Lincoln, Neb.: Univ. of Nebraska Press, 1997), p. 49; also Ingstad, *Westward*, pp. 70-76.

[45]Epaves Bay, just southwest of L'Anse aux Meadows.

[46]Wallace says it was not a "permanent settlement" but a "base camp" from which to explore and exploit the region ("L'Anse aux Meadows," pp. 169, 194).

[47]*Ibid.*, p. 192.

[48]For arguments against the identification, see Brown, "Norse Discovery," pp. 102-3; also Wallace, "L'Anse aux Meadows," pp. 191-4.

[49]The term is sometimes said to be derisive, meaning "wretches" (see *Vinland Sagas*, p. 27); but it may refer to the natives' short stature, deriving from from an Old Icelandic word meaning "shrink"; see Stuart Brown, rev. of B.D. Fardy, *Leifsburdir*, in *NS*, 10, 2 (1994), p. 288.

[50]See McGhee, *Canada Rediscovered*, p. 49.

Notes to Chapter 2

[1]On these alleged pre-Cabot voyages, see D.B. Quinn's biographies of Thomas Croft, Hugh Eliot, John Jay, *DCB*, vol. 1, pp. 239-40, 302, 386, and R.A. Skelton's biography of John Cabot, *Ibid.*, p. 147; also Quinn, *North America from Earliest Discovery to First Settlements* (New York: Harper & Row, 1977), pp. 60-64, and Stuart C. Brown, "Far Other Worlds and Other Seas," *NS*, 9, 2 (1993), p. 248. Quinn suggests that one voyage "was to find and exploit fishing grounds" (*DCB*, vol. 1, p. 240). See Alan Macpherson's skeptical treatment of these voyages in "Pre-Columbian Discoveries and Exploration of North America," pp. 66-9; also Olaf Janzen, "Review Essay: '1497 and all that...'," *NQ*, 92, 1 (1998), pp. 46-7.

[2]H.P. Biggar, *The Precursors of Jacques Cartier 1497-1534* (Ottawa: Government Printing Bureau, 1911), p. 9.

[3]The number 20 is given in John Day's letter (late 1497 or early 1498), likely to Christopher Columbus, in *NAW*, vol. 1, pp. 98-9; But Raimondo di Soncino said there were 18 in the crew (Biggar, *Precursors*, p. 20).

[4]Quinn, *North America*, p. 115, note 11; but see Samuel Eliot Morison, *The European Discovery of America* (New York: Oxford Univ. Press, 1971), p. 167.

[5]Biggar, *Precursors*, p. 14.

[6]But it could have been Cape Breton or Labrador. The location of the landfall is much disputed; see Quinn, *North America*, pp. 114-19, for a statement of some of the problems involved; also Morison, *European Discovery*, pp. 170-79; for a recent discussion, see Peter E. Pope, *The Many Landfalls of John Cabot* (Toronto: Univ. of Toronto Press, 1997), pp. 24-36.

[7]Details from John Day's letter. Day says "most of the land was discovered after turning back" from the land first sighted — a statement that on the surface doesn't seem to support Newfoundland as the landfall.

[8]Biggar, *Precursors*, p. 14.

[9]P. O'Flaherty, *The Rock Observed* (Toronto: Univ. of Toronto Press, 1979), p. 189. The fact the the tag "new found" attached itself quickly to Newfoundland and not to some other part of North America is a piece of evidence pointing to the island as the landfall.

[10]Skelton, "John Cabot," p. 151.

[11]See Quinn, *North America*, pp. 115, 127.

[12]The letters patent of 1496 authorized Cabot to acquire "for us [i.e., Henry VII] the dominion, title and jurisdiction" over the lands discovered.

[13]See Pedro de Ayala's letter to Ferdinand and Isabella of Spain, July 25, 1498; *NAW*, vol. 1, p. 101; in 1719 Spaniards were still claiming to be "the first discoverers of Newfoundland" (*CSP*, 1719-1720, p. 219).

[14]One historian claimed that Jacques Cartier in 1535 "hissa le drapeau français sur les côtes de Terre-Neuve." See F.F. Thompson, *The French Shore Problem in Newfoundland* (Toronto: Univ. of Toronto Press, 1961), p. 3. Louis XIII later included Newfoundland in the charter given to the Associates of New France (*Ibid.*, p. 5).

[15]L.-A. Vigneras, "Gaspar Corte-Real," *DCB*, vol. 1, pp. 234-6; see also Quinn, *North America*, pp. 122-3.

[16]Neary and O'Flaherty, *Part of the Main*, p. 23; see also *NAW*, vol. 1, appendix, maps 19 and 21.

[17]*NAW*, vol. 1, p. 151.

[18]Biggar, *Precursors*, pp. 63-7; see Marshall, *History and Ethnography*, pp. 15-16.

[19]Quinn (*North America*, p. 123) says they were "put up for sale" in Lisbon. See Morison, *European Discovery*, pp. 215-6.

[20]A. Davies, "João Fernandes," *DCB*, vol. 1, pp. 304-5; *HAC*, vol. 1, pl. 19; *NAW*, vol. 1, maps 43 and 46 (appendix).

[21]Raimondo di Soncino to the Duke of Milan, Dec. 18, 1497 (Biggar, *Precursors*, p. 20).

[22]D.B. Quinn, *The Voyages and Colonising Enterprises of Sir Humphrey Gilbert* (London: Hakluyt Society, 1940), vol. 1, p. 172.

[23]See Quinn's comments, *North America*, p. 60.

[24]Biggar, *Precursors*, p. 20.

[25]Quinn, *North America*, pp. 125-6; *NAW*, vol. 1, p. 110.

[26]But didn't cease; in 1522 we hear of the "New Found Isle landes flete" returning to England (Innis, *Cod Fisheries*, p. 13).

[27]J.A. Williamson, *The Voyages of the Cabots* (London: Argonaut Press, 1929), p. 91.

[28]I.e., Breton.

[29]*Ibid.*, p. 105.

[30]*Ibid.*, p. 104. The "mayne Land" was likely Labrador. See Alan Macpherson's comment on Rut, in "Early Perceptions of the Newfoundland Environment," *The Natural Environment of Newfoundland, Past and Present*, ed. Alan and Joyce Macpherson (St. John's: MUN, Dept. of Geography, 1981), pp. 1-2.

[31]See Keith Matthews, *Lectures on the History of Newfoundland* ([St. John's]: MUN, Maritime History Group, 1973), p. 69.

[32]Biggar, *Precursors*, p. 67.

[33]See *HAC*, vol. 1, pl. 22 for details about European ports involved in the organization, funding, and prosecution of the 16th-century Newfoundland fishery.

[34]For the organization of the English fishery and system of trading, see Gillian T. Cell, *English Enterprise in Newfoundland 1577-1660* (Toronto: Univ. of Toronto Press, 1969) .

[35]John Mason's phrase, in 1620, defining the common attitude towards fishing; in Gillian Cell, *Newfoundland Discovered* (London: Hakluyt Society, 1981), p. 95. See a similar comment by the colonist John Smith, *Ibid.*, p. 36.

[36]In *Pericles*, II, i.

[37]*The Tempest*, II, ii, 26-7.

[38]*DNE*, p. 387. (See also *OED*.)

[39]I.e., wooden props.

[40]For a description of these boats, see *HAC*, vol. 1, p. 47; also Cell, *English Enterprise*, pp. 4-5. Richard Whitbourne, in 1620, called the boats "fishing Pinnaces." See Cell, *Newfoundland Discovered*, p. 132.

[41]Perhaps meaning corned, i.e., cured with salt.

[42]Geoffrey H. Farmer, "The Cold Ocean Environment of Newfoundland," in *Natural Environment of Newfoundland*, p. 57.

[43]*HAC*, vol. 1, p. 47.

[44]*NAW*, vol. 4, p. 30.

[45]Termed train oil or train (as were the oils obtained from whales and seals).

[46]*The Voyages of Jacques Cartier* (Toronto: Univ. of Toronto Press, 1993), p. 7.

[47]Selma Barkham, C.B.C. radio interview, Sept. 24, 1998.

[48]Selma Barkham, C.B.C. radio interview, Sept. 24, 1998. See Selma Barkham, "The Basques: filling a gap in our history between Jacques Cartier and Champlain," *Canadian Geographical Journal*, 96, 1 (1978): 8-19, and "Documentary Evidence for 16th Century Basque Whaling Ships in the Strait of Belle Isle," in *Early European Settlement and Exploitation in Atlantic Canada*, ed. G.M. Story (St. John's: MUN, 1982), pp. 53-95; and James Tuck and Robert Grenier, *Red Bay, Labrador: World Whaling Capital A.D. 1550-1600* (St. John's: Atlantic Archaeology Ltd., 1989).

[49]C.O. 194/16, f. 227.

[50]See Tuck and Grenier, *Red Bay*, p. 37.

[51]Figures are from Selma Barkham, "The Basques."

[52]Selma Barkham, "The Spanish Province of Terranova," *The Canadian Archivist* 2, 5 (1974): 78.

[53]See Pastore, "The Sixteenth Century," p. 22.

[54]Tuck and Grenier, *Red Bay*, pp. 56-63.

[55]See Michael Barkham, "French Basque 'New Found Land' Entrepreneurs and the Import of Codfish and Whale Oil to Northern Spain," *NS*, 10, 1 (1994): 1-43, and his rev. of J.-P. Proulx, *Basque Whaling*

in Labrador in the 16th Century, in *NS*, 10, 2 (1994): 260-86; also Selma Barkham, "Two Documents written in Labrador, 1572 and 1577," *CHR*, 77, 2 (1976): 235-8.

[56]Selma Barkham, "Documentary Evidence," p. 85.

[57]Selma Barkham, "The Basques," p. 18.

[58]*Ibid.*, p. 11.

[59]*Ibid.*, p. 17. 38 Basques overwintered in 1604 (p. 18). See also Tuck and Grenier, *Red Bay*, p. 59.

[60]See Selma Barkham, "A Note on the Strait of Belle Isle during the period of Basque contact with Indians and Inuit," *Etudes Inuit Studies*, 4, 1-2 (1980): 51-8; also Pastore, "The Sixteenth Century."

[61]The term (also spelled without the -l) typically applied to aboriginals by Europeans, including Basques.

[62]W.C. Sturtevant, "The First Inuit Depiction by Europeans," *Etudes Inuit Studies*, 4, 1-2 (1980): 47-9.

[63]Whitbourne, *A Discourse and Discovery of Newfoundland* (1622), in Cell, *Newfoundland Discovered*, p. 117.

[64]Quinn, *Voyages and Colonising Enterprises*, vol. 2, p. 396.

[65]Morison, *European Discovery*, p. 624.

[66]See Selma Barkham, "A note on the Strait of Belle Isle," pp. 53-4.

[67]*Ibid.*, pp. 54-6.

[68]*Lectures*, p. 35.

[69]Armed vessels owned by private persons and authorized by the government to seize shipping of hostile nations (*OED*).

[70]Innis, *Cod Fisheries*, pp. 16, 31 n.5.

[71]Selma Barkham, "The Spanish Province of Terranova," pp. 77-8; "Documentary Evidence," p. 57. The fight took place at Los Hornos, whose location has not been identified (Selma Barkham, "The Basques," p. 14).

[72]*NAW*, vol. 1, p. 97. Innis identifies the port as St. John's (*Cod Fisheries*, p. 39).

[73]Selma Barkham, "Documentary Evidence," pp. 56-7.

[74]Cell (*English Enterprise*, p. 22) thinks Parkhurst may have deliberately underestimated the number.

[75]*NAW*, vol. 1, p. 5.

[76]Richard Hakluyt, *English Voyages*, 8 vols. (London: Everyman, 1926), vol. 5, p. 344; the Spanish cod fishing fleet would have included many Basque ships.

[77]*NAW*, vol. 4, p. 31. Hayes' account is pp. 23-42.

[78]Her captain, Richard Clarke, had raided Portuguese vessels in St. John's in 1582. See Quinn, "Sir Humphrey Gilbert," *DCB*, vol. 1, p. 334. Another of Gilbert's squadron, the *Swallow*, after arriving on the Newfoundland coast, boarded a fishing ship that was on her way back home, stole her tackle, sails, victuals, and the fishermen's clothing, and tortured the fishermen by "winding cords about their heads" (*NAW*, vol. 4, p. 30).

[79]*NAW*, vol. 4, p. 22.

[80]O'Flaherty, *Rock Observed*, p. 8.

[81]Cell, *Newfoundland Discovered*, pp. 155, 160. See N.H.'s comment in 1622 (*Ibid.*, p. 205). One of the clauses of the Western Charter of 1634 ordered that "noe person set fire in any of the woodes of the Country." Keith Matthews, *Collection and Commentary on the Constitutional Laws of Seventeenth Century Newfoundland* (St. John's: MUN, Maritime History Group, 1975), p. 74. The order was repeated in later regulations.

[82]Hakluyt, *English Voyages*, vol. 5, p. 344; see Hayes' similar comment, *NAW*, vol. 3, p. 125.

[83]*NAW*, vol. 4, p. 31.

[84]In St. John's, Hayes says, English masters were "Admirals by turnes over the fleetes." They chose a new admiral every week. This arrangement might have been unique to St. John's.

[85]Hakluyt, *English Voyages*, vol. 5, p. 344.

[86]See Matthews, *Lectures*, p. 67.

[87]*NAW*, vol. 4, p. 13. During the sixteenth century, the second English arrival came to be called vice-admiral and the third rear-admiral.

[88]Cell, *English Enterprise*, p. 6.

[89]*NAW*, vol. 4, p. 32. D.W. Prowse, in *A History of Newfoundland from the English, Colonial, and Foreign Records* (London: Macmillan, 1895), pp. 60-61, says "Sir Thomas Hampshire" was authorized by Elizabeth I to make "a new rule" to govern rooms in St. John's. But no such man existed. See Quinn, "Richard Clarke," *DCB*, vol. 1, p. 229.

[90]See Quinn, *North America*, p. 419; Innis, *Cod Fisheries*, p. 53; Cell, *English Enterprise*, p. 46.

[91]*NAW*, vol. 4, p. 32.

[92]O'Flaherty, *Rock Observed*, p. 6.

[93]The collective name given to the southwest English counties of Devon, Somerset, and Dorset.

[94]Cell, *English Enterprise*, pp. 31-2.

[95]*NAW*, vol. 4, p. 119; but the normal number would be lower (Cell, *English Enterprise*, p. 100).

[96]Cell, *English Enterprise*, p. 29.

[97]But Matthews notes that French and Portuguese vessels were at Ferryland and Harbour Grace in 1620. See "A History of the West of England-Newfoundland Fishery" (D.Phil. thes., Oxford Univ., 1968), pp. 186-7.

[98]Selma Barkham, *The Basque Coast of Newfoundland* (n.p.: Great Northern Peninsula Development Corporation, 1989), p. 6.

[99]See Quinn, "Newfoundland in the Consciousness of Europe in the Sixteenth and Early Seventeenth Centuries," in *Early European Settlement*, pp. 15-16; see also Alan Macpherson, "Early Perceptions of the Newfoundland Environment."

[100]*NAW*, vol. 3, p. 126.

[101]Hakluyt, *English Voyages*, vol. 5, pp. 345-6.

[102]*Ibid.*, p. 347.

[103]John Rastell, however, had recommended colonization c. 1517-19 (*NAW*, vol. 1, pp. 168-71). It was thought that a French attempt at a colony had been made in 1580, but "they all perished for want of necessaries for plantation" (*Ibid.*, vol. 4, p. 131). John Guy, in the House of Commons in 1621, said the French "planted there about 30 years [ago]" (*Proceedings and Debates of the British Parliaments respecting North America*, ed. L.F. Stock, vol. 1 [Washington: Carnegie Institution, 1924], p. 36). See also Quinn, *North America*, p. 421. Ralph G. Lounsbury refers to Portuguese "attempts" to settle Newfoundland "in the early sixteenth century" (*The British Fishery at Newfoundland 1634-1763* [n.p.: Archon Books, 1969], p. 20).

[104]Quinn, *North America*, pp. 419-21; *NAW*, vol. 3, pp. 124-38.

[105]Morison, *European Discovery*, pp. 656-79.

[106]The population can only be guessed at; Leslie Upton's guess is 2,000 at the period of European contact. See Ralph Pastore, "The Collapse of the Beothuk World," *Acadiensis*, 19, 1 (1989): 56.

[107]See Pastore, "The Sixteenth Century," pp. 30-32.

Notes to Chapter 3

[1]See Whitbourne's calculations of the profit from a fishing venture, in Cell, *Newfoundland Discovered*, pp. 176-8.

[2]For studies of the early 17th-century promotional literature on settlement, see Cell, *Newfoundland Discovered*, pp. 1-59; Quinn, "Newfoundland in the Consciousness of Europe," pp. 9-30; O'Flaherty, *Rock Observed*, pp. 6-13. The arguments for settling Newfoundland were similar to those advanced for other colonies.

[3]One of Whitbourne's arguments (Cell, *Newfoundland Discovered*, p. 163).

[4]*Ibid.*, p. 186.

[5]*Ibid.*, p. 127.

[6]*Ibid.*, p. 168. Gilbert had thought England "combred with loyterers, vagabonds, and such like idle persons" (D.B. Quinn, *The Voyages and Colonising Enterprises of Sir Humphrey Gilbert*, vol. 1, pp. 160-1).

[7]II, iii, 13-14.

[8]Meaning to found, establish. A "plantation" is a colony, a settler is a "planter" (though this word later acquired a more specialized meaning in Newfoundland; see *DNE*).

[9]Cell, *Newfoundland Discovered*, pp. 110, 125.

[10]*Ibid.*, pp. 149, 165.

[11]Gordon Handcock says there was "possibly casual overwintering" prior to 1610 (*So longe as there comes noe women: Origins of English Settlement in Newfoundland* [St. John's: Breakwater, 1989], p. 33). Lounsbury asserts "Sometimes caretakers wintered there" (*British Fishery*, p. 40). Prowse, writing of the 16th century, says "a few crews were left behind every winter" to build boats, etc., and that the shore fishery "could not be carried on ... without winter men" (*History*, p. 59). But to link boatbuilding with overwintering is speculative. In the early fishery boats were "transported overseas in sections" (*HAC*, vol. 1, p. 47) or constructed quickly from lumber brought on the ships; then left behind for the next season.

[12]The actual name given in the charter was "The Treasurer and the Company of Adventurers and Planters of the City of London and Bristol for the Colony of Plantation in Newfound Land" (*NAW*, vol. 4, p. 134).

[13]I.e., a document issued by the King, granting rights and privileges. Overseas possessions were thought to be the King's property, not Parliament's. For reasons why a royal charter was sought by merchants, see *Select Charters of Trading Companies, A.D. 1530-1707*, ed. Cecil T. Carr (New York: Burt Franklin, 1970), pp. xvi-xvii.

[14]For biographical information on the company's subscribers, see Cell, *English Enterprise*, pp. 53-8.

[15]*NAW*, vol. 4, pp. 131-2.

[16]The western boundary of the grant was the meridian "conceived to pass by" Cape St. Mary's, "which cape or headland," says the charter, "is to the eastward of the bay commonly called the Bay of Placentia." The phrasing may have been intended to exclude Placentia Bay. This appears to be Cell's view (*English Enterprise*, p. 74).

[17]*NAW*, vol. 4, p. 134. The odd feature of a specific grant within the general grant has not been explained.

[18]Cell, in "The Cupids Cove Settlement: A Case Study of the Problems of Early Colonisation," in *Early European Settlement*, p. 103, says "only those authorised by the company would, under the terms of the charter, be allowed ... *to trade* within its territory." I don't see this in the charter.

[19]*Ibid.*, p. 138. For the oath see *Select Documents of English Constitutional History*, ed. George B. Adams and H. Morse Stephens (New York: Macmillan, 1923), p. 299.

[20]But it merely repeats a clause in the second Virginia charter (1609); see *NAW*, vol. 5, p. 210.

[21]Gillian T. Cell, "John Guy," *DCB*, vol. 1, p. 350.

[22]The number 40 is given in the company's commission appointing Guy governor of the colony, May 26, 1610 (*NAW*, p. 142); but Guy himself gave a figure of 39 in his letter to the company in May, 1611 (*Ibid.*, p.147).

[23]Cell, *Newfoundland Discovered*, p. 63. Matthews says the settlers "were *not* to fish." To do so, he says, would be "to ignore the limitations of their Charter" ("History," pp. 104, 107). But there was nothing in the charter to prevent their going fishing.

[24]See Carl Bridenbaugh, *Vexed and Troubled Englishmen 1590-1642* (New York: Oxford Univ. Press, 1968), p. 128. For Guy's trading intentions, see his letter to Willoughby, Oct. 6, 1610 (Cell, *Newfoundland Discovered*, p. 63).

[25]See Matthews, "History," p. 104.

[26]Cell, *Newfoundland Discovered*, p. 61.

[27]In 1620 John Mason, the governor who succeeded Guy, referred to "our plantations ... in 2. places 16. miles distant from [the] other, on the northside the bay of conception" (*Ibid.*, p. 99).

[28]Cell, *English Enterprise*, p. 67.

[29]A site, likely that of Guy's colony, was being excavated by archaeologists in 1998 (William Gilbert, lecture, Newfoundland Museum, February 26, 1998).

[30]A plant thought to be effective against scurvy.

[31]Cell, *Newfoundland Discovered*, pp. 62-3.

[32]*NAW*, vol. 4, p. 148.

[33]Cell, *Newfoundland Discovered*, p. 63. It will be noted that he refers to a single "stage" or "place."

[34]*NAW*, vol. 4, p. 140. His commission is *Ibid.*, pp. 142-3.

[35]See the opening of Guy's letter of May 11, 1611 (*Ibid.*, p. 147); also Cell, "The Cupids Cove Settlement," p. 104; and Lounsbury, *British Fishery*, p. 40.

[36]But the admiral (i.e., first arrival) was allowed "an overplus, only for one boat more than he hath." Which is to say he was permitted a little more space than the number of boats he had justified. This right, repeated in the Western Charter of 1634, was already a custom in the fishery.

[37]*PC*, vol. 4, pp. 1715-6.

[38]But the fishermen evidently ignored the laws; see Lounsbury, *British Fishery*, pp. 42-3.

[39]Cell, *English Enterprise*, p. 65.

[40]Cell, "The Cupids Cove Settlement," p. 104.

[41]This remained a source of trouble after 1612. In 1618 Slany complained that the "very great damages" done by pirates was the reason the colony was "almost overthrown" (*PC*, vol. 4, p. 1717).

[42]*NAW*, vol. 4, p. 151.

[43]Two accounts of the episode survive: Cell, *Newfoundland Discovered*, pp. 68-78 (Guy's narrative); *Ibid.*, pp. 83-6 (Henry Crout's).

[44]Cell, *English Enterprise*, p. 71.

[45]See William Gilbert, "'Divers Places': The Beothuk Indians and John Guy's Voyage into Trinity Bay in 1612," *NS*, 6, 2 (1990), pp. 152-3. The map also shows a "great Lake or Sea" on the Burin Peninsula; the lake was said to be "discovered" by Mason in 1617.

[46]Cell, *Newfoundland Discovered*, p. 99.

[47]So says Cell (*Ibid.*, p. 22); R.J. Lahey says it was at Renews ("Avalon: Lord Baltimore's Colony in Newfoundland," *Early European Settlement*, p. 115).

[48]Cell, *Newfoundland Discovered*, pp. 13, 22, 135.

[49]In addition to its primary sense, "hope" also means an inlet or small bay.

[50]Cell, *Newfoundland Discovered*, p. 106.

[51]Cell claims Bristol's Hope "flourished" (*English Enterprise*, p. 87), but Handcock says the "alleged success" of the colony "cannot be documented" (*So longe*, p. 54).

[52]If, indeed, there were any; but see Cell, "Sir Francis Tanfield," *DCB*, vol. 1, p. 632.

[53]James A. Tuck, "Archaeology at Ferryland, Newfoundland," *NS*, 9, 2 (1993): 298; Tuck, lecture, Newfoundland Museum, January 22, 1998.

[54]Cell, *Newfoundland Discovered*, pp. 267-8.

[55]R.J. Lahey, "The Role of Religion in Lord Baltimore's Colonial Enterprise," *Maryland Historical Magazine*, 72, 4 (1977): 496-7. In a later article, Lahey says a clause in the charter "implicitly [required]" the oath of allegiance, which most Catholics felt able to take in good conscience ('Avalon: Lord Baltimore's Colony," p. 119). For the Oath of Allegiance, see note 97 below. The clause in question merely mentions "the allegiance due to us" (Cell, *Newfoundland Discovered*, p. 269); to see it as even impicitly requiring an oath is doubtful.

[56]The colonists were there said to "have and enjoy all liberties" as if they had been born in England (*NAW*, vol. 4, p. 137).

[57]Cell, *Newfoundland Discovered*, p. 268. The clause says Calvert could "have and enjoy all & singular the subsidyes, Customes, and Impositions payable, or accruable" within the colony. Lahey says this meant he could "impose his own taxes on imported goods" ("Avalon: Lord Baltimore's Colony," p. 118).

[58]The first settlers were "certainly not Roman Catholics" (Lahey, "The Role of Religion," p. 495).

[59]*Ibid.*, p. 504.

[60]*Ibid.*, pp. 506-7.

[61]Cell, *Newfoundland Discovered*, pp. 284-5; Lahey, "The Role of Religion," pp. 507-8.

[62]Barry Coward, *The Stuart Age: A history of England 1603-1714* (Longman: London, 1980), p. 272.

[63]Cell, *Newfoundland Discovered*, p. 279.

[64]*Ibid.*, p. 281.

[65]*Ibid.*, pp. 292-3.

[66]A calculation made in 1651 by Cecil Calvert, George Calvert's son, estimated the loss at £20,000.

[67]Peter E. Pope, "The South Avalon Planters, 1630 to 1700: Residence, Labour, Demand and Exchange in Seventeenth-Century Newfoundland" (Ph.D. thes., MUN, 1992), pp. 211-12.

[68]John G. Reid, *Acadia, Maine, and New Scotland* (Toronto: Univ. of Toronto Press, 1981), p. 43.

[69]*King Lear*, II, iii, 17-18. But Matthews pictures West Countrymen as "snug in their populous villages" ("17th Century English Settlement in Newfoundland," MS, CNS, 1974, p. 3) —elsewhere called "old established and comfortable villages" — whereas Newfoundland "had almost nothing to offer" (*Lectures*, p. 18).

[70]Handcock, *So longe*, pp. 29-30.

[71]But twice referred to ("plantacion" and "colony") in the charter for Avalon (Cell, *Newfoundland Discovered*, p. 259).

[72]See Handcock's discussion in *So longe*, pp. 34-6; also Cell, *English Enterprise*, p. 96.

[73]"South Avalon Planters," pp. 224-5.

[74]Matthews, "17th Century English Settlement in Newfoundland" (MS, CNS, 1974), p. 2. There were 50,000 in Barbados by 1712.

[75]"South Avalon Planters," pp. 216, 255.

[76]John G. Reid, *Acadia, Maine, and New Scotland: Marginal Colonies in the Seventeenth Century* (Toronto: Univ. of Toronto Press, 1981), pp. 114-24.

[77]Cell, "The Cupids Cove Settlement," p. 99; J.D. Rogers thought the development of Newfoundland was like "nowhere else in the world." See *A Historical Geography of the British Colonies*, vol. 5, pt. 4 (Newfoundland) (Oxford: Clarendon Press, 1911), p. vii.

[78]See "Of the Earths, and Soil," in Robert Beverley, *The History and Present State of Virginia* (1705), ed. Louis B. Wright (Chapel Hill: Univ. of North Carolina Press, 1947), pp. 123-8. Matthews says of Newfoundland that "agriculture was almost impossible given the technology of the era" ("17th Century English Settlement," p. 3), an extreme judgment.

[79]"South Avalon Planters," p. 251.

[80]Ralph Pastore, "The Collapse of the Beothuk World," *Acadiensis*, 19, 1 (1989): 52.

[81]*PC*, vol. 4, p. 1717. The petition is dated 1618.

[82]See Matthews' comment, "History," pp. 195-6.

[83]Reid, *Acadia, Maine, and New Scotland*, pp. 22-4.

[84]Stock, *Proceedings and Debates*, vol. 1, p. 30.

[85]*Ibid.*, p. 55. See Lounsbury's discussion, *British Fishery*, pp. 49-52.

[86]I.e., idea, notion.

[87]*PC*, vol. 4, pp. 1719-22. See Matthews' comments on the charter, *Collection and Commentary*, pp. 67-70.

[88]See Peter Pope, "Historical Archaeology and the Demand for Alcohol in 17th Century Newfoundland," *Acadiensis*, 19, 1 (1989): 72-90.

[89]*The Cambridge History of the British Empire*, vol. 6 (New York: Macmillan, 1930), p. 129.

[90]Anyone who committed offenses "upon the sea" was to be tried by the vice-admirals of Southampton, Dorset, Devon, and Cornwall.

[91]In the case of the London and Bristol Company, laws for the colony were to be made by the Council (resident in England), but "in defecte thereof in cause of necessitie" the Governors and Officers" could do so, provided such were "as neere as conveniently may be" to the laws of England. The Governor could also declare martial law.

[92]This is implied, not stated. Lounsbury says that under the charter the admiral "had first choice of the fishing grounds, stages, and boats' rooms" (*British Fishery*, p. 75). But the charter doesn't say that.

[93]*PC*, vol. 4, pp. 1723-37.

[94]Joseph Heller, *Catch-22* (New York: Dell, 1990), p. 40.

[95]*PC*, vol. 4, p. 1753.

[96]Matthews says of the Western Charter that "Neither this nor any of the later charters ever seem to have been taken seriously by the fishermen" (*Collection and Commentary*, p. 70). But inhabitants, to whom such charters were routinely read, might have responded differently.

[97]For the Oath of Allegiance, see *Constitutional Documents of the Reign of James I*, ed. J.R. Tanner (Cambridge: Univ. Press, 1960), pp. 90-91.

[98]Heller, *Catch-22*, p. 110. In 17th-century Furness it once took two teams of justices a full day to cope with a thousand oath-takers. See Paul Langford, *Public Life and the Propertied Englishman 1689-1798* (Oxford: Clarendon Press, 1991), p. 104.

[99]*Collection and Commentary*, p. 119.

[100]Tuck, "Archaeology at Ferryland, Newfoundland," p. 295. Little is known about settlers at St. John's at this time; the claim may be doubtful.

[101]Cell, *English Enterprise*, p. 115.

[102]Pope, "Historical Archaeology," p. 85.

[103]For French complaints in 1639, see A.M. Field, "The Development of Government in Newfoundland, 1638-1713" (M.A. thes., Univ. of London, 1924), pp. 59-60.

[104]Matthews, "History," pp. 142-3.

[105]Cell, *English Enterprise*, p. 115.

[106]Stock, *Proceedings and Debates*, vol. 1, p. 177; see also Pope, "Historical Archaeology," p. 85.

[107]Matthews says he "probably never had any intention of obeying [it]" (*Collection and Commentary*, p. 79).

[108]Louis D. Scisco, "Kirke's Memorial on Newfoundland," *CHR*, 7, 1 (1926): 48.

[109]So John Slaughter, a settler, claimed in 1652. A settler in 1667 said Kirke "imposed taxes and collected annual rents on their houses and fishing places" (Cell, *English Enterprise*, p. 122). There was nothing in Kirke's charter to prevent his collecting rents; although the King promised not to impose "any Imposition, Custome or other Taxation whatsoever" on the inhabitants, Kirke was evidently not restricted from doing so (Matthews, *Collection and Commentary*, p. 112; Pope, "South Avalon Planters," pp. 155-6).

[110]See Peter Pope, "Scavengers and Caretakers: Beothuk/European Settlement Dynamics in Seventeenth-Century Newfoundland," *NS*, 9, 2 (1993): 282.

[111]Field, "Development of Government," p. 56.

[112]*PC*, vol. 4, p. 1754.

[113]*DCB*, vol. 1, p. 406. The Clink was a famous prison in Southwark, a London borough south of the Thames. There is some doubt about where he died.

[114]L.D. Scisco, "Calvert's Proceedings against Kirke," *CHR*, 8, 2 (1927): 132-6. Newfoundland was restored to Cecil Calvert in 1661 by Order in Council (Matthews, *Collection and Commentary*, pp. 135-8). This had no apparent effect on settlement or law on the island.

[115]Louis D. Scisco, ""Testimony Taken in Newfoundland in 1652," *CHR*, 9, 3 (1928): 239-51. Cell's statement that the settlers "were almost uniformly hostile" to Kirke is inaccurate (*English Enterprise*, p. 121).

[116]Now Calvert.

[117]Or if they did, such views were not recorded.

[118]The 40-member Council of State took over the executive functions of the King shortly after the execution of Charles I in 1649.

[119]*PC*, vol. 4, pp. 1741-3.

[120]As such employees in the fishery were termed; see *DNE* under "servant"; also Matthews, "17th Century English Settlement," pp. 4-5, and Handcock, *So longe*, pp. 27-9.

[121]*PC*, vol. 4, pp. 1740-1.

[122]Presumably the "Adventurers" were the holders of the charter under which Kirke collected the tax.

[123]Prowse, *History*, p. 205.

[124]*PC*, vol. 4, p. 1746.

[125][James Yonge], *Some Considerations touching The present Debate between Owners And Fishermen, relating to The New-found-land Trade* (Oxford: 1671), p. 3.

[126]See *DNE*; also Handcock, *So longe*, pp. 25-7.

[127]For the merchants' arguments and Yonge's rebuttals, see [Yonge], *Some Considerations*, pp. 8-14.

[128]The count in 1675 was 1,580.

[129]Pope, "Scavengers and Caretakers," pp. 279-89.

[130]In the 17th century (and later) a general term for a medical man.

[131]*The Journal of James Yonge*, ed. F.N.L Poynter (London: Longmans, 1963), pp. 53-60.

[132]See Matthews' discussion, "17th Century English Settlement," pp. 4-6.

[133]Yonge listed 19 "Planters and Interlopers" in St. John's in 1669. (The "interlopers" were by-boat men.) These employed 175 men (*Journal*, pp. 119-20).

[134]*Ibid.*, p. 67.

[135]*Ibid.*, p. 133.

[136]*Some Considerations*, p. 9.

[137]*Journal*, p. 136. His pamphlet was *Some Considerations*, quoted above.

[138]Only one was there in 1675 (Handcock, *So longe*, p. 36). The buildings from the original settlement (around 13 in number) were burnt or otherwise destroyed c. 1660-70 (Gilbert lecture, 1998).

[139]Reid, *Maine, Charles II and Massachusetts*, p. 6.

[140]*Ibid.*, pp. 9-10.

[141]See Theodore Draper, *A Struggle for Power: The American Revolution* (New York: Vintage Books, 1997), pp. 33 ff.

[142]*Ibid.*, p. 28.

Notes to Chapter 4

[1]Daniel Defoe, *A Tour Through the Whole Island of Great Britain* (1724-6), 2 vols. (London: Dent, 1962), vol. 1, pp. 208, 215, 227.

[2]Peter Neary and P. O'Flaherty, *By Great Waters* (Toronto: Univ. of Toronto Press, 1974), p. 17.

[3]*Cambridge History of the British Empire*, vol. 6, p. 135. Yonge notes the Newfoundland fishery is a "vast Trade (not unfitly reckoned among the most profitable ones of the Nations)" (*Some Considerations*, p. 1).

[4]*DCB*, vol. 1, pp. 323-4.

[5]Though Englishmen "who turned Catholic" could stay (*CSP*, 1681-85, p. 107). And some did. A few French Protestants were living on the English shore by century's end. (I use Gordon Handcock's extracts of *CSP* documents, CNS.)

[6]Alan F. Williams. *Father Baudoin's War: D'Iberville's Campaigns in Acadia and Newfoundland 1696, 1697* (St. John's: MUN, 1987), pp. 24, 28.

[7]Gordon Handcock, "Settlement," *ENL*, vol. 5, p. 135; in 1685 a census placed the population at 640 (*DCB*, vol. 1, p. 530).

[8]*DCB*, vol. 1, p. 419.

[9]George MacBeath, "The Atlantic Region," *Ibid.*, p. 25.

[10]*CSP*, 1681-85, p. 709. Pope ("South Avalon Planters," p. 91) says both Renews and Trepassey functioned as points of "interface" between the two cultures.

[11]Matthews says the Dutch "burnt" Ferryland as well in the second Dutch War (*Collection and Commentary*, p. 147).

[12]*PC*, vol. 4, p. 1752.

[13]*Ibid.*, p. 1751.

[14]Dicky Glerum-Laurentius, "A History of Dutch Activity in the Newfoundland Fish Trade from about 1590 till about 1680" (M.A. thes., MUN, 1960), pp. 62-74. I rely mainly on this account of Dutch raids of 1665. In other accounts the date of the attack on St John's is given as June 6, using the Old Style (or Julian) calendar, employed in England until 1752. The New Style (or Gregorian) calendar suppressed ten days. E. Hunt (*DCB*, vol. 1, p. 496) says the Dutch "invaded and pillaged" St. John's again in 1667, and made yet another "attack" in 1673.

[15]Glerum-Laurentius, "History," pp. 80-81; see Prowse, *History*, p. 156.

[16]Pope, "South Avalon Planters," pp. 170-72.

[17]Shomette, Donald, and Robert Haslach, *Raid on America: The Dutch Naval Campaign of 1672-1674* (Columbia, S.C.: Univ. of South Carolina Press, 1988), pp. 203-5, 342.

[18]Matthews, *Collection and Commentary*, p. 147.

[19]*PC*, vol. 4, p. 1750; Matthews, "History," pp. 200-1.

[20]*PC*, vol. 4, p. 1750.

[21]The distinction being drawn is between criminal and non-criminal colonists. To transport here means to deport, to carry into banishment.

[22]*PC*, vol. 4, pp. 1755-6.

[23]"History," p. 205. Field says removal of the settlers was considered in 1655 ("Development of Government," p. 78).

[24]"South Avalon Planters," p. 205.

[25]That I know of.

[26]I.e., the King in Council.

[27]Matthews, *Collection and Commentary*, p. 151. The evolution of colonial administration and decision-making within the British government is complex. See Draper, *Struggle for Power*, pp. 30-33; also *The Oxford History of the British Empire*, ed. W.R. Lewis, vol. 2 ("The Eighteenth Century") (Oxford: Oxford Univ. Press, 1998), pp. 105-27.

[28]James Smith, appointed judge of a vice-admiralty court in Newfoundland in 1708, noted: "the inhabitants of ... H.M. Plantations, tho' they be H.M. subjects and belong to the Dominions of the Crown, yet cannot be said to belong to the Dominions of England" (*CSP*, 1714-15, p. 76).

[29]After this comes the phrase: "or in any part of the said Newfoundland." This, as the sentence is written, seems to mean that they couldn't settle within six miles of the shore between Cape Race and Cape Bonavista *or in any part of* that region, which makes no sense. It could mean that they were forbidden to go outside the coast between the two capes.

[30]The rules of 1653 forbad gardens only "upon or near the ground where fish is saved or dried."

[31]*OED*.

[32]*PC*, vol. 4, p. 1760. This last phrase is given somewhat differently by Matthews: "And that they all be provided for" (*Collection and Commentary*, p. 153). The intent seems to be: the settlers were not to take up rooms until *all* the ship fishermen had theirs.

[33]*PC*, vol. 4, p. 1760, has "their"; Matthews (*Collection and Commentary*, p. 153) has "other."

[34]Pope argues that parts of the English shore, "in particular the south Avalon, had already passed the frontier stage" by the late 17th century ("South Avalon Planters," p. 256).

[35]"History," p. 208.

[36]The rules applied to Ireland as well as England, since anyone who went to Newfoundland from Ireland before the mid-1670s would have gone on ships departing initially from England. It might be argued that settlers from other English *colonies* were not prevented by the regulations from going to Newfoundland, but there were few, if any, from this source in the 17th century.

[37]Matthews, *Collection and Commentary*, p. 161.

[38]*PC*, vol. 4, p. 1766.

[39]Field, "Development of Government," p. 120.

[40]A point made by Mason in 1620 (Cell, *Newfoundland Discovered*, p. 96).

[41]*CSP*, 1675-76, p. 179.

[42]*PC*, vol. 4, pp. 1768-71.

[43]Matthews, *Collection and Commentary*, p. 166.

[44]I.e., they would need poor relief.

[45]Matthews, *Lectures*, p. 18.

[46]*Ibid.*, p. 19.

[47]Pope, "South Avalon Planters," p. 406.

[48]*PC*, vol. 4, pp. 1772-5; C.O. 1/35.

[49]*PC*, vol. 4, p. 1776.

[50]*Ibid.*, pp. 1777-82.

[51]*Collection and Commentary*, p. 183.

[52]Field claims, though it is not clear on what evidence, that the fishing captains burnt stages, pulled down houses, looted, robbed, and persecuted the planters ("Development of Government," pp. 145-6).

[53]Matthews, "History," p. 223.

[54]A very high figure, likely misstated; unless Downing had adopted the West Country merchants' tactic of inflating numbers to make a point!

[55]*PC*, vol. 4, p. 1786.

[56]Prowse, *History*, p. 208.

[57]Matthews, *Collection and Commentary*, p. 185.

[58]*Ibid.*, p. 193.

[59]Pope, "South Avalon Planters," p. 55, following Matthews, "History," p. 226.

[60]Matthews, "History," pp. 230-33.

[61]"South Avalon Planters," pp. 84-7.

[62]That I know of.

[63]Though the admirals of course could do so.

[64]W.H. Whiteley, "James Cook and British Policy in the Newfoundland Fisheries, 1763-7," *CHR*, 54, 3 (1973): 257.

[65]A few English settlers were in Placentia when the French arrived in 1662.

[66]C.O. 1/35 (the 1675 Census); C.O. 1/38 (1676). But only 28 are listed in the 1708 census (C.O. 194/4, ff. 252-70).

[67]C.O.1/41. (Captain William Poole's census.)

[68]Williams, *Father Baudoin's War*, p. 65. Baudoin saw the shore south of St. John's after parts of it had been ransacked by Brouillan. Pope regards the southern Avalon as the most developed part of Newfoundland in the 17th century ("South Avalon Planters," pp. 256, 315).

[69]Baudoin says 20 men were found in the woods at Salmon Cove on February 1, 1697.

[70]See Philip E.L. Smith, "In Winter Quarters," *NS*, 3, 1 (1987): 1-36.

[71]Matthews, "History," pp. 174-5.

[72]I.e., those who owned boats and employed servants.

[73]In 1677 Carbonear had 11 inhabitants and planters, with 9 wives; the figures for Old Perlican and St. John's were: 13 (9) and 27 (15). The number of children in each place was: 35, 17, 45. C.O. 1/41.

[74]Handcock, *So longe*, p. 30.

[75]*CSP*, 1681-85, p. 707.

[76]I surmise this from observation of outport practices in the 1940s.

[77]"South Avalon Planters," pp. 70-74.

[78]C.O. 1/35.

[79]*PC*, vol. 4, p. 1789. See John Mannion's comments on agriculture in Newfoundland in "Victualling a Fishery: Newfoundland Diet and the Origins of the Irish Provisions Trade, 1675-1700" (MS, 1999), pp. 1-7.

[80]Iberville's men found horses to kill for food at Ferryland in 1696; others were located to carry booty from St. John's back to Placentia. Baudoin noted that the Newfoundland settlers travelled "from settlement to settlement by horse" (Williams, *Father Baudoin's War*, pp. 39, 53, 60).

[81]See an 1896 account of getting a horse ashore, in J.P. Howley, *Reminiscences* (Toronto: Champlain Society, 1997), p. 346.

[82]Williams, *Father Baudoin's War*, p. 35.

[83]*Journal*, p. 56.

[84]See Baudoin's comments, "Journal of Abbé Baudoin," trans. H. Bedford-Jones, *Daily News* (St. John's), 1923 (copy, CNS).

[85]Thompson, *French Shore Problem*, pp. 6-7.

[86]Matthews, *Collection and Commentary*, p. 195.

[87]The forts were: King William's Fort (or Fort William), on the western side of the harbour, commanding a view of the Narrows, Fort Mary, to the south of Fort William (also laid out by Lilly, but likely unfinished by 1696), an "old fort" south of the Narrows, and an unnamed fort at the head of the harbour; there was also a battery at Pigg's Point north of the Narrows; see Williams, *Father Baudoin's War*, pp. 43, 45, 46-7, 128-9; also Olaf Janzen, "New Light on the Origins of Fort William at St. John's,

Newfoundland, 1693-1696," *NQ*, 83, 2 (1987): 24-31. The original Fort William was probably on a different site from the later one bearing the same name.

[88]*DCB.*, vol. 1, p. 530; Williams, *Father Baudoin's War*, p. 28. Churches were used as prisons in French assaults as well.

[89]Accounts vary; see *DCB*, vol. 1, p. 546 and vol. 2, p. 510; Williams, *Father Baudoin's War*, pp. 28, 125.

[90]"A vessel filled with combustibles, and set adrift among ships, etc. to destroy them" (*OED*).

[91]A two-masted vessel rigged with mortars for bombarding (*OED*).

[92]*DCB*, vol. 2, p. 590. Matthews alludes to other raids ("History," p. 241).

[93]I follow the Abbé Baudoin's narrative of the "winter war" of 1696-7 (see note 84 above) and the scholarly treatment in Williams, *Father Baudoin's War*. Williams prints Baudoin's French text, pp. 173-91.

[94]The number given by Baudoin.

[95]Williams seems to conclude the others were Outounois (Ottawas); see *Father Baudoin's War*, pp. 23-4. Prowse (*History*, p. 220) assumed they were Abenakis, the allies of the French in their assaults on New England. The Abenaki chief Nescambiouit was on the expedition.

[96]See his calculations, *Father Baudoin's War*, pp. 10-12; Prowse says 400 (*History*, p. 216).

[97]Matthews, *Lectures*, p. 18.

[98]A small, fast-sailing vessel used for warlike purposes (*OED*).

[99]*DCB*, vol. 2, p. 666.

[100]"History," p. 240.

[101]Lilly had commented in 1680: "they did not...so much fear an enemy from the seaside as the Indians and the French together coming from Placentia overland to destroy and burn their habitations" (Janzen, "New Light," p. 27).

[102]Baudoin's figure, likely inflated.

[103]Baudoin's number is 88; another source says 84.

[104]Thus Baudoin; confirmed by an English account (*CSP*, 1696-97, p. 306).

[105]A map of the harbour from 1693 shows more than 50 houses stretched along the west side (Williams, *Father Baudoin's War*, p. 45). Baudoin noted St. John's was "very well settled along the north [i.e., west, or northwest] side of the harbour to a distance of about half a league."

[106]*DCB*, vol. 2, pp. 494-5.

[107]My italics.

[108]*Father Baudoin's War*, pp. 52, 55.

[109]Williams suggests they were slaughtered (*Ibid.*, p. 56).

[110]*DCB*, vol. 2, p. 626; so writes Louise Dechêne, Professeur d'histoire, Université d'Ottawa.

[111]*Ibid.*, p. 390; so writes Bernard Pothier.

[112]Williams, *Father Baudoin's War*, p. 71.

[113]For instance English Harbour, a very old settlement.

[114]Stock, *Proceeding and Debates*, vol. 2, pp. 178-89.

[115]*Ibid.*, p. 179.

[116]Which replaced the former Committee on Trade. In May, 1696, William III created "a special council or board for the purpose of promoting the trade of the kingdom and of inspecting and improving the plantations in America and elsewhere" (*PC*, vol. 4, p. 1795). This body, called by various names, the Board of Trade, Council of Trade, or Lords of Trade, lasted until the American Revolution (Draper, *Struggle for Power*, p. 31).

[117]*PC*, vol. 4, p. 1797.

[118]One source says 2,000 men came (*DCB*, vol. 4, p. 246).

[119]Janzen, "New Light," p. 27; *PC*, vol. 4, p. 1798.

[120]Stock, *Proceedings and Debates*, vol. 2, p. 250.

[121]See a table of the 1698 population in Williams, *Father Baudoin's War*, p. 112.

[122]"History," p. 243.

[123]*Father Baudoin's War*, p. 118.

[124]*History*, p. 495.

[125]"New Light," p. 25.

[126]Rev. of Williams, *Father Baudoin's War*, in *NQ*, 84, 4 (1989): 48.

[127]Draper, *Struggle for Power*, p. 29.

[128]Neary and O'Flaherty, *Part of the Main*, p. 35.

[129]*PC*, vol. 4, p. 1810.

[130]Stock, *Proceedings and Debates*, pp. 308-10.

[131]10 and 11 William III, c. 25. In John Reeves, *History of the Government of the Island of Newfoundland* (1793) (New York: Johnson Reprint Corporation, 1967), pp. i-xv.

[132]The specific clause guaranteeing freedom in the fishery reads, in part: "... from henceforth it shall and may be lawful for all his Majesty's subjects residing within this his realm of *England*, or the dominions thereunto belonging, trading or that shall trade to *Newfoundland* ... to have, use, and enjoy, the free trade and traffick, and art of merchandize and fishery, to and from *Newfoundland*." It has been assumed that this clause applies to residents of the island as well as to visiting fishermen. But the act does not say that. James Smith, appointed judge in a projected vice-admiralty court in Newfoundland in 1708, and therefore presumably someone with legal knowledge, thought that the phrase "his realm of England, or the dominions thereunto belonging" excluded inhabitants of "H.M. Plantations" (in America) and even the Irish from participating in the trade (see *CSP*, 1714-15, p. 76). In practice, however, the first four clauses of King William's Act applied to those (whether in England, Ireland, Scotland, or other "dominions," including the American plantations) "trading or that shall trade to" the island. But trading to is not the same as living in. Beginning at clause 5, we get a different set of regulations, for the "Inhabitants in Newfoundland, and other Persons." As the regulations make plain, these people do *not* have the same liberties as are outlined in the first four clauses. The inhabitants of Newfoundland are not specifically denied the right to fish by King William's Act, but neither are they specifically granted it.

[133]See Plymouth's petition of Dec. 11, 1696 (*CSP*, 1696-97, pp. 248-50); the Poole merchants on Dec. 9, 1696, said a governor was "very necessary" but only "during the war" (*Ibid.*, p. 244).

[134]Berwick, a border town in Northumberland, did not become officially English until 1885.

[135]It was recognized as such by Governor Milbanke in 1789 (C.O. 194/21, ff. 290-91).

[136]While it was recognized, for example by George Larkin in 1701 (*PC*, vol. 4, p. 1813), that "The late Act gives the Planters a title," it was by no means clear that clause 7 conferred ownership beyond an "estate for life." If it did not do so, the rooms could not be inherited. See the closely argued opinion of Francis Fane in Reeves, *History*, pp. 63-4. Fane argued that the words "to his or their own use" in clause 7 "seem to confine the possession to the builder," and such possession "would only last for the life of the builder." For the exact question on which Fane was asked for his opinion, see C.O. 194/8, ff. 183-4.

[137]"Settlement," *ENL*, vol. 5, p. 133.

[138]Reeves, *History*, p. 64.

[139]See Gov. F.H. Lee's comments, *CSP*, 1735-36, p. 71.

[140]Matthews, "History," pp. 257-8.

[141]Captain Philip Vanbrugh reported "some disputes" over rooms in 1738, but said they were "now in a fair way to be settled" (*CSP*, 1738, p. 236).

[142]Commodore Wheler in 1684 had pointed to the need for a "magistrate on the spot" to prevent abuses (*CSP*, 1681-85, p. 707).

[143]*CSP*, 1701, p. 529.

[144]*PC*, vol. 4, p. 1813.

[145]*Collection and Commentary*, pp. 200-01.

[146]For the proceedings, see GN2/1/A, vol. 11, pp. 106-11.

[147]Amid the wealth of statistics from the 18th century, there are none that I know of on this head. But "restoring" alleged ships' rooms to migratory fishermen was a regular feature of life for many years. See Commodore John St. Lo's comment in 1727 (*CSP*, 1726-27, p. 360).

[148]"History," p. 258; see his entire discussion, pp. 257-64.

[149]*PC*, vol. 4, p. 1811.

[150]Buying up, monopolizing. Engrossing land was widely recognized as an abuse in England, and various statutes were passed making it illegal. See *Agricultural Change: Policy and Practice, 1500-1750*, ed. Joan Thirsk (Cambridge: Cambridge Univ. Press, 1990), pp. 59-60, passim.

[151]*Some Considerations*, p. 17.

[152]*CSP*, 1701, p. 529.

[153]*PC*, vol. 4, pp. 1811-14.

[154]See Governor Clinton's comments, and his proclamation against it, *CSP*, 1731, pp. 96-7.

[155]The 1701 population was 3,575; Stock, *Proceedings and Debates*, vol. 2, p. 434; it was 2,402 in 1702 (*Ibid.*, vol. 3, p. 5).

[156]*CSP*, 1702-03, p. 723.

[157]Later renamed Winterton.

[158]Prowse, *History*, p. 239.

[159]Captured ships, later sold; the "prize money" was distributed after the sale.

[160]Stock, *Proceedings and Debates*, vol. 3, p. 5n.

[161]C.O. 194/3, f. 21.

[162]*DCB*, vol. 2, pp. 387-8.

[163]St. John's prize officer Colin Campbell's estimate was 150 (*Ibid.*, p. 118).

[164]*Ibid.*, p. 36; other estimates give 600 (pp. 118, 487); 430 was the number given in the Commons, Jan. 19, 1706 (Stock, *Proceedings and Debates*, vol. 3, p. 102).

[165]"History," pp. 243-4.

[166]Stock, *Proceedings and Debates*, vol. 3, p. 112.

[167]*CSP*, 1710-11, pp. 33, 321.

[168]Moody's estimate, "according to the best account he could have" (Stock, *Proceedings and Debates*, p. 110); the historian Charlevoix said there were "fifteen dead or wounded" (Prowse, *History*, p. 261).

[169]Quoted in Prowse, *History*, p. 261.

[170]*Ibid.*, p. 243.

[171]*DCB*, vol. 2, p. 626.

[172]Says Charlevoix (Prowse, *History*, p. 261).

[173]*DCB*, vol. 2, p. 37; doubtless exaggerated (this is René Baudry); Colin Campbell's contemporary count is 200, though this is said to be only the number taken by Subercase to Placentia (Prowse, *History*, p. 262).

[174]Stock, *Proceedings and Debates*, vol. 3, p. 102.

[175]See *Ibid.*, pp. 101-14, for petitions and discussion in the House of Commons.

[176]*CSP*, 1681-85, p. 709.

[177]Stock, *Proceedings and Debates*, vol. 3, p. 111.

[178]*DCB*, vol. 2, p. 511; or "a motley band of 164" (*Ibid.*, vol. 3, p. 454).

[179]*Ibid.*, vol. 3, p. 454; D.B. Quinn (vol. 2, p. 439), gives Dec. 22, 1708, as the date, using the Old Style calendar.

[180]*Ibid.*, vol. 3, p. 454.

[181]Prowse, *History*, pp. 271-2.

[182]*Ibid.*, pp. 272-3.

[183]J.K. Hiller, "Utrecht Revisited: The Origin of French Fishing Rights in Newfoundland Waters," *NS*, 7, 1 (1991): 25, 27.

Notes to Chapter 5

[1]*Oxford History of the British Empire*, vol. 2, p. 372.

[2]*Ibid.*, p. 373.

[3]See Stock, *Proceedings and Debates*, vol. 5, p. xiv.

[4]*CSP*, 1728-29, p. 281.

[5]*Ibid.*, p. 279.

[6]Draper, *Struggle for Power*, pp. 102-3.

[7]But see the discussion of Placentia below.

[8]See P. O'Flaherty, "Government in Newfoundland before 1832," *NQ*, 84, 2 (1988): 26-30.

[9]*Thoughts on the Present Discontents* (1770) (London: Cassell & Co., 1886), p. 49.

[10]*The New York Review of Books*, 45, 15 (1998): 42.

[11]"History," p. 603.

[12]Draper, *Struggle for Power*, pp. 37-8.

[13]*CSP*, 1714-15, p. 30.

[14]For a likely version of the oath (combining allegiance to the king and abjuration of Rome's power to excommunicate him), see *Select Documents of English Constitutional History*, ed. G.B. Adams and H.M. Stephens (New York: Macmillan, 1923), p. 466.

[15]*CSP*, 1716-17, pp. 14-15; Thompson, *French Shore Problem*, p. 8.

[16]*CSP*, 1735-36, p. 71.

[17]*CSP*, 1734, p. 27.

[18]Olaf Janzen, "'Une Grande Liaison': French Fishermen from Île Royale on the Coast of Southwestern Newfoundland, 1714-1766," *NS*, 3, 2 (1987): 183-200.

[19]*DCB*, vol. 2, p. 497.

[20]Olaf Janzen, "Military Garrisons," *ENL*, vol. 3, p. 542.

[21]*Eighteenth Century Newfoundland: A Geographer's Perspective* (Toronto: McClelland and Stewart, 1976), p. 59.

[22]*Memoirs of Lieut.-Colonel Samuel Gledhill*, ed. W.H. Chippindall (Kendal, Cumbria: Titus Wilson, 1910); see also D.B. Quinn's biography in *DCB*, vol. 2, pp. 249-51.

[23]*CSP*, 1726-27, pp. 224-5.

[24]*Memoirs*, p. 115.

[25]Matthews, "History," p. 352.

[26]*CSP*, 1719-20, p. 217.

[27]Matthews, "History," p. 334.

[28]*CSP*, 1732, p. 96.

[29]Janzen, "'Une Grande Liaison'," pp. 191-2.

[30]*CSP*, 1714-15, p. 74.

[31]*PC*, vol. 4, p. 1815; Lounsbury, *British Fishery*, pp. 217-8; *DCB*, vol. 2, pp. 117, 165.

[32]A vice-admiralty court was the colonial equivalent of the High Court of Admiralty; it would try cases of piracy and other crimes on the high seas, and deal with questions related to prizes and other maritime issues.

[33]*DCB*, vol. 2, pp. 610-11.

[34]However, he "left deputations to such as I believed to be persons of the greatest probity and knowledge" (*CSP*, 1714-15, p. 75).

[35]I.e., an officer whose duty is to receive copies of ships' manifests and entries in the customs house (*OED*). (There was as yet no customs house.)

[36]Various acts passed by the British Parliament in 1651-73 to support English merchant shipping and secure colonial markets.

[37]J. Paterson, "The History of Newfoundland 1713-1763" (M.A. thes., Univ. of London, 1931), pp. 199-202.

[38]The planter or by-boatman who hired them was answerable to the ship for the passage out from England or Ireland (paid for in what was termed "fish pay," i.e., cod); passage back, higher than that out, was paid by the servant in cash or bill of exchange.

[39]Paterson, "History," p. 193.

[40]Commodore Thomas Kempthorn, quoted in John E. Crowley, "Empire versus Truck: The Official Interpretation of Debt and Labour in the Eighteenth-Century Newfoundland Fishery," *CHR*, 70, 3 (1989): 320.

[41]Agents acting (on commission) for other merchants.

[42]For an instance in 1728, see C.O. 194/8, ff. 188-90. King William's Act gave the commodore power over admirals only in the area of disputes over fishing rooms, and then only on appeal from the admirals' decisions.

[43]I.e., those punishable by death.

[44]The King's commission of oyer and terminer empowered judges to hear cases of treason and other capital crimes; commissions of jail-delivery authorized periodic clearing of jails by bringing inmates before judges to be acquitted or condemned. For Newfoundland's early legal history, see Christopher English, "The Development of the Newfoundland Legal System to 1815," *Acadiensis*, 20, 1 (1990): 89-119.

[45]See William Keen's letter in 1728, complaining of having to send an accused murderer to England for trial (*CSP*, 1728-29, p. 218); and another such complaint in 1730 (C.O. 194/9, f. 66).

[46]*CSP*, 1717-18, p. 318.

[47]As Governor Fitzroy Henry Lee hinted in 1735; *CSP*, 1735-36, p. 67.

[48]Lee, again writing in 1735; *Ibid.*

[49]*CSP*, 1716-17, p. 35.

[50]*CSP*, 1717-18, pp. 257-8, 412-24.

[51]*Ibid.*, pp. 439-42.

[52]*Ibid.*, p. 319. Likely an underestimate. The official count for 1715 was 4049.

[53]Thereby halving the size of Gledhill's garrison.

[54]See *DCB*, vol. 2, p. 250; vol. 3, p. 516; Paterson, "History," pp. 35-9.

[55]Matthews, "History," p. 355.

[56]*CSP*, 1712-14, p. 311.

[57]Houses where food and drink were supplied (*OED*). "Cating" houses (from the obsolete verb "cate," meaning to provide cooked food) also existed in St. John's.

[58]*CSP*, 1718-20, p. 176.

[59]C.O. 194/7, ff. 246-52.

[60]C.O. 194/8, ff. 15-16.

[61]*CSP*, 1728-29, pp. 220-23.

[62]It was at this point that the Council on Trade asked Francis Fane for his opinion on the meaning of clause 7 in the 1699 Newfoundland act. His letter to them is dated Dec. 19, 1728. See Chapter 4, note 136.

[63]*CSP*, 1728-29, p. 283.

[64]C.O. 194/8, ff. 198-9. The Privy Council was a body of advisors selected by the King. It was not the same as the Cabinet council which, with the King, made government policy and key decisions.

[65]The naval commodore was appointed by the Admiralty. Normally the King then appointed the commodore Governor, but this did not always happen.

[66]C.O. 194/8, f. 210. He was back in his post, though subject to the Newfoundland governor, in 1731; *DCB*, vol. 2, p. 251.

[67]Stock, *Proceedings and Debates*, vol. 4, p. 73.

[68]His commission is in *PC*, vol. 4, pp. 1838-40; his instructions are in *CSP*, 1728-29, pp. 377-9.

[69]C.O. 194/8, f. 226. The number of districts was reduced to five in 1730, when there were 19 justices and 35 constables in place, but raised back to six in 1732 (C.O. 194/9, f. 6; Prowse, *History*, p. 301). By 1750, 27 justices were in place in Newfoundland.

[70]C.O. 194/9, ff. 2-4.

[71]Matthews says that the magistrates were not "to obstruct the fishing admirals in administering justice during the summer," and cites the commission appointing Osborne governor as his source ("History," p. 358). But Osborne's commission is silent on this point. He adds (p. 359) that the crown lawyers Philip Yorke and Francis Fane said the authority of the justices was confined to enforcing criminal law "*during winter only*." No source for this is given. Letters from the two lawyers in Apr.-May, 1730, commenting on the powers of the justices do not mention restriction of their activities to winter (C.O. 194/8, ff. 295-6, 307, 321).

[72]C.O. 194/8, ff. 228-31.

[73]See petitions from the merchants of Dartmouth and Poole, C.O. 194/9, ff. 83, 86.

[74]That of Attorney General Philip Yorke, in 1730 (*PC*, vol. 4, pp. 1841-2).

[75]See Yorke's opinion, C.O. 194/8, ff. 295-6; and Fane's, f. 307.

[76]He had 11 sets of books for 17 justices, so in places that had more than one justice the books presumably had to be shared.

[77]Their commissions of appointment make this clear.

[78]Joseph Shaw, *The Practical Justice of Peace: or, A Treatise shewing the Power and Authority of that Office in all its Branches*, 2 vols. (London: 1728), vol. 1, p. 7.

[79]"History," p. 365; see his entire discussion, pp. 354-65.

[80]The latter's considerable powers are outlined in Shaw's *Parish Law: or, a Guide to Justices of the Peace, Ministers, Churchwardens, Overseers of the Poor, Constables, Surveyors of the Highways, Vestry-Clerks, and all Others concerned in Parish Business* (1734), 7th ed. (London: 1750), pp. 361 ff.

[81]This point is made in Fane's letter of April 26, 1730 (C.O. 194/8, f. 307).

[82]Gledhill refers to "harlotts" keeping "bawdy houses" in Placentia in 1725 (*CSP*, 1724-25, p. 451).

[83]Clause 16 of King William's Act was aimed at Newfoundland sabbath-breakers, but no penalties or enforcers were named. They had now arrived.

[84]Shaw, *Practical Justice*, vol. 1, pp. 17 ff.

[85]During the first week after Michaelmas, Epiphany, and the close of Easter; and on the translation of Thomas à Becket, July 7.

[86]Shaw, *Parish Law*, p. 371.

[87]"The act of presenting or laying before a court or person in authority a formal statement of some matter to be legally dealt with" (*OED*).

[88]*CSP*, 1731, p. 279.

[89]"History," pp. 363-5.

[90]See, for instance, C.O. 194/11, f. 43; also Gov. Palliser's charges, C.O. 194/16, f. 216.

[91]Shaw, *Practical Justice*, vol. 1, p. 9.

[92]*King Lear*, IV, vi, 167.

[93]It was termed a "Colony," no doubt inadvertently, by Holles-Newcastle in 1730 (C.O. 194/9, f. 1).

[94]I deduce this from various reports by governors around the mid-century; see C.O. 194/11, f. 94; /12, ff. 119, 186; /13, ff. 13, 52.

[95]*CSP*, 1717-18, p. 393; 1728-29, p. 507.

[96]See Commodore Falkingham's comments, *CSP*, 1732, p. 224.

[97]*CSP*, 1728-29, p. 507.

[98]C.O. 194/12, f. 2.

[99]*CSP*, 1728-29, p. 509; 1738, p. 237.

[100]Salmon fisheries were also established in St. Mary's Bay and Biscay Bay in the 1720s.

[101]Dams would be constructed upriver in smaller streams. The inflowing tide would bring salmon into pools behind them; when the tide ebbed, the salmon would be trapped.

[102]Neary and O'Flaherty, *Part of the Main*, p. 41.

[103]*CSP*, 1722-23, p. 163; 1724-25, pp. 226, 363.

[104]C.O. 194/14, f. 5.

[105]See descriptions, C.O. 194/18, ff. 134-6, 161; Shannon Ryan, *The Ice Hunters: A History of Newfoundland Sealing to 1914* (St. John's: Breakwater, 1994), pp. 50-51; also *CSP*, 1732, p. 224.

[106]Matthews, "History," p. 319.

[107]*CSP*, 1717-18, p. 393.

[108]*CSP*, 1719-20, p. 235.

[109]Ryan, *Ice Hunters*, p. 49.

[110]*Ibid.*, p. 424 (Table: "Value of Seal Oil produced by Inhabitants: 1723-1802.") The value of oil does not, of course, tell the full story of the importance of the industry.

[111]See Handcock, "John Slade," *DCB*, vol. 4, pp. 711-14.

[112]C.O. 194/12, ff. 69, 186. Their ships were sometimes called "passage ships" (f. 47).

[113]C.O. 194/15, f. 190.

[114]*CSP*, 1714-15, p. 309.

[115]Handcock, *So longe*, p. 76.

[116]Matthews, "History," p. 374.

[117]By the end of the century the Lester firm of Trinity and Poole owned 48 dwelling houses in Trinity Bay and a large number of rooms along the coast north of Bay de Verde. For the extent of the Lester properties and those of other firms, see Handcock, *So longe*, pp. 226-32.

[118]The Newfoundland trader Joseph White of Poole died in 1771 with a fortune of £130-150,000 (Handcock, *So longe*, p. 222; *DCB*, vol. 5, p. 783); John Slade's estate (he died in 1792) was estimated "perhaps conservatively" at £70,000 (*DCB*, vol. 4, p. 714). For pictures of luxurious West Country homes built on cod profits, see Neary and O'Flaherty, *Part of the Main*, pp. 36-7.

[119]See Handcock, *So longe*, pp. 220-2.

[120]Meaning, harbours "other than the the the chief port of St. John's" (*DNE*). The earliet citation for the word in *DNE* is 1764. "Outport" (with the same meaning) starts occurring around the mid-1700s.

[121]C.O. 194/15, f. 200.

[122]Neary and O'Flaherty, *Part of the Main*, pp. 32-3, 35, 36.

[123]John Mannion, "Irish Merchants Abroad: The Newfoundland Experience, 1750-1850," *NS*, 2, 2 (1986): 127-90.

[124]The word seems to used for the first time in print to describe the Newfoundland-born in Griffith Williams' *An Account of the Island of Newfoundland* (London: 1765), p. 9.

[125]Matthews, "History," p. 377.

[126]Cook said "Wadhams Islands, Tilton Harbour, and Fogo Harbour [were] settled on or before the year 1729. Bay of Touliguet on or before the year 1735" (Whiteley, "James Cook," p. 257). Gov. Falkingham, in 1732, said Fogo and Twillingate were "new settlements this year" (*CSP*, 1732, p. 224).

[127]Janzen, "'Une Grande Liaison'," p. 189.

[128]C.O. 194/11, f. 24.

[129]See C.O. 194/15, f. 201.

[130]See Handcock, *So longe*, p. 102.

[131]Shannon Ryan, in *Fish Out of Water: The Newfoundland Saltfish Trade 1814-1914* (St. John's: Breakwater, 1986), p. 33, puts it at 8,225.

[132]*Ibid.* Gov. Palliser in 1765 gives an official figure of 16,000 for the overwintering population, but says "I am satisfy'd they are 20,000" (C.O. 194/16, f. 211). It is likely that the official population size was underestimated throughout the century.

[133]Many of the figures supplied were rough guesses. In 1765 he Council on Trade conceded that "It is difficult to ascertain with precision the present Number of Inhabitants" (*PC*, vol. 4, p. 1852). It was likely no more difficult in 1765 than in any other year.

[134]Robert V. Wells, *The Population of the British Colonies in America before 1776* (Princeton, N.J.: Princeton Univ. Press, 1975), p. 50.

[135]Figures suggest that servants "were not as common" in Nova Scotia as in Newfoundland; those in "bondage" in French Canada in 1762 were "less than 10%" of the population (*Ibid.*, pp. 62, 66).

[136]Thomas Graves in 1764 (C.O. 194/15, f. 193).

[137]For the costs (including wages of crew members) of maintaining a fishing boat for the year 1760, see C.O. 194/15, f. 23.

[138]Here meaning to buy up the whole of a commodity so as to gain a monopoly and sell at a high profit.

[139]C.O. 194/15, f. 193.

[140]Crawley, "Empire versus Truck," p. 318.

[141]C.O. 194/15, f. 192.

[142]C.O. 194/15, ff. 192, 197-8.

[143]C.O. 194/15, f. 193.

[144]C.O. 194/17, f. 26.

[145]C.O. 194/13, f. 121.

[146]See Gov. Graves' report in 1757 (C.O. 194/13, f. 220).

[147]Governors were instructed "to permit a liberty of conscience to all persons (except Papists)" (*CSP*, 1728-29, p. 378).

[148]C.O. 194/11, ff. 7-12.

[149]C.O. 194/11, ff. 41-4.

[150]C.O. 194/12, f. 1.

[151]C.O. 194/12, ff. 12-15.

[152]"Military Garrisons," p. 542.

[153]C.O. 194/12, ff. 72-3.

[154]The 1754 count was: 74 soldiers from a regiment of foot, and 55 artillery men (C.O. 194/13, f. 184).

[155]*PC*, vol. 4, pp. 1843-6; the court was sometimes referred to as the assizes. See note 44 above.

[156]The number of grand jurors in Newfoundland in the 1750s; the number varied elsewhere.

[157]O'Flaherty, "Government in Newfoundland," p. 26.

[158]C.O. 194/13, ff. 1-2.

[159]If no capital crimes had been committed, no court was held.

[160]C.O. 194/13, ff. 9, 14-17, 22, 69.

[161]Hoare was a common name in the West Country; but it might also be Irish.

[162]C.O. 194/13, ff. 54-7, 100.

[163]See Marshall, *History and Ethnography*, p. 485.

[164]C.O. 194/13, ff. 57-64.

[165]In 1764 Governor Palliser found that "all" the soldiers in Newfoundland were Irish (C.O. 194/16, f. 5).

[166]For the considerable powers justices exercised over soldiers, see Shaw, *Practical Justice*, vol. 1, pp. 68-71.

[167]See Matthews' biography of Keen in *DCB*, vol. 3, p. 324, for a list of his various positions.

[168]C.O. 194/13, f. 146.

[169]McGuire was a surname of Scotland too, but most Newfoundland McGuires were Irish. See E.R. Seary, *Family Names of the Island of Newfoundland* (St. John's: MUN, 1977), p. 308.

[170]C.O. 194/13, ff. 160-63.

[171]For the trial, see C.O. 194/13, ff. 163-71.

[172]C.O. 194/13, f. 186.

[173]C.O. 194/13, f. 31; see also ff. 35-8.

[174]C.O. 194/15, f. 42.

[175]C.O. 194/14, f. 15.

[176]C.O. 194/17, f. 6.

[177]C.O. 194/15, ff. 45-6.

[178]C.O. 194/14, f. 15.

[179]C.O. 194/14, f. 15; /15, f. 30.

[180]See Paterson, "History," p. 192; 128,000 gallons of rum were brought by Americans to Newfoundland in 1763 (C.O. 194/15, f. 197).

[181]C.O. 194/15, ff. 14-19.

[182]Palliser estimated American imports for 1764 at over £100,000 (C.O. 194/16, f. 212).

[183]A superior "cull" (grade) of dry fish (see *DNE*).

[184]As noted in petitions from 1758 (C.O. 194/14, ff. 16-23).

[185]C.O. 194/15, f. 130.

[186]C.O. 194/15, f. 42; this is part of Gov. Thomas Graves' account of the invasion. See also *DCB*, vol. 4, pp. 31-2, and Paterson, "History," pp. 224-33.

[187]Ruth M. Christensen, "The Establishment of S.P.G. Missions in Newfoundland, 1703-1783," *Historical Magazine of the Protestant Episcopal Church*, 20 (1951), p. 222.

[188]For the occupation of Trinity from July 1 to August 1, see Gordon Handcock, *The Story of Trinity* (n.p.: Trinity Historical Society, n.d.), pp. 15-20.

[189]Home-made anchors; the word was in use by 1760.

[190]Single-tined prongs.

[191]R.C. Simmons and P.D.G. Thomas, eds., *Proceedings and Debates of the British Parliaments Respecting North America 1754-1783*, 6. vols. (in progress) (Millwood, N.Y.: Kraus International Publications, 1982-6), vol. 1, p. 347.

[192]*Ibid.*, p. 468.

[193]Paterson, "History," p. 228. This topic awaits further study.

[194]C.O. 194/15, ff. 70-72.

[195]*DCB*, vol. 3, p. 133.

[196]Benjamin Lester's diary, which describes the occupation of Trinity, is an exception. See. Handcock, *Story of Trinity*, pp. 19-20.

[197]In 18th- and 19th-century discourse, the word (as here) meant deprivation and anxiety caused by poverty.

[198]Simmons and Thomas, *Proceedings and Debates*, p. 468.

[199]C.O. 194/15, f. 78.

[200]"Houses" (in addition to cook-rooms, wharves, and stages) were listed as part of the fishing admirals' establishments as early as 1731 (*CSP*, 1731, p. 274).

[201]In 1775 the merchant Benjamin Lester told the House of Commons that 8,000 residents were needed in Newfoundland "for carrying on the British fishery" (Simmons and Thomas, *Proceedings and Debates*, vol. 5, p. 502). There were then, by official count, 12,438 inhabitants in Newfoundland (Ryan, "Consolidated Census Returns," p. 67). But this is a low estimate. Palliser said there were 20,000 in 1765. See note 132.

[202]C.O. 194/15, f. 116.

[203]C.O. 194/15, ff. 116-36, 160, 164.

[204]See Dorothy Marshall, *Eighteenth Century England*, 2 ed. (London: Longman, 1974), pp. 322-4, for the fishery diplomacy leading up to the Treaty of Paris; for parliamentary debate on the preliminary articles of peace, see Simmons and Thomas, *Proceedings and Debates*, vol. 1, pp. 416-27.

[205]Thompson, *French Shore Problem*, p. 191.

[206]Arthur Kitson, *Captain James Cook* (London: John Murray, 1907), pp. 67-8; the "payment by France of £300,000" for the islands is stated as fact in Richard Hough, *Captain James Cook* (New York: Norton, 1995), p. 28.

Notes to Chapter 6

[1]E.J. Pratt, *Collected Poems*, ed. Northrop Frye, 2 ed. (Toronto: Macmillan, 1970), p. 115. My use of the word dory is anachronistic; dories date from the 19th century.

[2]*A Journal of Transactions and Events, during a Residence of nearly Sixteen Years on the Coast of Labrador*, 3 vols. (Newark: 1792); see O'Flaherty, *Rock Observed*, pp. 34-42.

[3]William Whiteley, "Sir Hugh Palliser," *DCB*, vol. 4, pp. 597-601; see also Whiteley, "Governor Hugh Palliser and the Newfoundland and Labrador Fishery, 1764-1768," *CHR*, 50, 2 (1969): 141-63.

[4]I allude to Frederick Alderdice, prime minister of Newfoundland, 1932-4, who had "no feet and only one leg." See *White Tie and Decorations: Sir John and Lady Hope Simpson in Newfoundland, 1934-1936*, ed. Peter Neary (Toronto: Univ. of Toronto Press, 1996), p. 27.

[5]C.O. 194/16, f. 35; *PC*, vol. 4, p. 1853.

[6]C.O. 194/16, ff. 35, 217.

[7]Shannon Ryan, "Newfoundland Consolidated Census Returns. 1698-1833" (MS, CNS), p. 38.

[8]*Ibid.*, p. 42.

[9]*Ibid.*, p. 44.

[10]C.O. 194/15, f. 193.

[11]See his grant to George Milner in 1760, C.O. 194/18, f. 89.

[12]GN2/1/A, vol. 20, pp. 47-8.

[13]See his "Remarks on the present state of the Newfoundland fishery," C.O. 194/16, ff. 211-18.

[14]See, for instance, C.O. 194/16, f. 184.

[15]*PC*, vol. 4, pp. 1848-55.

[16]*Ibid.*, pp. 1856-7.

[17]In 1766 he reported an increase of 62 in the number of fishing ships (C.O. 194/16, f. 316).

[18]See Palliser's comments in 1765, C.O. 194/16, f. 188.

[19]C.O. 194/30, ff. 119-20.

[20]There were 190 bankers fishing in 1772 (Ryan, "Newfoundland Consolidated Census," p. 62).

[21]C.O. 194/17, f. 166

[22]C.O. 194/31, f. 48.

[23]His successor was named in Feb., 1769.

[24]I mean as they relate to the island of Newfoundland. In Labrador, France could no longer have a legal fishery.

[25]Whiteley, "Governor Hugh Palliser," p. 143; Prowse, *History*, pp. 318-9.

[26]C.O. 194/16, f. 111.

[27]C.O. 194/16, f. 318.

[28]C.O. 194/18, f. 42 (1768 figures).

[29]See their 1765 petition to the Commons (Simmons and Thomas, *Proceedings and Debates*, vol. 2, p. 43); it occasioned a "heavy and long debate." Palliser was called before the House on April 3rd and 4th (pp. 44-6).

[30]See C.O. 194/18, f. 65; /30, ff. 102-5.

[31]C.O. 194/32, f. 55.

[32]W.H. Whiteley, "James Cook and British Policy in the Newfoundland Fisheries, 1763-7," *CHR*, 54, 3 (1973): 258-9.

[33]C.O. 194/16, f. 172.

[34]For their names, see C.O. 194/16, f. 184.

[35]C.O. 194/16, ff. 171-2.

[36]C.O. 194/30, f. 97.

[37]C.O. 194/16, f. 67; preventive officers were given specific powers to prevent smuggling.

[38]In different letters, Palliser calculates the number at 175 and 130.

[39]C.O. 194/16, ff. 302-5.

[40]C.O. 194/16, f. 305.

[41]C.O. 194/16, ff. 166, 168-9.

[42]G.O. Rothney, "The Case of Bayne and Brymer: An Incident in the Early History of Labrador," *CHR*, 15, 3 (1934): 264-75.

[43]Jens Haven, in C.O. 194/16, f. 62; Haven also comments on "their laziness."

[44]C.O. 194/16, f. 23.

[45]See W.H. Whiteley, "The Establishment of the Moravian Mission in Labrador," *CHR*, 45, 1 (1964): 29-50.

[46]C.O. 194/16, ff. 223-30.

[47]C.O. 194/30, f. 180.

[48]C.O. 194/16, ff. 181-2.

[49]The secretary of state in the British government responsible for the colonies.

[50]Simmons and Thomas, *Proceedings and Debates*, vol. 5, p. 90.

[51]C.O. 194/18, ff. 161-5.

[52]C.O. 194/18, ff. 162-3.

[53]Simmons and Thomas, *Proceedings and Debates*, vol. 2, pp. 558-9.

[54]See C.O. 194/31, ff. 3-4, 7-13, 15, 36, 88.

[55]See the debate in the Commons, Simmons and Thomas, *Proceedings and Debates*, vol. 5, pp. 89-96.

[56]C.O. 194/30, f. 167.

[57]A 1762 map of Trinity, sometimes attributed to Cook, was likely done by J.F.W. Des Barres. See Handcock, *Story of Trinity*, p. 21.

[58]For a bibliography, see R.A. Skelton and R.V. Tooley, "The Marine Surveys of James Cook in North America 1758-1768, particularly the Survey of Newfoundland," *Map Collectors' Circle*, no. 37 (1967).

[59]Whiteley, "James Cook," p. 247.

[60]*A Chart of the Island of Newfoundland with part of the Coast of Labradore* (n.p.: n.p., 1764).

[61]R.A. Skelton, *James Cook, Surveyor of Newfoundland, Being a Collection of Charts of the Coasts of Newfoundland and Labradore, &c. drawn from Original Surveys taken by James Cook and Michael Lane* (San Francisco: David Magee, 1965).

[62]See Whiteley, "James Cook," pp. 265-6. "A Chart of the Sea-Coast of Newfoundland between St. Laurence and Point-May," for instance, displays brooks, hills, and ponds some distance back from the coast. See See Sotheby's *Travel, Natural History, Atlases and Maps* catalogue (June 7, 1999), p. 106.

[63]For his comment, see J.P. Howley, *A Historical Sketch of the Discovery and Development of the Coal Areas of Newfoundland Up to Date* (St. John's: "Evening Telegram" Job-Print, 1896), pp. 3-4.

[64]C.O. 194/16, f. 2.

[65]O'Flaherty, *Rock Observed*, p. 43.

[66]Neary and O'Flaherty, *Part of the Main*, p. 46. The map on p. 41 is also Cartwright's. See Marshall, *History and Ethnography*, pp. 88-9.

[67]*A General Chart of the Island of Newfoundland* (London: Thomas Jeffreys, 1770; 1775).

[68]Cook's 11-p. pamphlet *Directions For Navigating the West-Coast of Newfoundland, with a Chart thereof* (London: 1768), was sold by Nicholas Gill, naval officer at St. John's.

[69]C.O. 194/30, f. 7. The Conception Bay population rose to over 5,069 in 1772 (f. 140).

[70]C.O. 194/32, f. 98.

[71]Though Handcock says that Trinity was "the major centre of trade and commerce on the northeast coast of Newfoundland" in the 1760s, "and indeed ranked among the principal colonial ports in North America." See *Story of Trinity*, p. 14.

[72]*DCB*, vol. 3, p. 189.

[73]Christensen, "Establishment of S.P.G. Missions," pp. 207-29.

[74]*CSP*, 1728-29, p. 378.

[75]P. O'Flaherty, "Laurence Coughlan," *DCB*, vol. 4, pp. 175-7; Hans Rollmann, "Laurence Coughlan and the Origins of Methodism in Newfoundland," in *The Contribution of Methodism to Atlantic Canada*, ed. C.H.H. Scobie and J.W. Grant (Montreal & Kingston: McGill-Queen's Univ. Press, 1992), pp. 53-76.

[76]Petition dated October 30, 1766 (United Society for the Propagation of the Gospel, 15 Tufton St., Westminister, London; p.c.)

[77]Or perhaps 1769; Coughlan worked "for near three years" before the revival commenced, but it is unclear whether he dates his work from 1766 or 1767.

[78]Coughlan, *An Account of the Work of God, in Newfoundland, North-America* (London: 1776), p. 9.

[79]Meaning the Newfoundland-born, not aboriginal people. Coughlan uses the word in *Account*, p. 15.

[80]*Ibid.*, pp. 10, 14, 79.

[81]*Ibid.*, pp. 79-81; the letters occupy pp. 50-168.

[82]*Ibid.*, p. 77.

[83]O'Flaherty, *Rock Observed*, pp. 26-7.

[84]See Rollmann, "Laurence Coughlan," pp. 66-7.

[85]In L.A. Anspach, *A History of the Island of Newfoundland* (London: 1819), p. 191, a "formidable riot" is said to have taken place in Conception Bay in 1765.

[86]*Account*, pp. 18-19.

[87]*Ibid.*, p. 13.

[88]C.O. 194/4, f. 255. I thank Edward-Vincent Chafe for this reference.

[89]C.O. 194/16, f. 156; Matthews, "History," p. 440.

[90]C.O. 194/16, f. 300.

[91]C.O. 194/18, ff. 72-4; /28, f. 95.

[92]C.O. 194/29, ff. 58-60.

[93]C.O. 194/31, ff. 31-4.

[94]C.O. 194/21, ff. 346-7.

[95]Simmons and Thomas, *Proceedings and Debates*, vol. 4, pp. 414, 476.

[96]C.O. 194/19, ff. 1, 31-6, 41.

[97]15 Geo. III, c. 31. Printed in Reeves, *History*, Appendix, pp. xvi-lii.

[98]Palliser had a public career in Britain after leaving Newfoundland. He was comptroller of the Navy, 1770-75; was made a lord of the Admiralty, 1775; and was elected to the Commons, 1774. He appeared before the House of Lords to discuss the New England Prohibitory Bill, March 15, 1775 (Simmons and Thomas, *Proceedings and Debates*, vol. 5, p. 526); he later gave evidence in the 1793 inquiry into the Newfoundland fishery.

[99]Enacted as 15 Geo. III, c. 10; House of Commons, *Sessional Papers of the Eighteenth Century*, ed. Sheila Lambert, 145 vols. (Wilmington, Del.: Scholarly Resources Inc., 1975), vol. 27, pp. 1-10. For parliamentary debate, see Simmons and Thomas, *Proceedings and Debates*, vol. 5, pp. 430 ff.; minutes of hearings into the Newfoundland and related fisheries are pp. 482-96, 501-3 (Benjamin Lester's testimony), 530-3.

[100]Matthews, "History," p. 448.

[101]See objections from Dartmouth and Teignmouth, C.O. 194/19, ff. 37-8, 41; for the Poole petition, see Simmons and Thomas, *Proceedings and Debates*, vol. 5, p. 480.

[102]C.O. 194/21, f. 155.

[103]See the Dartmouth petition of of 1776, C.O. 194/19, f. 38. In 1785 Holdsworth's bill (never enacted) specified that bounties should be available to ships with "only Twelve Men each" (House of Commons, *Sessional Papers*, vol. 46, p. 2), and the 1786 amended fisheries act, 26 Geo. III, c. 26 (Reeves, *History*, Appendix, pp. liii-lxxxiii) accepted this number.

[104]C.O. 194/34, f. 66; for St. John's petitions against the act, see f. 33, and Prowse, *History*, pp. 341-2n.

[105]House of Commons, *Sessional Papers*, vol. 46, pp. 2-3.

[106]See C.O. 194/21, ff. 91-2, 95, 97; and Chapter 8, below, where this issue surfaces again.

[107]"History," p. 451.

[108]Ryan, "Newfoundland Consolidated Census," p. 67. But official figures from the period are suspect. Reeves would later comment that the "great Increase" in the population began "at the Time the War with the Colonies broke out" (*PC*, vol. 4, p. 1915).

[109]For the impact of the Revolution, see Head, *Eighteenth Century Newfoundland*, pp. 196-202 and Matthews, "History," pp. 455-82. Anspach (*History*, pp. 204-11) wrote when the Revolution was part of living memory on the island.

[110]C.O. 194/32, f. 79.

[111]C.O. 194/32, f. 70.

[112]C.O. 194/32, ff. 104-5.

[113]C.O. 194/32, f. 78.

[114]1776 statistics, C.O. 194/33, f. 38b.

[115]C.O. 194/33, ff. 1-3.

[116]C.O. 194/33, f. 34.

[117]C.O. 194/34, ff. 34-8; Prowse, *History*, p. 340.

[118]C.O. 194/33, ff. 31-2.

[119]C.O. 194/33, f. 33.

[120]C.O. 194/33, f. 130. She was recaptured shortly afterwards.

[121]C.O. 194/34, f. 1.

[122]C.O. 194/33, f. 139; /34, f. 25.

[123]W.H. Whiteley, "Jeremiah Coghlan," *DCB*, vol. 4, pp. 158-9.

[124]C.O. 194/34, ff. 25, 31-2.

[125]"Cut out" is a naval term, meaning to steal (a ship) from a harbour, by getting between her and the shore, cutting ropes, etc., and taking her away (from *OED*).

[126]C.O. 194/34, f. 62.

[127]Cartwright, *Journal*, vol. 2, pp. 361-4.

[128]C.O. 194/34, f. 32.

[129]C.O. 194/34, f. 69. Damage was estimated at £60,000.

[130]C.O. 194/34, ff. 78, 102.

[131]C.O. 194/35, f. 37.

[132]C.O. 194/35, ff. 7, 28-30.

[133]C.O. 194/35, f. 76.

[134]C.O. 194/35, f. 88.

[135]C.O. 194/35, f. 76.

[136]C.O. 194/35, ff. 123, 131.

[137]Called "fishing ships" in the returns; C.O. 194/35, f. 130.

[138]Bank fishery, 18,850 qtls.; by boatmen, 68,150; inhabitants, 260,350.

[139]C.O. 194/35, f. 152. Bankers, 25,300 qtls.; by boatmen, 60,400; inhabitants, 300,050.

[140]See Edwards' comments, C.O. 194/20, ff. 8-9; and Matthews, "History," p. 469.

[141]See Edward Langman's comment on unemployment in 1779, Christensen, "Establishment of S.P.G. Missions," p. 223.

[142]Balfour in 1779 said "thousands" were emigrating from Conception Bay to "the Continent of America" (*Ibid.*, p. 228).

[143]See tables of Newfoundland imports and exports, 1786-7 (C.O. 194/21, ff. 46-7).

[144]C.O. 194/20, f. 7.

[145]Cartwright, *Journal*, vol. 3, p. 215.

[146]C.O. 194/21, f. 291.

[147]Paul O'Neill, *The Oldest City: The Story of St. John's, Newfoundland* (Erin, Ont.: Press Porcepic, 1975), p. 50.

[148]Matthews, "History," p. 466.

[149]So called by John Elford in 1787 (C.O. 194/37, f. 102).

[150]See C.O. 194/35, ff. 84, 133-4.

[151]That I have seen.

[152]C.O. 194/92, f. 64. For some of the discussion over use of the word "exclusif," demanded by France, see /37, ff. 112-8. An English negotiator noted that the difference between "exclusive" and the alternative phrasing in the Declaration "was hardly worth objecting to." The French version of "by their competition" in the Declaration was "par leur concurrence," by which some, if not all, of the ambiguity is removed. See the discussion, /98, ff. 297-313.

[153]For the treaty see Thompson, *French Shore Problem*, pp. 191-3; negotiations prior to the treaty are discussed *Ibid.*, pp. 14-18. See also R.A. MacKay, ed., *Newfoundland: Economic, Diplomatic, and Strategic Studies* (Toronto: Oxford Univ. Press, 1946), pp. 275 ff.

[154]C.O. 194/35, f. 345 (the Duke of Manchester to the Count de Vergennes, July 20, 1783); Britain refused, however, to extend the right of cutting beyond the end of 1785 (/36, ff. 9-10).

[155]C.O. 194/35, ff. 286-7.

[156]C.O. 194/36, f. 194.

[157]C.O. 194/36, f. 210.

[158]C.O. 194/36, ff. 129-32, 155-6, 169.

[159]C.O. 194/36, f. 88.

[160]See C.O. 194/37, ff. 15-16. The cabinet minute is ff. 19-20; Elliott's instruction, f. 22.

[161]28 Geo. III, c. 35; see House of Commons, *Sessional Papers*, vol. 61, pp. 389-94.

[162]See governor Elliott's additional instruction in 1788 (C.O. 194/21, f. 368).

[163]C.O. 194/21, ff. 172-4.

[164]See 1788 memos on salmon, C.O. 194/37, ff. 192-3, 243-5.

[165]C.O. 194/35, f. 278.

[166]See the Dartmouth petition, April 16, 1784, C.O. 194/35, f. 331; and Holdsworth's letter, Dec. 3, 1784, ff. 343-4.

[167]See William Pitt's letter, dated January 10, 1785, C.O. 194/37, ff. 134-5.

[168]C.O. 194/19, f. 34.

[169]I.e., a customs official; not an officer in the navy.

[170]C.O. 194/35, ff. 326-30.

[171]25 Geo. III, c. 1; in House of Commons, *Sessional Papers*, vol. 46, pp. 221-5.

[172]28 Geo. III, c. 6; *Ibid.*, vol. 61, pp. 1-10.

[173]C.O. 194/21, f. 263.

[174]C.O. 194/35, f. 274.

[175]*PC*, vol. 2, p. 518; "Papists" had been prohibited from practising their religion as late as 1775 (*Ibid.*, p. 484). The various issues surrounding the freedom to Catholics are discussed in Hans Rollmann, "Religious Enfranchisement and Roman Catholics in Eighteenth-Century Newfoundland," in *Religion and Identity: The Experience of Irish and Scottish Catholics in Atlantic Canada*, ed. Terrence Murphy and Cyril J. Byrne (St. John's: Jesperson Press, 1987), pp. 34-52. Rollmann relates the "introduction of change" to "a new legal situation for Catholics in England" (p. 37).

[176]R.J. Lahey, *James Louis O'Donel in Newfoundland 1784-1807: The Establishment of the Roman Catholic Church* (St. John's: Newfoundland Historical Society, 1784), pp. 1-9.

[177]C.O. 194/36, f. 14.

[178]The word "chapel" was used of places of worship other than those of the established church (from *OED*).

[179]John FitzGerald, "Conflict and Culture in Irish-Newfoundland Roman Catholicism, 1829-1850" (Ph.D. thes., Univ. of Ottawa, 1997), p. 42.

[180]Lahey, *James Louis O'Donel*, p. 10.

[181]See governor Milbanke's letter to O'Donel in 1790 (GN2/1/A, vol. 12, pp. 102-3).

[182]Lahey, *James Louis O'Donel*, p. 13.

[183]The obligation to go to confession, if in a state of sin, and to receive the Eucharist, at least once a year.

[184]See J. Elford's letter, May, 14, 1785, C.O. 194/36, ff. 13-14.

[185]Their petition, Dec. 16, 1784, is C.O. 194/35, ff. 276-7.

[186]C.O. 194/36, f. 13.

[187]C.O. 194/36, f. 14.

[188]C.O. 194/21, f. 154.

[189]Memo, perhaps for cabinet, [1788], C.O. 194/37, f. 245.

[190]26 Geo. III, c. 26; Reeves, *History*, Appendix, p. lx.

[191]Which offered food and lodging as well as alcoholic beverages.

[192]C.O. 194/37, ff. 44-5.

[193]C.O. 194/21, f. 226.

[194]C.O. 194/21, ff. 300-1.

[195]House of Commons, *Sessional Papers*, vol. 79, pp. 505-11.

[196]GN2/1/A, vol. 11, pp. 61-3; Elliot had been told not to allow any buidings except those for the fishery "within six hundred yards distant from high water mark" (C.O. 194/23, f. 348). See also Matthews, "History," pp. 549-50.

[197]C.O. 194/23, f. 347.

[198]C.O. 194/23, ff. 371-95.

[199]C.O. 194/21, ff. 224-5.

[200]*A Brief State of the Evidence laid before the Committee of the House of Commons* ([London]: 1793), p. 4; elsewhere in the hearings skepticism was expressed about the extent of the decline and the cause of the merchants' losses (see p. 9). For the year-to-year figures, see Ryan, "Newfoundland Consolidated Census," p. 65, and Prowse, *History*, p. 695; also Matthews, "History," pp. 534-8.

[201]*Brief State of the Evidence*, p. 7.

[202]Matthews, "History," p. 552.

[203]Down by 50%, according to the merchants of Dartmouth, Exeter, etc. (C.O. 194/21, ff. 327, 329), but this was likely rhetorical.

[204]C.O. 194/21, ff. 271, 327.

[205]C.O. 194/21, f. 278; his full report is ff. 275-302.

[206]See *DCB*, vol. 4, p. 259; *Brief State of the Evidence*, p. 18.

[207]C.O. 194/21, f. 308.

[208]C.O. 194/23, f. 385.

[209]On May 4, 1790 (C.O. 194/21, f. 333).

[210]31 Geo.III, c. 29; House of Commons, *Sessional Papers*, vol. 79, pp. 209-14; see Christopher P. Curran, "The Judicature Act: A History of the Early Acts," in *Legislative History of the Judicature Act 1791-1988* ([St. John's]: Newfoundland Law Reform Commission, 1989), pp. 1-18.

[211]32 Geo. III, c. 46; House of Commons, *Sessional Papers*, vol. 79, pp. 495-502.

[212]Chief Justice D'Ewes Coke called it into session in 1797 (GN2/1/A, vol. 13, p. 176); and there were various later instances. Governor Cochrane's commission in 1832 authorized him to appoint courts of oyer and terminer. See *PC*, vol. 2, p. 726.

[213]Governor Waldegrave was told in June, 1798, after he'd objected to the practice of the chief justice of going "home" annually, that in future he (the judge) will "constantly reside" in Newfoundland, C.O. 194/40, f. 89. This of course meant he was available for year-round duties.

[214]Note the carefully chosen word.

[215]C.O. 194/21, ff. 333-4.

[216]Peter Neary, "John Reeves," *DCB*, vol. 6, pp. 636-7.

[217]C.O. 194/38, f. 310.

[218]C.O. 194/38, ff. 300-26.

[219]*PC*, vol. 4, pp. 1911-18.

[220]C.O. 194/38, f. 316.

[221]Reeves, *History*, p. [1]. For a discussion of Reeves' book, see O'Flaherty, *Rock Observed*, pp. 51-4.

[222]See C.O. 194/41, ff. 77-81, 84-5.

[223]C.O. 195/15, p. 248.

[224]GN2/1/A, vol. 12, p. 243.

[225]GN2/1/A, vol. 12, pp. 294-301.

[226]GN2/1/A, vol. 12, p. 356.

[227]C.O. 194/41, f. 103.

[228]GN2/1/A, vol. 12, pp. 252-4.

[229]For accounts of the French in Newfoundland in 1796, see GN2/1/A, vol. 12, pp. 369-77; C.O. 194/39, ff. 19-25.

[230]See statistics from 1787-97, C.O. 194/23, f. 427.

[231]C.O. 194/23, ff. 453-6.

[232]In 15 Geo. III, c. 31; Reeves, *History*, Appendix, p. xxx. A strong clause against desertion to "foreign states" was added in 26 Geo. III, c. 26 (*Ibid.*, pp. lxvii-lxix).

[233]Numbers are uncertain. Ambrose Crofton, commander of H.M.S. *Pluto*, told governor Waldegrave in 1798 that "fishermen and people of all descriptions went to America late in the season in the most public and official manner."

[234]The period of anxiety might be dated from 1789, when 114 Irish convicts were landed at Bay Bulls and Petty Harbour in mid-July; they were sent back to England in October (see C.O. 194/38, ff. 86 ff.) The incident has been extensively studied: Ged Martin, "Convict Transportation in Newfoundland in 1789," *Acadiensis*, 5, 1 (1975): 84-98; Bob Reece, "'Such a Banditti': Irish Convicts in Newfoundland, 1789," *NS*, 13, 1 (1997): 1-29 (pt. 1); 13, 2 (1997): 127-41 (pt. 2). See also Ch. 7, n. 3, above.

[235]P. O'Flaherty, "William Waldegrave," *DCB*, vol. 6, pp. 795-7.

[236]C.O. 194/39, ff. 86-8.

[237]C.O. 194/23, ff. 476-7.

[238]An Irish revolutionary movement of the 1790s, led by Wolf Tone and Napper Tandy.

[239]For an account of the rising, see C.O. 194/42, ff. 167-8.

[240]*Gentlemen-Bishops and Faction Fighters*, ed. Cyril Byrne (St. John's: Jesperson Press, 1984), p. 225; see also *DCB*, vol. 5, p. 633, and Lahey, *James Louis O'Donel*, pp. 26-8. A report in 1801 noted "many thousands of united Irishmen" in Newfoundland, "encouraged by some of the priests" (GN2/1/A, vol. 43, p. 192).

[241]C.O. 194/42, f. 15.

[242]C.O. 194/42, f. 66.

[243]GN2/1/A, vol. 14, pp. 403-08.

[244]GN2/1/A, vol. 14, p. 410.

[245]C.O. 194/42, f. 113.

Notes to Chapter 7

[1]The chapter draws on my article "The Seeds of Reform: Newfoundland, 1800-18," *Journal of Canadian Studies*, 23, 3 (1988): 39-59, and my other writings on the reform movement. I am indebted to R.J. Lahey's work, especially his paper "Religion and Politics in Newfoundland: The Antecedents of the General Election of 1832" (MS, 1979). This chapter was largely written before I read either Jerry Bannister, "The Campaign for Representative Government in Newfoundland," *Canadian Historical Association Journal*, N.S., 5 (1995): 19-40, or John FitzGerald's Ph.D. thesis, "Conflict and Culture," both valuable contributions to the literature. I have reexamined my own conclusions in the light of their findings. See also Keith Matthews, "The Class of '32: St. John's Reformers on the Eve of Representative Government," *Acadiensis*, 6, 2 (1977): 80-94.

[2]See justice John Dingle's comments, GN2/1/A, vol. 12, pp. 252-4; vol. 13, f. 160. Ferryland's Robert Carter had the same notion.

[3]See O'Flaherty, "Government in Newfoundland before 1832." For a study of how the colonial administration dealt with one crisis, see Jerry Bannister, "Convict Transportation and the Colonial State in Newfoundland, 1789," *Acadiensis*, 27, 2 (1998): 95-123.

[4]In 1 Geo. IV, c. 51, "An Act to regulate the rebuilding of the Town of *Saint John's*," the approval of the grand jury is specifically stated to be required before additional "Cross Streets" in the town can be made (House of Commons, "Newfoundland Acts, 1786-1820").

[5]C.O. 194/45, f. 117.

[6]A typical presentment from 1802 is GN2/1/A, vol. 17, pp. 10-13.

[7]The terms "justices" and "magistrates" are often used interchangeably in Newfoundland documents. But by 1800, and increasingly in the 19th century, the words take on different meanings. Magistrates become "stipendiary magistrates," i.e., they receive stipends (salaries) from government. This starts happening in the closing years of the 18th century. Justices, though they have equivalent powers to magistrates, are "honarary magistrates," i.e., they receive no salaries.

[8]See Gambier's letter of Oct. 9, 1802, to the magistrates and grand jury (GN2/1/A, vol. 16, pp. 338-9).

[9]GN2/1/A, vol. 28, p. 406-08

[10]For an illustration, see *Royal Gazette*, Jan. 26, 1815.

[11]Sheriff John Bland in 1815 said "the Parliament of Great Britain is the best and fittest legislature for the prosperity of Newfoundland" (GN2/1/A, vol. 27, p. 78).

[12]6 Geo IV, c. 73; *SUK*, vol. 4 (1826), pp. 170-73.

[13]I.e., streets crossing Water and Duckworth streets.

[14]1 Geo. IV, c. 51; *SUK*, vol. 8 (1822), p. 101; House of Commons, "Newfoundland Acts, 1786-1820."

[15]41 Geo. III, c. 77; in House of Commons, "Newfoundland Acts, 1786-1820."

[16]GN2/1/A, vol. 13, pp. 134-6, 307 ff.; vol. 14, pp. 334-5.

[17]Schools "which provided meagre and inefficient education for the very poor" (Dickens, *Oliver Twist* [London: Penguin Books, 1981], p. 487). The original suggestion for the schools came from Walde-grave; see Sister Mary Nolasco Mulcahy, "The St. John's Schools of Industry," *NQ*, 78, 4 (1983): 17. A comment by F.W. Rowe on the charity schools (*The Development of Education in Newfoundland* [Toronto: Ryerson Press, 1964), p. 34) is misconstrued by FitzGerald, who says the schools "were only Sunday schools and did not provide a daily education" ("Conflict and Culture," p. 25).

[18]GN2/1/A, vol. 16, pp. 338-41.

[19]C.O. 194/43, ff. 174-5.

[20]C.O. 194/43, f. 175; his full report is ff. 173-8.

[21]C.O. 194/44, f. 233.

[22]C.O. 194/44, f. 29. The term "charity school" was often still used of the schools of industry.

[23]C.O. 194/44, ff. 30-31.

[24]GN2/1/A, vol. 31, p. 231.

[25]See Sean Cadigan, "Artisans in a Merchant Town: St. John's, Newfoundland, 1775-1816," *Canadian Historical Association Journal*, N.S., 4 (1993): 95-119.

[26]600 yards in instructions to Elliot and Milbanke.

[27]C.O. 194/45, ff. 75-8, 69, 256-8.

[28]C.O. 194/44, f. 333; the full response is ff. 332-42.

[29]Since the migratory fishery was virtually at an end, the act of 1801 on bounties (see above) was in fact an encouragement to the resident fishery.

[30]GN2/1/A, vol. 20 (i), p. 55; vol. 25, pp. 101-02.

[31]P. O'Flaherty, "John Ryan," *DCB*, vol. 7, pp. 763-6.

[32]See the letter from the crown lawyers, Feb. 25, 1814, indicating that setting up a printing press was a common law right over which the Crown had no power; a person had the right to set up a newspaper without the governor's licence (C.O. 194/55, ff. 127-8).

[33]GN2/1/A, vol. 19 (ii), pp. 63-4.

[34]GN2/1/A, vol. 19 (ii), p. 175.

[35]It is unclear exactly how far it filled this role, since the file of the paper is incomplete. See the bibliography in *DCB*, vol. 7, p. 766.

[36]P. O'Flaherty, "William Carson," *DCB*, vol. 7, pp. 151-6; "In Search of William Carson," *NQ*, 83, 1 (1987): 28-34.

[37]*Aris's Birmingham Gazette*, Dec. 29, 1806.

[38]*Newfoundland Patriot*, Sept. 8, 1835.

[39]He told Duckworth in 1810 that "Ever since I came to this country my mind has been ardently bent upon plans calculated for the improvement of the fisheries" (C.O. 194/49, f. 32). He had by then concocted an elaborate new way to kill whales; see ff. 34-5.

[40]The 1808 population; GN2/1/A, vol. 20 (ii), p. 45.

[41]Keith Matthews, "James MacBraire," *DCB*, vol. 6, pp. 417-20.

[42]GN2/1/A, vol. 20 (ii), ff. 53-5.

[43]GN2/1/A, vol. 20 (ii), p. 51.

[44]GN2/1/A, vol. 21, p. 33.

[45]49 Geo. III, cap. 27; *SUK*, vol. 3, pp. 691-4. See GN2/1/A, vol. 20, p. 137.

[46]J.M. Bumstead and Keith Matthews, "Thomas Tremlett," *DCB*, vol. 6, pp. 784-6; for the merchants' complaints against Tremlett, see GN2/1/A, vol. 20 (ii), pp. 125-7; vol. 21, pp. 136-44.

[47]GN2/1/A, vol 20 (ii), pp. 169-70; vol. 21, p. 181.

[48]The report (which exonerated Tremlett) is GN2/1/A, vol. 21, pp. 302-9.

[49]GN2/1/A, vol. 15, pp. 278-9. Also vol. 21, p. 111; permission in the latter case was later granted (p. 123).

[50]GN2/1/A, vol. 21, p. 107.

[51]"No more than nine," according to Duckworth (*PC*, vol. 2, p. 648).

[52]No fishing ships were reported in Newfoundland in 1805 and 1810; none were in St. John's in 1807 and 1808 (though a very few were operating elsewhere).

[53]GN2/1/A, vol. 21, p. 10.

[54]See his letter to Nicholas Gill, Sept. 17, 1810 (GN2/1/A, vol. 21, pp. 121-2).

[55]*PC*, vol. 2, pp. 648-9. He was not the first governor to make this recommendation. See Gower's letter to Earl Camden, Feb. 6, 1805, C.O. 194/44, ff. 80-81.

[56]The estimated charges for the civil establishment in 1811 were put at £3,901 (GN2/1/A, vol. 21, f. 295). In 1812 Parliament increased duties on rum and spirits entering Newfoundland.

[57]51 Geo. III, c. 45; *PC*, vol. 1, pp. 197-8.

[58]GN2/1/A, vol. 22, p. 151.

[59]GN2/1/A, vol. 21, pp. 430-1.

[60]The sheriff was normally asked to convene meetings of inhabitants.

[61]GN2/1/A, vol. 21, pp. 374, 378-80.

[62]*Royal Gazette*, Nov. 28, 1811.

[63]*Royal Gazette*, Dec. 5, 12, 19, 26, 1811; Jan. 2, 9, 1812.

[64]See Duckworth's letter, July 24, 1812, conveying His Majesty's regret "that it is not in his power to direct a compliance with the prayer of [the] Address" (C.O. 194/84, f. 182). Duckworth was instructed, in June, 1812, to carry out consultations in St. John's on "the laws by which Newfoundland is governed," and did so. His report (/53, ff. 3-8) of Nov. 2, 1812, while conceding that "a revision of the laws should take place," stressed the importance of "preventing his Majesty's subjects in Newfoundland from forming themselves into a colony."

[65]Crown lawyers advised against instituting "any kind of proceeding" against him for writing the pamphlet (C.O. 194/53, f. 138).

[66]*A Letter to the Members of Parliament of the United Kingdom* (Greenock: 1812), pp. 18-21.

[67]*Reasons for Colonizing the Island of Newfoundland, in a Letter addressed to the Inhabitants* (Greenock: 1813), pp. 8, 24.

[68]Shannon Ryan, *Newfoundland-Spanish Saltfish Trade: 1814-1914* (St. John's: Harry Cuff Publications, 1983), p. 5; for other economic data relating to the fishery, see Ryan, "Fishery to Colony: A Newfoundland Watershed, 1793-1815," *Acadiensis*, 12, 2 (1983): 34-52.

[69]44 Geo. III, c. 44 (House of Commons, "Newfoundland Acts, 1786-1820").

[70]When regulations were imposed in 56 Geo. III, c. 83 (*Ibid.*).

[71]GN2/1/A, vol. 21, p. 275.

[72]GN2/1/A, vol. 22, pp. 24, 297; vol. 25, pp. 99-100; vol. 26, p. 84; vol. 27, pp. 1-4; C.O. 194/56, f. 106. See John Mannion, "Patrick Morris," *DCB*, vol. 7, pp. 626-34; P. Maureen White, "A Study of Patrick Morris's Political Rhetoric" (M.A. thes., MUN, 1987), pp. 1-18.

[73]See John Mannion, "John O'Brien," *DCB*, vol 8, pp. 658-9.

[74]GN2/1/A, vol. 26, p. 254.

[75]Now Marystown.

[76]I judge this from figures for the year 1813-14 (GN2/1/A, vol. 26, pp. 85-6).

[77]The estimate of "not less than 70,000" was made by governor Keats (GN2/1/A, vol. 26, p. 103; see also pp. 85-6 for a much lower estimate, with Protestants barely outnumbering Catholics). For official population figures from 1796 to 1820 — likely underestimated — see Ryan, "Fishery to Colony," p. 40. A "very careful return" of the population made in 1827-8 —in effect a census — gave a figure of 60,088 (C.O. 194/85, f. 15).

[78]Matthews says (*DCB*, vol. 6, p. 419) that "ecumenism flourished in Newfoundland during this era." Certain actions by Scallan, in particular, might well bear this out, and it is possible to find statements about the "cordiality" existing between Protestants and Catholics in the early 19th century. Morris, never known for understatement, said that the various religious sects in Newfoundland "*love one another*" (*Remarks on the State of Society* ([London]: 1827), p. 17). But there is often a superficial cordiality between the powerful and the vulnerable, felt especially by the latter towards the former. Cordiality does not necessarily signify either real "ecumenism" or equality. Yet Lahey also refers to the "harmony" between Catholics and Protestants at this time ("Religion and Politics," p. 2). I am not willing to reject altogether the views of these two scholars.

[79]C.O. 194/43, ff. 192, 315.

[80]C.O. 194/45, ff. 5-8.

[81]For the typical attitude, see GN2/1/A, vol. 14, pp. 307-8.

[82]I.e., those who came without O'Donel's (or other) ecclesiastical sanction; see Lahey, *James Louis O'Donel*, pp. 13-16.

[83]GN2/1/A, vol. 18, p. 210; see *Gentlemen-Bishops*, pp. 238, 330, for comments by Lambert and Scallan on the Irish.

[84]GN2/1/A, vol. 18, pp. 195-6, 207; vol. 25, p. 209. See Lahey's comments, *James Louis O'Donel*, p. 30.

[85]GN2/1/A, vol. 21, p. 298.

[86]GN2/1/A, vol. 21, p. 12.

[87]See Lahey, "Religion and Politics," p. 4. The instructions given governor Cochrane in 1832 illuminate the colonial office's understanding of the governor's responsibilities vis-à-vis the Anglican religion. He was generally to "be aiding and assisting" to the Bishop of Nova Scotia (in whose see Newfoundland

fell) in the exercise of his charge. But he had many specific duties, including taking care that the *Book of Common Prayer*, "as by law established," was read each Sunday and holiday, ensuring that "all orthodox churches" be well kept "and that more be built," and that "besides a competent maintenance," a house and glebe be provided for each minister. See *PC*, vol. 2, pp. 740-43. From these and other parts of the instructions, it might reasonably be deduced that the colonial officials thought the Church of England legally "established" in Newfoundland. Cochrane certainly thought so. See C.O. 194/85, f. 25.

[88] GN2/1/A, vol. 21, p. 12; see C.O. 194/43, f. 174; /45, ff. 258-9.

[89] For typical contributions, see GN2/1/A, vol. 20 (i), p. 27; vol. 22, pp. 155-8, 223-4; vol. 23, pp. 264-5.

[90] See GN2/1/A, vol. 19 (i), p. 133, and vol. 19 (ii), pp. 230-31, for payments to the Anglican priest in St. John's for his services as a magistrate. The ministers at Harbour Grace and Trinity often served as surrogates, a paid position; L.A. Anspach, for example, was a Conception Bay surrogate; see GN2/1/A, vol. 21, pp. 127-32, for typical correspondence; see also vol. 17, p. 294; for direct payments to Anglican clergy in 1811, see vol. 21, p. 295, where five priests are paid £50 each.

[91] For typical payments, see GN2/1/A, vol. 20 (i), p. 27; vol. 25, pp. 16-17.

[92] GN2/1/A, vol. 18, pp. 354-6; vol. 21, pp. 311-12.

[93] GN2/1/A, vol. 19 (ii), p. 17. The Benevolent Irish Society was formed in 1806.

[94] Pauline Maier, *American Scripture: Making the Declaration of Independence* (New York: Vintage Books, 1998), p. 12.

[95] John Mannion, *Point Lance in Transition: The Transformation of a Newfoundland Outport* (Toronto: McClelland and Stewart, 1976).

[96] GN2/1/A, vol. 26, p. 85.

[97] P. O'Flaherty, "Richard Goodwin Keats," *DCB*, vol. 6, pp. 371-3.

[98] GN2/1/A, vol. 25, pp. 24, 120-23, 329-40.

[99] Patrick J. Corish, "The Irish Catholics at the End of the Penal Era," in *Religion and Identity*, p. 4.

[100] See Keats's comments, C.O. 194/56, ff. 107-8.

[101] C.O. 194/54, ff. 164-6.

[102] C.O. 194/56, f. 109.

[103] C.O. 194/55, f. 128.

[104] C.O. 194/55, f. 100.

[105] Ryan, "Fishery to Colony," p. 45.

[106] GN2/1/A, vol. 26, p. 67.

[107] GN2/1/A, vol. 25, pp. 109-16.

[108] GN2/1/A, vol. 25, pp. 169-71.

[109] Thompson, *French Shore Problem*, p. 192.

[110] The fact that the Americans were allowed to fish on the west coast, concurrently with the French, would be later cited by the British to question the French claim to exclusiveness (*Ibid.*, p. 28).

[111] *Ibid.*, p. 193.

[112] They were in fact borrowed from the Treaty of Versailles of 1783, where the Americans were given the right to dry and cure fish in the unsettled bays of Labrador. This right was restated in 1818.

[113] 59 Geo. III, c. 38 (House of Commons, "Newfoundland Acts, 1786-1820").

[114] Ryan, *Newfoundland-Spanish Saltfish*, p. 7; see House of Commons, *Report from Select Committee on Newfoundland Trade* ([London]: 1817), p. 5.

[115] GN2/1/A, vol. 26, pp. 106-07, 176-86; John Mannion, "The Irish Migrations to Newfoundland" (MS, CNS, 1973), p. 11.

[116] GN2/1/A, vol. 26, pp. 197-215, 222-8.

[117] GN2/1/A, vol. 27, pp. 98-102.

[118] GN2/1/A, vol. 27, pp. 104-06.

[119] C.O. 194/57, ff. 24-5.

[120] C.O. 194/40, ff. 23-4; Ryan, *Ice Hunters*, pp. 52-4.

[121] C.O. 194/42, f. 142; for an account of the seal fishery early in the 19th century, see Anspach, *History*, pp. 413-28.

[122] Ryan, *Ice Hunters*, p. 56.

[123]For the French bounties now in effect, see Thompson, *French Shore Problem*, p. 22.

[124]C.O. 194/57, f. 134.

[125]House of Commons, Select Committee (1817), *Report*, p. 5.

[126]C.O. 194/60, f. 301.

[127]GN2/1/A, vol. 27, pp. 341-4. The removals took place from Dec. 6, 1816, to Jan. 31, 1817; see vol. 28, pp. 203-7.

[128]By Mar., 1817, it was reported that 3,000 persons were being given relief (C.O. 194/59, f. 94).

[129]C.O. 194/60, f. 301; *Mercantile Journal*, Apr. 4, 1817.

[130]GN2/1/A, vol. 28, p. 270.

[131]See C.O. 194/60, f. 294; GN2/1/A, vol. 28, pp. 310-14; *Mercantile Journal*, Mar. 28, 1817.

[132]GN2/1/A, vol. 28, pp. 310-14.

[133]C.O. 194/60, f. 211.

[134]House of Commons, Select Committee (1817), *Report*, p. 9.

[135]GN2/1/A, vol. 28, pp. 104-5, 151-2, 251-3, 257-8.

[136]GN2/1/A, vol. 28, pp. 115-17, 145-6.

[137]GN2/1/A, vol. 28, pp. 172-5; see also pp. 403-07.

[138]See C.O. 194/64, f. 129.

[139]O'Flaherty, "Seeds of Reform," pp. 55-6.

[140]Their formal request to Bathurst, dated Feb. 8, 1817, was read to the Select Committee of the Commons in June (*Report*, pp. 19-22).

[141]GN2/1/A, vol. 27, p. 78.

[142]*Newfoundland Mercantile Journal*, Mar. 14, 1817; see also Oct. 22, 1818.

[143]See his long letter to colonial secretary Bathurst, Feb. 8, 1817, C.O. 194/60, ff. 130-42, containing an attack on Pickmore along with general remarks on the system of government.

[144]*Colonial Journal*, no. 6 (June, 1817), p. 360; *Newfoundland Mercantile Journal*, Mar. 28, 1817.

[145]P. O'Flaherty, "James Lundrigan (sic)," *DCB*, vol. 6, pp. 409-11.

[146]See Chapter 2, note 39.

[147]*Newfoundland Mercantile Journal*, Nov. 20, 1816; Feb. 7, 1817.

[148]P. O'Flaherty, "Sir Francis Forbes," *DCB*, vol. 7, pp. 301-4.

[149]For the court cases, see GN5 2/A/1 (1820-21), under Nov. 8 and 9, 1820.

[150]GN5 2/A/1 (1820-21), under Nov. 11, 1820.

[151]See, for instance, GN5 2/A/1 (1806-11), pp. 316-22.

[152]See, for instance, governor Hamilton's letter to St. John's magistrates on Sept. 11, 1822, in which he complains of the cost of having surgeon John Bunting "attend the infliction of punishment" (GN2/1/A, vol. 33, pp. 15-16).

[153]The petition is C.O. 194/64, ff. 239-47.

[154]C.O. 194/64, ff. 237-54.

[155]C.O. 194/64, f. 59.

[156]See Mannion's comments, *DCB*, vol. 7, pp. 628-9.

[157]C.O. 195/17, f. 66.

[158]C.O. 195/17, ff. 67-8.

[159]GN2/1/A, vol. 32, pp. 337-42.

[160]C.O. 194/65, f. 7.

[161]There were other such internal restraints, among them the crown lawyers in London who were frequently consulted about affairs in Newfoundland and whose decisions sometimes curbed gubernatorial action. See O'Flaherty, "Government in Newfoundland," p. 27.

[162]GN2/1/A, vol. 30, p. 122.

[163]As far as it was applicable to circumstances there; Forbes, "Decisions of the Supreme Court of Judicature," State Library of New South Wales, Mitchell Library, MS A740, p. 58. This applied to both common law and statute law. He stated the principle elsewhere: English laws were "a common fund, from which the colony may draw as often and as largely as its exigences may require" (*Ibid.*, p. 252). The principle allowed Forbes to proceed through court business with considerable dispatch. His

successor, R.A. Tucker, took a different view, holding that "only so much of the statute law of England as was in existence at the period of the first settlement of the colony" applied to Newfoundland — likely a more cumbersome approach. See attorney general James Simms' comments, C.O. 194/84, ff. 264-5, 280-82. Forbes did also, however, take into account local customs in the fishery.

[164]Forbes, "Decisions," pp. 111-14.

[165]See GN2/1/A, vol. 30, pp. 49-71 for the fire engine episode; Forbes, "Decisions," pp. 135-8.

[166]*Ibid.*, pp. 159-64; see also Forbes's letter of Sept. 21, 1821, to Hamilton on the question of private property, GN2/1/A, vol. 32, pp. 102-6.

[167]Thomas Portanger Wescote was appointed in May, 1821 (GN2/1/A, vol. 32, pp. 218-9). According to governor Cochrane, he was "ignorant" and a "sot" (C.O. 194/85, f. 117).

[168]Forbes, "Decisions," pp. 213-25.

[169]*Ibid.*, pp. 253-6.

[170]See ["Britannicus"], *Observations on the Present State of Newfoundland* (London: 1823), pp. 7-10, for a local account of the episode.

[171]See James E. Candow, "The British Army in Newfoundland, 1697-1824," *NQ*, 79, 4 (1984): 21-8, and Janzen, "Military Garrisons," *ENL*, vol. 3, pp. 540-49, for studies of the British military in Newfoundland.

[172]["Brittanicus"], *Observations*, pp. 30-7.

[173]Reeves had made similar observations in the 1790s. See Ch. 6.

[174]C.O. 194/69, f. 35; the points are restated at greater length, ff. 55-6.

[175]See Dawe to Bathurst, Mar. 19, 1821 (C.O. 194/64, ff. 237-8); Bannister, "Campaign," p. 36, n. 102.

[176]Now Old Bonaventure.

[177]J.P. Howley, *The Beothucks or Red Indians* (Cambridge: University Press, 1915), pp. 132-3; for Cormack's account of west and south coast settlements, see pp. 158-68.

[178]Termed by him St. George's Bay Harbour.

[179]Near or at what is now Robinsons.

[180]C.O. 194/81, f. 60.

[181]["Britannicus"], *Observations*, p. 42.

[182]C.O. 194/65, f. 7.

[183]*Newfoundland Mercantile Journal*, Oct. 1, 1818.

[184]C.O. 194/65, ff. 130-31.

[185]Actually two islands, divided by a narrow tickle.

[186]GN2/1/A, vol. 32, pp. 517-25 (report by John Leigh, Aug. 31, 1822).

[187]C.O. 194/65, ff. 137-8.

[188]GN2/1/A, vol. 32, pp. 515-6.

[189]C.O. 194/65, ff. 143-5, 151-4.

[190]Interest in mining in Newfoundland goes back to Gilbert. A copper mine was operating in Shoal Bay, south of St. John's, in the 1770s (*PC*, vol. 2, p. 520). See Cormack's account of the mine (Howley, *Beothucks*, p. 131); and Wendy Martin, *Once upon a Mine: Story of Pre-Confederation Mines on the Island of Newfoundland* (Montreal: Canadian Institute of Mining and Metallurgy, 1983), p. 8.

[191]There had of course been interest in the interior before Cormack's journey. See remarks on John Cartwright and Cook in Chapter 6. Griffith Williams went "between Twenty and Thirty Miles into the Country" before 1765, and made a comment on it (*Account*, pp. 1-2); George Kemp told the 1817 Commons committee that he had been in the "interior." He too described it (House of Commons, *Report* [1817], p. 28).

[192]In the *Edinburgh Philosophical Journal*, 10 (1824): 156-62; on Cormack's journey, see O'Flaherty, *Rock Observed*, pp. 44-8.

[193]See the committee of inhabitants' report to Bathurst, Dec. 6, 1822, C.O. 194/66, f. 285: "there can remain but very little doubt, that there are many parts of the interior more favourable to agriculture than the sea coast."

[194]Howley, *Beothucks*, pp. 161, 163.

[195]Neary and O'Flaherty, *By Great Waters*, pp. 60-66; see Marshall, *History and Ethnography*, pp. 137-53.

[196]Howley, *Beothucks*, p. 215.

[197]*Newfoundland Mercantile Journal*, Nov. 4, 1819.

[198]For an account of his pamphleteering, see O'Flaherty, *Rock Observed*, pp. 56-8; also White, "Study."

[199]Pronounced Kehoe, as it was sometimes spelled. See Fabian O'Dea, "Patrick Kough," *DCB*, vol. 9, pp. 435-6.

[200]The schools of industry, though notionally non-denominational, were in effect Church of England schools, as were S.P.G. schools elsewhere in the island; the Orphan Asylum School in St. John's and St. Patrick Free School in Harbour Grace, both established in 1826, were Roman Catholic, though again supposedly open to all; schools established by the Newfoundland Society for Educating the Poor, commencing in 1824, were Protestant evangelical in tendency. On the last named, which is normally called the Newfoundland School Society, see Gordon Handcock, "Samuel Codner," *DCB*, vol. 8, pp. 164-7.

[201]On the Catholic petition of 1823 (see below) the overwhelming majority of the 600 signatories did not employ marks.

[202]*Newfoundland Mercantile Journal*, July 13, Aug. 31, Oct. 5, 1820.

[203]P. O'Flaherty, "Henry David Winton," *DCB*, vol. 8, pp. 947-51; "The Road to Saddle Hill," *NQ*, 89, 3 (1995): 21-6.

[204]C.O. 194/66, 283-6.

[205]The memorial noted that "local governments" had been granted to other colonies such as Nova Scotia and the Canadas. These of course now included assemblies.

[206]C.O. 194/66, ff. 345-61.

[207]C.O. 195/17, f. 89.

[208]C.O. 194/67, ff. 88-94. It is dated Oct. 27, 1823.

[209]57 Geo. III, c. 51 (in House of Commons, "Newfoundland Acts, 1786-1820"); see Lahey, "Religion and Politics," pp. 13-16. According to the Act, marriages were to be celebrated by persons in Holy Orders (which included Catholic priests).

[210]R.J. Lahey, "Michael Anthony Fleming," *DCB*, vol. 7, pp. 292-300. Fleming's name is not on the petition.

[211]An Act to repeal several Laws relating to the Fisheries, 5 Geo. IV, cap. 51; An Act for the better Administration of Justice, 5 Geo. IV, cap. 67; An Act to repeal ... An Act to regulate the Celebration of Marriages, 5 Geo. IV, cap. 68; *SUK*, vol. 9 (1824), pp. 692-5, 743-52.

[212]A.H. McLintock, *The Establishment of Constitutional Government in Newfoundland, 1783-1832* (London: Longmans, Green and Co., 1941), p. 161.

[213]The word had a particular meaning, i.e., "anything obnoxious to the community or individual by offensiveness of smell or appearance, by causing obstruction or damage, etc." (*OED*).

[214]I.e., granting by will.

[215]See Lahey, "Religion and Politics," pp. 16-18

[216]The provision in 15 Geo. III, cap. 31, clause 4, stipulated that the right of drying fish in Newfoundland "shall not be held and enjoyed by any of His Majesty's subjects arriving ... from any other country except from *Great Britain*, or one of the *British* dominions in *Europe*" (Reeves, *History*, appendix, pp. xxiii-iv). This was repeated in 29 Geo. III, cap 53 (An Act for further encouraging the *Newfoundland* ... Whale Fisheries) in 1789. See *PC*, vol. 1, p. 286. But 59 Geo. III, c. 38 (in 1819) had, in forbidding any but "a natural-born subject of His Majesty" to fish within three miles of his North American possessions, implied that any subject, including of course inhabitants of the colonies, could fish there.

[217]See James Stephen's letter to Robert Wilmot-Horton, 12 Mar., 1824 (C.O. 194/68, ff. 112-30). Stephen, a barrister of Lincoln's Inn, was under-secretary for the colonies, 1836-47, prior to which he was an advisor and counsel in the colonial office. Wilmot-Horton was under-secretary for the colonies, 1821-8.

[218]*Public Ledger*, June 1, June 4, 1824; the inhabitants' committee in 1822 had objected to such a structure as "most obnoxious" (C.O. 194/66, f. 286).

[219]See his commission, dated Aug. 20, 1825 (*PC*, vol. 2, pp. 718-22); also C.O. 195/17, ff. 106-7; 194/70, f. 153.

[220]See Lahey, "Religion and Politics," p. 19.

[221]C.O. 194/70, f. 252; 195/17, f. 135. Cochrane also put forward Morris's name.

[222]For documents relating to the controversy, see C.O. 194/72, ff. 158-78. Dawe had warned Bathurst in 1824 not to exclude absentee landowners from taxes (GN2/1/A, vol. 34, pp. 328-9); see also Melvin Baker, "The Government of St. John's 1800-1921" (Ph.D. thes., Univ. of Western Ontario, 1980), pp. 30-2.

[223]C.O. 194/67, f. 67.

[224]C.O. 194/72, f. 332.

[225]C.O. 194/72, f. 157.

[226]See McLintock, *Establishment*, pp. 207-10.

[227]See Ryan, *Newfoundland-Spanish Saltfish*, pp. 5-23.

[228]C.O. 194/74, f. 285.

[229]C.O. 194/74, f. 115; GN2/1/A, vol. 34, p. 260; C.O. 194/76, f. 162.

[230]C.O. 194/76, f. 162.

[231]*Public Ledger*, May 2, 1828; but a packet boat, the *Lively*, had operated between Portugal Cove and Harbour Grace in 1821-2.

[232]GN2/1/A, vol. 35, p. 375 (insert); C.O. 194/76, f. 163; Cochrane later argued that the cost to Britain of governing Newfoundland had actually decreased with the introduction of the system of circuit judges. Naval surrogating had ended, so "several" men-of-war were no longer required and the Admiralty saved money (C.O. 194/85, f. 26).

[233]C.O. 194/77, ff. 6-7.

[234]C.O. 194/77, ff. 6-8; also (for duties) /78, ff. 225-6.

[235]By 6 Geo. IV, c. 114. See C.O. 194/74, f. 281.

[236]Bannister notes that Cochrane had suggested an ad valorem duty to Bathurst in 1826 ("Campaign," p. 26).

[237]C.O. 194/74, ff. 275-82; see the *Public Ledger*, Apr. 22, 1828. The Chamber of Commerce was the "executive body" of the St. John's Commercial Society; see David Davis, "William Bickford Row," *DCB*, vol. 9, pp. 694-5.

[238]*Public Ledger*, Apr. 22, 1828.

[239]Draper, *Struggle for Power*, pp. 89-90.

[240]C.O. 194/76, f. 282.

[241]Keith Matthews, in his essay "The Class of '32," argues (and argues well) that reformers' agitation for change reflected their newly imported European ideas and their desire to assert "their own rightful position as the leaders and rulers of Newfoundland society" — and was not a response to real abuses and grievances in local society. My essay "The Seeds of Reform" is in part a reply to Matthews' paper.

[242]Which, among other requirements, stated that office-holders, to qualify, take communion in the Church of England.

[243]Nativist sentiment was felt in Carbonear in the 1820s; see Marjorie Doyle, *Newfoundlander in Exile: The Life and Times of Philip Tocque (1814-1899)* (Halifax: John W. Doull Books, 1997), p. 5; also the *Newfoundlander*, Oct. 15, 1829 (the proprietor of the paper, John Shea, was a Newfoundlander) and James Stokes's letter to Edward Stanley in the colonial office, Nov. 25, 1833 (C.O. 194/86, ff. 254-5). There was a nativist plank in the pledges taken by prospective candidates in Harbour Grace in 1832 (see below). See also Bannister, "Campaign," pp. 31, 39.

[244]C.O. 194/84, ff. 303-5.

[245]Clause 11 of 5 Geo. IV, cap. 51 gave, it was thought, considerable latitude to a servant who wilfully neglected his work or refused to work; he could absent himself for fourteen days without being deemed a deserter and forfeiting his wages. If the servant was a key employee —a splitter, salter, or master of voyage, say — the catch of fish could be damaged or altogether ruined by such neglect or absence. Attorney general Simms thought that this defect was responsible for mobilizing outport opinion in favour of a local assembly.

[246]The Harbour Grace petition of 1831 noted that government from London had proved inefficient "owing to the difficulty of legislating at such a distance for a people and trade whose habits and avocations so essentially differ from those of the mother country," and that this was nowhere more evident than in the 1824 acts. See C.O. 194/84, f. 252; also ff. 287-91.

[247]See *Harbour Grace and Carbonear Weekly Journal*, Jan. 29, 1829; *Public Ledger*, Dec. 19, 1828. For the St. John's petitions see *Ibid.*, Jan. 20 & 23, 1829.

[248]*Newfoundlander*, July 23, 1829.

[249]*Public Ledger*, June 10, 1831.

[250]*Royal Gazette*, May 19 & Aug. 25, 1829; *Public Ledger*, May 12, 1829.

[251]*Public Ledger*, May 12, 1829.

[252]Quoted in *Newfoundlander*, Aug. 20, 1829.

[253]Quoted in *Public Ledger*, Sept. 4, 1829.

[254]*Harbour Grace and Carbonear Weekly Journal*, May 14, 1829.

[255]Lahey, "Religion and Politics," pp. 21-2; see GN2/2 (1829), pp. 197-206 for the legal opinion.

[256]C.O. 195/18, p. 51.

[257]*Royal Gazette*, May 18, 1830.

[258]*Newfoundlander*, Dec. 31, 1829.

[259]*Newfoundlander*, Jan. 28, 1830.

[260]C.O. 194/74, f. 135.

[261]R.J. Lahey, "Timothy Browne," *DCB*, vol. 8, pp. 106-8.

[262]*Gentlemen-Bishops*, pp. 348-9.

[263]C.O. 194/82, f. 283.

[264]*Royal Gazette*, Sept. 28, 1830. Cochrane had direct access to the *Gazette*; see Stark's letter of Jan. 1, 1837, Cochrane papers, Nat. Lib. Scot., 2278, f. 1.

[265]*Public Ledger*, Nov. 23, 1830.

[266]C.O. 194/83, f. 185.

[267]C.O. 194/82, ff. 344 ff.

[268]C.O. 194/84, f. 253; *Royal Gazette*, Oct. 19, 1830.

[269]GN2/2 (Sept.-Dec., 1830), pp. 71-84.

[270]C.O. 194/84, f. 254.

[271]Cochrane had advised against the assembly. Chief justice Tucker thought "the time for it had not arrived" (C.O. 194/86, f. 275); Attorney general Simms was still finding ways to obstruct the Assembly in 1832 (C.O. 194/84, ff. 301-2); the Poole petition of Jan. 30, 1832, is ff. 325-6.

[272]*Royal Gazette*, Sept. 6, 1831.

[273]*Royal Gazette*, Oct. 4, 1831.

[274]For an account of "plebian" behaviour in Conception Bay in the period, see Linda Little, "Collective Action in Outport Newfoundland: A Case Study from the 1830s," in *Labour and Working-Class History in Atlantic Canada: A Reader*, ed. David Frank and Gregory S. Kealey (St. John's: Institute of Social and Economic Research, MUN, 1995), pp. 41-70.

[275]C.O. 194/74, ff. 103-4.

[276]C.O. 195/17, ff. 154-5.

[277]*Public Ledger*, June 22, 1830; see also GN2/2 (Jan.-Dec., 1830), # 197.

[278]*Public Ledger*, Jan. 11 & 25, 1831.

[279]*Public Ledger*, June 3, 1831.

[280]C.O. 194/83, f. 34.

[281]Tucker said "more than three thousand"; another estimate was "about four thousand" (C.O. 194/83, f. 41; *Public Ledger*, Mar. 13, 1832). The magistrate John Stark, writing from Harbour Grace to Cochrane, said there were "about 2000" (National Library of Scotland, Edin., Cochrane papers, 2274, f. 26). Stark's account (ff. 26-7) is the best short description of the affair.

[282]This is a quotation from an original notice of the meeting, dated Jan. 5. See G.N. 2/2 (Jan.-Mar., 1832, unpaged). The date of Jan. 9 for the meeting is given here. This notice (with two others) is in Little, "Collective Action," p. 70.

[283]Proclamation by R.A. Tucker, Feb. 22, 1832 (private collection).

[284]In which a fisherman is given credit for supplies, gear, etc., against the anticipated catch of fish. The word truck means generally: payment of wages otherwise than in money (*OED*). For a recent scholarly treatment of truck, especially as it applies to Conception Bay, see Sean T. Cadigan, *Hope and Deception in Conception Bay: Merchant-Settler Relations in Newfoundland, 1785-1855* (Toronto: Univ. of Toronto Press, 1995).

[285]Nat. Lib. Scot., Cochrane Papers, 2274, f. 26.

[286]In a letter to the Conception Bay *Mercury*, dated Mar. 1, 1832; repr. in *Public Ledger*, Mar. 13, 1832. Normally, it seems, the men were paid for their share of the seal catch in cash, "according to a price previously agreed upon." See Anspach, *History*, pp. 423-4.

[287]The Carbonear fisherman; see note 286.

[288]But Little thinks the sealers were "demanding concessions rather than resisting encroachments on previously existing benefits." See "Collective Action," p. 66.

[289]Stark gives a higher number: "a mob from Carbonear of about 200 joined by men of this place [i.e., Harbour Grace]."

[290]*Public Ledger*, Feb. 21, 1832.

[291]See the account in the *Public Ledger*, Mar. 13, 1832.

[292]Nat. Lib. Scot., Cochrane Papers, 2274, f. 50.

[293]Little, "Collective Action," pp. 64-7.

[294]Though, to be fair, he gave some observers with different views access to his paper.

[295]*Public Ledger*, Apr. 19, 1831.

[296]Nat. Lib. Scot., Cochrane Papers, 2273, f. 6.

[297]*Public Ledger*, Feb. 7, 1832.

[298]*Public Ledger*, Dec. 27, 1831.

[299]*Public Ledger*, March 27, 1832.

[300]A stock description of Ireland among Irish orators.

[301]*Public Ledger*, April 3, 1832.

[302]2-3 William IV, c. 78; in *PC*, vol. 1, pp. 321-2.

[303]His commission, dated Mar. 28, 1832, is in *PC*, vol. 2, pp. 723-30; see also his instructions, dated July 26, 1832, *Ibid.*, pp. 731-44; and the royal proclamation establishing electoral districts and setting out qualifications for voters and members, dated also July 26, *Ibid.*, pp. 745-8.

[304]Some ambiguity exists as to the number. In Cochrane's commission the number seven is mentioned, but in his instructions, six are specifically named as to be appointed, and six were appointed, the effective date being July 26, 1832; three members formed a quorum. See *PC*, vol. 2, pp. 725, 731; C.O. 194/85, f. 264.

[305]*Newfoundlander*, Aug. 30, 1832.

[306]Chief justice H.J. Boulton's comment in 1833; see C.O. 194/85, ff. 115-6.

[307]I.e., to withhold assent until the King's pleasure was known.

[308]A community called Bonne Bay (later McCallum) existed at this time.

[309]*PC*, vol. 2, p. 723. 6 Geo. IV, cap. 59 set the western limit of the portion of the Labrador coast now within the government of Newfoundland at "the bay or harbour of Ance Sablon" (i.e., Blanc Sablon). See Leslie Harris, "Labrador Boundary Dispute," *ENL*, vol. 3, p. 217.

[310]Gerald M. Craig, *Upper Canada: The Formative Years, 1784-1841* (Toronto: McClelland and Stewart, 1963), p. 18.

[311]The regulation did not say that he could stand for election only in the district he lived in (*PC*, vol. 2, p. 747).

[312]*Public Ledger*, Apr. 11, 1834. Joseph Shea said Kent was "just out of his uncle's [i.e., Morris's] counting-house," but "he was going to be married to the bishop's sister, and to give him a little consequence he was to be made a member of the House of Assembly" (House of Commons, Select Committee [1841], "Minutes of Evidence," p. 83).

[313]*Newfoundlander*, Sept. 6, 1832. The ad appeared in the *Public Ledger* as well.

[314]GN2/2 (Apr.-June, 1838), pp. 207-9.

[315]Sept. 13, 1832.

[316]The circular is alluded to in the *Public Ledger*, Sept. 18, 1832.

[317]To Fleming the cross was "the sacred emblem of salvation." See Fleming, *Letters on the State of Religion in Newfoundland* (Dublin: 1844), p. 10.

[318]"Conflict and Culture," p. 122.

[319]*Newfoundlander*, Oct. 4, 1832; Winton replied in the *Ledger* on Oct. 5, saying he walked the public streets, where "both our falsehood and our cowardice are in a fair way of being put to the test." Kent took the matter no further.

[320]See Joseph Shea's testimony, House of Commons, Select Committee (1841), "Minutes of Evidence," p. 80. A plumper is a vote given to one candidate only, when the ballot permits a vote to more than one. Shea once heard Fleming say "he had it in his power to return all the representatives" (p. 95).

[321]Two others, Gill and Henessy, had offered themselves earlier, but withdrew before voting started.

[322]I.e., secret voting. *Public Ledger*, Nov. 13, 1832. Voting was carried on, not through a ballot, but by supporters presenting themselves to the returning officer in groups of agreed-on numbers, often ten, in rotation, for each of the candidates, and verbally stating their preference. Polling in St. John's took place over eight days.

[323]*Newfoundlander*, Oct. 11, 1832; for a contemporary discussion of "the propriety of extracting pledges" from candidates, see the *Public Ledger*, Oct. 26, 1832.

[324]Perhaps "mob rule" would be a more accurate description of certain aspects of the sealers' strike.

Notes to Chapter 8

[1]See Ryan, *Fish Out of Water*, pp. 258, 261. I am indebted to this book as I am to the standard work on the period, Gertrude E. Gunn, *The Political History of Newfoundland 1832-1864* (Toronto: Univ. of Toronto Press, 1966). The quantity of salt fish exported had dropped since 1828 — most dramatically in 1831. Prices in overseas markets remained low; the value of Newfoundland exports, mostly fish, in 1832 fell by nearly £100,000 from the previous year (C.O. 194/85, f. 207). The fish *catches* in both 1831 and '32 were poor, so stocks of fish for winter food were reduced.

[2]See Cochrane's comments, Nov., 1833, C.O. 194/85, f. 336. The population had tripled, he said, during the past thirty years, while cod production "has actually decreased."

[3]"... in sectors with a constrained resource, improved labour productivity ... may be unable to either improve export performance for the region or increase living standards" (Doug May and Dane Rowlands, "Atlantic Canada in Confederation: Uncharted Waters with Dangerous Shoals" [MS, MUN, Dept. of Economics, 1991], p. 11).

[4]*JHA* (1834), 4th Session, p. 17.

[5]C.O. 194/85, f. 77. The remark was made of Bonavista.

[6]C.O. 194/85, f. 85.

[7]GN2/2 (Jan.-June, 1833), pp. 158-60, 177-8.

[8]C.O. 194/85, f. 305. He likely was not referring to the French shore, which had no resident magistrates to send reports, nor was it visited by the circuit court.

[9]C.O. 194/85, f. 70.

[10]A doorkeeper replaced the messenger in subsequent motions, and in time more officers were added. For a history of the long dispute between the Crown and House on this point, see C.O. 194/115, ff. 128-36.

[11]Fleming referred to him as "the government carpenter" and noted he had wrongly been referred to as a "merchant" (C.O. 194/99, f. 218). See Joseph Shea's comment on Kough's qualities; House of Commons, Select Committee (1841), "Minutes of Evidence," p. 94.

[12]*JHA* (1833), pp. 10-11. The petition, presented Jan. 2, was withdrawn Jan. 14.

[13]P. O'Flaherty, "Peter Brown," *DCB*, vol. 7, pp. 112-4.

[14]*JHA* (1833), p. 18.

[15]3 Wm. IV, c. 1; *ALN* (1833), pp. 1-17.

[16]As Cochrane described it. See his comments on the first session, C.O. 194/85, ff. 290-94. The Nuisances' Act is 3 Wm. IV, c. 8; *ALN* (1833), pp. 45-8.

[17]The equivalent of the Assembly's speaker.

[18]C.O. 194/86, f. 286.

[19]C.O. 194/86, f. 302.

[20]C.O. 195/18, p. 140. He had tendered his resignation before leaving Newfoundland.

[21]C.O. 194/86, ff. 312-8. He estimated that the cost to the public of maintaining Cochrane was about £12,000 per year.

[22]Notes on Tucker's letters betray concern on the part of officials. See C.O. 194/86, f. 313.

[23]C.O. 194/87, ff. 50-51 (Assembly); ff. 84-93 (Council).

[24]He also recommended that John Bingley Garland, the Assembly's speaker, be appointed to the Council. This advice was followed as well, and in December W.B. Row was returned, without opposition, in Garland's district of Trinity Bay.

[25]The origins of the paper are obscure, but Carson was known as the "head of a coterie" that set it up (*Public Ledger*, Jan. 4, 1832). The prospectus of the *Patriot*, with all the marks of Carson's authorship, is in the *Ledger*, Jan. 11, 1833. The first number of the paper appeared July 15, 1833; the *Royal Gazette*, on July 16, noted that "It is generally understood to be under the editorship of a *Medical Gentleman* of the town." The surviving file of the *Patriot* dates from Dec. 16, 1834.

[26]In the *Patriot*, Jan. 20, 1835, it is said that Carson had "long ago" been "superseded" as editor. Cochrane said he was still "proprietor and editor" in April, 1834 (C.O. 194/88, f. 63).

[27]See Fleming's letter to Monsignor Francis Capaccini, under-secretary of state at the Vatican, June 13, 1835 (C.O. 194/92, f. 92).

[28]See *Public Ledger*, Aug. 16, Nov. 26, 1833. Carson gave scandal early in his Newfoundland career by denying Jesus' divinity. His pamphlet on cholera in 1832 had allegedly contained heresy. See *Ledger*, Aug. 28, Sept. 4, Sept. 11, 1832.

[29]C.O. 194/87, f. 128 (withdrawal); f. 129 (apology).

[30]It had commenced Aug. 15, 1832, under the editorship of the youthful John McCoubrey.

[31]*Public Ledger*, Dec. 10, 1833.

[32]*Public Ledger*, Dec. 17, 1833.

[33]*Public Ledger*, Dec. 24, 1833.

[34]"... several persons were bayoneted," writes Lahey (*DCB*, vol. 7, p. 294), repeating a charge made in the resolutions of the meeting on Dec. 17 (C.O. 194/87, f. 121). FitzGerald says the same ("Conflict and Culture," p. 147). Five years later James Kent reported seeing one man bayoneted (C.O. 194/99, ff. 230-1). FitzGerald speculates that mummers were in the crowd around Winton's home.

[35]Phyllis Creighton, "Edward Troy," *DCB*, vol. 10, pp. 687-8.

[36]*Public Ledger*, Dec. 27, 1833; *Newfoundlander*, Dec. 26, 1833; the latter account differs slightly from Winton's. For Cochrane's account, see C.O. 194/88, ff. 74-7.

[37]Jan. 2, 1834.

[38]Here meaning the secretary to the governor.

[39]James Crowdy, colonial secretary (in St. John's), to Fleming, Dec. 28, 1833, C.O. 194/88, ff. 74-7.

[40]Even FitzGerald, Fleming's most astute defender, calls attention to this aspect of the bishop's character, noting his success even "in evading Rome's requests" ("Conflict and Culture," p. 355). See also pp. 268-70 for Fleming's evasive dealings with Rome over Troy. FitzGerald elswhere comments on Fleming's "perpetually imprecise" use of figures (p. 95) and notes how he "gilded ... the lily" to suit his purposes (p. 118).

[41]C.O. 194/87, f. 121.

[42]C.O. 194/87, ff. 124-6. The letter was published in the local press. See *Public Ledger*, Jan. 21, 1834.

[43]For sympathetic depictions of his character and actions, see Lahey's in *DCB*, vol. 7, p. 292-300, FitzGerald's, throughout "Conflict and Culture," and Phillip McCann's, in "Bishop Fleming and the Politicization of the Irish Roman Catholics in Newfoundland, 1830-1850," in *Religion and Identity*, pp. 81-97. The phrase quoted is Stephen's in 1838 (C.O. 194/100, f. 33).

[44]Fleming, *Letters on the State of Religion*, p. 11.

[45]See his letter to Lord Duncannon, July 4, 1835 (C.O. 194/92, ff. 112-3).

[46]But a slight one. Edward Kielley, Joseph Shea, and of course Kough found employment under the government; Patrick Doyle and Peter Brown were appointed justices of the peace in 1834; Patrick Morris was a J.P. in 1835. Fleming himself got a government salary of £75 p.a. In 1838 Prescott told Glenelg that every salaried officer appointed since his arrival had been Protestant (C.O. 194/100, f. 305). Fleming said that no Catholic was allowed to enjoy government favour until he "distinguished himself" by abusing the clergy — a preposterous charge (C.O. 194/99, f. 228).

[47]He claimed, and perhaps believed, that the Catholics amounted to four-fifths of the population. By official count in the census of 1836 Catholics numbered slightly more than Protestants. See Prescott's dispatch, C.O. 194/95, ff. 324-6. Neither Fogo nor the French shore was included in this census. In counting Catholics and Protestants, Prescott assumed that figures for Fogo district had not changed since the previous count, i.e., 1827.

[48]Carson's son-in-law and eldest son of the Irish merchant Henry Shea; see John Mannion, "Henry Shea," *DCB*, vol. 6, pp. 709-12; also Shea's testimony to the House of Commons, Select Committee (1841), "Minutes of Evidence," pp. 79-97.

[49]FitzGerald, "Conflict and Culture," p. 83.

[50]P. O'Flaherty, "Edward Kielley," *DCB*, vol. 8, pp. 467-70.

[51]See his comments on Shea and Eliza Boulton, C.O. 194/92, ff. 98, 101. Eliza Boulton, H.J. Boulton's wife, challenged other points of Catholic practice, including holy water and Easter water. She not only married a Protestant but declined to have her children baptized as Catholics. Fleming's remarks on her character provide one of the earliest sketches in the documents of a resident Newfoundland woman of European descent.

[52]See *JHA* (1833), p. 25.

[53]It is possible to find remarks by him that might suggest otherwise; but these were strategic and rhetorical.

[54]In the National Library of Scotland, MSS 2268 ff., especially the letters of Stark, Simms, Christopher Ayre, and John Inglis, Bishop of Nova Scotia.

[55]Edward Wix, *Six Months of a Newfoundland Missionary's Journal* (London: 1836). See in particular the "Appeal" prefaced to the 2nd. edit. (1836), pp. ix-xi.

[56]C.O. 194/92, ff. 114-5. In 1834 the British government agreed to give the SPG £2,170 p.a. in support of Church of England priests. See C.O. 194/100, ff. 95-6.

[57]C.O. 194/88, f. 69.

[58]FitzGerald, "Conflict and Culture," p. 178; McCann, "Bishop Fleming," p. 87.

[59]R.J. Lahey, "James W. Duffy," *DCB*, vol. 8, pp. 246-7.

[60]They were "Irish nationalists and strong supporters of O'Connell," writes FitzGerald (see "Conflict and Culture," pp. 99-100).

[61]*Six Months*, pp. 27-8. But his statement was challenged in the *Newfoundland Patriot*, Nov. 19, Dec. 3, 1836.

[62]And neither did the reformers.

[63]But there were merchant-reformers too: the Conception Bay MHA Robert Pack, for instance, Brown, and even Kent.

[64]The "reformers" or "popular party" often used the word "liberals" to describe themselves. See *Newfoundland Patriot*, Dec. 23, 1834. They also on occasion called themselves "whigs." They were more accurately termed, though not by themselves, the "Catholic party" or "Priests' party" (C.O. 194/90, ff. 164-5; Nat. Lib. Scot. MS 2279, f. 11). The words "conservative" and "tories" were used of their opponents, the latter derogatively. (The term "conservative party" was first used in England in 1831.) They were also termed the "mercantile party." See House of Assembly, *Address of the House of Assembly* (1839), pp. 6, 18. Fleming referred to "tories" as the "official party," "government party," or even "monopolists," this last term doubtless picked up from Morris. For Winton's acerbic comment on the use of the words "tory" and "whig" in Newfoundland, see *Public Ledger*, July 28, 1837.

[65]See Lahey, "Fleming," *DCB*, p. 294.

[66]See his comment on Carson, C.O. 194/99, f. 217.

[67]C.O. 194/87, ff. 109-10; the petition is ff. 116-20.

[68]4 Wm. IV, c. 7; *ALN* (1834), pp. 33-4. See C.O. 194/88, ff. 172-3.

[69]4 Wm. IV, c. 8; *Ibid.*, pp. 37-9.

[70]4 Wm. IV, c. 5; *Ibid.*, pp. 21-2.

[71]Hereward and Elinor Senior, "Henry John Boulton, *DCB*, vol. 9, pp. 69-72.

[72]See his *Rules and Regulations to be observed in the Legislative Council of Newfoundland* (St. John's: 1834), which contains fifty rules. The official response to Boulton's tinkering with the Council, drafted by Stephen in the colonial office, is C.O. 194/90, ff. 69-71, 73-8.

[73]See Boulton's charge to the grand jury, *Public Ledger*, Jan. 14, 1834. For J.V. Nugent's cogent (but partisan) summary of the Irish objections to Boulton's changes to the impanelling of juries, see *Newfoundland Vindicator*, May 7, 1842.

[74]C.O. 194/97, f. 325.

[75]And that they were very occupied. See the three supreme court judges' comments on the case, C.O. 194/97, ff. 326-8.

[76]C.O. 194/89, ff. 376-9. It was written by J.V. Nugent.

[77]C.O. 194/89, f. 374.

[78]C.O. 194/95, f. 368.

[79]See the account of the hanging in *Public Ledger*, Jan. 14, 1834.

[80]A jury of married women with expert knowledge of matters of pregnancy, etc. (*OED*).

[81]For documents relating to Snow, see C.O. 194/87, ff. 55-9; /88, ff. 78-80; *Newfoundlander*, July 24, 1834.

[82]This was an office under the government, as was "gaol surgeon," also held by Kielley. The district surgeon's principal task was to provide medical attendance to the poor.

[83]GN2/2 (May-Aug., 1834), pp. 349-54.

[84]See C.O. 194/88, ff. 81-2.

[85]Elizabeth A. Wells, "John Valentine Nugent," *DCB*, vol. 10, pp. 552-3.

[86]Troy confessed to being the author of the attacks (see C.O. 194/88, f. 65), but might have done so to protect Nugent, who was also thought to have written them. In the *Patriot*, Feb. 17, 1841, R.J. Parsons attributed the letters of Junius to Nugent. For a sample of Junius from Feb., 1834, see C.O. 194/99, f. 209.

[87]See her account of Troy's words in church, Nat. Lib. Scot. MS 2275, ff. 239-40.

[88]C.O. 194/88, f. 348; /90, f. 165.

[89]C.O. 194/90, f. 56.

[90]Capaccini to Fleming, Nov. 9, 1834 (C.O. 194/89, ff. 73-4). Capaccini did not bring Fleming's activities to the attention of Pope Gregory XVI, but had he done so they would, he told Fleming, have excited "his heavy displeasure."

[91]*Newfoundland Patriot*, Dec. 23, 1834, quoting the *Ledger* of Dec. 16.

[92]Jan. 6, 1835.

[93]*JHA* (1835), pp. 8-9, 36; *Newfoundland Patriot*, Feb. 24, 1834.

[94]*Newfoundland Patriot*, Feb. 10, 1835.

[95]For petitions against taxes, see *JHA* (1835), pp. 16, 39, 40-1; see p. 9 for a typical request (this from Grand Bank) for a sum to build a jail.

[96]5 Wm. IV, c. 1; *ALN* (1835), pp. 1-5.

[97]"Bishop Fleming," p. 82.

[98]See his letter to O'Connell, June 10, 1835 (C.O. 194/93, f. 263).

[99]FitzGerald, "Conflict and Culture," p. 139.

[100]See his petition, dated Mar. 21, 1835 (C.O. 194/90, ff. 167-77). Little, like Shea, had married a Protestant.

[101]See letters of apology in *Patriot*, Feb. 10, Feb. 24, Mar. 10, 1835, the last from Timothy Hogan.

[102]It is printed in the *Public Ledger*, June 5, 1835.

[103]He might not have been convicted if he had divulged the author of the offending paragraph, but he refused to do so. He was sentenced on May 26. In addition to the jail sentence and fine, he was to give

security for good behaviour for 12 months, himself in £200, and two securities in £100 each; he was to remain in custody until the securities were in place. See GN5/2/A/1 (1832-35) (Central Circuit Court), p. 253; *Royal Gazette*, June 2, 1835.

[104] *Public Ledger*, Apr. 10, 1835.

[105] See the *Newfoundland Patriot*, Feb. 10, 1835, for Winton's remark (the *Ledger* of Feb. 3 is missing). It is not easy to explain the insult, since the wording is obscure; but it was thought to be sexual in nature. The correct name of the order is: The Order of the Presentation of Our Blessed Lady. See Peter Neary, "Miss Kirwan" (Sister Mary Bernard), *DCB*, vol. 8, 474-6.

[106] See Shea's account of the proceedings, House of Commons, Select Committee (1841), "Minutes of Evidence," pp. 82-4.

[107] Winton said it was "red ochre or some colouring of that description"; Churchyard called it "red and a little yellow ochre" (C.O. 194/90, ff. 190, 193).

[108] For Winton's account of the incident, see *Public Ledger*, June 2, 1835. Christopher Ayre's, dated May 22, 1835, is in Nat. Lib. Scot. MS 2350, ff. 147-8. For a list of documents relating to Winton's mutilation, see *DCB*, vol. 8, p. 951. Philip Henry Gosse said one "Dr. Molloy, a surgeon of Carbonear," cut off Winton's ears. See *NS*, 6, 2 (1990), p. 260.

[109] See his letters to Prescott, July 1, Dec. 31, 1835 (C.O. 195/18, pp. 331-2, 428).

[110] C.O. 194/90, f. 236.

[111] C.O. 194/90, f. 207.

[112] "Croppy Boy" may mean Protestant in Irish balladry; here, of course, there is a play on the word. See Corish, "The Irish Catholics," pp. 15, 17.

[113] July 28, 1835.

[114] C.O. 194/90, 319-37. See Prescott's comment, f. 317. He believed "a very large proportion" of signatories "are neither acquainted with its contents, nor feel any interest in its result." Boulton said the petition was not shown to the signers; instead, sheets of paper were spread out on tables at the doors of the Catholic chapel in St. John's, and people entering were induced to sign them; "some were told they should not go in to hear mass unless they did" (/93, f. 89).

[115] See Browne's letter to Prescott, Jan. 9, 1836, C.O. 194/100, ff. 56-64. Browne refers to Fleming's "intolerance, bigotry and prejudice" and says his ambition is for "absolute power, civil and ecclesiastic."

[116] See Thompson's comment, *French Shore Problem*, p. 26.

[117] C.O. 194/87, ff. 272-3.

[118] C.O. 194/89, ff. 467-8.

[119] C.O. 194/90, ff. 24-5.

[120] C.O. 194/92, f. 47. See /93, ff. 361-3 for internal British memos on the matter in Feb., 1835.

[121] C.O. 194/94, ff. 131-2.

[122] C.O. 194/97, ff. 531-3.

[123] See C.O. 194/102, ff. 43-7.

[124] C.O. 194/109, f. 236.

[125] See J. Lack's letter of July 1834, C.O. 194/92, ff. 58-67; esp. ff. 64-5.

[126] Thompson, *French Shore Problem*, pp. 23-4.

[127] C.O. 194/87, ff. 34-5.

[128] C.O. 194/89, ff. 58-9.

[129] C.O. 194/92, f. 68.

[130] Thompson, *French Shore Problem*, p. 31.

[131] I.e., trawl; a long fishing line with baited hooks strung at intervals.

[132] Spawning cod.

[133] Captain Thomas Bennett of H.M.S. *Rainbow* told Prescott in 1836 that Fortune Bay men who had petitioned against the French "were themselves deeply engaged in the capelin trade" to St. Pierre (C.O. 194/95, f. 114).

[134] C.O. 194/90, ff. 120-23; see *JHA* (1835), pp. 101, 108-9, 114-5.

[135] C.O. 194/92, f. 70.

[136]See Prescott to Glenelg, Jan. 29, 1836, and the Chamber of Commerce petition of Jan. 26, 1836 (C.O. 194/94, ff. 129-32).

[137]See C.O. 194/94, ff. 388-9, 396; 6 Wm. IV, c. 3; *ALN* (1836), pp. 13-15.

[138]C.O. 194/95, ff. 114-5.

[139]See Wix, *Six Months*, pp. 120-4.

[140]*Ibid.*, p. 99.

[141]C.O. 194/95, ff. 324-6; 4 Wm. IV, c. 14; *ALN* (1834), pp. 65-9. The eastern boundary of the new district was actually "the shore, which is situate and lying Westward of Jersyman's Harbour." It was to include St. George's Bay, Bay of Islands, and Bonne Bay on the west coast.

[142]C.O. 194/91, ff. 16-17.

[143]C.O. 194/91, f. 15.

[144]*Population Returns 1836* (n.p.: n.d.), pp. 14-15.

[145]The suggestion was made in Prescott's speech opening the legislature on Jan. 7, 1836.

[146]C.O. 194/94, ff. 253-7.

[147]GN2/2 (Sept.-Dec., 1835), pp. 92-4; C.O. 194/94, f. 81.

[148]C.O. 194/94, ff. 63-6 (Harbour Grace petition). See Kent's letter about the Carbonear petition, Dec. 24, 1835, f. 72.

[149]*Public Ledger*, Feb. 12, 1836.

[150]Carson had published Neaven's account of this in 1834 in the *Patriot*. See C.O. 194/88, ff. 90-91, 117.

[151]For an account of the episode, including Fleming's letter, see C.O. 194/94, ff. 178-84; also *Public Ledger*, Feb. 26, 1836.

[152]6 Wm. IV, c. 13; *ALN* (1836), pp. 57-8.

[153]C.O. 194/94, f. 318.

[154]C.O. 194/94, ff. 375-6.

[155]C.O. 194/95, ff. 50-64.

[156]C.O. 194/95, ff. 65-6.

[157]See Glenelg's response, C.O. 194/95, ff. 46-9.

[158]*Public Ledger*, July 12, 1836.

[159]See C.O. 194/95, ff. 9-13.

[160]See *Public Ledger*, Sept. 13, 1836.

[161]*Public Ledger*, Aug. 23, 1836; see the *Patriot*, Oct. 26, 1836.

[162]As Prescott described them in December, C.O. 194/95, f. 194. The Carbonear crowd included women and children.

[163]See the magistrates' report on the election, C.O. 194/95, ff. 206-12; for depositions, see ff. 228-41.

[164]Levi's house was attacked twice. See C.O. 194/95, f. 220.

[165]C.O. 194/95, ff. 360-5.

[166]C.O. 194/95, f. 166; see also ff. 159-63.

[167]The terms "orange Catholics," "mad dogs," and "wolves" were applied to Catholics who were politically opposed to the priests. See C.O. 194/95, f. 284. It was Morris who evidently started using "mad dogs" of such people in Newfoundland. It was an import from Ireland (FitzGerald, "Conflict and Culture," p. 190).

[168]*Public Ledger*, Nov. 25, 1836. Winton had informers who kept him abreast of transactions in the Catholic chapel. The events (including the sermon) are mostly confirmed by depositions given afterwards. See C.O. 195/95, ff. 304-8.

[169]In an account of the subsequent trial of Patrick Brawders, Troy is said to have "advanced towards the gallery stairs leading to Mr. Scanlan's pew" (C.O. 194/97, f. 105); but Joseph Shea later said the Troy did not leave the altar (House of Commons, Select Committee [1841], "Minutes of Evidence," p. 90). Shea was not present at the mass, but was told of events by one who attended.

[170]See his deposition, C.O. 194/95, ff. 306-7.

[171]For a list of such atrocities, most attested to in other documents, see C.O. 194/97, f. 420-3.

[172]*Newfoundlander*, Oct. 20, 1836.

[173]Simms said, in Feb., 1837, that the military wasn't called out until the 15th (C.O. 194/97, f. 100); but this conflicts with earlier accounts by Winton and Prescott.

[174]See the three defeated candidates' letter of protest, C.O. 194/95, ff. 266-73; various depositions, ff. 276-310; *Public Ledger*, Nov. 15, 25, 1836.

[175]For a list of elected members, with their politics, when known, defined, see *Public Ledger*, Dec. 2, 1836.

[176]See Winton's comments, *Public Ledger*, Dec. 9, 1836.

[177]Especially Carson and Kent; the latter threatened that St. John's would be burnt if a soldier killed a reform supporter.

[178]House of Assembly, *Address of the House of Assembly of Newfoundland* ([St. John's], 1839), p. 5.

[179]See Boulton's letter of Aug. 25, 1836, and the answer to it, C.O. 194/96, ff. 187-90; also ff. 191-2. The position in question was commissioner for the sale of crown lands and clergy reserves.

[180]For accounts of the trials, see C.O. 194/97, ff. 97-113.

[181]He was also sentenced to enter into recognizances to keep the peace for 12 months, himself in £50 and two sureties of £25 each; the court normally added such recognizances to the sentences in these trials.

[182]C.O. 194/97, ff. 105-6.

[183]And to enter into recognizances of the peace for 12 mos., himself in £100, and two sureties of £50 each.

[184]Petty juries were the normal trial juries in civil or criminal cases. These jurors were, said Simms, "chiefly shopkeepers, coopers, carpenters and other tradesmen." He estimated that seven-tenths of them were Irish and Catholic. See C.O. 194/97, f. 118.

[185]C.O. 194/97, f. 94.

[186]A trial jury; under normal circumstances it would be used much less frequently than petty juries, but in Newfoundland in the mid to late 1830s it was in fact often called. The jurors were of a higher station in life from those on petty juries, and in Newfoundland were "nearly all Protestants." See Simms' comment, C.O. 194/97, f. 118.

[187]And to enter into recognizances to keep the peace for 12 months, in sum of £100 each, and two sureties of £50 each. See C.O. 194/97, ff. 110-13. Thomey had earlier been separately convicted of an assault against Thomas Gosse.

[188]*Newfoundland Patriot*, Mar. 11, 1837.

[189]C.O. 194/97, ff. 157-72.

[190]See the comments by Boulton and the two assistant judges, C.O. 194/97, ff. 340-41.

[191]Fleming to Glenelg, Jan. 10, 1837 (C.O. 194/99, ff. 212-28).

[192]See Fleming's pastoral letter in Dec., 1837 (*Newfoundland Patriot*, Dec. 30, 1837). A jubilee is a time of rejoicing, pardon, and "enlarged Indulgence."

[193]C.O. 194/100, f. 33.

[194]C.O. 195/19, pp. 11-12.

[195]His proclamation on the invalid writs is C.O. 194/97, ff. 34-5; the crown lawyers' view, that the election was in fact valid, is dated Oct. 17, 1837 (/98, ff. 357-8).

[196]C.O. 194/97, ff. 147-50.

[197]*Public Ledger*, Nov. 22 & 25, 1836.

[198]See Stephen's comment in Apr., 1837, C.O. 194/97, f. 77.

[199]*Public Ledger*, July 28, 1837.

[200]For an accurate list of returned candidates, see Gunn, *Political History*, p. 195.

[201]McCann, "Bishop Fleming," p. 90.

[202]See *Newfoundland Patriot*, May 6, 1837; Carson was awarded £10 damages.

[203]See C.O. 194/97, ff. 441-520; *Public Ledger*, May 19, 1837. The trial ended in a nonsuit.

[204]*Public Ledger*, June 20, 1837; the petition to the Queen (C.O. 194/98, ff. 256-65), with 3,268 signatures, was sent to London in December.

[205]For comments on the Nisbet case, see C.O. 194/101, ff. 83-4, 96-100.

[206]*Newfoundlander*, July 6, 1837.

[207]See Simms' comment, C.O. 194/98, f. 266.

[208]C.O. 194/97, f. 437; see Winton's comment, *Public Ledger*, July 28, 1837.

[209]See surveyor general Joseph Noad's answers to Prescott's queries, C.O. 194/98, ff. 185-8.

[210]*Public Ledger*, May 3, 1836.

[211]*Newfoundland Patriot*, Mar. 11, 1837.

[212]C.O. 194/96, f. 170. On the Newfoundland School Society, see chapter 7, note 200. A Low-Churchman was a member of the Church of England, but evangelical in outlook.

[213]"Entomologia Terrae Novae" (1828-35). It remains in manuscript in the National Museum of Natural Sciences, Ottawa.

[214]Doyle, *Newfoundlander in Exile*, pp. 11-13.

[215]See C.O. 194/98, ff. 508-10.

[216]Gosse, "Anecdotes and Reminiscences," ed. Ronald Rompkey, *NS*, 6, 2 (1990): 260-64.

[217]C.O. 194/98, ff. 499-501.

[218]Morris, *Speech delivered in the House of Assembly, on Friday, August 25, 1837* ([St. John's, 1837]), p. 12.

[219]Colbert v. Howley; see Boulton's account of it and related cases, C.O. 194/99, ff. 146-65.

[220]The law in 1817 still gave the servant access to the merchant's fish and oil for his wages. See House of Commons, Select Committee (1817), *Report*, p. 8. Clause 10 of 5 Geo. IV (1824) ordered "That all the Fish and Oil which shall be taken and made by the Person or Persons who shall hire or employ [fishermen] shall be subject and liable in the first Place to the Payment of the Wages or Shares of every such [fisherman]." This law had expired; but Boulton ruled that while the clause gave "a sort of lien" on the fish and oil while the planter had it, it did not do so once the supplying merchant possessed it. See Cadigan's analysis of this case and its repercussions, *Hope and Deception*, pp. 147-55.

[221]For Bolton's plea of trespass, see C.O. 194/103, f. 431. The case was tried in the supreme court in December, 1837, but the two assistant judges, Augustus Wallet DesBarres and Brenton, decided they were "not competent" to proceed with it (f. 437). For the Assembly petition, see C.O. 194/98, ff. 171-6.

[222]*Times* (St. John's), Nov. 28, 1838.

[223]*Petition of the Merchants, Traders, and other Inhabitants of St. John's* ([St. John's], 1837), pp. 4, 9, 13-14.

[224]*Petition of the Chamber of Commerce of St. John's, Newfoundland* (1) ([St. John's], 1838).

[225]"Supplies" were moneys needed to defray the costs of the public service.

[226]Contingent expenses were those miscellaneous and other charges needed for the operation of the legislature. They were normally met by a separate contingency bill.

[227]See his letter on this subject, *Public Ledger*, July 6, 1838.

[228]GN2/2 (July-Dec., 1837), pp. 679 ff.; (Jan.-Dec., 1838), pp. 1, 15-17, 20-01, 28-30.

[229]House of Commons, Select Committee (1841), Correspondence, 1835-8, pp. 103-6 (Council); C.O. 194/98, ff. 416-8 (Assembly). Both are dated Nov. 18, 1837.

[230]The House repeated the request for amalgamation in a petition to Lord Durham in 1838. See *JHA* (1838), p. 81.

[231]Morris spent most of his time overseas in Ireland. Carson soon went to visit his brother James Carson, M.D., in Liverpool, and his ancestral home in Kircudbright, Scotland. Nugent did most of the delegation's work.

[232]See the instructions, C.O. 194/103, ff. 6a-6b.

[233]See Prescott's answers to them, C.O. 194/100, ff. 299-308, /101, ff. 70-90.

[234]Thompson, *French Shore Problem*, p. 29.

[235]*Newfoundland Patriot*, Dec. 16, 1837. Boulton's removal, Carson says, is his "sole purpose" in going to England.

[236]Mar. 3, 1838.

[237]Select Committee (1841), Correspondence, 1835-8, pp. 101-2.

[238]*Ibid.*, p. 102.

[239]Synonymous here with supply bill.

[240]*Ibid.*, pp. 123-4.

[241]Select Committee (1841), Correspondence, 1838-9, pp. 1-2.

[242]In fact, he had to wait a while longer to get it. He was finally given the land in Apr., 1839 (C.O. 194/102, ff. 105-6).

[243]In his commission, Durham was appointed governor general of Newfoundland as well as of the other colonies, and his *Report* includes brief passages relating to the island. But he didn't visit Newfoundland and admitted he knew little about it. Nugent may have contributed to the misunderstanding about Newfoundland that is evident in the report. See *Lord Durham's Report*, ed. Gerald M. Craig (Toronto: McClelland and Stewart, 1968), pp. 13-15, 52, 109-10, 166-7.

[244]It didn't actually do so until 1839 (C.O. 194/101, ff. 209-11).

[245]See the *Newfoundland Patriot*, Apr. 7, May 5, 1838.

[246]July 21, 1838.

[247]*Newfoundland Patriot*, May 12, 1838.

[248]It predates the recommendation to the same effect in Lord Durham's *Report* by eight months. See *Lord Durham's Report*, pp. 166-7. But news of Durham's plan circulated in Sept., 1838; Winton opposed the *"federal union of the Provinces."* The inclusion of Newfoundland, he said, was "fraught with the most serious mischiefs" (*Public Ledger*, Sept. 24, 1838).

[249]*Public Ledger*, July 6, 1838.

[250]House of Commons, Select Committee (1841), Correspondence, 1835-8, p. 123.

[251]Lahey (*DCB*, vol. 7, pp. 293) notes that Fleming recruited 36 priests for Newfoundland. I gather from his carefully written paragraph that they were all Irish, but he doesn't specifically say that. He notes that Fleming "refused to accept native Newfoundlanders as candidates for the priesthood."

[252]The sermon (at least a version of it) was widely circulated. See *Public Ledger*, Mar. 8, 1836.

[253]A trace of such feeling can be detected in some of his comments, e.g., this, during the 1836 election: "we will serve [the tories] like Newfoundland dogs — we will give them a good thrashing and they will like us the better for it" (C.O. 194/95, f. 298). But his remarks at the St. Patrick's Day dinner in 1838 sound a different tune (*Patriot*, Mar. 31, 1838).

[254]*Newfoundland Patriot*, Aug. 4 & 11, 1838 (reporting July debates).

[255]Winton said bail ("which was of course very shortly found") was given for his appearance next day at the House (*Public Ledger*, Aug. 7, 1838), but in his later plea to the supreme court Kielley said he was kept in Beck's house overnight (C.O. 199/19, f. 27).

[256]*Public Ledger*, Aug. 10, 1838.

[257]Morris and Nugent weren't in the House during these proceedings. The latter didn't return from Europe until October; nor did Fleming.

[258]*JHA* (1838), pp. 69-70.

[259]The details of his interrogation are from Kielley's sworn deposition of August 9. See House of Commons, Select Committee (1841), Correspondence, 1838-9, p. 5.

[260]P. O'Flaherty, "George Lilly," *DCB*, vol. 7, pp. 507-8.

[261]The writ had been applied for by Bryan Robinson, lawyer for Kielley, on Aug. 9; Lilly granted the writ, returnable before him, on the 10th. For Kielley's petition to Lilly from jail on the 9th, see C.O. 194/100, f. 221; Lilly's discharge order is f. 230.

[262]See *Newfoundland Patriot*, Aug. 18, 1838. Beck and his men were refused admittance at Winton's home.

[263]See Lilly's account of his arrest, House of Commons, Select Committee (1841), Correspondence, 1838-9, pp. 12-13.

[264]Stephen in the colonial office appeared to doubt the "propriety" of proroguing the House in these circumstances. See C.O. 194/102, f. 94.

[265]His judgment is C.O. 194/100, ff. 231-51. How far Lilly was responsible for the judgments he delivered is not clear. E.M. Archibald, chief clerk and registrar of the supreme court, and Bryan Robinson, Kielley's lawyer, later took credit for them, or part of them. But they may have presented arguments which Lilly then rendered into his judgments.

[266]*Public Ledger*, Aug. 17, 1838; *Royal Gazette*, Aug. 21, 1838.

[267]See Parsons' comments, *Patriot*, July 21, 1838.

[268] *JHA* (1838; 3rd session), pp. 28-9.

[269] *Public Ledger*, Aug. 14, 1838; there had, in fact, been no "charter" as such, but his point was clear.

[270] Cited in *NQ*, 83, 1 (87), p. 33.

[271] House of Commons, Select Committee (1841), Correspondence, 1838-9, p. 1.

[272] FitzGerald, "Conflict and Culture," pp. 191-2.

[273] *Public Ledger*, Aug. 21, 1838.

[274] See his cringing letter to Fleming on Aug. 2, 1838 (C.O. 194/102, ff. 286-7).

[275] *Public Ledger*, Aug. 31, 1838. Fleming was thought to have been born in Co. Tipperary.

[276] *Public Ledger*, Aug. 17, 1838.

[277] *Patriot*, Dec. 30, 1837; see *Public Ledger*, Jan. 2, 1838. Winton had been drawing links between local and Canadian reformers since 1835.

[278] House of Commons, Select Committee (1841), Correspondence, 1838-9, pp. 24-6.

[279] House of Commons, *Newfoundland. Return to an Address of the Honourable The House of Commons* ([London], 1839), pp. 15-17.

[280] *Ibid.*, pp. 18-20.

[281] *Petition of the Chamber of Commerce of St. John's, Newfoundland* (2) ([St. John's], 1838), pp. 7, 14, 16.

[282] See *Public Ledger*, Jan. 1 & 4, 1839.

[283] *Newfoundlander*, Jan. 10, 1839.

[284] *Royal Gazette*, Apr. 16, 1839. In their decision of Dec. 3, 1838, the crown lawyers expressed some hesitation, and recommended the issue be sent to the judicial committee.

[285] C.O. 194/101, f. 291.

[286] House of Commons, *Newfoundland. Return to an Address*, pp. 18-29.

[287] See a report of the Lords' proceedings, *Royal Gazette*, May 28, 1839.

[288] *A Letter to the most noble the Marquis of Normandy* (London, 1839), p. 20.

[289] *Petition of the Chamber of Commerce* (1), p. 11.

[290] *Public Ledger*, Apr. 9, 1839.

[291] *Public Ledger*, Oct. 26, 1838.

[292] His full report, dated Sept. 12, 1838, is C.O. 194/101, ff. 18-33, 47-51.

[293] Jukes, *Excursions in and about Newfoundland, during the Years 1839 and 1840*, 2. vols. (London: 1842), vol. 1, p. 121.

[294] He was actually directed to the coal by others. The Micmac Sulleon showed him the coal deposit near Grand Lake, and a settler named Stephen Shears did the same in St. George's Bay.

[295] I.e., advantage (*OED*).

[296] *Ibid.*, vol. 1, p. 41.

[297] *Ibid.*, pp. 134-5.

[298] An inlet of Bonavista Bay.

[299] For his comments on politics and society, see *Ibid.*, pp. 232-44.

[300] C.O. 194/102, ff. 55, 57; *DCB*, vol. 10, p. 688.

[301] C.O. 194/105, f. 153.

[302] Demands came from the coast between Twillingate and Bay Bulls, including St. John's (C.O. 194/106, ff. 270-2).

[303] See C.O. 194/105, ff. 313-30 for relevant correspondence.

[304] House of Commons, *Papers relative to the Constitution of Newfoundland* ([London, 1839]), pp. 4-8.

[305] C.O. 194/106, f. 22.

[306] Who told the House of Lords in late August, 1839, that reports of "general confusion" in Newfoundland were "much exaggerated" (C.O. 194/109, f. 226).

[307] C.O. 194/108, f. 13.

[308] House of Assembly, *Address of the House of Assembly*, pp. 5, 18, 20.

[309] Dated Jan. 13, 1840 (C.O. 194/108, ff. 108-10).

[310] C.O. 194/108, ff. 67-73.

[311]Along with two others sent in February; see an extract from an address by the Assembly to Prescott, Apr. 23, 1840 (C.O. 194/108, ff. 231-3).

[312]I.e., one that authorized the raising of revenue, in this case through duties.

[313]C.O. 194/108, ff. 240-51.

[314]See Carson's letter, *Newfoundland Patriot*, May 2, 1840.

[315]See C.O. 194/108, ff. 229, 329-32.

[316]House of Assembly, *Address of the House of Assembly*, p. 9.

[317]The treasurer's office became vacant on the death of Newman Hoyles in February, 1840. Morris immediately assumed the duties of treasurer. For the relevant correspondence, see C.O. 194/108, ff. 135-7; also House of Commons, Select Committee (1841), "Minutes of Evidence," p. 103.

[318]*Newfoundland Patriot*, Apr. 18, 1840; for Carson's response, see *Newfoundlander*, Apr. 23, 1840.

[319]GN2/2 (Sept.-Dec., 1840), p. 138; (Jan.-Mar., 1841), p. 24. This second letter reveals that Fleming had signed a recognizance for Morris, but now (Jan. 11, 1841) wanted to have his signature returned "as early as convenient." His signing of the bond was reported in the press, and his change of heart was said to be due to this. But he could also have learned unsettling news in the confessional — or perhaps from a priest who'd heard it there.

[320]C.O. 194/112, f. 58.

[321]From the medical report by Dr. Stirling, May 16, 1840 (GN2/2 [Jan.-June, 1840], p. 160). Lott said simply that his ears were "cut off." His ears were in fact located near the scene of the assault. See pp. 119 ff. for other details of the Lott case.

[322]See *Public Ledger*, May 22, 1840, for an account of the interrogation.

[323]A secret society dedicated to the overthrow of Protestantism and British rule in Ireland.

[324]So Winton said; *Public Ledger*, May 22, 1840.

[325]See their letter to Prescott on Apr. 13, 1840 (C.O. 194/108, f. 357).

[326]C.O. 194/108, ff. 339, 358.

[327]See Prescott's description of him, C.O. 194/109, f. 9. Other documents are ff. 8-11. See David Davis, "Laurence O'Brien," *DCB*, vol. 9, pp. 604-6.

[328]*Newfoundland Patriot*, May 22, 1840.

[329]See C.O. 194/109, ff. 40-1.

[330]GN2/2 (Jan.-June, 1840), pp. 180-1.

[331]C.O 194/109, f. 9.

[332]C.O. 194/109, f. 12.

[333]See Aubin's letter, Dec. 5, 1840 (C.O. 194/110, ff. 50-2; also ff. 41-6).

[334]*DCB*, vol. 7, p. 297.

[335]*Newfoundland Patriot*, July 11, 1840.

[336]See *Newfoundland Patriot*, Aug. 25, 1840.

[337]See letters from "Copper-coloured native" and "Another 'copper-coloured native'" in *Public Ledger*, June 12 & 16, 1840. Winton noted (on the 16th) that Nugent's "offence" was "given under exciting circumstances, in the course of an election." See Winton's comment (*Ledger*, June 19), affirming that Nugent had made the remark. Parsons also said Nugent made it (*Newfoundland Patriot*, Sept. 22, 1840) and noted its "stimulus" to the forming of the Natives' Society.

[338]See his letter to the *Newfoundlander*, June 18, 1840.

[339]P. O'Flaherty, "The Newfoundland Natives' Society," *ENL*, vol. 4, pp. 21-7. Phillip McCann has argued that successive British administrations in 1832-55 "fostered and promoted a nativist culture" so that "patriotism and local culture" might be "invented." See his "Culture, State Formation and the Invention of Tradition: Newfoundland 1832-1855," *Journal of Canadian Studies*, 23, nos. 1-2 (1988): 86-103. This view lacks support in the documents I have seen.

[340]July 11, 1840.

[341]*Newfoundland Patriot*, Sept. 15, 1840.

[342]*Newfoundland Patriot*, Oct. 17, 1840.

[343]See *Public Ledger*, Sept. 8, 1840. On Sept. 11, Winton commented: "the fact is notorious that the Roman Catholic clergy are opposed to the establishment of this Natives' Society, and what more natural than that they should oppose it from the Altar."

[344]See, for instance, the letters by "Cato" and "An Elector" in *Public Ledger*, June 5 & July 17, 1840,

[345]See relevant documents, C.O. 194/109, ff. 285-90, 330, 334, 337, 342-3, 356.

[346]This was H.A. Emerson's conclusion, after an 11-day inquiry (C.O. 194/111, f. 4).

[347]See the magistrates' report, Dec. 10, 1840 (C.O. 194/109, f. 342); Emerson later said 700 men had been in arms on Dec. 8 and 9 to fend off the Carbonear "ruffian band" (/111, f. 4)

[348]C.O. 194/109, f. 342.

[349]C.O. 194/109, f. 290.

[350]C.O. 194/109, f. 285.

[351]C.O. 194/109, f. 337.

[352]C.O. 194/111, f. 29.

[353]See his pamphlet, *A Sketch of the State of Affairs in Newfoundland* (London: 1841), pp. 16-18.

[354]C.O. 194/111, f. 37.

[355]C.O. 195/19, pp. 387-8.

[356]C.O. 194/111, f. 393.

[357]*Newfoundland Patriot*, Apr. 21, 1841.

[358]So limited by 6 Wm. IV, c. 7; *ALN* (1836), p. 28.

[359]C.O. 194/111, f. 108.

[360]I.e., decided.

[361]C.O. 194/114, f. 39. This is from an internal colonial office memo written in 1842 by Lord Stanley, who is describing the actions of "the late govt.," i.e., Melbourne's ministry. Stanley, colonial secretary in Peel's administration, received the seals of the colonial department on Sept. 6, 1841. Shortly after assuming his office, he wrote of the action of "Her Majesty's late servants" in "directing the suspension of the Representative and Legislative privileges conferred upon the Island in 1832" (see Stanley to governor Harvey, Nov. 19, 1841, C.O. 194/112, ff. 302-3). I assume he refers to a formal decision taken by the prior administration, though they might simply have chosen not to call the Assembly together until modifications in the constitution were made. Either way, what amounts to a suspension took place. When O'Connell in the Commons debate of 1842 "denied that the noble lord had found the constitution suspended," Stanley answered that his new bill (see below) would "confer certain rights which had been suspended by his predecessors" — again pointing to a formal suspension. See also Gunn, *Political History*, pp. 77 ff., where, however, this question is not directly addressed.

[362]C.O. 194/112, f. 306.

[363]Though the evidence of Henry Geary, a soldier and Catholic convert, has to be read as a counter to Shea's. See House of Commons, Select Committee (1841), "Minutes of Evidence," pp. 79-97 (Shea) and 97-108 (Geary). O'Connell, a member of the committee, was evidently not present to hear Shea, but carefully drew out Geary's views.

[364]Keith Matthews, "Thomas Holdsworth Brooking," *DCB*, vol. 9, pp. 84-6; for Brooking's testimony, see House of Commons, Select Committee (1841), "Minutes of Evidence," pp. 21-49.

[365]House of Commons, Select Committee (1817), *Report*, p. 21.

[366]C.O. 194/87, f. 88.

[367]The Queen dissolved Parliament June 23, thereby interrupting, and in effect ending, the committee's work.

[368]*Newfoundlander*, May 13, 1841.

[369]*Public Ledger,* May 21, 1841.

[370]C.O. 194/112, ff. 259-60.

[371]See C.O. 194/112, ff. 270-2, and Stephen's comment, f. 276.

[372]*Public Ledger*, Dec. 3, 1841. There were, Winton wrote, "various reasons" why Morris should not have been appointed councillor and colonial treasurer. See Morris's letter in the *Newfoundlander*, May 5, 1842.

[373]House of Commons, Select Committee (1841), "Minutes of Evidence," p. 46.

[374]C.O. 194/112, ff. 308-11.

[375]Kent, O'Brien, Brown, and, as chairman, Nugent. Their representations to the colonial office (or rather those of the last three; Kent's signature is missing) are C.O. 194/113, ff. 410-43.

[376]See his long article, *Newfoundland Patriot*, Sept. 29, 1840.

[377]C.O. 194/113, ff. 218-9.

[378]See their petition to Stanley of Sept. 5, 1842 (C.O. 194/115, ff. 39-41).

[379]See "A Few Words to the Labouring Classes," *Newfoundlander*, Dec. 8, 1842.

[380]*Public Ledger*, Aug. 16, 1842.

[381]C.O. 194/114, f. 143.

[382]C.O. 194/114, f. 250; for a report on the meeting, see *Public Ledger*, Mar. 25 & 29, 1842; also Apr. 12, for ridicule of the petition.

[383]*Royal Gazette*, June 28, 1842.

[384]For the petition, see *Public Ledger*, Aug. 30, 1842; the Commons debates in July and August are reported Aug. 23 and Sept. 6.

[385]*Public Ledger*, Aug. 23, 1842. Stanley told Harvey of the meeting with Fleming in London: "I think that he was sensible of the injury which had been done by [his clergy's] active interference on former occasions" (C.O. 195/20, p. 108). Fleming had returned to St. John's from Europe in late April.

[386]C.O. 194/115, f. 66; see *Royal Gazette*, Sept. 23, 1842, for Harvey's new commission; for the act, see *PC*, vol. 1, pp. 323-5.

[387]C.O. 195/20, pp. 99-108.

[388]*Public Ledger*, May 1, 1846. But on July 5, 1842, he said, reluctantly, that Stanley's bill was "the best that could have been devised."

[389]And the as yet unchosen speaker (C.O. 194/114, f. 90).

[390]C.O. 194/114, ff. 336-8.

[391]*Public Ledger*, Mar. 4, 1842.

[392]*Newfoundlander*, Nov. 10, 1842.

[393]*Newfoundlander*, Dec. 1, 1842.

[394]*Newfoundlander*, Dec. 22, 1842.

[395]For documents on the libel suits, see GN5/2/A/1 (supreme court) (1839-42), June 13, 1842 (Carter v. Nugent); (central circuit court) (1839-44) May 13-20, 1842 (Simms v. Nugent); also *Newfoundlander*, May 16, 1842, *Newfoundland Patriot*, Dec. 14, 21, 1842.

[396]See Harvey to Stanley, Dec. 21, 1842 (C.O. 194/115, ff. 183-5) for a full account of the incident.

[397]See GN2/2 (Sept.-Dec., 1842), pp. 171-84.

[398]Pamela Bruce, "Richard Barnes," *DCB*, vol. 7, pp. 48-9.

[399]J.K. Hiller, "Robert Carter," *DCB*, vol. 10, p. 141.

[400]*JHA* (1843), pp. 19, 21. Carter seconded the motion to elect Archibald.

[401]*Newfoundland Patriot*, Jan. 25, 1843.

[402]*Newfoundland Patriot*, Feb. 22, 1843.

Note to Chapter 9

[1]See P. O'Flaherty, "'Holding the Baby': Parliamentary Responses in Britain and Newfoundland to the Crisis of [1933]," *NQ*, 91, 2 (1997): 23-32.

[2]*The New York Review of Books* (Mar. 18, 1999), p. 50.

[3]*Public Ledger*, Aug. 23, 1842. At this point O'Connell was actually quoting an unnamed "writer."

[4]Stephen's description, C.O. 194/100, ff. 43-4.

[5]Maier, *American Scripture*, pp. 59 ff.

Abbreviations
(asterisked items have entries in the Bibliography)

ALN   *Acts of the Legislature of Newfoundland*
CHR   *Canadian Historical Review*
CNS   Centre for Newfoundland Studies, Queen Elizabeth II Library, MUN
C.O.   Colonial Office documents, PRO (mfm., CNS or Maritime History Archive, MUN)
CSP   *Calendar of State Papers, Colonial Series, America and West Indies*
DCB   *Dictionary of Canadian Biography**
ENL   *Encyclopedia of Newfoundland and Labrador**
GN   Government of Newfoundland, papers and correspondence, PANL
HAC   *Historical Atlas of Canada**
JHA   *Journals of the House of Assembly of Newfoundland*
mfm.   microfilm
MUN   Memorial University of Newfoundland, St. John's
NAW   *New American World**
NQ   *Newfoundland Quarterly*
NS   *Newfoundland Studies*
OED   *The Oxford English Dictionary*
PANL   Provincial Archives of Newfoundland and Labrador, St. John's
p.c.   personal communication
PC   *In the Privy Council**
PRO   Public Record Office, Kew, London, England
RA   review article
SUK   *Statutes of the United Kingdom**

Bibliography
(Included are books, pamphlets, articles, reports, unpublished papers, and theses cited in the text or notes.)

Anspach, Lewis Amadeus, *A History of the Island of Newfoundland* (London: 1819)
Baker, Melvin, "The Government of St. John's, Newfoundland 1800-1921" (Ph.D. thes., Univ. of Western Ontario, 1980)
Bannister, Jerry, "The Campaign for Representative Government in Newfoundland," *Canadian Historical Association Journal*, N.S., 5 (1994): 19-40
——————, "Convict Transportation and the Colonial State in Newfoundland, 1789," *Acadiensis*, 27, 2 (1998): 95-123
Barkham, Michael, "French Basque 'New Found Land' Entrepreneurs and the Import of Codfish and Whale Oil to Northern Spain, c. 1580 to c. 1620 ...," *NS*, 10, 1 (1994): 1-43
——————, rev. of J.-P. Proulx, *Basque Whaling in Labrador in the 16th Century*, in *NS*, 10, 2 (1994): 260-86

Barkham, Selma, "The Spanish Province of Terranova," *The Canadian Archivist*, 2, 5 (1974): 73-83
——————, "Two documents written in Labrador, 1572 and 1577," *CHR*, 57, 2 (1976): 235-8
——————, "The Basques: filling a gap in our history between Jacques Cartier and Champlain," *Canadian Geographical Journal*, 96, 1 (1978): 8-19
——————, "A note on the Strait of Belle Isle during the period of Basque contact with Indians and Inuit," *Etudes Inuit Studies*, 4, 1-2 (1980): 51-8
——————, "Documentary Evidence for 16th Century Basque Whaling Ships in the Strait of Belle Isle," in *Early European Settlement*, pp. 53-95
——————, *The Basque Coast of Newfoundland* (n.p.: Great Northern Peninsula Development Corp., 1989)
Baudoin, Jean, "Journal of Abbé Baudoin," trans. H. Bedford-Jones, *Daily News* (St. John's: 1923) (CNS)
Beverley, Robert, *The History and Present State of Virginia* (1705), ed. Louis B. Wright (Chapel Hill: Univ. of North Carolina Press, 1947)
Biggar, H.P., *The Precursors of Jacques Cartier 1497-1534* (Ottawa: Government Printing Bureau, 1911)
[Boulton, Henry John], *Rules and Regulations to be observed in the Legislative Council of Newfoundland* (St. John's: 1834)
Bridenbaugh, Carl, *Vexed and Troubled Englishmen 1590-1642* (New York: Oxford Univ. Press, 1968)
["Britannicus"], *Observations on the Present State of Newfoundland, in reference to its Courts of Justice, Local Government, and Trade* (London: 1823)
Brown, Stuart C., "Far Other Worlds and Other Seas: The Context of Claims for Pre-Columbian European Contact with North America," *NS*, 9, 2 (1993): 235-59
——————, rev. of B.D. Fardy, *Leifsburdir*, in *NS*, 10, 2 (1994): 287-95
Bruce, Pamela, "Richard Barnes," *DCB*, vol. 7 (1988), pp. 48-9
Bumstead, J.M., and K. Matthews, "Thomas Tremlett," *DCB*, vol. 6 (1987), pp. 784-6
Burke, Edmund, *Thoughts on the Present Discontents, and Speeches* (London: Cassell & Co., 1886)
Cadigan, Sean, "Artisans in a Merchant Town: St. John's, Newfoundland, 1775-1816," *Canadian Historical Association Journal*, N.S., 4 (1993): 95-119
——————, *Hope and Deception in Conception Bay: Merchant-Settler Relations in Newfoundland, 1785-1855* (Toronto: Univ. of Toronto Press, 1995)
The Cambridge History of the British Empire, ed. J.H. Rose, A.P. Newton, and E.A. Benians, vol. 6 (Canada and Newfoundland) (New York: Macmillan, 1930)
Candow, James E., "The British Army in Newfoundland, 1697-1824," *NQ*, 79, 4 (1984): 21-8
Carson, William, *A Letter to the Members of Parliament of the United Kingdom* (Greenock, Scot.: 1812)
——————, *Reasons for Colonizing the Island of Newfoundland, in a Letter addressed to the Inhabitants* (Greenock: 1813)
Cartwright, George, *A Journal of Transactions and Events, during a Residence of nearly Sixteen Years on the Coast of Labrador*, 3. vols. (Newark: 1792)
Cell, Gillian T., "John Guy," *DCB*, vol. 1 (1966), pp. 349-51
——————, "Sir Francis Tanfield," *DCB*, vol. 1, p. 632
——————, *English Enterprise in Newfoundland 1577-1660* (Toronto: Univ. of Toronto Press, 1969)
——————, ed. *Newfoundland Discovered: English Attempts at Colonisation, 1610-1630* (London: Hakluyt Society, 1982)

—————, "The Cupids Cove Settlement: A Case Study of the Problems of Early Colonisation," in *Early European Settlement*, pp. 97-114

Christensen, Ruth M., "The Establishment of S.P.G. Missions in Newfoundland, 1703-1783," *Historical Magazine of the Protestant Episcopal Church*, 20 (1951): 207-29

Clark, Charles E., *The Eastern Frontier: The Settlement of Northern New England 1610-1763* (New York: Alfred A. Knopf, 1970)

Constitutional Documents of the Reign of James I: A.D. 1603-1625, with commentary by J.R. Tanner (Cambridge: Univ. Press, 1960)

Cook, James, *Directions For Navigating the West-Coast of Newfoundland, with a Chart thereof* (London: 1768)

Corish, Patrick J., "The Irish Catholics at the End of the Penal Era," in *Religion and Identity*, pp. 1-17

Cormack, W.E., "Account of a journey across the island of Newfoundland," *Edinburgh Philosophical Journal*, 10 (1824): 156-62

Coughlan, Laurence, *An Account of the Work of God, in Newfoundland, North-America* (London: 1776)

Coward, Barry, *The Stuart Age: A history of England 1603-1714* (London: Longman, 1980)

Craig, Gerald M, *Upper Canada: The Formative Years, 1784-1841* (Toronto: McClelland and Stewart, 1963)

Creighton, Phyllis, "Edward Troy," *DCB*, vol. 10 (1972), pp. 687-8

Crowley, John E., "Empire versus Truck: The Official Interpretation of Debt and Labour in the Eighteenth-Century Newfoundland Fishery," *CHR*, 70, 3 (1989): 311-36

Curran, Christopher P., "The Judicature Act: A History of the Early Acts," in *Legislative History of the Judicature Act 1791-1988* ([St. John's]: Newfoundland Law Reform Commission, 1989), pp. 1-18

Davies, A., "João Fernandes," *DCB*, vol. 1 (1966), pp. 304-5

Davis, David J., "William Bickford Row," *DCB*, vol. 9 (1976), pp. 694-5

—————, "Laurence O'Brien," *DCB*, vol. 9, pp. 604-6

Defoe, Daniel, *A Tour Through the Whole Island of Great Britain* (1724-6), 2 vols. (London: Dent, 1962)

Dickens, Charles, *Oliver Twist* (Harmondsworth, U.K.: Penguin Books, 1981)

Dictionary of Canadian Biography, 14 vols. (Toronto: Univ. of Toronto Press, 1966-98, in progress)

Doyle, Marjorie, *Newfoundlander in Exile: The Life and Times of Philip Tocque* (Halifax: John Doull Books, 1997)

Draper, Theodore, *A Struggle for Power: The American Revolution* (New York: Vintage Books, 1997)

Early European Settlement and Exploitation in Atlantic Canada: Selected Papers, ed. G.M. Story (St. John's: MUN, 1982)

Encyclopedia of Newfoundland and Labrador, ed. J.R. Smallwood and Cyril Poole, 5 vols. (St. John's: Newfoundland Book Publishers [1967] Ltd., and Harry Cuff Publications Ltd. [for the J.R. Smallwood Heritage Foundation], 1981-94)

Farmer, G.H., "The Cold Ocean Environment of Newfoundland," in *Natural Environment*, pp. 56-82

Field, A.M., "The Development of Government in Newfoundland, 1638-1713" (M.A. thes., Univ. of London, 1924)

FitzGerald, John, "Conflict and Culture in Irish-Newfoundland Roman Catholicism, 1829-1850" (Ph.D. thes., Univ. of Ottawa, 1997)

Fleming, M.A., *Letters on the State of Religion in Newfoundland, addressed to the Very Rev. Dr. A. O'Connell* (Dublin: 1844)

Gentlemen-Bishops and Faction Fighters: The Letters of Bishops O Donel, Lambert, Scallan and Other Irish Missionaries, ed. C.J. Byrne (St. John's: Jesperson Press, 1984)

Gilbert, William, "'Divers Places': The Beothuk Indians and John Guy's Voyage into Trinity Bay in 1612," *NS*, 6, 2 (1990): 147-67

Glerum-Laurentius, Dicky, "A History of Dutch Activity in the Newfoundland Fish Trade from about 1590 till about 1680" (M.A. thes., MUN, 1960)

Gosse, Philip Henry, "Anecdotes and Reminiscences," ed. Ronald Rompkey, *NS*, 6, 2 (1990): 213-66

——————, "Entomologia Terrae Novae" (MS, National Museum of Natural Sciences, Ottawa, 1828-35)

Gunn, Gertrude E., *The Political History of Newfoundland 1832-1864* (Toronto: Univ. of Toronto Press, 1966)

Hakluyt, Richard, *English Voyages*, 8 vols. (London: Everyman, 1926)

Handcock, W. Gordon, "John Slade," *DCB*, vol. 4 (1979), pp. 711-14

——————, "Samuel Codner," *DCB*, vol. 8 (1985), pp. 164-7

——————, *So longe as there comes noe women: Origins of English Settlement in Newfoundland* (St. John's: Breakwater, 1989)

——————, *The Story of Trinity* (n.p.: Trinity Historical Society, n.d.)

——————, "Selected Newfoundland Extracts 1667-1738 from ... Calendar of State Papers, Colonial Series: America and the West Indies" (CNS)

Harris, Leslie, "Labrador Boundary Dispute," *ENL*, vol. 3, pp. 216-21

Head, C. Grant, *Eighteenth Century Newfoundland: A Geographer's Perspective* (Toronto: McClelland and Stewart, 1976)

Heller, Joseph, *Catch-22* (New York: Dell Publishing, 1990)

Hiller, J.K., "Robert Carter," *DCB*, vol. 10 (1972), p. 141

——————, "Utrecht Revisited: The Origins of French Fishing Rights in Newfoundland Waters," *NS*, 7, 1 (1991): 23-39

Historical Atlas of Canada, ed. R. Cole Harris, et al., 3 vols. (Toronto: Univ. of Toronto Press, 1987-90)

Hood, Bryan C., "The Maritime Archaic Indians of Labrador: Investigating Prehistoric Social Organization," *NS*, 9, 2 (1993): 163-84.

Hough, Richard, *Captain James Cook* (New York: Norton, 1995)

House of Assembly, *Address of the House of Assembly of Newfoundland* ([St. John's], 1839)

House of Commons, "Newfoundland Acts, 1786-1820" (CNS)

——————, *A Brief State of the Evidence laid before the Committee of the House of Commons, upon the Newfoundland Trade and Fishery, in the last Session* ([London]: 1793)

——————, *Report from Select Committee on Newfoundland Trade: with Minutes of Evidence taken before the Committee; and an Appendix* ([London], 1817)

——————, *Newfoundland. Return to an Address of the Honourable The House of Commons* ([London], 1839)

——————, *Papers relative to the Constitution of Newfoundland* ([London, 1839])

——————, Select Committee (1841), "Minutes of Evidence" [with other documents] ([London]: 1841)

——————, *Sessional Papers of the Eighteenth Century*, ed. Sheila Lambert, 145 vols. (Wilmington, Del.: Scholarly Resources Inc., 1975)

Howley, J.P., *A Historical Sketch of the Discovery and Development of the Coal Areas of Newfoundland* (St. John's: 1896)

——————, *The Beothucks, or Red Indians: The Aboriginal Inhabitants of Newfoundland* (Cambridge: Cambridge Univ. Press, 1915)

—————, *Reminiscences of James P. Howley: Selected Years*, ed. W.J. Kirwin, G.M. Story, and P. O'Flaherty (Toronto: Champlain Society, 1997)

Ingstad, Helge, *Westward to Vinland: The Discovery of Pre-Columbian Norse House-sites in North America* (Toronto: Macmillan, 1969)

In the Privy Council. In the Matter of the Boundary between the Dominion of Canada and the Colony of Newfoundland in the Labrador Peninsula, 12 vols. (London: n.p., n.d.)

Innis, Harold A. *The Cod Fisheries: the History of an International Economy*, rev. ed. (Toronto: Univ. of Toronto Press, 1978)

Janzen, Olaf Uwe, "'Une Grande Liaison': French Fishermen from Île Royale on the Coast of Southwestern Newfoundland, 1714-1766 — A Preliminary Survey," *NS*, 3, 2 (1987): 183-200

—————, "New Light on the Origins of Fort William at St. John's, Newfoundland, 1693-1696," *NQ*, 83, 2 (1987): 24-31

—————, rev. of Williams, *Father Baudoin's War*, in *NQ*, 84, 4 (1989): 47-8

—————, "Military Garrisons," *ENL*, vol. 3 (1991), pp. 540-49

—————, "Review Essay: '1497 and all that...'," *NQ*, 92, 1 (1998): 46-8

John, Brian S., *The Ice Age: Past and Present* (London: Collins, 1977)

Jukes, J.B., *Excursions in and about Newfoundland, during the Years 1839 and 1840*, 2 vols. (London: 1842)

Kitson, Arthur, *Captain James Cook, R.N., F.R.S* (London: John Murray, 1907)

Lahey, R.J., "The Role of Religion in Lord Baltimore's Colonial Enterprise," *Maryland Historical Magazine*, 72, 4 (1977): 492-511

—————, "Religion and Politics in Newfoundland: the Antecedents of the General Election of 1832" (MS, 1979)

—————, "Avalon: Lord Baltimore's Colony in Newfoundland," in *Early European Settlement*, pp. 115-37

—————, *James Louis O'Donel in Newfoundland 1784-1807: The Establishment of the Roman Catholic Church* ([St. John's]: Newfoundland Historical Society, 1984)

—————, "Timothy Browne," *DCB*, vol. 8 (1985), pp. 106-8

—————, "James W. Duffy," *DCB*, vol. 8, pp. 246-7

—————, "Michael Anthony Fleming," *DCB*, vol. 7 (1988), pp. 292-300

Langford, Paul, *Public Life and the Propertied Englishman 1689-1798* (Oxford: Clarendon Press, 1991)

A Letter to the most noble the Marquis of Normanby (London: 1839)

Little, Linda, "Collective Action in Outport Newfoundland: A Case Study from the 1830s," in *Labour and Working-Class History in Atlantic Canada: A Reader*, ed. David Frank and Gregory S. Kealey (St. John's: Institute of Social and Economic Research, MUN, 1995), pp. 41-70

Lord Durham's Report, ed. Gerald M. Craig (Toronto: McClelland and Stewart, 1968)

Lounsbury, Ralph G., *The British Fishery at Newfoundland 1634-1763* (1934) (n.p.: Archon Books, 1969)

MacBeath, George, "The Atlantic Region," *DCB*, vol. 1 (1966), pp. 21-6

McCann, Phillip, "Bishop Fleming and the Politicization of the Irish Roman Catholics in Newfoundland, 1830-1850," in *Religion and Identity*, pp. 81-97

—————, "Culture, State Formation and the Invention of Tradition: Newfoundland 1832-1855," *Journal of Canadian Studies*, 23, nos. 1-2 (1988): 86-103

McGhee, Robert, *Canada Rediscovered* ([Ottawa]: Canadian Museum of Civilization, 1991)

—————, *Ancient People of the Arctic* (Vancouver: UBC Press, 1996)

MacKay, R.A., ed., *Newfoundland: Economic, Diplomatic, and Strategic Studies* (Toronto: Oxford Univ. Press, 1946)

McLintock, A.H., *The Establishment of Constitutional Government in Newfoundland, 1783-1832: A Study of Retarded Colonisation* (London: Longmans, Green and Co., 1941)

Macpherson, Alan G., "Early Perceptions of the Newfoundland Environment," in *Natural Environment*, pp. 1-23

——————, "Pre-Columbian Discoveries and Exploration of North America," in *North American Exploration*, vol. 1, ed. John Logan Allen (Lincoln, Neb.: Univ. of Nebraska Press, 1997), pp. 13-70

Maier, Pauline, *American Scripture: Making the Declaration of Independence* (New York: Vintage Books, 1998)

Mannion, John, "The Irish Migrations to Newfoundland" (MS, CNS, 1973)

——————, *Point Lance in Transition: The Transformation of a Newfoundland Outport* (Toronto: McClelland and Stewart Ltd., 1976)

——————, "John O'Brien," *DCB*, vol. 8 (1985), pp. 658-60

——————, "Irish Merchants Abroad: The Newfoundland Experience, 1750-1850," *NS*, 2, 2 (1986): 127-90

——————, "Henry Shea," *DCB*, vol. 6 (1987), pp. 709-12

——————, "Patrick Morris," *DCB*, vol. 7 (1988), pp. 626-34

——————, "Victualling a Fishery: Newfoundland Diet and the Origins of the Irish Provisions Trade, 1675-1700" (MS, 1999)

Marshall, Dorothy, *Eighteenth Century England*, 2 ed. (London: Longman, 1974)

Marshall, Ingeborg, *A History and Ethnography of the Beothuk* (Montreal & Kingston: McGill-Queen's Univ. Press, 1996)

Martijn, Charles A., "An Eastern Micmac Domain of Islands," in *Actes du Vingtième Congrès des Algonquinistes*, ed. William Cowan (Ottawa: Carleton Univ., 1989), pp. 208-31

——————, RA on Marshall, *A History and Ethnography of the Beothuk*, in *NS*, 12, 2 (1996): 105-31

Martin, Ged, "Convict Transportation to Newfoundland in 1789," *Acadiensis*, 5, 1 (1975): 84-99

Martin, Wendy, *Once upon a Mine: Story of Pre-Confederation Mines on the Island of Newfoundland* (Montreal: Canadian Institute of Mining and Metallurgy, 1983)

Matthews, Keith, "A History of the West of England-Newfoundland Fishery" (D.Phil. thes., Oxford Univ., 1968)

——————, *Lectures on the History of Newfoundland* (St. John's: Maritime History Group, MUN, 1973)

——————, "17th Century English Settlement in Newfoundland" (MS, CNS, 1974)

——————, "William Keen," *DCB*, vol. 3 (1974), pp. 323-4

——————, *Collection and Commentary on the Constitutional Laws of Seventeenth Century Newfoundland* (St. John's: MUN, Maritime History Group, 1975)

——————, "Thomas Holdsworth Brooking," *DCB*, vol. 9 (1976), pp. 84-6

——————, "The Class of '32: St. John's Reformers on the Eve of Representative Government," *Acadiensis*, 6, 2 (1977): 80-94

——————, "James MacBraire," *DCB*, vol. 6 (1987), pp. 417-20

May, Doug, and Dane Rowlands, "Atlantic Canada in Confederation: Uncharted Waters with Dangerous Shoals" (MS, MUN, Dept. of Economics, 1991)

Morison, Samuel Eliot, *The European Discovery of America; the Northern Voyages, A.D. 500-1600* (New York: Oxford Univ. Press, 1971)

Morris, Patrick, *Remarks on the State of Society, Religion, Morals, and Education at Newfoundland* (London: 1827)

——————, *Speech delivered in the House of Assembly, on Friday, August 25, 1837* ([St. John's: 1837])

Mulcahy, Sister Mary Nolasco, "The St. John's Schools of Industry," *NQ*, 47, 4 (1983): 17-22

The Natural Environment of Newfoundland, Past and Present, ed. Alan and Joyce Macpherson (St. John's: MUN, Dept. of Geography, 1981)

Neary, Peter, "Miss Kirwan" (Sister Mary Bernard), *DCB*, vol. 8 (1985), pp. 474-6

——————, "John Reeves," *DCB*, vol. 6 (1987), pp. 636-7

——————, and Patrick O'Flaherty, *By Great Waters* (Toronto: Univ. of Toronto Press, 1974)

——————, and ——————, *Part of the Main: An Illustrated History of Newfoundland and Labrador* (St. John's: Breakwater, 1983)

New American World; A Documentary History of North America to 1612, ed. D.B. Quinn, 5 vols. (New York: Arno Press, and Hector Bye, Inc., 1979)

Newfoundland. Return to an Address of the Honourable The House of Commons ([London]: 1839)

O'Flaherty, Patrick, *The Rock Observed: Studies in the Literature of Newfoundland* (Toronto: Univ. of Toronto Press, 1979)

——————, "Laurence Coughlan," *DCB*, vol. 4 (1979), pp. 175-7

——————, "Edward Kielley," *DCB*, vol. 8 (1985), pp. 467-70

——————, "Henry David Winton," *DCB*, vol. 8, pp. 947-51

——————, "In Search of William Carson," *NQ*, 83, 1 (1987): 28-34

——————, "William Waldegrave," *DCB*, vol. 6 (1987), pp. 795-7

——————, "Government in Newfoundland before 1832: The context of reform," *NQ*, 84, 2 (1988): 26-30

——————, "The Seeds of Reform: Newfoundland, 1800-18," *Journal of Canadian Studies*, 23, 3 (1988): 39-59

——————, "William Carson," *DCB*, vol. 7 (1988), pp. 151-6

——————, "George Lilly," *DCB*, vol. 7, pp. 507-8

——————, "John Ryan," *DCB*, vol. 7, pp. 763-6

——————, "Peter Brown," *DCB*, vol. 7, pp. 112-14

——————, "The Newfoundland Natives' Society," *ENL*, vol. 4 (1993), pp. 21-7

——————, "The Road to Saddle Hill," *NQ*, 89, 3 (1995): 21-6

——————, "'Holding the Baby': Parliamentary Responses in Britain and Newfoundland to the Crisis of [1933]," *NQ*, 91, 2 (1997): 23-32

O'Neill, Paul, *The Oldest City: The Story of St. John's, Newfoundland* (Erin, Ont.: Press Porcepic, 1975)

The Oxford History of the British Empire, ed. W.R. Louis, vol. 2 (The Eighteenth Century) (Oxford: Oxford Univ. Press, 1998)

Pastore, Ralph, *Newfoundland Micmacs: A History of their Traditional Life* ([St. John's]: Newfoundland Historical Society, 1978)

——————, "The Collapse of the Beothuk World," *Acadiensis*, 19, 1 (1989): 52-71

——————, *Shanawdithit's People: The Archaeology of the Beothuks* (St. John's: Atlantic Archaeology Ltd., [1992]

——————, "The Sixteenth Century; Aboriginal Peoples and European Contact," in *The Atlantic Region to Confederation: A History*, ed. P.A. Buckner and J.G. Reid (Toronto: Univ. of Toronto Press, 1994), pp. 22-39

Paterson, J., "The History of Newfoundland 1713-1763" (M.A. thes., Univ. of London, 1931)

Petition of the Chamber of Commerce of St. John's, Newfoundland, to the Queen's Most Excellent Majesty (1) ([St. John's]: 1838)

Petition of the Chamber of Commerce of St. John's, Newfoundland, to the Queen's Most Excellent Majesty (2) ([St. John's]: 1838)

Petition of the Merchants, Traders, and other Inhabitants of St. John's, Newfoundland to Her Most Excellent Majesty ([St. John's]: 1837)

Pope, Peter, "Historical Archaeology and the Demand for Alcohol in 17th Century Newfoundland," *Acadiensis*, 19, 1 (1989): 72-90

——————, "The South Avalon Planters, 1630 to 1700: Residence, Labour, Demand and Exchange in Seventeenth-Century Newfoundland" (Ph.D. thes., MUN, 1992)

——————, "Scavengers and Caretakers: Beothuk/European Settlement Dynamics in Seventeenth-Century Newfoundland," *NS*, 9, 2 (1993): 279-93

——————, *The Many Landfalls of John Cabot* (Toronto: Univ. of Toronto Press, 1997)

Population Returns 1836 (n.p.: n.d.) [Nfld. census]

Pratt, E.J., *Collected Poems*, ed. Northrop Frye, 2nd ed. (Toronto: Macmillan, 1970)

[Prescott, Henry], *A Sketch of the State of Affairs in Newfoundland* (London, 1841)

Prowse, D.W., *A History of Newfoundland from the English, Colonial, and Foreign Records* (London: Macmillan, 1895)

Quinn, David B., *The Voyages and Colonising Enterprises of Sir Humphrey Gilbert*, 2 vols. (London: Hakluyt Society, 1940)

——————, "Richard Clarke," *DCB*, vol. 1 (1966), pp. 228-9

——————, "Thomas Croft," *DCB*, vol. 1, pp. 239-40

——————, "Hugh Eliot," *DCB*, vol. 1, p. 302

——————, "Sir Humphrey Gilbert," *DCB*, vol. 1, pp. 331-6

——————, "John Jay," *DCB*, vol. 1, p. 386

——————, "Samuel Gledhill," *DCB*, vol. 2 (1969), pp. 249-51

——————, *North America from Earliest Discovery to First Settlements; the Norse Voyages to 1612* (New York: Harper & Row, 1977)

——————, "Newfoundland in the Consciousness of Europe in the Sixteenth and Early Seventeenth Centuries," in *Early European Settlement*, pp. 9-30

Reece, Bob, "'Such a Banditti': Irish Convicts in Newfoundland, 1789," *NS*, 13, 1 (1997): 1-29 (pt. 1); 13, 2 (1997): 127-41 (pt. 2).

Reeves, John, *History of the Government of the Island of Newfoundland* (1793) (New York: Johnson Reprint Corp., 1967)

Reid, John G , *Maine, Charles II and Massachusetts: Governmental Relationships in Early Northern New England* (Portland: Maine Historical Society, 1977)

——————, *Acadia, Maine, and New Scotland: Marginal Colonies in the Seventeenth Century* (Toronto: Univ. of Toronto Press, 1981)

Religion and Identity: The Experience of Irish and Scottish Catholics in Atlantic Canada, ed. Terrence Murphy and Cyril J. Byrne (St. John's: Jesperson Press, 1987)

Renouf, M.A.P., "Palaeoeskimo Seal Hunters at Port au Choix," *NS*, 9, 2 (1993): 185-212.

——————, "Prehistory of Newfoundland Hunter-Gatherers: Extinctions or Adaptations?" *World Archaeology*, 30, 3 (1999): 403-20

A Report of Certain Proceedings of the Inhabitants of the Town of St. John, in the Island of Newfoundland; with the View to Obtain a Reform of the Laws ... and an Independent Legislature (St. John's: 1821)

Rogers, J.D., *A Historical Geography of the British Colonies*, vol. 5, pt. 4 (Newfoundland) (Oxford: Clarendon Press, 1911)

Rollmann, Hans, "Religious Enfranchisement and Roman Catholics in Eighteenth-Century Newfoundland," in *Religion and Identity*, pp. 34-52

——————, "Laurence Coughlan and the Origins of Methodism in Newfoundland," in *The Contribution of Methodism to Atlantic Canada*, ed. C.H.H. Scobie and J.W. Grant (Montreal & Kingston: McGill-Queen's Univ. Press, 1992), pp. 53-76

Rothney, G.O., "The Case of Bayne and Brymer: An Incident in the Early History of Labrador," *CHR*, 15, 3 (1934): 264-75

Rowe, Frederick W., *The Development of Education in Newfoundland* (Toronto: The Ryerson Press, 1964)

Ryan, Shannon, "Fishery to Colony: A Newfoundland Watershed, 1793-1815," *Acadiensis*, 12, 2 (1983): 34-52

—————, *Newfoundland-Spanish Saltfish Trade: 1814-1914* (St. John's: Harry Cuff Publications Ltd., 1983)

—————, *Fish Out of Water: The Newfoundland Saltfish Trade 1814-1914* (St. John's: Breakwater, 1986)

—————, *The Ice Hunters: A History of Newfoundland Sealing to 1914* (St. John's: Breakwater, 1994)

—————, "Newfoundland Consolidated Census Returns. 1698-1833" (MS, CNS)

Schultz, Gwen, *Ice Age Lost* (Garden City, N.Y.: Anchor Press/Doubleday, 1974)

Scisco, Louis D., "Kirke's Memorial on Newfoundland," *CHR*, 7, 1 (1926): 46-51

—————, "Calvert's Proceedings Against Kirke," *CHR*, 8, 2 (1927): 132-6

—————, "Testimony Taken in Newfoundland in 1652," *CHR*, 9, 3 (1928): 239-51

Seary, E.R., *Family Names of the Island of Newfoundland* (St. John's: MUN, 1977)

Select Charters of Trading Companies A.D. 1530-1707, ed. Cecil T. Carr (New York: Burt Franklin, 1970)

Select Documents of English Constitutional History, ed. George B. Adams and H. Morse Stephens (New York: Macmillan, 1923)

Senior, Hereward and Elinor, "Henry John Boulton," *DCB*, vol. 9 (1976), pp. 69-72

Shaw, Joseph, *The Practical Justice of Peace: or, A Treatise shewing the Power and Authority of that Office in all its Branches*, 2 vols. (London: 1728)

—————, *Parish Law: or, a Guide to Justices of the Peace, Ministers, Churchwardens, Overseers of the Poor, Constables, Surveyors of the Highways, Vestry-Clerks, and all Others concerned in Parish Business* (1734), 7th ed. (London: 1750)

Shomette, Donald G., and Robert D. Haslach, *Raid on America: The Dutch Naval Campaign of 1672-1674* (Columbia, S.C.: Univ. of South Carolina Press, 1988)

Simmons, R.C., and P.D.G. Thomas, *Proceedings and Debates of the British Parliaments Respecting North America 1754-1783*, 6 vols. (in progress) (White Plains, N.Y.: Kraus International Publications, 1982-6)

Skelton, R.A., *James Cook, Surveyor of Newfoundland, Being a Collection of Charts of the Coasts of Newfoundland and Labradore, &c. drawn from Original Surveys taken by James Cook and Michael Lane* (San Francisco: David Magee, 1965)

—————, and R.V. Tooley, "The Marine Surveys of James Cook in North America, 1758-1768, particularly the Survey of Newfoundland," *Map Collectors' Circle*, no. 37 (1967)

Smith, Philip E.L., "In Winter Quarters," *NS*, 3, 1 (1987): 1-36

The Statutes of the United Kingdom of Great Britain and Ireland, ed. T.E. Tomlins, John Raithby, and N. Simons, vols. 1, 2, 3, 8, 9, 12 (London: 1804-32)

Stith, William, *The History of the First Discovery and Settlement of Virginia* (1747), intro. Darrett B. Rutman (New York: Johnson Reprint Corp., 1969)

Stock, Leo F., *Proceedings and Debates of the British Parliaments respecting North America*, 5 vols. (Washington: Carnegie Institution of Washington, 1924-41)

Sturtevant, W.C., "The first Inuit depiction by Europeans," *Etudes Inuit Studies*, 4, 1-2 (1980): 47-9

Thirsk, Joan, ed., *Agricultural Change: Policy and Practice, 1500-1750* (Cambridge: Cambridge Univ. Press, 1990)

Thompson, Frederic F., *The French Shore Problem in Newfoundland: An Imperial Study* (Toronto: Univ. of Toronto Press, 1961)

Travel, Natural History, Atlases and Maps (London: Sotheby's, 1999) (L09206 "FIESTA")

Tuck, James A., *Newfoundland and Labrador Prehistory* (Ottawa: National Museum of Man, 1976

——————, "Maritime Archaic Tradition," *ENL*, vol. 3, pp. 462-5.

——————, "Archaeology at Ferryland, Newfoundland," *NS*, 9, 2 (1993): 294-310

——————, and Robert Grenier, *Red Bay, Labrador; World Whaling Capital A.D. 1550-1600* (St. John's: Atlantic Archaeology Ltd., 1989)

Vigneras, L.-A., "Gaspar Corte-Real," *DCB*, vol. 1 (1966), pp. 234-6

The Vinland Sagas; The Norse Discovery of America, trans. Magnus Magnusson and Hermann Pálsson (London: Penguin Books, 1965)

The Voyages of Jacques Cartier, intro. Ramsay Cook (Toronto: Univ. of Toronto Press, 1993)

Wallace, Birgitta, "L'Anse aux Meadows: Gateway to Vinland," *Acta Archaeologica*, 61 (1990): 166-97

Wells, Elizabeth A., "John Valentine Nugent," *DCB*, vol. 10 (1972), pp. 552-3

Wells, Robert V., *The Population of the British Colonies in America before 1776* (Princeton, N.J.: Princeton Univ. Press, 1975)

White, Maureen, "A Study of Patrick Morris's Political Pamphlets" (M.A. thes., MUN, 1987)

White Tie and Decorations: Sir John and Lady Hope Simpson in Newfoundland, 1934-1936, ed. Peter Neary (Toronto: Univ. of Toronto Press, 1996)

Whiteley, W.H., "The Establishment of the Moravian Mission in Labrador and British Policy, 1763-83," *CHR*, 45, 1 (1964): 29-50

——————, "Governor Hugh Palliser and the Newfoundland and Labrador Fishery, 1764-1768," *CHR*, 50, 2 (1969): 141-63

——————, "James Cook and British Policy in the Newfoundland Fisheries, 1763-7," *CHR*, 54, 3 (1973): 245-72

——————, "Sir Hugh Palliser," *DCB*, vol. 4 (1979), pp. 597-601

——————, "Jeremiah Coghlan," *DCB*, vol. 4, pp. 158-60

Williams, Alan F., *Father Baudoin's War: D'Iberville's Campaigns in Acadia and Newfoundland 1696, 1697* (St. John's: Dept. of Geography, MUN, 1987)

Williams, Griffith, *An Account of the Island of Newfoundland* (London: 1765)

Williamson, J.A., *The Voyages of the Cabots* (London: Argonaut Press, 1929)

Wix, Edward, *Six Months of a Newfoundland Missionary's Journal*, (London: 1836; 2nd ed., 1836)

[Yonge, James], *Some Considerations Touching The present Debate between Owners, &c. And Fishermen, relating to The New-found-land Trade* (Oxford: 1671)

——————, *The Journal of James Yonge (1647-1721)*, ed. F.N.L. Poynter (London: Longmans, 1963)

Index

AGMV Marquis

MEMBRE DE SCABRINI MEDIA

Québec, Canada
2001